VISUAL MEDIA AND THE HUMANITIES

VISUAL MEDIA
AND THE
HUMANITIES

A Pedagogy of Representation

Edited by

KECIA DRIVER MCBRIDE

Tennessee Studies in Literature,
VOLUME 42

THE UNIVERSITY OF TENNESSEE PRESS / Knoxville

CONTENTS

FIGURES

ACKNOWLEDGMENTS

The scholars and teachers who contributed to this volume have greatly enriched my understanding of the intersections between the visual media and the humanities, and I appreciate their hard work and thoughtful expression. I wish to acknowledge gratefully the support of the Ball State English Department in completing this project, as well as the individual efforts of my research assistants Julie Goodspeed, Andrea Powell, and Laura Swartz, and the extra work by Fred Johnson. Thanks are due to Chuck Maland and Mary Papke for setting me down this path long ago, and to Bill Larson for his companionship along the way, and I am especially indebted to Don Cox for his generous support and patience. This project would not have been completed without the encouragement of Lauren, Bob, Pat, and Rebecca. Most importantly, for his fierce belief in my ability to untangle the chaos and his complete willingness to support me every step of the way, I reserve my deepest appreciation for Paul Joseph.

INTRODUCTION
Kecia Driver McBride

The past ten years have produced a remarkable growth in the areas of film studies and visual culture, as evidenced by course offerings, textbook publications, and conference panels devoted to these subjects. Yet, despite this interest, Rey Chow argued recently that the field of film studies has "remained relatively marginalized in the teaching of the humanities at most universities" (1391) when compared to more traditional subjects such as literature, history, and philosophy. Chow describes film as a "phantom-like" academic discipline "because it is inextricably linked to every other type of knowledge production" (1391); professors in the humanities include films on their syllabi as a matter of course, and there is an abundance of publications on film from "amateurs" (a category in which Chow modestly includes herself) who work primarily in other disciplines but are drawn to film. In fact, at most universities, film studies (as opposed to film production) is still taught at the undergraduate level as an interdisciplinary program, rarely existing as a separate major with its own scholars, resources, financial support, office space, and research agenda.

At the same time, critics such as Christine Gledhill and Linda Williams have argued that film might soon be absorbed within the current trend towards "globalized multimedia" (1). Since the late 1980s, media studies scholars have increasingly (and understandably) turned to the development of new technologies, including hypertext and hypermedia, as the wave of the future. Technical support, materials, and training are increasingly available in many academic departments, even in the face of budget woes and the threat of recession. No one wants to be labeled a luddite; indeed, technical skills are a measurement of how well one keeps up, a reflection of one's fitness and relevance as a twenty-first-century scholar. It is an exciting and challenging time to teach, especially since our students come to us more comfortable with certain types of technology than some of our colleagues. Even while we struggle to learn new skills and suffer through tech workshops that eat up our precious time for research and writing, we marvel at the ways in which technology has changed our profession, improved our writing, and expanded our control over information.

In recent years, humanities scholars have also become more interested in issues of pedagogy, a development that might strike the outside observer as both obvious and long overdue. A glance at the programs from the MLA conventions in December of 2001 and 2002 reveal presentations devoted to teaching on virtually every page, and panels devoted to pedagogy are often the most interesting as well as the best-attended at academic conferences. We have become attentive to the ways in which we think and talk about what we do in the classroom for a variety of reasons: growing pressure from local and state governments for accountability, increased emphasis on assessment and evaluation, recent challenges to the tenure system, and the need to satisfy university-wide goals and standards, just to name a few. We are also eager to become better teachers, to reach our students more fully, to increase their critical thinking skills, improve their writing, engage their interest. A focus on the connections between cultural studies and critical pedagogy is certainly not new, as evidenced by the work of such critics as Paulo Freire, Henry Giroux, Peter McLaren, and bell hooks. According to Giroux and Simon, pedagogy can exist at any site where a practice "intentionally tries to influence the production of meaning," and film can be a particularly fruitful example of Giroux's "pedagogy of representation." However, as we who love film pause to reflect on the past half-century of film studies in American universities, and look towards the new technologies of the twenty-first century with a mingling of excitement and anxiety, it seems clear that we must more specifically connect our enthusiasm for the subject of film to our broader pedagogical goals. There is currently not a body of writing that specifically links film and critical pedagogy, and I fear that the current emphasis on technical skills might only exacerbate this lack.

Those of us who teach in the humanities need to more fully assess the pedagogical implications of the ways in which the media have been invited into our classrooms. Historically, our British and the Australian colleagues have done a much better job of theorizing and teaching approaches to the media—drawing from the model of British cultural studies and the Frankfort school—than North American critics. Particularly in the humanities, where media literacy is increasingly a goal of teacher training and the semiotic interrogation of texts is routine, we need to carefully examine the critical context of our classroom practices in terms of curricula, teaching strategies, materials, texts, assignments, and assessment. We need to be attentive as well to the differences that exist among the various media, including print, and, while technical skills are certainly valuable and increasingly necessary, those skills mean little unless we find practical ways to use the visual media to help accomplish our pedagogical goals.

Until quite recently, media literacy was commonly assumed to be a necessary measure to protect students, a sort of inoculation against the evils of either capitalism or hedonism, depending on who was teaching. Under this system, students were taught a sort of structuralist rhetoric, through which they learned to analyze cinematic codes of representation, recognize stereotypes, and hopefully evaluate the content of the message as linked inextricably to its form. Because the media shape our knowledge of ourselves, teach dominant beliefs and values, and encourage consumerism, viewers "should" be able to recognize, deconstruct, and resist these codes. With the development of feminist film theory and the groundbreaking work of such scholars as Laura Mulvey, Teresa De Lauretis, and Claire Johnston, film studies became more specifically engaged with issues of race, class, and gender, reflecting theoretical trends in other disciplines in the humanities. Like language, like literature, film is a signifying practice through which students make meaning. However, unlike English studies, for example, film has never had the same firmly established boundaries—such as a stable canon of texts and universally accepted teaching standards—to rebel against, and film's marginalized status makes it a more open and experimental discipline. Whereas the inoculation approach assumes the students are passive and uncritical viewers, film studies has, since the late 1970s and with the growing acceptance of poststructuralist theories, emphasized active and engaged viewers who must participate in the viewing experience in order to create meaning, an approach that is mirrored in literary studies by the various reader-based theories of critical reading.

The growing popularity of visual culture, combined with rapid increases in technology, have encouraged theorists to explore texts as complex sites of knowledge and information, but also of entertainment and pleasure. While these readings can produce rich and sophisticated possibilities, some critics have also become sensitive to the perception of a type of uncritical media populism, where every text has equal value and the reading of those texts becomes personal instead of dialectical. A further concern here is that computer culture will "kill" the cinema, and there is certainly evidence, as Douglas Kellner has recently pointed out, that digital technology might well do away with the celluloid, an issue that creates a crisis of identity for cinema studies. Thus, issues of canonicity are recast: is there a canon of sophisticated and complex films that should be taught? Should we incorporate films into our more mainstream courses, sacrificing F. Scott Fitzgerald for Orson Welles, Richard Wright for Spike Lee, John Steinbeck for Barbara Kopple? While issues of the canon have become commonplace enough to produce groans and eye-rolling from even my undergraduate students, the fact remains that we have not solved them. If complex, engaged critical thinking and writing are the primary goals, however, as they are for many of these contributors, then film can serve as a touchstone for Giroux's pedagogy of representation.

This collection of essays is intended for those of us who are trained in the humanities and, while teaching within a "traditional" discipline, are interested in incorporating the visual media into our courses, in support of our overall pedagogical goals. It does our students little good if films are used only as a substitute on a day when we are gone to a conference, or if films are shown and then discussed only as narratives, or if adaptations are used only to demonstrate the superiority of the original literary texts. The voices here are diverse, from the wisdom and experience of Scott MacDonald and Gerald Duchovnay, to the fresh perspectives of Adrienne McCormick and James Miles. The contributors teach in a range of different classroom environments, from the Ivy League and flagship state universities to small liberal arts schools and community colleges. These scholars recognize the differing needs of their student bodies, as well as their varying degrees of media literacy and technological competency. This collection is not, then, intended to be a blueprint for a universal pedagogy, but rather it is intended to open up dialogue, to suggest fresh approaches, and to share the thoughtful and innovative ways in which our fellow workers are incorporating the visual media into their pedagogical theories and practices, to teach rhetoric, literature, history, research methods, and cultural studies to their students.

The essays collected here have several concerns in common which highlight the debates surrounding cinematic representation more broadly.

In different ways, they transgress boundaries between high and low culture, the mainstream and the marginal. In addition, they conceive of film as a system of codes or signs, as opposed to one of mimesis or transparent realism; this is true even in a discussion of documentary filmmaking. Recognizing or "reading" these codes enables the viewer to participate in the process of making meaning from a film text, in much the same way that readers learn to recognize language codes when reading literature. These pieces are also concerned with the intersections between technology and art as they are specifically framed within the classroom. The increasing technological savvy of our students challenges us to keep up, to tap into their interests and fully integrate developing technologies in our course plans. Finally, these teachers all engage the rhetorical positioning of text, text-makers, audience, and context, focusing on the ways in which meaning is produced through these interactions and teaching our students the necessary skills with which to engage this dialectical process.

The first four essays address the impact of technology and visuality in the classroom. In "Visualizing Feminist Theatre History on the Web," Thomas Crochunis takes the reader on an adventure back through theatre history, discussing the benefits of visual access to elements of performance like manuscripts, posters, performance clips, and 3D spatial models in order to expand the limiting, text-based experience most students have of theater. In another move away from the traditional classroom, Stephanie Tripp points out in "Haunting in the Age of Electronic Post-literacy" that the computerized classroom is not just a conduit through which students learn to master the practices of print literacy, but one site of an emerging form of post-literacy that joins written text with multimedia. Tripp uses the metaphor of haunting as an approach to writing and research, arguing that semiotics should not be discarded in a new pedagogy for the electronic classroom, but its focus should shift from identifying and treating symptoms to recognizing symptoms as sites for conjuring textual ghosts.

John Zuern demonstrates, in "Diagram, Dialogue, Dialectic: Visual Explanations and Visual Rhetoric in the Teaching of Literary Theory," how visual materials, whether they take the form of graphics, cartoons, photographs, digital animation, or film footage, can help students not only to understand theoretical concepts, but to engage these ideas critically and productively, thus developing their own theoretical vision. In a similar vein, James Miles argues in "Simulation Machines, Media Boundaries, and the Re-expansion of Composition" that the academy must more effectively utilize the ever-widening array of media around us, and questions how multiple mediation or alternating mediation makes our students' works, and ours, vastly more effective, given the surging developments in communications outside of school.

The use of film in the composition classroom is the focus of the next three essays. In "The Guises of Martin Guerre: Pedagogical Applications," Joonna Smitherman Trapp uses three versions of the historic story of Martin Guerre to discuss the social and artistic issues concerning gender, religion, social class, identity, and the nature of reality and truth. Trapp discusses a capstone project for an argumentative writing course that engages oral, written, and visual discourse, and explores the concepts of logos, ethics, and pathos through both written and filmic texts. Using the heavily-anthologized example of Plato's *Allegory of the Cave,* Maria Bachman in "'Strange Prisoners': Plato Goes to Pleasantville" introduces the recent Hollywood film *Pleasantville* as a transformation of Plato's essay that enables her to teach critical reasoning. Pushing students to explore the similarities in the two texts, Bachman frames a discussion of mimesis, authenticity, and representation, as well as revealing enlightenment or knowledge as both painful and pleasurable. Moving from analysis to production, Dale Jacobs in "Where Can I Get a Camera?: Documentary Film, Visual Literacy, and the Teaching of Writing" asserts that students learn best by producing artifacts. He shares a course design for introductory composition courses in which students create their own "mock documentaries" mimicking the research, organization, and presentation of documentary film, which he defines as "visual rhetoric."

Shifting to the medium of television, Rai Peterson shares her experiences over the past nine years of teaching a composition course on literature through the distance education program. Dubbed "the metaphor lady," Peterson discusses the challenges of on-air scrutiny, managing a video persona (and becoming something of a local celebrity), viewer mail, and the rewards of working with nontraditional learners who sometimes aren't even registered students. Ultimately, Peterson sees televised classes as a medium that is becoming obsolete, replaced by rapidly developing (and more cost-effective) Web-based learning, but her narrative of television learning as an in-between technology is both instructive and entertaining, providing us with important clues about how to continue to adapt to technological innovations. An alternate vision of the use of television in the classroom comes from Barbra Morris in "The Televised Interview as Focus Group Research Text," in which she looks at the Monica Lewinsky interview with Barbara Walters aired originally on March 3, 1999, on *20/20*. Based on research gathered during a Study Abroad program conducted by the University of Michigan and student studies of focus group questionnaires, Morris discusses the advantages of using material of interest to students, with volatile content but significant cultural resonances, and how to teach students to analyze this material through an academic lens.

Film can also, obviously, be used to engage issues of culture and ideology, as revealed in the next four essays. In "'An Imitation of Life: Deconstructing Racial Stereotypes in Popular Culture," Stephanie Thompson compares Fannie Hurst's 1933 novel *Imitation of Life* to its 1934 and 1959 film adaptations as a way to discuss America's racial dilemmas at pivotal points in American history. Thompson focuses on the prevalence of racial stereotypes, and the problematic depictions of interracial relationships throughout the twentieth century, with attention to the subtle changes in the representation of ideology over time. Focusing on popular culture in "The Gumpification of Academia? Teaching the Ideological Analysis of Popular Film and Television," Diane Negra and Walter Metz explore the ways in which quite sophisticated critical thinking skills can be taught through the deconstruction of popular texts such as hit television shows and blockbuster films. Metz and Negra are interested in the ways in which we encode pleasure and entertainment, and they challenge the perceived split between content and critical theory in the study of film and popular culture. The way to engage students with theory, they claim, is to employ pop culture as the site for analysis.

In a related investigation of popular culture and pedagogy, Gerald Duchovnay, in "The World in a Frame: Introducing Culture through Film," discusses an interdisciplinary course which introduces students to issues concerning culture and intercultural communication, using film as a catalyst. Duchovnay focuses on nonverbal communication, the deep structure of culture, cultural diversity, and the ways in which communication and culture interact to shape our perceptions of reality. By contrast, in the essay "To Show or Not to Show: The Use of Film in Teaching Cross-Cultural Courses," Ban Wang explores the ways television and film both enhance and impede the teaching of humanities courses in a cross-cultural context, using trauma as a central transcultural experience. Emphasizing the difficulties implicit in teaching cross-cultural courses, which are usually taught in the United States through translation and interpreted via media images and stereotypes, Wang warns against a focus on the exotic elements of Asian culture instead of the specific context of production implicit in any film text.

The next four essays discuss the ways in which film can be used to teach literature; moving beyond the predictable, these teachers stretch the ways in which their students experience adaptation. Kamilla Elliott discusses the usefulness of film adaptations for teaching literary criticism and theory in "Through the Looking Glass: Pedagogical Uses of Literary Film Adaptations," using a wide range of literary examples to prove that adaptations are performative acts of criticism, artistic responses to art, and rich sources of historical and cultural responses to a text. In contrast, Elyse Blankley proposes an alternative model for rereading film adaptations and the fictional sources on which they are based by focusing on a commercially successful cinematic adaptation of an E. M. Forster novel. Her "Merchant-Ivory Tames the Shrew in *Howards End*" uses the changes made in one character in the film version of *Howards End* to discuss the historical and cultural anxieties embedded in those changes. In "I Don't Want to Talk about It: Using Spanish Feature Films to Teach Literature," Carmen Chávez discusses the problem of a lack of literature in foreign language classes, and how instructional technologies can be used to improve listening and reading comprehension. Films, she suggests, can be used to teach students how to comprehend and also express more complicated and subtly nuanced ideas in Spanish, greatly improving their oral and written proficiency in the process of teaching language, literature, and culture.

Finally, the last two articles in this collection explore the ways in which avant-garde filmmaking can stretch our students' experiences with film. Adrienne McCormick explores feminist filmmaking in "Veiling Practices, Invisibility, and Knowledge Production in the Documentary Films of Trinh T. Minh-ha, Barbara Hammer, and Lourdes Portillo," using the veil image as a site for the intersection of theories of identity and authenticity, the filmmaking apparatus, and the in/visibility of knowledge production in documentary film. In contrast, Scott MacDonald draws from his extensive interviews with independent filmmakers and his years of experience in the classroom to advocate for the use of experimental film as a crucial teaching strategy. He argues in "There's No Light without Heat, and No Heat without Friction: Avant-Garde Film in the College Classroom" that learning to analyze complicated and sometimes alienating films is the best way to encourage critical thinking in undergraduate students, as well as offering them intelligent alternatives to mainstream, commercial media.

These pieces together offer a rich and varied array of approaches to the visual media, from the exploration of new technologies and their usefulness to the humanities, to case studies of individual texts and their attendant adaptations, to practical discussions of classroom practices, to the development of more abstract theoretical frameworks within which to situate these issues. If we accept the premise that the influence of the visual media is likely to continue to increase, then the time is ripe for scholars in the humanities to reconceptualize the intersections between the humanities classroom and visual rhetoric.

Visualizing Feminist Theatre History on the Web

THOMAS CROCHUNIS

In August of 1997, Tracy Davis and Ellen Donkin held a small conference at Northwestern University in Evanston, Illinois, for contributors
to their then-forthcoming volume *Women and Playwriting in Nineteenth
Century Britain* (Cambridge University Press, 1999). Contributors presented
versions of their essays for the volume and other invited participants gave
responses to these essays. Over the two-plus days of the conference, however, participants shared more than just a series of drafts. In informal conversation and open discussion, colleagues raised historical and theoretical
issues about women and playwriting in the British nineteenth century. We
discussed what kinds of evidence were important, how authorship could
be understood, what approaches one could use to explore and interpret play
scripts, and how the significance of social and economic conditions could
be studied in relation to women in the nineteenth-century British theatre.
Less directly related to the volume itself, people talked about their other
projects and invited contributions to journals, participation in conference
sessions, or submissions to edited volumes of essays. For me, the most
important thing was meeting in person many of those whose work I had
read and getting a glimpse of the complex social processes involved in forming a community of inquiry. The event was like having many of those
whose work most influences your own suddenly appear in your scholarly
life as a part of your own department, if only for a few days. Because of this
conference, both the collaboration and the contention produced by historians working in a common field visibly embodied the performance of feminist theatre historiography.

Afterwards, I thought about how to advance scholarship on women
playwrights of the British eighteenth and nineteenth centuries through fur-
thering development of a common space of inquiry. Someone from the
conference initiated a discussion list, but it never took off—such lists often

have difficulty becoming working communities because they seem like they're "just talk." Later that year, at the Modern Language Association conference in Toronto, I met to have coffee with Michael Eberle-Sinatra. For several years Michael had been serving as general editor of *Romanticism on the Net,* one of the most successful online periodicals in the humanities. We had both come to MLA to participate in the session "British Women Playwrights around 1800: Rethinking the Paradigms" that I organized and Michael chaired.[1] Michael was interested in exploring what a Web-based working group and site might offer in support of the ongoing scholarship on women's writing of drama and theatre scripts in the years around 1800.[2] As we improvised some ideas about how the Web could open new avenues for scholarship on this topic, we began to realize that we were outlining a project we would need to undertake gradually over time. Building a community online is painstaking work.

The rest, as they say, is history—or in this case, historiography. Naturally, a site and working group that aims to support a community of inquiry centered on women's roles as theatre writers and authors[3] cannot limit itself to textual sources, and so, though limited resources have restricted what has gone up at the *British Women Playwrights around 1800* site to date, plans for the future include additions of visual materials such as images of theatres, playbills, periodical sketches, and portraits of authors and performers. However, we have been reminded during the early stages of the project's development that the Web is, even when textual, a medium whose cultural *visibility* has complex social, cognitive, and theoretical implications. In fact, this project has reminded us repeatedly that the same is true of print as a medium; the processes and forms of its production also have complex implications, though scholarship—so invested in participating in print culture—often ignores them. The site has led us to confront questions about the limitations of print culture's media and social processes for those investigating theatre history. If, as many have noted of electronic textuality, we are reminded of the specificity of print as a medium by encounters with new media (Sutherland), how much more important is it for theatre history studies to examine critically the book's role within cultural histories that have positioned both theatre and scholarship.

Our work in developing the site has led us to discuss—and in some cases to publish commentary on—questions of editorial practice and text encoding; of collegial collaboration and review; of appropriate and legal use of texts, images, and scholarly commentary; of the economics of research as a form of labor; and many other matters that go to the heart of scholarly practice. The site has become a microcosm—if not necessarily a representative one—of feminist historiography as a social process, perpetuating the collegial visibility that the Evanston conference initiated, though of course this visibility is skewed by the peculiarities of the Web as emerging social medium. The site also provides one possible medium through which a loosely formed community of inquiry can *perform*—both *do* and *display*—its work. Without forcing vision metaphors to balance too precariously between the literal and metaphoric, I would argue that the perceptual *visuality* of the Web as medium lends a kind of social *visibility* to feminist historiography's processes. This visibility both displays and invites collegial exchange, revisionary thinking about women in dramaturgical history, and formation of less specialized communities of inquiry that include students, professors, and performers. Web visibility's feedback loop of display and access provides important social stimulation to our project's work.

In this essay, I want to tease out some of the subtle ways in which this particular portion of women's theatre history looks different on the Web, but I should say at the outset that I am as much interested in how users of the site might socially navigate, read, and interpret the materials online or in how historiography appears when performed online as I am in how visual images can be mounted or used in a Web-based archive.[4] The *British Women Playwrights around 1800* project—and this essay—is particularly concerned with the theoretical and social implications of making visible online historiographic practices and collaborations. Therefore, although I do write about "visual materials" in this essay as one kind of artifact that the Web might allow scholars to use when working together on theatre history, it is really the Web's capacity for increasing—beyond the products of print publication—the "visibility" of scholarly work in women's dramaturgical history that lies at the heart of my discussion of the theoretical and practical implications of working on feminist theatre historiography on the Web. The chief contribution the Web makes to "the visual in the humanities" is not its capacity to reproduce visual material—though that potential has great promise for the future—but rather that the Web can simply and with minimal production cost make knowledge work visible to a wide audience. The constraints placed on collaboration by print production's expense need no longer dictate how we think together as colleagues.

THEATRE/HISTORIOGRAPHY/WOMEN'S WRITING

There are fundamental intellectual problems, however, in how historiography has handled dramaturgical history in the past. While there is a long tradition of theatre history scholarship focused on production practices and the theatre's social history, there is a competing literary history of drama. These two histories have sometimes been woven together, but for the most part, they occupy different historical studies, scholarly careers, and even departments in institutions of higher education. The disjunction is particularly significant in scholarship on British theatre in the years around 1800, since legal restrictions on the performance of "legitimate" (spoken and not musical) drama, and censorship of the content of performed drama were defining features of the period's politically anxious public culture, and limited how a writer of drama could engage audiences of the time (Conolly 11). These limitations continue to affect what we know about theatre writing in Britain in the years before and after 1800. For many women playwrights, the dialogue between dramatic publication and performance was central to their professional lives.[5]

The historiographic record has inadequately represented women's work in the British theatre previous to the mid-nineteenth century for some time. Only in the past few years have scholars begun to identify the gaps in the record and study many of the women writers, performers, critics, and business people who were active in the British theatre around 1800. At the same time as research has set about recovering the lives of women in the theatre, theoretical questions have emerged in performance studies about how we have understood the relationship between theatre writing, production, and performance.[6] These theoretical questions have particular importance for how we study the histories of women working in and around the British theatre at the end of the eighteenth and beginning of the nineteenth centuries. This period is particularly significant as a case study in historiographic method for two main reasons. Broadly speaking, it was a period both of increased opportunity for women as cultural producers (writers, performers, theatre managers) and of intense concern about the influence of writing and performance on political life.[7] And yet, the work of women in relation to the theatre in this period has perhaps been less fully investigated and taught than any other comparably rich period in British cultural history. Women playwrights in Britain in the years around 1800 are especially significant subjects for feminist historiography because their histories provoke questions about how we frame historical inquiries about public institutions like the theatre, what kinds of writing matter, and how our research and teaching about drama can produce new cultural histories for an audience beyond specialists in theatre or literary history. Because these women writers traveled between the worlds of theatre and print publishing, their histories have significance for feminist literary and theatre history, as well as for feminist cultural history generally.

When historians of women's theatre writing avoid choosing between production-based or drama-based models of history, they place attention on the complex social negotiation that women's theatrical and literary careers required in Britain around 1800. Refusing to choose too easily between literary and theatre historiography is a crucial feminist gesture because this refusal forces us to choose a much more complex object of historical study than the dramatic text. In many cases, the women playwrights to be studied have not been widely republished or read. Therefore, the historian who wishes not only to understand the writer's work but also to influence others' knowledge must take into account that few will have read widely in the dramatic works under consideration. While this might seem a matter little worth noting, it helps to explain why much scholarship on women writers initially involves preparing editions of the works of one or more women playwrights.[8] Like other feminist historians, scholars of women's theatre writing must study, stimulate interest in, and often provide access to texts, for textual access remains an essential component of developing knowledge about women who wrote for the theatre. But in republishing women's theatre writing scholars make an implicit argument for certain ways of valuing these texts—literary ways.

While the styles and subjects of women's theatre writing deserve to be studied in detail, investigating the history of women playwrights only by scrutinizing their dramatic texts ignores the cultural "performances" these women may have been giving when they published or staged their works. We cannot assume that women writers could unproblematically claim a normative "authorship" when they wrote for the public in any form, but their authorship was especially complicated in the theatre of the British nineteenth century because the writer's play script was only one factor in determining the meanings of performance. Competing with the writer for authorship were leading actors, theatre managers and the trademark styles of their companies, and even the political climate at the time of a particular performance which sometimes threatened to overwrite a play text's meanings.[9] A woman playwright's texts are therefore complicated sites of "authorship"—because of their writer's gender, because of the medium of their delivery to the public, and because of each writer's potential self-consciousness about how these conditions of production might be addressed.

Yet, to explore women's roles as authors of drama and theatre in Britain around 1800, theatre historians also have to engage with more than women's dramatic texts. Without looking at other artifactual materials, a historian risks narrowing consideration of women's theatre writing to literary evaluation, framing out of view these writers' acts of social assertion and authorial strategy and uncritically endorsing literary valuations that are legacies of the very contemporary biases that disparaged women's writing in their own era. In addition, although the three-dimensional, visual, sound-filled theatre event itself cannot be recovered in any integrated way, a variety of materials can provide starting points for speculation about how the varied elements of theatre events participated in cultural discourses. For instance, a caricature of an actor in a periodical or a painting by a contemporary artist provides a glimpse of the ways in which the performer, the play, or the role were read, allowing us to view the social reception which the writer of the play might well have anticipated. Images of men's and women's bodies allow us to speculate about how a woman playwright formulated gender in ways that affected dramatic gesture, speech, action, and set design. In fact, any graphic image can be cross-referenced with other images or with written commentaries to uncover patterns of response and interpretation that reveal the cultural *mise en scène* within which women's critical, personal, or dramatic writing was discursively set.[10] Although a scholar's theories about a playwright's role in authoring performer gesture must remain speculative, visuality has an important role to play in any history of women's dramaturgy that seeks to interpret women's writing as contextualized cultural—not just literary—gestures. Furthermore, women's theatre writing needs to be studied in relation to the social activity that its publication and staging involved. Not only is the sociality of women's careers as playwrights significant to how and what they wrote, but it also helps to connect the significance of women's sociability as playwrights with their roles as theatre managers, journalists, and political agents in British culture at large.[11] So in addition to studying the texts that women produced and the visual images related to the theatre in which they were involved, historians need to investigate these women's professional activities—their negotiating of contracts, fending off assaults by sexually presumptuous theatre managers, or exchanging ideas with each other either through private correspondence or public commentary about the works of other women writers. A richly multifarious history of women's writing for the theatre in Britain around 1800 engages with a mixture of textual, visual, and social data.

VISUAL MATERIAL AND NEW HISTORIOGRAPHIC SPACES

The institutions and discourses surrounding theatre artifacts and their availability provide challenges to the practice of historical inquiry, for few of the materials related to women's dramaturgical history—playbills, posters, play manuscripts, unpublished correspondence—are available in published form. As a result, these materials are only available in a limited number of archival collections. Furthermore, the mixture of types of materials—images from advertising, manuscripts, inexpensively published books—have similarly mixed legal status: a scholar might be able to find a microfiche copy of a published play text easily and make photocopies of it without encountering legal restrictions, but may receive permission to use an image from a play bill only personally in an archive or by following accepted legal procedures when preparing material for professional print publication. These variations in the status of theatre history artifacts —which reflect the tangled legal histories of publishing, scholarship, and theatrical culture—influence the kinds of inquiry and collaborative learning about women's theatre history that seem institutionally possible.

So, too, do the economic realities of historical inquiry, given these institutional barriers to access. With a limited number of archives holding these materials, only scholars with travel budgets can hope to perform theatre historiography. Not only students but also many teachers at less well-endowed colleges and universities have little chance, barring winning a substantial competitive grant, of developing historical projects that might depend on trips to the archive. Those interested in pursuing theatre history inquiry must also have the credentials to obtain access to the materials housed in many different collections. Those who investigate theatre history not as scholars but as theatre practitioners are subtly discouraged by these current conditions of historical inquiry (not to minimize the ways in which their interests in such inquiry are also influenced by cultural values regarding who is authorized to produce history).[12] With such limitations on access, literary interpretation of drama becomes more appealing than historical work on theatre culture. But it is only when the theatre writing of women in Britain around 1800 is read within the social milieu embodied by artifactual remains that these texts reveal the significance of their discursive gestures. Remaining a specialists' business, then, research into women's theatre history prevents a change in the performance of cultural or dramaturgical history, either in British eighteenth- or nineteenth-century studies in academia or in theatre production. However lamentable this marginalization may be, my point is that theatre historiography—including not just writing but other forms of producing history—could change if alternatives to traditional archival research became available. I believe the visuality and sociality of the Web can give feminist investigations of theatre history a new influence.

To understand the potential significance of using online media to support feminist theatre history, one needs to consider how the history of women's work in the British theatre has been constrained by not only the limited availability of materials and the inaccessibility of archives but also by professional prohibitions on methods of inquiry. Reconsidering the history of women's writing for the theatre in the years around 1800 in Britain involves reformulating both the historical questions asked and the methods of inquiry that might be used.[13] Specialist discourses about historical knowledge and social structures impede collaboration, shared inquiry, and to some extent changes in thinking. As I have suggested earlier, the material conditions someone must navigate in order to engage with historical materials support specialization. Furthermore, specialization constitutes how scholars perform their roles as teachers since typically students cannot work with essential materials for historical investigation unless provided access to them by their professors. These professors face an uncomfortable choice. They can either violate the conventionally accepted methods of teaching and inquiry with which they are most at ease—by, for example, using performance as a primary method of making historical knowledge. Or they can embrace hierarchies of expertise—by choosing to disseminate historical knowledge rather than collaborate in inquiry with students. Either way, feminist theatre historians must make compromises when they seek to stimulate new historical knowledge. Even so, as the examples of using performance as a method of historical inquiry and developing a provisional collaborative online archive suggest, there are options that can change substantially not just what we know about women in theatre history but how we go about making knowledge.[14] The limitations that might seem to be natural to the performance of professional scholarship can be overcome.

Placing different kinds of evidence in the theatre history archive enables varied methods of interpretation and inquiry that will effect changes in historiographic practice. While contemporary theatre historians range across these mixtures of materials in developing their published work, the development of a common workspace in which materials of interest are shared and discussed might well re-clutter theatre histories that scholarly monographs tend to present in the form of organized, thesis-driven arguments or continuous narratives. While engaging with the clutter of diverse materials and their potential significance can be rewarding for theatre historiography generally, marginal or seemingly unreadable materials (partial manuscripts, box office receipts, glancing references in a journal, irrationally vitriolic criticism in the press) can prove absolutely central to interpreting the history of women in the theatre. A cluttered archive might well be the best venue for staging feminist theatre history.

In reality, the dispersal of theatre history artifacts among many different institutions limits the likelihood of creating productively cluttered material archives, but the benefits of even a partially stocked but cluttered electronic archive are many—including offering the potential to browse before visiting an actual archival collection, thus leveraging limited travel expenses and making them extend further. While any particular artifact available online might not itself contribute to a researcher's project, the value of that *type* of artifact (say, for example, a playbill) might send a scholar to an online listing of relevant playbill collections (if one exists), and then to a particular collection of materials in search of the specific artifact that could contribute to her work. However, while a cluttered online archive might produce these kinds of efficiencies, it might produce benefits for almost opposite reasons. By presenting more of theatre history's messiness, the online archive might actually complicate inquiry, making it difficult to interpret the wider selection of information or to determine what is and is not relevant to an investigation. In fact, it seems very likely that an online archive might unsettle familiar historiographic practices and epistemologies.[15] Both existing accounts of women's roles in British theatre and scholarly methods of investigation grounded in literary analysis or positivist social science methodology now seem inadequate and flawed.

As a result, while women playwrights' texts may demand new strategies of interpretation, so too do any visual materials related to their work invite new ways of reading images. Whether seemingly representational portraits or caricatured sketches in the popular press, even those images that claim to represent characters from a woman writer's works exist on a continuum of visual styles and strategies that demands careful interpretation. For example, the 1806 engraving of a scene from act 5 of Elizabeth Inchbald's "Such Things Are" shows a woman fainting into the arms of a compassionate British colonial prison reformer while the sultan looks on with concern. In interpreting this image one needs to consider the play's relevance, when first performed in 1787, to the Hastings affair in which issues related to Britain's colonial administration in India were aired publicly, most emotionally in a speech by Richard Brinsley Sheridan— the well-known theatre manager and playwright—before the House of Commons. Then, one can further consider the critical introduction to the play that was published alongside the engraving in *The British Theatre* series in 1806, in which Inchbald herself cannily reminds readers of the historical moment of the play's first performance while strategically calling into question her own presumption in daring to tackle such a subject in the first place. In a case like this one, the complications of "authorship" underlying a visual image are foregrounded. Where do meaningful details of the image originate? Was an actor's interpretation the main source of meaning for the image's portrayed postures? Does the image represent the script's thematic material? Is the choice of actor posture or affect a deliberate part of the publisher's marketing of the volume of collected plays that includes both plays by women writers and critical introductions by one of the best known of these women playwrights? What has the creator of the image conveyed through the style of drawing and affective emphasis? Unlike play texts that are read as literary works, visual images related to women's plays remind us of the complexity of authorship of theatrical work and of its cultural reception.[16] Likewise, interpreting drawings of set designs, of character costumes, or of the public attending a play written by a woman playwright calls for sensitivity to the wider cultural scene in which these plays were staged. If visual materials require users to consider the multiple sources of an image's authorship, an online archive that includes a mixture of materials from period images and play texts to modern performance experiments and critical essays further unsettles a user's belief in a written play's "authorship." Mixed materials—to which an online archive so readily lends itself—denaturalize the limits of any one kind of historical material and remind users of the role they must play in assembling connected readings from the images, commentaries, and primary texts available.

METHODOLOGICAL SELF-REFLECTION AND THE COLLABORATIVE ARCHIVE

Underlying many diverse kinds of historiographic projects are assumptions about what kinds of subjects can be studied, how knowledge emerges, and how inquiry should articulate knowledge. While the subjects of historiography arc seemingly without limits, in order to develop a publishable manuscript some boundary to the subject of inquiry must be defined and some coherent body of knowledge articulated (however provisionally). In contemporary historiographic works, clearly boundaried topics (particular authors, periods, institutions, movements) have increasingly come to be questioned, but still a project's definition of its boundaries makes possible the delivery of a resulting product (a scholarly volume, typically). With the goal of coherent knowledge of a defined object of study in mind, inquiry pursues a progressive and ends-driven path. Only historiographic projects that can be accepted as valid and worthwhile within these parameters receive the support of publication, institutional credit, and even collegial validation, and, as a result, the forms of scholarly production dictate the structures of emerging knowledge. Though the dividing lines between valid and invalid projects are blurry and less clearly delineated than my brief comments suggest, the coarse outline of historiographic assumptions I have provided helps to explain why some inquiry that might easily take place does not.

For instance, while the encyclopedic scholarship of David and Susan Garland Mann has provided a valuable resource for work on women playwrights in England, Scotland, and Ireland, their volume remains only a beginning for those who would desire further engagement with these women's writing and careers.[17] If even a representative sample of the authors and works referenced in the Manns' book were in fact available online in the form of theatre scripts, playbills, contemporary periodical reviews, and references in letters and journals, an ingenious scholar could easily query the data in ways that might reveal important patterns of discourse, circles of affiliation, or social themes. Perhaps someone would notice that the public reputation of Elizabeth Inchbald, then an actress, seemed to undergo an important change when her husband died. Such an observation, if noted online in a discussion thread, might then stimulate a second generation of queries that would ask what other women writers might have said about Inchbald at the time, or how later in her career her public reputation might have influenced how performers of her plays created characterizations or how theatre managers determined which of her plays seemed most marketable. Rather than producing a single published volume that advances a single thesis, a collaborative space of inquiry advances a series of interconnected *essais* into remaking our historiographic discourse. While including visual materials in the online archive challenges interpretive assumptions based on literary interpretation, providing spaces for visibly constructing meaning through mounting, linking, and otherwise using the online archive to perform theatre historiography challenges familiar institutional assumptions about how we write history.

In questioning the methodological and epistemological restrictions placed on historiography by print publishing, of course, I must also acknowledge the institutional structures that bolster the intellectual models that influence much historiographic work. Scholars are evaluated for their individual work. Within departments of English or theatre, there are seldom several scholars with similar areas of specialization and therefore seldom supportive conditions for sustained collaborative work. Though I know that scholars sometimes arrange to meet colleagues socially by coordinating scheduled trips to archives with each other, serial archival pilgrimages are more common than collective working gatherings of specialists. In fact, some of us have been known to deputize a colleague to check something in archival materials for us in order to avoid duplication of travel expenses. As a result, the processes of excavation, showing of findings, and presentation of interpretations are separated from one another in the public professional life of many scholars. The underlying assumptions about both the intellectual shape of historiography and the way historical inquiry functions in the institutions of higher education in which many scholars work block the development of projects that produce knowledge as a sort of by-product of collaborative exchange. Publication of scholarly products—not ongoing historiographic performances—structures how we work.

These assumptions about the practice of professional historiography do not suit the history of British women playwrights in the years around 1800. While the inadequacy of text-based study of performance history has long been obvious, the limitations of traditional forms of scholarly historiography for the study of women in the theatre in the British eighteenth and nineteenth centuries only gradually has come into focus. The reasons for this incompatibility of women's dramaturgical history and scholarly historiography are hard to pin down for they are engrained in our theories of historical knowledge, our institutions, and our forms of historiographic production. When a collaborative online archive and scholarly performance space starts to evolve into not a stable collection of artifacts but a potentially malleable site where excavation, showing of findings, and presentation of interpretations can all be made visible, then the archive becomes a new kind of site for the social performance of historiographic work. One person's inquiry can add to someone else's in surprising ways, and an accumulation of images, texts, and commentary can be supplemented by an additional accumulation of connections among projects and their distinct strategies of historiographic inquiry and performance. With plans to develop over the next year a hypertext archive on Joanna Baillie's 1798 play *De Monfort,* Michael Eberle-Sinatra has begun to contact a number of scholars working on projects related to Baillie. Judith Slagle, editor of two volumes of Baillie's letters, expressed interest in contributing material from her work.

A bibliography on Baillie by Ken Bugajski that has already been published in *Romanticism on the Net* can be linked to the archive. Information and an interview about a volume of essays on Baillie's drama that I am editing for Routledge will further add content to the archive. So, too, will an interview with Catherine Burroughs, who has both edited a volume of essays on women in British Romantic theatre, many of which discuss Baillie, and written a book on Baillie. Not only will these sources provide a rich set of resources on Joanna Baillie, but they will invite and enable additional projects that might add images or texts related to Baillie's plays or to her role as member of a literary circle or as supporter of other women's writing. In online projects, presentation of historiographic work opens social processes, enabling collaborative projects, frequent sharing of findings, and conversation. Online archives are less like a museum than a feminist theatre company, less a collection of inert displays and more a venue for a series of historiographic performances.

Within the archive, a user's self-consciousness about her or his own historiographic performances is invited and—through the potential interactivity of discussion lists and annotation software—made a topic of commentary.[18] Reflection on the performance of historical interpretation itself is a crucial counterpart to the study of particular periods in women's theatre history, as those whose commentaries on method and women's history have argued.[19] Reevaluating how evidence is interpreted and juxtaposed becomes a crucial gesture in the performance of feminist theatre historiography, a gesture that the online archive permits to become a part of a site's emerging collaborative culture. For example, since the online archive must have some structure for its information—whether play texts, other linguistic materials, visual images, or critical commentary—what is online and how it is linked becomes an important gesture by those who mount the material. If an image is linked to a particular play or particular scene from the play, the interpretive juxtaposition invites commentary from the viewer that can then be displayed. If a digital video clip of a performance experiment is mounted, it signifies a choice of object for inquiry, of method, and of style and interpretation within the performance. Even if a group of play texts are mounted and prefaced with critical commentaries, their selection meta-critically establishes and shifts the terms of what texts matter; commentary may further explicate a choice of text, or move beyond such rationalization to pursue biographical significances, thematic material, or stylistic strategies in the play. For example, the *British Women Playwrights around 1800* site has chosen to add texts for a number of different reasons—because the texts had otherwise limited availability, because a scholar already doing research offered to transcribe them, or because their inclusion strategically extended the historical range of the site. The benefit of an online site is that it allows many different participants to "mount"—a verb that wonderfully connects both Web design and theatre performance language—their own mini-archives within the larger social and informational structure of the site. These displayed historiographic gestures become an essential part of the process of interpretation of women's theatre history at the site. Therefore, the visual is both essential historical material for feminist theatre history and a crucial modality in the online performance of new historiographies. In the syntax of historiography the visual is both object and subject. The more we include mixed materials that activate varied ways of reading, the more the strategies of inquiry and interpretation that site participants display demonstrate expanded ways of viewing women and playwriting.

By enabling the social processes that can support historiographic work, the online archive can better suit how we work to the subjects of our inquiry. For example, because dramatic texts are artifacts of theatre's complex gendered social processes, the contexts surrounding a woman playwright's texts are as significant to a feminist theatre historian as literary form. Whether a play script was prepared for the licenser, for a member of the acting company, or for a publisher, its material details bear traces of social processes. While these traces have often been ignored by literary history—whose biases have led it to dwell on textual variants and the authorial or counter-authorial actions they betray—they situate a textual artifact within the complex material circumstances of theatre history and offer an entry point to the gendered history of women in the theatre. Scholarly publishing seldom reproduces the complex layers of visual detail that ephemeral textual artifacts like play scripts offer; even when print publication reproduces facsimiles, its media are inadequate and prohibitively expensive. Although the creation of images for the Web is considerably more flexible and less expensive than for print production, we are still far from being able to outstrip print facsimiles of archival texts. But there is more to the comparison of these media than matters of image quality. Print's limitations come from the necessity of controlling quality—and managing costs—of production; because online reproduction allows for variable quality of delivery to users (depending on their hardware and software of choice), a wider range of visual outputs is permissible. This range allows for economies of cost that could eventually lead to a wider range of reproductions of artifactual images being made available. The Blake Archive is one experiment in this direction (see note 4), though its work does not seem inexpensive unless compared to the costs of making comparable images available in print facsimiles or of traveling to each of the archives in which its originals are held.

I have pursued the example of facsimiles of artifactual materials at length in order to suggest how online media provide significant alternatives to print. While online archives might eventually provide economies that will enable wider engagement with evidence of the social history of women's writing for theatre, in the short term, online workspaces might also produce social processes among scholars that increase access to the social history data available in theatre archives. Even without facsimiles of manuscripts or visual materials online, projects can provide those who visit archives with a venue for sharing their observations about what they find and how they interpret it. By enabling annotation of electronic texts and encouraging updates on interesting findings in archives, an online site allows exchange of information that might otherwise only be found by traveling to an archive or reading the published results of a colleague's research. Print publication only provides a venue for feminist theatre historians' completed interpretations, not for the social processes of inquiry that constitute archival exploration—it supports historiographic "authorship" but not provisional historiographic "performances." Online work nurtures collective social engagement with the social history that archival materials can reveal.[20]

While greater sociability in the archive can play an important role in changing how we think historically, some recent work in theatre history uses performance itself as a method of investigation through which historiographic actors embody words, social spaces, and gestures, and perform speculative interpretations.[21] Rather than seeing performance as a resulting outcome of completed historical investigation, this work uses performing as inquiry, providing provisional interpretations for others to see and participate in revising. Just as essential as handling and viewing the archive's artifacts is trying on styles of dress, behavior, and speech to see what they show us and what we reveal about them. Performance historiography has the potential to explore important questions about the cultural *mise en scène* in which British women playwrights operated in the years around 1800—questions about gendered styles of behavior, about public space, and about theatre as a cultural venue. While performance is currently difficult to mount on a Web site (due to the technical limitations of many users' home computers), the online archive offers the potential of sharing performance clips in the future. In the meantime, it can provide useful resources that might enable more groups to explore archival images and materials through performance. Without such a highly accessible archive of images, students and other performers would be unlikely to encounter, manipulate, or query archival materials themselves. Online resources make images, texts, and commentary widely available, allowing actors to draw on them as the basis for performance exploration. Ultimately, performance experiments can become another kind of historiographic interpretation occupying virtual space alongside critical essays, still images, and play scripts. Again, visual material—particularly in the case of theatre history— is both a powerful stimulus and a form of response to online historiography.

NEW COMMUNITIES, NEW STANDARDS AND VALUES

The kinds of materials that users might soon be able to view within an online theatre archive—encoded play texts, facsimile manuscripts, posters advertising performances, 3D spatial models, and digital video recordings of performance experiments—will require varied forms of "reading" or "viewing" and methods of cross-referencing that stimulate users of theatre history materials to reflect on the performance of historical interpretation. For example, a user might search an encoded manuscript for evidence of a link between a leading actor and certain thematic material in the play's text. She might also scan a promptbook copy of the play for marked changes to the play text that may not have been reflected in subsequent published versions. She might study the postures and clothes of figures on a poster for hints of themes promoted by the theatre management. Potentially, in the not-too-distant future, she might "walk on stage"—in a 3D virtual simulation of one of London's theatres of the early nineteenth century—and gauge the optics of the space from the actor's perspective. Finally, she might look at recorded scenes to note how a particularly heightened moment of character revelation was embodied by the modern actor playing the lead in a recent student production; and then she might compare these performances to reviews of a star actor's performance in the early nineteenth century. Any of these ways of viewing or reading the archive can lead a user to ask follow-up questions that might be pursued by exploring other parts of the archive. She might form a theory about how the complex social process of theatre writing, production, and promotion created the public persona of one of the era's actors. She might speculate about how our modern approaches to performance and gestural idiom lead us to read textual evidence. She might posit that typical audiences today lack key social knowledge that audiences of a particular historical period drew on when interpreting performances. She might recognize lost traces of complex cultural understandings in the performance reviews of another era. An archive stimulates its users to engage in complex performances of theatre historiography that can inform classroom practice and the field's structures of knowledge. Perhaps most significantly, the online archive allows the "she" of whom I speak to be either an undergraduate student, performance practitioner, or a professor.[22]

The significance of professors, students, and performance practitioners using the same online archive does not lie primarily in their being able to consume the same materials. After all, research libraries provide a comparable array of resources; but the socially defined interests of distinct communities of users provide a much greater barrier than material accessibility to participation in shared inquiry. More importantly, as *producers* of material for the online archive, each of these groups has a potential reason for expanding their interest in what their work has in common. The online archive makes it possible to involve a wide range of people in preparing material so that it can change the ways we learn from our students and each other. Of course, allowing a wider community to produce and display interpretations alters longstanding rules about who controls historiographic performances and how standards are negotiated. There is not space in this essay for me to take up these questions fully, but I would suggest that the online collaborative community I envision will function more like a classroom than a refereed journal in terms of its structures or authority. That is, rather than attempting to prevent the visibility of error, the online archive will make negotiations over accuracy, quality, and significance a key part of its intellectual discourse and learning process. Participants will need to develop appreciation for others' expertise and earn authority within the community's discourse.

There are of course challenges to an archive of materials produced from many different sources. While standards for quality become increasingly hard to uphold, the cultural specificity of what scholars call "standards" becomes more apparent when the values and standards of other groups with interests in using the archive are seriously considered. What might be an essential matter of version distinction and authority in scholarly textual editing might be less important to some theatre practitioners; expectations that scholars might have that only images of high quality should be posted online might seem less essential to students for whom any opportunity to view images from British periodicals in the early nineteenth century comes as a pleasurable and enlightening surprise. Negotiation about what standards and values will determine online contributions to a theatre history archive are essential; in fact, such discussions are one of the most important ways in which scholars can teach—and learn—about the communities of inquiry that form around Web-based projects. At the *British Women Playwrights around 1800* site, we have worked with members of an editorial board both to identify colleagues engaged in interesting work that could be added to the site, and to discuss explicitly some of the issues raised in establishing standards of quality and accuracy and the processes needed to realize them. Email discussions about these topics have become part of the site's content. I suspect, however, that scholars are unprepared to answer the complex questions involving newly formed communities and their standards, and won't learn how to approach these issues until they are part of our daily work. But will projects like the *British Women Playwrights around 1800* site become a part of many scholars' lives? A further challenge to the management and development of a site like ours is the lack of financial or institutional support for the work of general editors. Both Michael Eberle-Sinatra and I put in hours of unpaid time to keep the site developing, but our full-time jobs—either in or out of academia—do not much support us in sustaining the project.[23] And yet, the role of such a site's general editors in facilitating the social process of site development and in guiding quality control processes (such as identifying and working with reviewers) is crucial to the long-term project of building an online archive and collaborative community.

If fifteen or twenty professors anywhere in the world are teaching courses that touch upon the theatre writing of women in Britain around 1800, each of their classes can potentially use and contribute to the developing online archive. If a teacher doesn't find the materials she would like to use with her class online at the site, she could simply make them available to a small group through photocopying, but, with the aid of those participating in an online working group, she could post the materials to the site so that many others can use them as well. Little by little, the materials teachers want their students to use become part of a wider collection, providing not only resource materials but an anthology constituted by interest and classroom practice. What develops is a new kind of canon building, but rather than simply providing a play text and perhaps some related transcribed letters or a critical introduction, teachers can add their syllabi and other classroom materials to the site, allowing other teachers to be stimulated by the pedagogical approaches being tried elsewhere. Furthermore, many teachers with graduate students or advanced undergraduates might assign as one project option the development of a "suite" in the expanding archive.[24] Some might prepare the text of a play along with related excerpts from reviews and other writing of the time that provides interesting ways into the play text itself. Others might prepare listings of available resources housed in other artifactual archives, even linking to online sites for those institutions and thus bridging the gap between historical information and the social practices of historiographic inquiry.

A trend in this direction could radically change the relationships between teachers and students, removing the boundaries created by the local limitations of the classroom—in which the knowledge, experience, and resources that a single teacher can make available establish the horizon of student work—and encouraging teachers to focus on becoming effective coaches of student inquiry. Though direct instruction remains an essential part of the classroom we might envision, a new group of workshop activities drawing on the online archive and other comparable resources becomes more easily accessible and makes project-based learning for students of women's theatre history a real possibility. Not only would more material become available for students and their teachers to *consume,* but students—as *producers* of material for the online archive—can explore beyond their local professor's inquiry. As a result, even a seemingly "over-specialized" field such as feminist theatre historiography could begin to develop an ongoing loop of production-exchange-consumption that repositions the classroom—or potentially the rehearsal hall—as a newly visible venue of historiographic performance.

Online archives and working groups have the potential to stimulate and nourish historical work on under-researched and unlikely-to-be-republished writings like those of women playwrights in Britain around 1800. A large part of the initial interest stimulated by projects such as the *British Women Playwrights around 1800* site comes from their making accessible texts and materials that are otherwise unavailable to all but a few. But, as the project develops, a second kind of interest takes over: interest in collegial participation and dialogue in an emerging community of inquiry that goes beyond listserv exchanges. This second kind of interest has applicability to projects that are not focused on inaccessible historical materials; it provides the motive for a new kind of teaching and learning space that combines elements of the scholarly journal, the conference, the rehearsal hall, and the potential of newly organized departments consisting of scholarly colleagues and students. The Web's ability to influence scholarly performance emerges from its literal and social visibility as a medium. While that visibility sometimes produces hesitancy in professionals as cautious about display as academics sometimes are, it is a visibility that women playwrights both sought in the years around 1800 in Britain—though in many cases they were aware of its potential dangers—and deserve now because their works and histories are essential to the full picture of British cultural history. The *British Women Playwrights around 1800* project aims to serve the histories of these women and to influence the future of scholarly collaboration.

NOTES

1. This session included papers by Tracy Davis, Catherine Burroughs, Nora Nachumi, and me on how studying the work of these women playwrights might alter our understanding of cultural history; Margaret Ezell responded to our papers. The papers that constituted this session later became part of "British Women Playwrights around 1800," volume 12 of *Romanticism on the Net.*

2. I use the phrase "women's writing of drama and theatre scripts" or, more simply, "women's theatre writing," deliberately to mark the social complexities of women's writing

in these forms in Britain in the era around 1800. Women writers of this period both wrote and published poetic dramas primarily intended for reading and, at the far end of the spectrum, wrote speeches, songs, and fragments of dialogue for performance that were never published. Because gaining access to theatrical performance was for women writers of this era sometimes personally and socially difficult, historians of this portion of literary and theatre history need to avoid assuming normative ideas of "drama" or "theatre scripts" in order to engage with the wide range of important textual evidence of women's activity in this field of writing. See Donkin for a group of related studies of women playwrights of this era.

3. I use the terms "writer" and "author" to mark an important distinction in the roles that women active in British theatre in the years after 1800 play. Moody provides a thoughtful analysis of the complexity of determining women's theatrical authorship in this era. Other essays in the Davis and Donkin collection also offer interesting perspectives on the relationship between playwriting and authorship for women in the theatre of this era.

4. Approaches to encoding and presenting images via the Web have been pioneered by the University of Virginia and the William Blake Archive. See "Editorial Principles: Methodology and Standards in the Blake Archive"; McGann for a discussion of the issues involved; and Carson for discussion of the strategies behind *The Cambridge King Lear CD-ROM: Text and Performance History Archive.*

5. I discuss the ways in which women playwrights used both publication and production of their works in creating their public personae in my essay "Authorial Performances in the Criticism and Theory of Romantic Women Playwrights."

6. See, for example, Worthen and Rouse.

7. See, for example, Baer, Simpson, Hoagwood, and Cox ("Ideology and Genre").

8. Several editions of plays by women of the era lay the groundwork for further critical work on the authors involved: Inchbald (ed. Manvell), Gore et al. (ed. Franceschina), and Burney (ed. Sabor). Manvell published his *Elizabeth Inchbald, England's Principal Woman Dramatist and Independent Woman of Letters in 18th Century London: A Biographical Study* in the same year as his facsimile edition of her plays. Both Franceschina and Sabor build critical discussions into their editions.

9. For discussions of the place of (mainly male) playwrights in the theatre of Britain in the late eighteenth and early nineteenth centuries, see Stephens and Donohue.

10. In my essay "Authorial Performances in the Criticism and Theory of Romantic Women Playwrights," I consider the value of adapting Patrice Pavis's analysis of the interaction of dramatic text and *mise en scène* to analysis of British women playwrights' writing for the theatrical culture of the era just after the French Revolution.

11. For the most thorough discussions of women's social navigation of playwriting careers, see Donkin and also Tracy Davis ("Sociable Playwright").

12. In a recent year-long series of public readings in New York City titled "The First 100 Years: The Professional Female Playwright," organizers Mallory Catlett and Gwynn MacDonald invited a number of small companies to explore and present plays by Aphra Behn, Susanna Centlivre, Hannah Cowley, Elizabeth Inchbald, and Joanna Baillie. The significance of problems of access to theatrical investigation of women's dramatic materials is illustrated by the important role that Catlett, MacDonald, and scholars working with them played simply through making electronic texts of the plays and historical information about the playwrights readily available.

13. See, for example, Ezell (*Writing Women's Literary History,* "Revisioning Responding"), Davis ("Sociable Playwright"), and Crochunis ("Function of the Dramatic Closet").

14. See Newey's discussion of using online resources in teaching women's theatre history. As I see it, the "over-specialization problem" much remarked upon in academia recently is mainly due to the current configuration of institutions of higher education. Departments consist of colleagues unable to engage or evaluate each other's specialized work, and scholars/teachers need to teach more "general" subjects in order to provide basic knowledge to students in prescribed sequences that support disciplinary coherence within departments (as they are currently constituted). With the emergence of online media as a viable alternative teaching and learning space, wider selections of specialization or expertise will be available to learners and to colleagues, profoundly challenging the inevitability of the discipline or department as institutional or epistemological structures.

15. For examples of several discussions of the complexities of theatre historiography, see Quinn, Vince, Roach, and McConachie. Also, see Tracy Davis's approach to applying economic analysis to social and feminist historiographic practice, in particular in *Actresses as Working Women* and *The Economics of the British Stage.*

16. Bennett provides a thoughtful overview of the theoretical issues involved in theatre's cultural reception.

17. Their book *Women Playwrights in England, Ireland, and Scotland, 1660–1823* provides thorough chronological lists and short descriptive entries on a large number of theatre pieces and dramas written by women that were published or performed in the period covered by their volume. The book documents in detail women's theatre writing activity in the late eighteenth and early nineteenth centuries. Through an agreement with Indiana University Press, much of the material from the Manns' book will be mounted at the *British Women Playwrights around 1800* site, thereby making it possible for other contributors to the site to link the Manns' work hypertextually and use such linkages to inflect their own additions to the site.

18. Carson notes of projects like *The Cambridge King Lear CD-ROM: Text and Performance History Archive* that to some scholars "exposing the workings of the scholarly process may seem threatening; however, for the discipline as a whole this process must be seen as a means of dramatically increasing the variety and scope of the work that can be undertaken" (435).

19. See, for example, Tracy Davis (*Actresses as Working Women,* "Editorial") and also Bratton ("Miss Scott and Miss Macauley"). Ezell (*Writing Women's Literary History*) provides a thorough discussion of this kind of methodological self-reflexivity.

20. Carson suggests that multi-media materials on theatre might shift the emphasis of scholarship from production to rehearsal and other theatre creation processes, processes that can now be documented through audio and video and whose designer sketches and other working documents can be electronically archived (438–39). A similar case can be made for the role online multi-media could play in opening up historiographic process to ongoing collaboration, perhaps even changing where matters of standards get addressed from reviews afterwards to expert guidance during the process of inquiry. In fact, this change is already occurring in many online working groups.

21. I am indebted to Jacky Bratton for sharing with me copies of the journal *Studies in Theatre Production,* published by the University of Exeter; this journal frequently publishes articles dealing with historiographic work done through performance. Similarly,

occasional articles in *Theatre Topics,* published by The Johns Hopkins University Press, also deal with performance as a form of historiographic inquiry. Bratton has also shared materials from some of her courses at Royal Holloway, University of London, in which she, her colleague Gilli Bush-Baily, and their students employ this method of inquiry.

22. As Carson remarks of the *King Lear CD-ROM* project, "the reasoning behind the construction of this archive has always been to provide an opportunity not only to see the primary materials which support research in this area, but also to provide sufficient materials to question, contest or confirm the opinions that 'experts' put forward" (435).

23. While my co-editor, Michael Eberle-Sinatra, was hired for a tenure track position, I continue to work a full-time job in education research. In the past year or so, development of new content for the *British Women Playwrights around 1800* Web site has been slowed by our increasing work responsibilities. Work on the site used to fit snugly between the cracks of our other scholarly work, but now it competes unsuccessfully for time with our families and our paid work. Some of our efforts have gone toward collaborating with Alex Dick and Catherine Burroughs on a working-group conference, "Drama and Theatre History, 1770–1840," that was held in conjunction with the August 2002 North American Society for the Study of Romanticism conference in London, Ontario. It was striking to me that the kind of sustained work needed to keep developing the Web site has now become more difficult for us to perform than the intensive work needed to stage a conference.

24. The Corvey Collection's online project (http://www2.shu.ac.uk/corvey/CW3/) uses this approach, inviting students to develop electronic suites of historical materials on women writers whose works are in the library's collection (though the works themselves are not accessible at the collection's Web site).

WORKS CITED

Baer, Marc. *Theatre and Disorder in Late Georgian London.* Oxford: Clarendon Press, 1992.

Bennett, Susan. *Theatrical Audiences: A Theory of Production and Reception.* 2nd ed. New York: Routledge, 1997.

Bratton, J. S. "Miss Scott and Miss Macauley: 'Genius Comes in All Disguises.'" *Theatre Survey* 37.1 (May 1996): 59–74.

Bratton, Jacky. "Jane Scott the Writer-Manager." *Women and Playwriting in Nineteenth-Century Britain.* Ed. Tracy C. Davis and Ellen Donkin. Cambridge: Cambridge UP, 1999. 77–98.

British Women Playwrights around 1800: New Paradigms and Recoveries. Spec. issue of *Romanticism on the Net* 12 (November 1998). 2 November 2003 <http://www.erudit.org/revue/ron/1998/v/n12/005827ar.html>.

Burney, Frances. *The Complete Plays of Frances Burney.* Ed. Peter Sabor. 2 vols. Montreal: McGill-Queen's UP, 1995.

Carson, Christie. "Creating and Context: The Case of *King Lear.*" *Theatre Journal* 51.4 (1999): 433–41.

Conolly, L. W. *The Censorship of English Drama 1737–1824.* San Marino, CA: Huntington Library, 1976.

Cox, Jeffrey N. "Ideology and Genre in the British Antirevolutionary Drama in the 1790s." *British Romantic Drama: Historical and Critical Essays.* Ed. Terence Allan Hoagwood and Daniel P. Watkins. Madison, NJ: Fairleigh Dickinson UP, 1998. 84–114.

Crochunis, Thomas C. "Authorial Performances in the Criticism and Theory of Romantic Women Playwrights." *Women in British Romantic Theatre: Drama, Performance, and Society, 1790–1840.* Ed. Catherine B. Burroughs. Cambridge: Cambridge UP, 2000. 223–54.

———. "The Function of the Dramatic Closet at the Present Time." *British Women Playwrights around 1800: New Paradigms and Recoveries.* Spec. issue of *Romanticism on the Net* 12 (November 1998). 8 February 2003 <http://www-sul.stanford.edu/mirrors/romnet/bwpcro.html>.

Davis, Jim. "Sarah Lane: Questions of Authorship." *Women and Playwriting in Nineteenth-Century Britain.* Ed. Tracy C. Davis and Ellen Donkin. Cambridge: Cambridge UP, 1999. 125–47.

Davis, Tracy C. *Actresses As Working Women: Their Social Identity in Victorian Culture.* London: Routledge, 1991.

———. *The Economics of the British Stage, 1800–1914.* Cambridge UP, 2000.

———. Editorial introducing the book review section. *Nineteenth Century Theatre* 24.1 (summer 1996): 36–41.

———. "The Sociable Playwright and Representative Citizen." *Women and Playwriting in Nineteenth-Century Britain.* Ed. Tracy C. Davis and Ellen Donkin. Cambridge: Cambridge UP, 1999. 15–34.

Donkin, Ellen. *Getting into the Act: Women Playwrights in London 1776–1828.* New York: Routledge, 1995.

Donohue, Joseph. *Theatre in the Age of Kean.* Totowa, NJ: Rowman and Littlefield, 1975.

"Editorial Principles: Methodology and Standards in the Blake Archive." *William Blake Archive.* 24 January 2003; 2 November 2003 <http://www.blakearchive.org/public/about/principles/index.html>.

Ezell, Margaret J. M. "Revisioning Responding: A Second Look at Women Playwrights around 1800." *British Women Playwrights around 1800: New Paradigms and Recoveries.* Spec. issue of *Romanticism on the Net* 12 (November 1998). 2 November 2003 <http://www.erudit.org/revue/ron/1998/v/n12/005821ar.html >.

———. *Writing Women's Literary History.* Baltimore: Johns Hopkins UP, 1993.

Gore, Catherine. *Gore on Stage: The Plays of Catherine Gore.* Ed. John Franceschina. New York: Garland, 1999.

Gore, Catherine, et al. *Sisters of Gore: Seven Gothic Melodramas by British Women, 1790–1843.* Ed. John Franceschina. New York: Garland, 1997.

Hoagwood, Terence Allan. "Romantic Drama and Historical Hermeneutics." *British Romantic Drama: Historical and Critical Essays.* Ed. Terence Allan Hoagwood and Daniel P. Watkins. Madison, NJ: Fairleigh Dickinson UP, 1998. 22–55.

Inchbald, Elizabeth. *Selected Comedies.* Ed. Roger Manvell. Lanham, MD: UP of America, 1987.

Mann, David D., and Susan Garland Mann, with Camille Garnier. *Women Playwrights in England, Ireland, and Scotland, 1660–1823.* Bloomington: Indiana UP, 1996.

Manvell, Roger. *Elizabeth Inchbald, England's Principal Woman Dramatist and Independent Woman of Letters in 18th Century London: A Biographical Study.* Lanham, MD: UP of America, 1987.

McConachie, Bruce A. "Towards a Postpositivist Theatre History." *Theatre Journal* 37 (1985): 465–86.

McGann, Jerome. "The Rossetti Archive and Image-Based Electronic Editing." *The Literary Text in the Digital Age.* Ed. Richard J. Finneran. Ann Arbor: U of Michigan P, 1996. 145–83.

Moody, Jane. "Illusions of Authorship." *Women and Playwriting in Nineteenth-Century Britain.* Ed. Tracy C. Davis and Ellen Donkin. Cambridge: Cambridge UP, 1999. 99–124.

Newey, Kate. "Women's Theatrical Texts and Contexts." *British Women Playwrights around 1800.* Ed. Michael Eberle-Sinatra and Thomas C. Crochunis. 1 March 1999, 11 November 2003 <http://www-sul.stanford.edu/mirrors/romnet/wp1800/essays/newey1.html>.

Pavis, Patrice. "From Page to Stage: A Difficult Birth." Trans. Jilly Daugherty. *Theatre at the Crossroads of Culture.* London: Routledge, 1992. 24–47.

Quinn, Michael. "Theatrewissenschaft in the History of Theatre Study." *Theatre Survey* 32 (1991): 123–36.

Roach, Joseph R. Introduction to "Theatre History and Historiography" section. *Critical Theory and Performance.* Ed. Janelle G. Reinelt and Joseph R. Roach. Ann Arbor: U of Michigan P, 1992. 293–98.

Rouse, John. "Textuality and Authority in Theater and Drama: Some Contemporary Possibilities." *Critical Theory and Performance.* Ed. Janelle G. Reinelt and Joseph R. Roach. Ann Arbor: U of Michigan P, 1992. 146–57.

Simpson, Michael. Introduction. *Closet Performances: Political Exhibition and Prohibition in the Dramas of Byron and Shelley.* Stanford: Stanford UP, 1998. 1–24.

Stephens, John Russell. *The Profession of the Playwright: British Theatre 1800–1900.* Cambridge: Cambridge UP, 1992.

Sutherland, Kathryn. "Looking and Knowing: Textual Encounters of a Postponed Kind." *Beyond the Book: Theory, Culture, and the Politics of Cyberspace.* Ed. Warren Chernaik, Marilyn Deegan, and Andrew Gibson. Oxford: Office for Humanities Communication, 1996. 11–22.

Vince, R. W. "Theatre History As an Academic Discipline." *Interpreting the Theatrical Past: Essays in the Historiography of Performance.* Ed. Thomas Postlewait and Bruce A. McConachie. Iowa City: U of Iowa P, 1989. 1–18.

Worthen, W. B. "Drama, Performativity, and Performance." *PMLA* 113.5 (October 1998): 1093–1107.

Haunting in the Age of Electronic Post-literacy

STEPHANIE TRIPP

As soon as one stops searching for
knowledge, or if one imagines that it
need not be creatively sought in the depths
of the human spirit but can be assembled
extensively by collecting and classifying
facts, everything is irrevocably and forever
lost, lost for learning which soon vanishes
so far out of the picture that it even leaves
language behind like an empty pod, and
lost for the state as well.[1]

—WILHELM VON HUMBOLDT
(*Humanist Without Portfolio* 134)

As soon as one no longer distinguishes spirit
from specter, the former assumes a body, it
incarnates itself, as spirit, in the specter. . . .
It becomes, rather, some "thing" that remains
difficult to name: neither soul nor body, and
both one and the other.

—JACQUES DERRIDA
(*Specters of Marx* 6)

Perhaps it is fitting for an essay on haunting to begin with a tale of déjà vu. The tale originates in Berlin in 1809 as Wilhelm von Humboldt sketches out his plan for a new German university. His dilemma seems eerily familiar: How can a university founded on secular reason justify the study of what we now call the humanities against an instrumentalist appeal to practical knowledge? Upon what authority can the humanities base the pursuit of common human self-understanding at a time when populations are growing more mobile and when knowledge

is becoming more specialized? Humboldt, the linguist as well as the diplo-
mat, narrates in the epigraph above a cautionary tale of loss, of a hollowing
out so thorough that it renders language itself "an empty pod." What ostensibly fills this pod—and delivers the humanities scholar from bereave-
ment—is not God, or Reason, but *Geist*. For nearly two centuries, *Geist,* as
collective "mind" or "spirit," has conceptually joined the scholar to the university and, thus, the improvement of the individual to the good of the
whole. But as Humboldt's tale repeats itself in the present day of multicultural college campuses, vast virtual libraries untethered from the traditional
hierarchies that classify and evaluate knowledge, and scholars wired to
high-speed telecommunications networks, this conceptual linkage grows
increasingly untenable; instead of *Geist,* all we see are ghosts.

Corresponding to a resurgence in the Gothic aesthetic in the culture at
large, there has been a marked predilection for ghostly rhetoric among
humanities scholars in recent years, especially in discussions of the history
and structure of the disciplines themselves. Within the logic of grammatology,[2] the study of the theory and history of writing, the movement from print
culture to electronic culture requires new methods of organizing and presenting ideas. In its emphasis on organizing knowledge across the disciplines,
this article approaches the haunting of humanities discourse from within the
framework of the "grammatological apparatus," which Gregory L. Ulmer
defines as "an interactive mix of technology, institutional practices, and ideological subject formation" (*Heuretics* 17). This approach assumes that the
current challenges facing the humanities arise from profound shifts during
the past thirty years not only in classroom and research technology, but also
in practices of evaluating and legitimating knowledge, and in notions of individual and cultural identity. Ulmer suggests that adapting the humanities
to the twenty-first-century classroom requires more than adjusting for technological change: "The goal is not to adapt digital technology to literacy (anyway, that is happening as a matter of course), but to discover and create an
institution and its practices capable of supporting the full potential of the
new technology" (*Internet Invention* 29). Ulmer has dubbed the institution
he is trying to discover "electracy," a neologism that combines "electronic"
and "literacy" ("I Untied" 581). Electracy involves more than stylistic innovation; it shifts the focus of academic writing from argument to invention.
"The theory of the apparatus in grammatology indicates that electracy

should be to invention what literacy has been to proof," Ulmer writes. "The first step toward making good on this possibility is to introduce into schooling the aesthetic register of thought; learning, that is, may simulate discovery. Electracy is the prosthesis of discovery, augmenting it, democratizing it, making discovery writable" ("I Untied" 581).

My own pursuit of new humanities practices for the age of electracy—or, if you prefer, electronic post-literacy—is informed both by Ulmer's insights into creative invention and the rhetoric of haunting that wafts through so many discussions of the humanities these days. I began speculating about the convergence of humanities scholarship, electronic new media, and haunting when I encountered Jacques Derrida's *Specters of Marx* shortly after its translation into English in 1994. In *Specters,* Derrida not only deconstructs the claims of inheritance, disinterestedness, and ontological grounding that have surrounded Marxist scholarship—and, by extension, humanities scholarship in general—but it also provides an alternate approach to figures of the Western canon, beginning with one of the most canonical: Shakespeare's *Hamlet.* Specifically, the method of research and writing I seek to develop derives from what Derrida has called "hauntology." A pun on ontology, hauntology offers rich possibilities for engaging narratives in ways that displace, without completely replacing, my discipline's dominant model of hermeneutics. The goal is to theorize from hauntology a scholarly method that may be for the humanities in the twenty-first century what hermeneutics was to the humanities in the past two centuries. A good starting point would be to explore what any new method must hold in common with hermeneutics: an interest in how one's culture officially remembers its dead. Perhaps the rise in scholarly discussions of ghosts and haunting can be attributed, at least in part, to anxious speculation about what happens to the dead when our memory technologies are altered as dramatically as they have been in the past few decades.

The penchant for writing about haunting has extended across a number of scholarly works in the humanities. A case in point is Kathleen Brogan's *Cultural Haunting: Ghosts and Ethnicity in Recent American Literature* (1998). While watching the opening performance of August Wilson's *The Piano Lesson* in 1987, Brogan first developed the insight that "ghosts were populating African-American literature in growing numbers" (Brogan 1). Further observation convinced Brogan that the spectral proliferation was not limited to African American literature but was, "in fact, a pan-ethnic phenomenon, registering a widespread concern with questions of ethnic identity and cultural transmission" (4).

The same year Brogan's book announced a new genre of "cultural haunting," David Punter published *Gothic Pathologies: The Text, the Body, and the Law,* a book that makes broader connections between haunting and literary theory, arguing, in fact, that haunting "is the form of all textuality" (1). Other books since the early 1990s that have explored various registers of haunting in the humanities include Jean-Michel Rabaté's *The Ghosts of Modernity* (1996), Avery F. Gordon's *Ghostly Matters: Haunting and the Sociological Imagination* (1997), Peter Buse and Andrew Stott's edited collection *Ghosts: Deconstruction, Psychoanalysis, History* (1999), and Jeffrey Sconce's *Haunted Media: Electronic Presence from Telegraphy to Television* (2000). Commenting on the ascendant "Gothic mode" in the "fin-de-siècle academic world," Mark Edmundson traces ghostly elements in the work of contemporary theorists from Derrida to Michel Foucault to Slavoj Zizek: "Much, though surely not all, of what is called theory draws on Gothic idioms. Its subject is haunting" (40).

While the aforementioned texts, and other books and articles too numerous to list, cover an array of topics and rhetorical approaches, their references to ghosts and haunting seem to cluster around two representational problems: the inability of the whole to comprehend its parts and the lacuna between a thing and what it is presumed to represent. Derrida illustrates the first type of problem in *Specters of Marx* when he refers to specters as *plus d'un*.[3] The term's dual meaning of both "no more one" and "more than one" provides a prescient view of the university's current predicament. "University" comes to English speakers, through the French, from the ancient Latin *universum,* which means "the whole world." *Universum* is the singular form of *universus,* which the OED defines as "all taken collectively, universal." Ironically, as the university becomes more "universal" in one sense—more widely accessible through social, economic, and technological globalization—its claim to universality in the other sense—one standard that applies to all—grows more attenuated.

The second group of humanities texts employing ghostly figures converges around a notion of the ghost as marker of a gap, something missing or left out. For the most part, these texts address haunting through the discourse of psychoanalysis: trauma, "the uncanny," and repressed memories. The consistent recourse to psychoanalytic narrative in treating the subject of haunting is not surprising considering that, since as far back as the early nineteenth century, Western culture has viewed ghosts as products of the mind. Terry Castle suggests that this "very significant transformation in human consciousness over the past two centuries" coincides with a "rhetorical displacement" in the discourse of post-Enlightenment debunking of the supernatural phenomena (141). "What we find," Castle writes, "is that the demystifying project was peculiarly compromised from the start. The rationalists did not so much negate the traditional spirit world as displace it into the realm of psychology" (161).

Rather than disappearing, the ghost becomes internalized and, as Freud informs us a century later, manifests itself in the human psyche as the experience of "something familiar and old-established in the mind that has been estranged only by the process of repression" (Freud 394). Castle argues that "the uncanny" Freud describes in the early twentieth century actually is an "invention" of the late eighteenth century: "[T]he historic Enlightenment internalization of the spectral—the gradual reinterpretation of ghosts and apparitions as *hallucinations,* or projections of the mind—introduced a new uncanniness into human consciousness itself. The mind became a 'world of phantoms' and thinking itself an act of ghost-seeing" (Castle's emphasis; 17).

The Enlightenment disavowal of ghosts arises from a rationalist tradition whose genesis is bound inexorably to the emergence of the printing press. Print culture's emphasis on uniformity and standardization "functionally matched an intellectual interest in the systematic comparison and critical evaluation of knowledge that characterized the new science" (Deibert 77). Around 1800, at the height of what Friedrich A. Kittler describes as the "discourse network" of print,[4] a spate of ghost-debunking publications began emerging from England, France, and Germany (Castle 163). These treatises brandished the methods of the new science to attack notions of a spirit world supported by orthodox religion. Further, the theocracy criticized by intellectuals such as the Young Hegelians in early-nineteenth-century Germany was itself a product of a moribund manuscript culture. In this way, the transformation of ghosts from incarnations of souls of the dead to mental hallucinations can be viewed in conjunction with what Benedict Anderson describes as the rise of "print capitalism" (37–38).

The rise of literacy, print capitalism's burgeoning production of books, and a proliferation of fields of study posed challenges for European universities that had remained largely unchanged since the Renaissance. The printing press gave scholars the means to pursue their own interests through independent reading, and pressures for increasing specialization threatened to undermine the rationale for a more liberal education. A group of prominent German thinkers, concerned over this unexamined tendency toward specialization, undertook reforms "to provide university studies with a basis clearly detached from the narrowly vocational, utilitarian arguments of the Enlightenment" (Röhrs 14).

Educational reform in Germany fell to a group of intellectuals steeped in the philosophical tradition of Immanuel Kant, among them Wilhelm von Humboldt, Johann Gottlieb Fichte, and Friedrich Schleiermacher. Their efforts produced the first modern research university, which was founded at Berlin in 1810 (Röhrs 16). The reformers successfully advocated a policy of academic freedom and led the movement away from practices of rote memorization and toward the modern lecture format. More than half a century later, a general hermeneutics predicated on universal understanding would become the official method of a new discipline. The human sciences, or *Geisteswissenschaften* (literally the sciences of "mind" or "spirit"), were so named by Wilhelm Dilthey, who published his *Introduction to the Human Sciences* in 1883. Dilthey believed the various human sciences had a common structure that made it possible for them to share a common methodology. He organized the multiple disciplines—those that today would correspond to a combined humanities and social sciences—under a general grouping of the human sciences and the shared methodology of hermeneutics.

The *Geist* in *Geisteswissenschaften,* as we have seen, carries with it complex philosophical connotations, and the appropriateness of its use has been a matter of contemporary scholarly debate.[5] *Geist* plays an indispensable role in organizing the human sciences as a discipline. The *Geisteswissenschaften*— aesthetics, history, theology, political science, sociology, and literary criticism—all take as their subject matter "mental objects" or "objectifications of life" (Bontekoe 41). As an object of study, the mental object must reside in fact; in other words, it requires a physical instantiation. This instantiation occurs through the sensual mediation of common understanding. Dilthey states this explicitly in "The Rise of Hermeneutics" (1900):

> We therefore call understanding that process by which we recognize, behind signs given to our senses, that psychic reality of which they are the expressions. Such understanding ranges from grasping the babblings of children to *Hamlet* or the *Critique of Pure Reason*. Through stone and marble, musical notes, gestures, words, and texts, actions, economic regulations and constitutions, the same human spirit addresses us and demands interpretation. (236–37)

Hence, Dilthey's hermeneutic method for the human sciences depends on a certain number of archetypal experiences and basic mental states common to all human beings (Bontekoe 42).

In developing a practice of hermeneutics applicable to all the human sciences, Dilthey found a way to tie together various texts and fields of study according to what they most held in common. He responded to challenges that were very similar to those of today: the opening of educational institutions to different types of peoples (in the nineteenth century the lower classes, today multiple racial and ethnic groups); an unwieldy collection of fields and departments; and a compulsion to justify work that falls outside the realm of the natural or physical sciences. Dilthey's response to those challenges has persevered for more than a century, but since the 1960s, the humanities and the social sciences have been under increasing stress. Pressures to diversify the curriculum and student body, a crisis in representation articulated by poststructuralist critique,[6] and enormous shifts in technology have forced those of us working in the humanities to reevaluate our goals and methods. As Elaine Showalter notes, "We all know that the humanities are in trouble everywhere in terms of enrollments and declining undergraduate majors. . . . In short, one major source of our present malaise is our inability to articulate a shared vision of our goal that can provide a sense of ongoing purpose and connection" (B9).

Accompanying the social and cultural diversification taking place in the contemporary Western university is "the crisis of information and visual overload in everyday life" associated with what Nicholas Mirzoeff calls "visual culture" (8). Visualizing, Mirzoeff explains, is a technique of comprehending complex information simultaneously rather than sequentially (5–6). A student visualizes when she conducts a library search on her personal computer at the same time she is watching a video clip of the lunar landing and monitoring her e-mail for a message from her professor. This "multi-tasking" usually takes place outside the traditional structures of learning and, thus, lacks the markers of relevance or importance that students had grown accustomed to before the advent of the Internet. Increasingly, data produced by the culture at large merges with that produced by the academy, and the two are, in fact, often indistinguishable. This blurring of boundaries occurs most noticeably in the milieu of digitized information, where words and images that fill a scholar's computer screen may come from several academic, government, community, or commercial sources. Thus, from a practical standpoint, the computerized teaching and research environment is a mélange of texts, interests, and motivations that resists any central "filtering" system. Thomas Bender, Dean of Humanities at New York University, argues that traditional scholars cannot afford to dismiss knowledge produced beyond the gates of the academy:

> Alternative, not-for-profit sites for knowledge-making are being developed to assemble vital knowledge not being produced by universities. Research and advocacy groups are undermining the university's presumed monopoly on authoritative knowledge. . . . If we academics disdain such work, we not only risk marginalization, but also cut ourselves off from a needed stimulus. We must acknowledge the inherent value of multiple sites and styles of knowledge production. (8)

To respond seriously to Bender's call to "acknowledge the inherent value of multiple sites of knowledge production" one must examine how changes occur in the production of knowledge within a particular institution or the culture at large, taking into account all the elements of the grammatological apparatus.

Consider the observations of Alvin B. Kernan. Kernan, well known for his polemics against the influence of theory and cultural studies within English departments, acknowledges that changes in academic publishing, research, and pedagogy are part of a more fundamental movement away from the print literacy that has shaped his professional values, like those of so many of his contemporaries. Kernan characterizes the changes as the "shifts of these huge tectonic plates—demographic, cultural, technological." He further observes that even the conception of knowledge, "the primary product of higher education," will be affected by these seismic rumblings: "We have, therefore, to speak of a fourth major shift, an epistemological one, which tended like the other revolutions in a democratic direction by questioning established authority and 'empowering' a much wider intellectual competence" (Kernan xvi).

In his memoirs, Kernan laments that few students from even the nation's elite institutions care about reading literature nowadays. He illustrates his frustrations with the following anecdote taken from his final semesters of teaching at Princeton, when the long-familiar terrain of the literature course became for him a tortuous series of problems to negotiate:

> In my last years of teaching an undergraduate lecture course in Shakespeare, even with very intelligent students, I found myself looking for ways of getting around the fact that they had not read the texts, or had read them with almost no comprehension. Easy enough in the lectures—you simply filled in the story, read and explained key passages; but in the discussion sections I had to devise the method of picking a central scene, assigning students parts to read in it, having them play the scene, and then, only then, talking about what it meant. One student complimented me, he thought, by saying at the end of the term that I had made the plays sound sufficiently interesting that he hoped that he would have time to read them someday. (240–41)

The story points out in these students of the information age an absence of careful and patient reading—a skill valorized by print literacy. It also shows that the meritocratic ideal associated with the Great Books curriculum is being supplanted by a notion of "competition for attention" found in consumer entertainment culture: A Shakespeare play warrants a reading only if it proves "sufficiently interesting."

I find it compelling, and not entirely coincidental, that Kernan's anecdote focuses on Shakespeare, around whose work "English" was founded as a national literature. Shakespeare seems to function as a sort of limit case for confirming our professional anxieties in English departments. Certainly, Kernan is not alone in invoking the Bard when English literature itself appears to be at stake. Murray Krieger alludes to *Hamlet* when the topic turns to contemporary strife in literature departments: "I have seen the poem and its antireductive interpreters as playing Hamlet to the theorist's Horatio" (Krieger 81). And Showalter suggests that a promising model for teaching literature centers on Shakespearean drama: "Since the 1960s, many

Shakespeare scholars have made performance their primary pedagogical tool, pioneering a revolutionary approach both to teaching and to understanding dramatic literature" (B9). One could argue that specters of Shakespeare haunt Anglophone literary studies in the same way that specters of Marx haunt "history." *Specters of Marx* itself fits the pattern: Derrida noted in his keynote address at the 1994 "Deconstruction Is/In America" conference at New York University that "Hamlet in fact haunts the book . . ." (18).

For Derrida, haunting is more than a plague of uninvited guests or repressed psychological traumas. The logic of hauntology, like that of difièrance, points to the impossibility of knowing self or other from a position of presence. Opposed to the model of the hermeneutic circle, which posits a projection of self onto the other as a vehicle of self-knowledge, hauntology instructs us to create spaces that hold the promise of encountering the other as other. Derrida makes it clear from the beginning of *Specters* that a concern for justice to the other motivates him to address the question of Marxism after the collapse of Soviet communism:

> If I am getting ready to speak at length about ghosts, inheritance, and generations, generations of ghosts, which is to say about certain *others* who are not present, nor presently living, either to us, in us, or outside us, it is in the name of *justice*. Of justice where it is no longer *present*, and where it will never be, no more than the law, reducible to laws or rights. It is necessary to speak *of the* ghost, indeed *to the* ghost and *with* it, from the moment that no ethics, no politics, whether revolutionary or not, seems possible and thinkable and *just* that does not recognize in its principle the respect for those others who are no longer or for those others who are not yet *there*, presently living, whether they are already dead or not yet born. (Derrida's emphasis; xix)

How, then, do we address these discursive ghosts? When we choose to speak to, of, or about the dead we necessarily undertake acts of representation. How does one represent oneself to the dead? How does one represent the dead to others? These are difficult ethical and political choices, not matters of factual determination. And any new approach to humanities studies must take on the ethical and political considerations implicit in a call for just representation.

I believe that hauntology offers the basis for such an ethically informed approach. To begin with, Derrida's phrase *"plus d'un"* must be regarded as a promise every bit as much as a set of problems to overcome. While spectral apparitions signaling both "no more one" and "more than one" undoubtedly mark a crisis in the humanities, they also challenge us to think about our writing and teaching in ways that do not depend upon unity or stability as a mark of success. In this way, they shift the meaning of the "crisis" itself. Additionally, an approach to scholarship that does not tie its representations to an idea of objective and unchanging truth broadens our rhetorical possibilities just as the electronic apparatus extends our technologies of communication.

Although Derrida may provide a theoretical basis for a new pedagogy, the question remains how we might apply his spectral logic to the electronic classroom. To this end, we might do well to explore Derrida's engagement with the performative aspects of language. For instance, he speaks of hauntology as a "dimension of performative interpretation, that is, of an interpretation that transforms what it interprets" (*Specters* 51). In this vein, he invokes Marx's 11th Thesis on Feuerbach: "The philosophers have only interpreted the world in various ways; the point, however, is to change it" (qtd. in *Specters* 51). Our own version of this dictum might read: Traditional scholarship has only interpreted textual ghosts in various ways, but the charge of hauntology is to write with them.

How do we write with ghosts? Because the logic of hauntology precludes any prescriptive gestures, it makes sense to approach this question as an experiment. The computerized classroom provides the ideal laboratory in which to conduct such an experiment. Although a pedagogy informed by hauntology should by no means be limited to the literal requirements of the circuit board and pixelized screen, it does emerge from a cultural milieu saturated by electronic technology: television, digitized imaging, advanced telecommunications, interactive virtual environments, the Internet. The computer, more so than the book, foregrounds the instability of language. Derrida calls for a hauntological approach to the new media, stating, "the medium of the media themselves . . . this element itself is neither living nor dead, present nor absent: it spectralizes. It does not belong to ontology, to the discourse on the Being of beings, or to the essence of life or death" (*Specters* 50–51). Rather than attempting to sort out the authentic words of the dead from the inauthentic, or the true inheritance from the false one—the dilemmas that held Hamlet transfixed at Elsinore—hauntology redirects the creative energies of scholarship toward cultivating a hospitality toward the specter on the off chance that it might visit someday. In practical terms, the focus of student research shifts from solving the mysteries of the past to setting the stage for future invention. Rather than rehearse the common narratives of what has already taken place, students are encouraged to participate in a collaborative narrative that continues to reshape itself. The Internet seems an obvious venue for this kind of student writing, but it can be simulated in a non-networked teaching environment. Similarly, materials for a hauntologically inspired project need not involve the topic of haunting and can, in fact, come from any humanities discipline.

To demonstrate what a research project inspired by hauntology might be like, I would like to perform a speculative experiment. For the sake of convenience, I will cull the necessary ingredients for my experiment from *Specters of Marx,* which can provide theoretical prompts as well as good props for ghosts and a rich spectral cast. To begin with, we have *Hamlet,* a stalwart of humanities studies that continues to pique the popular imagination.[7] We have the body (the work, the corpus) of Karl Marx, whose status presents the occasion of Derrida's remarks, suspended under the equivocal sign of "Whither?" We have sundry texts and cultural references spanning centuries and continents, from *Titus Andronicus* to *Les Miserables,* from Hegel's Germany to Chris Hani's South Africa. Finally, we have Elsinore, a propitious setting, indeed. (What could be more conducive to spectral writing than a haunted castle?)

While Derrida draws on the theme of haunting in *Hamlet* to discuss specters and the spectral in Marx, his engagement with the text exceeds mere explication or comparison through analogy. On one level, he conveys the story of Marx's multifarious intellectual filiation as a ghost story, while on another he presents Elsinore as a site to conjure figures that act out his rhetorical gestures. For example, the ghost of Hamlet's father serves as a topos from which Derrida extrapolates spectral effects: "*Hamlet* already began with the expected return of the dead King. After the end of history, the spirit comes by *coming back* [*revenant*], it figures *both* a dead man who comes back and a ghost whose expected return repeats itself, again and again" (Derrida's emphasis; 10). The figure of the ghost, then, serves as a sort of prosthesis that enables Derrida to conceive a notion of the event that proves indispensable in his discussion of Marx and history, but also to the staging of *Specters of Marx* itself.

I wish to call attention to the term "staging" because of its strategic value for an experiment in hauntology and its significance to Derrida's notion of the event. Derrida uses *mise en scène,* the French term for staging or directing, in a defining passage on hauntology: "Mise en scène pour une fin de l'histoire. Appelons cela une *hantologie*"[8] (*Spectres de Marx* 31, his emphasis). For Derrida, the spectral logic of hauntology is crucial to thinking the event outside the constraints of ontology. The Western tradition of metaphysics ties the event to a particular time and place. Hauntology, however, conceives the time and place of the event as necessarily indeterminate. In this way, the performance of the event depends on the spectral nature of language; neither can occur without a paradoxical interruption between presence and absence, past and future. Derrida himself addresses the paradoxes of the event through Hamlet's well-known remark "The time is out of joint." According to hauntology, events perform in spectral border worlds defined by language, and these borders are porous, behaving as conduits as well as barriers.

While *Specters of Marx* hints at what the staging of a spectral event might be like, the text itself is as far from such an event as a group of recipes is from a meal. *Specters* does, however, provide us with a good set of stage directions and some promising examples. We can envision our scene—Elsinore—as a sort of border town through which textual ghosts pass. Because these ghosts travel through the medium of language, instead of time or space, their passage is not restricted by any common understanding of history or geography. They carry no passports that insist on exact correspondences between specters and people—living, dead, or not yet born. In this sense, our practice of staging could be viewed as an antithesis of *You Are There,* the popular 1950s television program hosted by Walter Cronkite that represented historical events such as the Battle of Waterloo from a fly-on-the-wall perspective. While a spectral staging would share *You Are There*'s attitude of scholarly enthusiasm, its tone would be speculative rather than declarative. Instead of creating a scene as evidence (as in "the scene of the crime") to support a hypothesis, the goal would be to create a scene out of curiosity, to see where it leads. Thus, while a pedagogy inspired by hauntology would not exclude traditional aspects of critical reasoning and scholarship—it would, indeed, value them—it would shift the emphasis in learning from mastery to improvisation.

The staging of learning as improvisation calls for a new type of student protagonist who performs a new approach to the unknown. For Derrida, the encounter with the armored ghost outside Elsinore in the opening scene of *Hamlet* exemplifies the Western academy's traditional stance toward the unknown other. "There has never been a scholar who really, as a scholar, deals with ghosts," he writes. "A traditional scholar does not believe in ghosts— nor in all that could be called the virtual space of spectrality" (*Specters* 11). In Shakespeare's play, this traditional scholar is, of course, figured by Hamlet's friend Horatio, who is called by the officers standing watch at the castle to identify and address the apparition. "By charging or conjuring him to speak, Horatio wants to inspect, stabilize, *arrest* the specter in its speech" (Derrida's emphasis; 12). In place of Horatio's traditional scholar, Derrida imagines another answering Marcellus's call to speak to the ghost: "Marcellus was perhaps anticipating the coming one day, one night, several centuries later, of another 'scholar.' The latter would finally be capable, beyond the opposition between presence and non-presence, actuality and inactuality, life and non-life, of thinking the possibility of the specter, the specter as possibility" (12).

This future scholar cannot break from the past, but must inherit from it in a complex skein of violence, debt, secrets, and responsibility. To illustrate the violent burden of inheritance, Derrida invokes Prince Hamlet's famous lament: "The time is out of joint; O cursed spite, / That ever I was born to set it right!" (*Ham.* 1.5.188–89). Derrida observes: "Hamlet is 'out of joint' because he curses his own mission, the punishment that consists in having to punish, avenge, exercise justice and right in the form of reprisals" (*Specters* 20). Scholarship invokes an inheritance as intricate, violent, and binding as Hamlet's. Yet inheritance as Derrida defines it in *Specters of Marx* is not a matter of patrilineal or any other form of presumed succession. There is more than one spirit of Marx, he states, and one must choose to be faithful to a particular spirit: "An inheritance is always the reaffirmation of a debt, but a critical, selective, and filtering reaffirmation" (91–92). Derrida demonstrates this process of filtering not only in his oath of fidelity to "a certain spirit of Marx" but also in his engagement with *Hamlet*.

The staging of Shakespeare's tragedy in *Specters of Marx* is not meant to be exegetic, but generative. It occurs in conjunction with a host of other spectral revivals, including texts by Freud, Heidegger, Paul Valéry, Maurice Blanchot, Victor Hugo, Walter Benjamin, and Francis Fukuyama. These textual ghosts weave themselves in and out of scenes through a series of tropes, including "Old Europe," "the visor effect," and, of course, the specter. They participate in a collaborative tradition exemplified by theater in Shakespeare's time. In this model, "staging" is not the sole venue of a single authority but an aggregation of many interdependent performances. Although Derrida's practice of staging juxtaposes texts from a variety of time periods and genres, it differs from pastiche in its critical—if often playful—investigation of the resulting connections. Following this example, students could combine scholarship in a diverse range of fields without resorting to an overarching interpretive frame. They stage their scenes as points of connection among topics drawn from their scholarly fields, their cultural backgrounds, their roles within a larger community, and their family histories. The spectral actors—themes, quotations, stylistic gestures, historical anecdotes—are not cast in advance but take their places in the performance according to their frequency.

By "frequency" I mean several things, drawing on the word's etymology and on Derrida's allusions to the term in *Specters of Marx*. First, the word suggests the recurrence of a pattern of information. In broadcast communications, frequency is determined by wave patterns; on the Internet it is determined by search engines and hit counters. Following this logic, a student recognizes that a research element belongs in a project because it keeps showing up across a variety of topics and discourses. In addition, frequency suggests attunement, as in, "Are we on the same frequency?" In his work on Internet pedagogy, Ulmer describes attunement as a state of mind that can cue memories and he traces it to the role of music in classical education, which was "based on the idea of morality as a tuning of the individual soul to . . . world harmony" (*Internet Invention* 58-59). Finally, I note that haunting can be defined as the frequency of visitation by specters (frequentation).

The scene I am staging takes place along the ramparts of Elsinore. Hamlet, Horatio, and Marcellus are in the foreground. In front of them flicker an assortment of images, among them Marx in London, Derrida behind a lectern at New York University, a bust of Shakespeare in a college library. Horatio holds some sort of tuning device, and the three men bicker over how to operate it. Their voices trail off as one image—one that cannot be completely discerned—begins to appear at a greater frequency than the others. The images continue to flicker as Marcellus says, "Thou art a scholar; speak to it, Horatio."

The scene establishes an initial attunement, or mood framework, out of which spectral actors will emerge and begin to improvise a collective performance. The varying frequencies of the performance depend on the attunement established by the scene a student creates. The scene, in turn, is the product of research in a discipline, cultural commemoration, personal and family history, and the whirl of icons and artifacts that suffuse everyday life. The specters, those hybrids of intangible idea and material instantiation, haunt us in the words of dead playwrights, in pop melodies, in the zigzagging lines of the stock markets, in cinematic images. It is through the performance of frequencies—of personal and collective spectral encounters—that hauntology promises an alternative way of connecting the individual to the universal. Instead of approaching the other as an object of interpretation (as the model of the hermeneutic circle instructs) we assume that the other is spectral, is always *plus d'un*.

The computerized classroom provides a number of venues for spectral staging. Although the most obvious appears to be hypermedia, with its graphic, sound, and linking capabilities, the Multi-user Object-Oriented domain, or MOO, would nicely accommodate experiments in staging, as would graphically based virtual worlds and three-dimensional game spaces. The specific technology employed seems less important than the method that motivates its use. Seven years of teaching in the Networked Writing Environment at the University of Florida have exposed me to student work produced on a simple word processor that is inventive, unconventionally insightful, and non-hierarchical. Conversely, I often have seen the most sophisticated multimedia programs turn out what are essentially slick versions of the traditional academic essay; images, animations, and hyperlinks are drafted into the service of hierarchy, rigid classification, and authoritative interpretation.

Read as a set of stage directions, *Specters of Marx* shows teachers and students how to develop a writing space that encourages the transformative, rather than the revelatory, practice of research and interpretation. What happens in those spaces can be predicted no more exactly than it can be prescribed. Of course, the work of spectral staging could never be about final results. For me, the teaching methods informed by hauntology promise less of a pedagogical revolution than an ongoing, self-revising practice.

NOTES

1. Translated from the German by Marianne Cowan in *Humanist Without Portfolio: An Anthology of the Writings of Wilhelm von Humboldt* (134). Humboldt's original essay, also included in the collection, reads: "Sobald man aufhört, eigentlich Wissenschaft zu suchen, oder sich einbildet, sie brauche nicht aus der Tiefe des Geistes heraus geschaffen, sondern könne durch Sammeln extensiv aneinandergereiht werden, so ist Alles unwiederbringlich und auf ewig verloren; verloren für die Wissenschaft, die, wenn dies lange fortgesetzt wird, dergestalt entflieht, dass sie selbst die Sprache wie eine leere Hülse zurücklässt, und verloren für den Staat" ("Über die innere und ässere Organisation der höheren wissenschaftlichen Anstalten in Berlin" 253).

2. While this term was popularized by Derrida's publication of *De la grammatologie* in 1967 and its English translation in 1976, Gregory L. Ulmer notes at least one earlier instance of its use: one edition of a book on the history of writing by I. J. Gelb was titled *Grammatology (Applied Grammatology: Post(e)-Pedagogy from Jacques Derrida to Joseph Beuys.* [Baltimore: Johns Hopkins UP, 1985], 5).

3. I would be remiss not to note that the term *plus d'un* itself performs the same representational slippage that it describes when viewed in the context of Derrida's other work. Specifically, it alludes to *plus d'une langue* ("both more than one language and no more of just one language"), a phrase that he uses to describe deconstruction in *Mémoires: For Paul de Man* (15). In the keynote address for the 1994 "Deconstruction Is/In America" conference at New York University, Derrida describes the phrase as "the only definition that I have ever in my life dared to give of deconstruction" ("Time is Out of Joint" 27).

4. See Kittler's *Discourse Networks, 1800/1900,* trans. Michael Metteer (Stanford: Stanford UP, 1990).

5. In their introduction to Friedrich A. Kittler's *Gramophone, Film, Typewriter* (Stanford: Stanford UP, 1999), translators Geoffrey Winthrop-Young and Michael Wutz note that Kittler and other German scholars addressed the subject in a collection first published in 1980 entitled *Austreibung des Geistes aus den Geisteswissenschaften: Programme des Poststrukturalismus [Expulsion of the Spirit from the humanities: programs of poststructuralism]* (xxiii).

6. An early and well-known instance of such critique is, of course, Derrida's 1966 presentation at Johns Hopkins University, "Structure, Sign, and Play in the Discourse of the Human Sciences." An English version of the paper appears in *Writing and Difference* (Chicago: U of Chicago P, 1978), 278–93.

7. Three popular film versions of *Hamlet* have been produced in the past fifteen years: one directed by Franco Zeffirelli and starring Mel Gibson in 1990, one directed by and starring Kenneth Branagh in 1996, and one directed by Michael Almereyda and starring Ethan Hawke in 1999.

8. In the English edition, Peggy Kamuf translates the passage as, "Staging for the end of history. Let us call it *hauntology*" (10).

WORKS CITED

Anderson, Benedict. *Imagined Communities: Reflections on the Origin and Spread of Nationalism*. 1983. Rev. ed. London: Verso, 1991.

Bender, Thomas. "Locality and Worldliness." *The Transformation of Humanistic Studies in the Twenty-First Century: Opportunities and Perils*. ACLS Occasional Paper. Ed. Thomas Bender. New York: American Council of Learned Societies, 1997. 1–10.

Bontekoe, Ronald. *Dimensions of the Hermeneutic Circle*. Atlantic Highlands, NJ: Humanities Press, 1996.

Brogan, Kathleen. *Cultural Haunting: Ghosts and Ethnicity in Recent American Literature*. Charlottesville: UP of Virginia, 1998.

Castle, Terry. *The Female Thermometer: Eighteenth-Century Culture and the Invention of the Uncanny*. Ideologies of Desire. New York: Oxford UP, 1995.

Deibert, Ronald J. *Parchment, Printing, and Hypermedia: Communication in World Order Transformation*. New Directions in World Politics. New York: Columbia UP, 1997.

Derrida, Jacques. *Specters of Marx: the State of the Debt, the Work of Mourning, and the New International*. Trans. Peggy Kamuf. New York: Routledge, 1994.

———. *Spectres de Marx: L'État de la dette, le travail du deuil et la nouvelle Internationale*. La Philosophie en Effet. Paris: Éditions Galilée, 1993.

———. "The Time is Out of Joint." *Deconstruction Is/In America: A New Sense of the Political*. Ed. Anselm Haverkamp. New York: New York UP, 1995.

Dilthey, Wilhelm. "The Rise of Hermeneutics." *Wilhelm Dilthey: Selected Works*. Vol. 4 of *Hermeneutics and the Study of History*. Ed. Rodolf Makkreel and Frithjof Rodi. Trans. Fredric Jameson and Rodolf Makkreel. Princeton: Princeton UP, 1996. 235–58.

Edmundson, Mark. *Nightmare on Main Street: Angels, Sadomasochism, and the Culture of Gothic*. Cambridge: Harvard UP, 1997.

Freud, Sigmund. "The Uncanny." *Sigmund Freud: Collected Papers*. Trans. Joan Riviere and James Strachey. 1st American ed. Vol. 4. New York: Basic Books, 1959. 368–407.

Humboldt, Wilhelm von. *Humanist Without Portfolio: An Anthology of the Writings of Wilhelm von Humboldt*. Trans. Marianne Cowan. Detroit: Wayne State UP, 1963.

Kernan, Alvin B. *In Plato's Cave*. New Haven: Yale UP, 1999.

Mirzoeff, Nicholas. *An Introduction to Visual Culture*. New York: Routledge, 1999.

Punter, David. *Gothic Pathologies: the Text, the Body, and the Law*. New York: St. Martin's, 1998.

Röhrs, Hermann. "The Classical Idea of the University: Its Origin and Significance As Conceived by Humboldt." *Tradition and Reform of the University Under an International Perspective: An Interdisciplinary Approach*. Ed. Hermann Röhrs. Frankfurt: Peter Lang, 1987. 13–27.

Shakespeare, William. *Hamlet*. 1601. Ed. Shane Weller. Dover Thrift Editions. Mineola, NY: Dover, 1992.

Showalter, Elaine. "What Teaching Literature Should Really Mean." *Chronicle of Higher Education* 17 January 2003: B7–B9.

Ulmer, Gregory L. *Heuretics: The Logic of Invention.* Baltimore: Johns Hopkins UP, 1994.

———. "I Untied the Camera of Tastes (Who Am I?): The Riddle of Chool (A Reply and Alternative to A. Sahay)." *New Literary History* 28.3 (1997): 569–94.

———. Internet Invention: From Literacy to Electracy. New York: Longman, 2003.

Diagram, Dialogue, Dialectic

Visual Explanations and Visual Rhetoric in the Teaching of Literary Theory

JOHN ZUERN

n the second book of his 1605 treatise *The Advancement of Learning,* Francis Bacon offers a series of suggestions for rejuvenating the art of rhetoric as it is applied to teaching. When he turns to the canon of *memoria,* the now neglected techniques of remembering a composition as one is delivering it, he makes a cogent argument for the pedagogical value of visual media: "Emblem," he writes, "reduceth conceits intellectual to images sensible, which strike the memory more" (3:399). Bacon goes on to suggest that the mnemonic power of emblem—what we might now call visualization—is not sufficiently incorporated into the teaching practices of his day. Out of the "axiom" that visual images have a greater *capacity* than words alone to fix ideas in the memory "may be drawn much better practique than that in use" (3:399). Taking up Bacon's recommendation, this essay suggests how visual media can advance learning in courses dealing with contemporary literary theory and methodology,[1] an area of study with a wide range of "conceits intellectual" that some students find extremely difficult to comprehend, let alone to employ in their own interpretations of literature and culture.

I will accompany my practical examples of visually oriented teaching methods with an examination of the capacity of visual representations, ranging from simple diagrams to the complex moving images of feature films, to place students in a critical, questioning relationship with the concepts they are learning. Rather than serving as mere vehicles of ideas, visual materials engage us in a dialogue with those ideas out of which we gain an understanding based less on memorization and mastery than on critical, intellectually supple inquiry. Moreover, visualization can spark invaluable "ah-ha"

experiences that push learners' understanding of concepts beyond an instrumental "application" of ideas in a particular discipline—for example, literary studies—and open them to philosophical reflection on their own social,
cultural, and political lives.

WHAT KIND OF LIGHT DOES AN ILLUSTRATION SHED?

Most teachers have at some time or another attempted to explain a concept
by way of a quick diagrammatic sketch on the chalkboard or through a
verbal presentation of a visual analogy. We turn from words to images in
an effort to clarify, but what do we really gain by moving into the domain
of the visual? Can our impulse to *show,* a desire born of a certain disappointment with the ambiguities and abstractions of verbal communication
(born, too, of a frustration with the incomprehension of our interlocutors,
and perhaps also of uncertainty and anxiety about our own understanding), be any more satisfied than our impulse to *tell*?

Many of the foremost writers and teachers in the fields that have directly
contributed to present-day literary and cultural theory appear to have had
considerable faith in the explanatory efficacy of images. Ferdinand de
Saussure's famous graphics representing his concept of the linguistic sign,
Jacques Lacan's infamous diagrams and formulae of the relations between
language and the unconscious, Claude Lévi-Strauss's representations of the
painted faces of the Caduveo in the Amazon Basin, and Julia Kristeva's interpretations of the paintings of Giotto and Bellini are only a few of the more
obvious examples of how theorists have turned to non- or extra-verbal modes
of representation to convey their complex ideas about language, social organization, the psyche, and representation itself.[2] Edward Tufte describes such
"visual explanations" as "pictures of verbs, the representation of mechanism
and motion, of process and dynamics, of causes and effects, of explanation
and narrative" (10). The rhetorical function of the visual materials included
in philosophical and theoretical work cannot be easily subsumed under the
category of "illustration." As much as they clarify theoretical ideas and processes, images complicate and raise questions about the process of theoretical speculation. In the following account of my own attempt to teach a
particular set of theoretical concepts with the help of images, I will try to
demonstrate that the visual is as complex and as potentially powerful a

medium of instruction as the verbal, not because of its superior precision or immediacy, but precisely because of its own forms of ambiguity and opacity.

My approach to using visual materials in the classroom has been shaped by the work of a number of thinkers in a variety of disciplines. In the field of social semiotics, Gunther Kress and Theo van Leeuwen are working toward a "grammar of images" that accounts for visual forms of communication. Their approach to the relationship between images and the texts that incorporate them stresses that "the visual component of a text is an independently organized and structured message—connected with the verbal text, but in no way dependent on it: and similarly the other way around" (17). Visual design elements are therefore not simply "versions" of verbal originals. Kress and van Leeuwen go on to argue that rather than thinking of images as ancillary to verbal discourse, an "incessant 'translation' or 'transcoding' between a range of semiotic modes represents . . . a more adequate understanding of representation and of communication" (37). This argument challenges the optical metaphors with which we understand images used as illustrations: they can be neither revelatory projections of the verbal material nor mirror reflections, in a different medium, of what the text "says." The visual is another order of discourse with its own grammar—and, by extension, its own logic and rhetoric.

While Kress and van Leeuwen emphasize the difference between the verbal and visual domains, W. J. T. Mitchell concerns himself with the inextricability of these two realms, asserting in Picture Theory that "there are no 'purely' visual or verbal arts" (5). Mitchell formulates what he calls "a critical iconology" (28) that enables a study of visual representation to perform a analysis of how those representations operate to shore up or critique particular ideologies; for Mitchell, ideology can be defined as "a historical, cultural formation that masquerades as a universal, natural code" (31). He is careful to note, however, that a critical iconology cannot operate as a detached metadiscourse that presumes to diagnose the ideological inflections of images, but is rather a discourse always already implicated in the visual materials it addresses. "It intervenes and is itself subjected to intervention by its object," he argues. "That is why I've called this notion of iconology critical and dialectical" (30). Especially valuable for a visual pedagogy of literary theory is Mitchell's assertion that any "picture theory" must also comprise a means of "picturing theory" and accounting for how theoretical discourse itself engages both words and images to develop its representations—and advances its ideologies (see 6).

Mitchell's analysis, informed by the work of art historian Erwin Panofsky and Marxist philosopher Louis Althusser, emphasizes the importance of recognition in an understanding of the semiotic and ideological function of visual images. The obvious fact that we know what a picture is "of" because we recognize what it represents in a manner analogous to our recognition of the meaning of words in a text places our encounter with images within a "recognition scene" in which our social and cultural background, our ideological life-world, comes to bear upon our experience of a visual representation. Mitchell takes up this experience of recognition as a way of connecting the function of pictures and the operations of ideology. "The main importance of recognition as the link between ideology and iconology," Mitchell writes, "is that it shifts both 'sciences' from an epistemological 'cognitive' ground . . . to an ethical, political, and hermeneutic ground" (35). Images, Mitchell insists, must be interpreted, and that interpretation is always situated within historical, social, and cultural contexts. Together with his outline of a critical iconology, Mitchell's concern with the role of recognition in our understanding of images can help us imagine teaching practices that employ visual materials but eschew naïve assumptions about what or how images signify. Although their projects take different points of departure regarding the relationship between the verbal and visual, Mitchell's efforts to establish a "critical iconology," and Kress and van Leeuwen's account of the "grammar of images," remind us that pictures, belonging as they do to a semiotic register, pose the same interpretive challenges as the texts to which they are too often subordinated.

Another point of reference for my understanding of how images can work to teach theory lies in philosophy, for the images I employ in my classes on theory are by and large meant to represent, in various ways, philosophical concepts. Gilles Deleuze and Félix Guattari's *What is Philosophy?* opens with an analysis of our concept of the concept. "There are no simple concepts," these writers argue. "Every concept has components and is defined by them" (15). This point is important to our present concerns about the visual, since visual representations of concepts are almost inevitably enlisted to depict the different components of the concept and their interrelations. Deleuze and Guattari themselves turn to a diagrammatic presentation of

the Cartesian cogito which relates the components of the doubting, thinking, and being "I" (25).

The argument of *What is Philosophy?* also supports a visual pedagogy
of theory insofar as the writers emphasize the need to view concepts as entities bound up with acts of creation, and the criticism of concepts as an operation productive of new concepts. Juxtaposing the presentation of a
theoretical concept in a text with a set of images that bear some relation to
it—only initially and heuristically a relationship based on the notion of
"illustration"—almost always turns out to be a dialectical, critical, and at
least potentially creative gesture. "Even the history of philosophy is completely without interest," Deleuze and Guattari write, "if it does not undertake to awaken a dormant concept and to play it again on a new stage, even
if this comes at the price of turning it against itself" (83). The theoretical
work of these philosophers and teachers, which has been widely and productively engaged by critics of art, film, multimedia, and other visual forms
of cultural production, testifies to their own capacity to perform this kind
of critical renewal of philosophical concepts.

The most complicated and ultimately most productive aspect of the
transition from word to image in teaching is the capacity of images to do
more than simply restate verbal messages, to resist, in fact, any mere repetition of the verbal statement and to raise in its place an insistent question. Anyone who has turned to "idea mapping" or "concept clustering"
exercises to jump start the writing process has recognized that diagrams
return us to words, asking "what are you trying to say?" Saussure insists
that "writing obscures language; it is not a guise for language but a disguise" (30). This provocative assertion underscores Saussure's effort to privilege the connection between the spoken sound-image (signifier) and the
mental concept (signified) as the focus of linguistic research, but it also
raises questions about other graphical representations we employ to signify abstract mental structures of philosophy and theory.

In the domain of concepts, then, do illustrations also disguise the phenomena they purportedly render visible? We might ask this question in
another way: if these images are indeed illustrations, if they really eluci-
date, what kind of light do they shed, and on what, exactly? Illustrations
do not simply turn a spotlight onto a concept, making it stand out on the
dim stage of language, brighter than when it was shrouded in words, but

essentially the same. Instead, features of a concept often appear in the light of a graphical representation (as does the skeleton under the x-ray, or areas of warmth under infrared) that might have remained invisible had the concept remained strictly verbal. Images can reveal the complex structures of concepts as well as the functions that derive from the interactions of the component parts; the right pictures have the capacity to reveal the physiology of ideas.

The ideas I attempt to convey to the students in my graduate and undergraduate classes on contemporary literary theory involve active processes and dynamic interactions. In the history of ideas, they often intersect with one another to produce even more complex models of processes and conditions in language, culture, and human experience. Saussure's theory of the linguistic sign, for example, contributes substantially to Lacan's reinterpretation of Freudian models of the psyche, which in turn inspire Louis Althusser's conception of the interpellation of the human subject through ideological state apparatuses. This trio of theorists represents three major philosophical strands within literary theory—linguistics, psychoanalysis, and Marxism. Each offers students important insights into the fundamental categories of language, subjectivity, and society. In my experience, teaching these thinkers as an "ensemble" also helps students understand how innovative concepts and models emerge out of those that precede them. By incorporating various forms of visualization into my presentation of the interconnected concepts of Saussure, Lacan, and Althusser, I both supplement the visual material already present in their works and offer students different perspectives from which to analyze and test their ideas.

LISTENING TO IMAGES, PICTURING CONCEPTS: GRAPHICAL LANGUAGE IN SAUSSURE AND LACAN

Many of the major texts of both Saussure and Lacan are the transcripts of oral performances— seminars, lectures, and conference presentations. The graphical material they contain possesses a definite pedagogical thrust; the reader must imagine them scribbled on a chalkboard in the course of a presentation—built up and altered, perhaps, as the verbal explanation unfolds. The convention of printing texts with illustrations tends to obscure the dialectical role of drawing in the practice of teaching, in which the teacher's speech (and the speech of the students) eddies around the sketch, enters into dialogue with it, shapes it as the drawing itself shapes the verbal discourse through explication, clarification, and, as sometimes happens, distortion and obfuscation. Examining how these thinkers employ graphical diagrams as they elaborate their ideas—and in the case of Lacan the occasional curious avoidance of graphics—can offer practical examples of the pedagogical implementation of images as well as theoretical insights into the role of visualization in capturing and concretizing abstract thought.

Saussure's *Course in General Linguistics,* a compilation of student notes from seminars between 1906 and 1911, employs both striking graphical representations and visual metaphors to convey its concepts. Saussure's representation of the linguistic *sign* as a compound of the *signified* (the mental concept, e.g. a tree) and the *signifier* (the sound-image of the word "tree") remains one of the best-known graphics in the discourse of literary theory. Saussure later translates this graphical representation into a verbal metaphor of a visual and tactile phenomenon. "Language," he writes, "can also be compared with a sheet of paper: thought is the front and the sound the back; one cannot cut the front without cutting the back at the same time; likewise in language, one can neither divide sound from thought nor thought from sound" (113). Reading Saussure at the other end of the twentieth century, when computer graphics allow us to construct three-dimensional models with relative ease, it is tempting to interpret his toggling between two-dimensional drawings and verbal metaphors of concrete sensory and spatial experiences as a struggle to overcome the limitations of his media. Saussure's model of the sign is resolutely three-dimensional and animated; one can imagine the sign as a revolving sphere, a kind of atomic particle in which the paired elements are fused without any stable hierarchy.[3]

In his presentation of the idea of the arbitrary nature of the sign, Saussure develops an extended analogy to the game of chess in which "the respective value of the pieces depends on their position on the chessboard just as each linguistic term derives its value from its opposition to all the other terms" (88). Another useful (and portable) visual metaphor for the arbitrary nature of the linguistic sign, this one borrowed from Claude Lévi-Strauss's *Structural Study of Myth,* is a deck of cards. The cards assume different values in relation to one another depending upon the game one is playing; in this analogy, the individual cards correspond to the signs, the rules of play correspond to Saussure's concept of *langue* (the diachronic, historically developing structures of a given language), and the unfolding of play in a particular game corresponds to *parole* (the synchronic, transient, particular instances of speech).

Bringing a chessboard and several decks of cards into class and having students at least initiate games provides a direct engagement with the logic of Saussure's analogies and can raise productive questions, such as "who decides on the rules?," "Who enforces them?," "Is it possible to 'cheat' in language as it is in games?," "Is literary language a form of 'cheating'?" Calling attention to the feudal social relations fossilized in the game of chess offers an occasion to reflect on how hierarchical power structures might inhere in the structures of language, reflections that preview developments in cultural theory based on Saussurian linguistics, such as Lacanian psychoanalysis.

In "The Agency of the Letter in the Unconscious or Reason since Freud," an essay that was originally presented as a lecture in 1957, Lacan outlines some of his main arguments about the centrality of language in the formation and function of the psyche, drawing explicitly on the work of Saussure. To diagram his understanding of the unconscious as having the structure of a language, Lacan exploits a tension in the diagrammatic representation of Saussure's theory of the sign: the hierarchical position of the components of the sign, the signified above the bar, the signifier below. With the simple graphical gesture of reversing the stacking order of the two elements, Lacan achieves a simple visual formulation that allows him to explain a set of complex interactions (149):

$$\frac{S}{s}$$

The "S" corresponds to Saussure's signifier, the "s" to the signified. The horizontal bar in Lacan's typographical schema represents the psychical operation of repression; the lowercase "s" occupies the domain of the unconscious, which the diagram locates in the signifying operations of language itself. With Lacan's adoption of Saussurian models of signification, Elizabeth Grosz notes, "Freud's neurological model is transposed into linguistic form" (96). Comparing Lacan's "algorithm" to the conventional tripartite Freudian schema of the ego, id, and superego gives students a visual sense of Lacan's transformation of traditional Freudianism, and can also lead to explorations of Lacanian theory. Asking students to locate the unconscious in Lacan's graphic reinforces its most straightforward message—that the unconscious lies "beneath" the signifiers of "conscious" speech as a repressed dimension of signification. Asking students to find the *ego,* however, introduces them to Lacan's challenge to naïve conceptions of consciousness and identity, for the ego is not "there," but is implied as a kind of literal "sum" of Lacan's quasi-mathematical formula for the ongoing (but never fully stable) production of consciousness.

Lacan's inversion of Saussure's graphic offers an example of what theory has to gain from a dialogue with a visual representation, asking it questions that at first appear simple: Why is this element on top of that element? Does the diagram represent a static condition or a dynamic process? Is the process unidirectional or reversible? We must listen to images, giving our attention to the subtle ways in which their initially straightforward presentation of an idea point to possibly unexamined assumptions about value (is what is pictured in the lower half of the field subordinate to what is above?), agency (do elements positioned on top of a vertical series or at the beginning of a horizontal sequence exert some kind of force on the elements that follow?), temporality (does the diagram represent a fixed state or only a stage in a process?), and many other dimensions of our conceptualization. This attention to the often unacknowledged rhetoric of visual presentations—what images tell us about ideas as they show us their structures—can lead to striking insights into the omissions and limitations of a theoretical model as well as into its relevance and utility.

The elegant simplicity of Lacan's adaptation of Saussure's graphical schema, for example, can spur questions about the scope of Lacan's theory. Students who are convinced by Saussure's diagram, and who can imagine all languages operating in the terms Saussure outlines, are sometimes less satisfied with Lacan's representation of language's relation to psychic life. I am, of course, asking students to entertain the ideas of both Freud and Lacan, since one has to concede the existence of the unconscious before one can reinterpret it in linguistic terms. During the unit on Freud earlier in the semester, at least one student generally objects to Freud's cultural biases—his assumption of the nuclear family as the norm, for example.

Lacan makes no less universal a claim for his theory than does Freud, and in some respects the lack of historical or cultural qualification of Lacan's claims is even more striking. The clarity of his graphic S/s, viewed in the light of a critical iconology, can begin to appear sterile, deracinated, and arrogant. Can we encompass the psychic and linguistic life of all human subjects in all cultures in this notation? What is at stake for Lacan in making such a claim? Careful attention to the figural language of a theoretical text can reveal unacknowledged impulses, repetitions, and tensions that we might locate in the text's cultural context, a shared (and also contested) zone of imaginary formations that pervade and interrupt the text's verbal structures. A critical reading of Lacan's graphical notations turns such a method back onto Lacan's argument, diagnosing, perhaps, not only a scientistic desire for control over a domain of knowledge expressed in the deployment of mathematical symbols but also a conflicting desire to educate and at the same time to mystify.

STAGING IDEAS:
NARRATIVES OF "CATCHING SIGHT" AND CATCHING SIGHT OF NARRATIVES IN LACAN AND ALTHUSSER

As Lacan draws upon Saussure's theory of language to reinterpret Freud's theory of the psyche, Louis Althusser turns to Lacan's model of the psychic life of the human subject to elaborate a Marxist, structuralist account of how ideology shapes consciousness. Neither of the key texts that offer an account of the subject's imaginary relations to the formations of culture—Lacan's brief paper "The Mirror Stage as Formative of the Function of the I as Revealed in Psychoanalytic Experience" (developed as conference presentations and published in 1949), and Althusser's 1970 article "Ideology and Ideological State Apparatuses (Notes towards an Investigation)"—use diagrams to illustrate the concepts they present. They do, however, require the reader to visualize by presenting dramatic "scenes" which are meant to capture the structural and functional characteristics of their central concepts.

In the "mirror stage," according to Lacan, the human infant acquires an image of himself as a separate, complete entity in relation to other objects and persons in the world. Prior to this moment in the child's development, the child experiences the boundaries between himself and other things, especially the mother, as fluid and contiguous. (The exclusive use of the mascu-line gender here is deliberate; I will discuss the gender bias of Lacanian psy-choanalysis shortly.) Lacan asks his readers to visualize this scene by imagining a baby who "identifies" himself in his reflected image. The image need not be literally reflected in a mirror, but can also be surmised from the mother's eyes—the child recognizes himself as the object of the maternal gaze and intimates, too, that the mother's vision extends "past" his actual physical being to an idealized child "beyond" him. For Lacan, it is crucial that the child's reflected image is incommensurate with the actual physical status of the infant. The infant glimpses a whole, autonomous image of him-self while remaining in a state of "motor incapacity and nursling depen-dence" (2). This split between the ideal image of the self and the actual state of affairs locks the human subject into a lifelong pursuit of completion, sat-isfaction, and stability out of which emerges all of his intellectual and social accomplishments, as well as his anxieties and neuroses. In a 1954 seminar, Lacan reminds his audience that the mirror stage is not only an isolated stage in psychic development but rather exemplifies the subject's ongoing rela-tionship with his imaginary self-image (*Seminar* 74).

Despite his fascination with diagrams, Lacan offers no graphic repre-sentation of the mirror stage. As an event unfolding over time, the concept may resist static depictions; elsewhere, however, Lacan engages in highly complex schematizations of dynamic psychical processes for which the mirror stage model provides a foundation.[4] In an attempt to help students "see" and conceptualize the mirror stage as both a developmental event and an ongoing condition of the psyche, I have turned to the moving images of computer animation and film.

For the past several years, I have been developing a set of World Wide Web resources to assist in the teaching of literary theory and methodology. In the materials devoted to Lacan's mirror stage I include an animated dia-gram of the concept, which I produced using the Macromedia Flash appli-cation program for Web-based animation (fig. 3.1). The animation aims, in part, to reveal the implicit spatial and temporal metaphors that structure the model of the mirror stage. The external image reflected in the mirror (or in the mother's gaze) "returns" to the subject to be internalized as an imagi-nary picture, but one that exists, as an ideal, in an imaginary "beyond" out-side the range of the subject's capacity to master—and become—that Ideal-I.

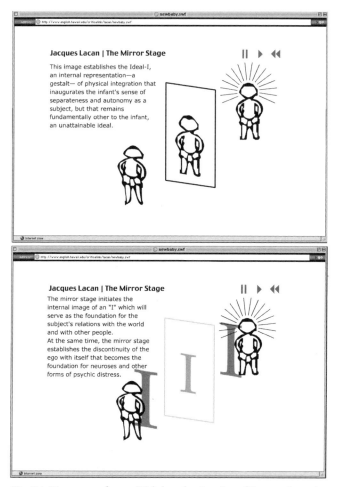

Fig. 3.1. Two scenes from a Web-based animation of Jacques Lacan's account of the mirror stage. Designed by John Zuern. Reproduced by permission of John Zuern.

The simplified presentation in the animation at once points out the basic structure of the model and, like Lacan's algorithms, divorces the model from any particular context. Asking students to identify the gender of the diapered infant-symbol points them toward important feminist critiques of Lacan's model such as that of analyst and philosopher Luce Irigaray, who argues in *The Speculum of the Other Woman* that Lacan's version of the mirror stage can apply convincingly only to male children and excludes or misrepresents the experience of women, both as children and as mothers.[5] It is not the case that students inevitably view the animated baby as a male, but the question about gender does almost always lead to them to ask why Lacan offers only one model for both genders. Does his account apply to male and female infants in exactly the same way? The initially appealing clarity of the diagram exposes the potentially universalizing, homogenizing effects of the concept it seeks to represent.

While the animated diagram is able to guide a student through the process Lacan describes, it is less able to demonstrate the dynamic operation of the concept of the mirror stage in Lacanian psychoanalytic theory in individual cases: it is, in other words, a diagram and not an example. Film offers a way to situate Lacan's idea in historical and individual contexts, in particular films that are themselves concerned about human development. When I teach Lacan's mirror stage essay, I show students clips from three films: François Truffaut's *The Wild Child* (1969), which tells the story of Victor, a feral child discovered in the woods of Aveyron in 1799; and Werner Herzog's *Everyman for Himself and God Against All* (1974) and Peter Sehr's *Kaspar Hauser* (1994), both of which explore the case of Kaspar Hauser, a mysterious foundling who appeared in Nurnberg in 1828. Each of these films includes a scene in which the main character, who has been cut off from human society and language for a critical portion of his development, encounters his own reflected image. Provided with basic background information on the historical cases of Victor and Kaspar, students can engage these episodes as both examples of and challenges to Lacan's model.

Forensic evidence suggests that Victor had his throat cut and was abandoned to die in the forest as a very early age.[6] In *The Wild Child,* the scene with the mirror follows directly from the medical examination that establishes these facts. Victor wanders over to a full-length mirror in the examining room. He sniffs at the mirror, as if trying to catch the scent of this other creature. Agitated and apparently frustrated, he scratches at the mirror's surface. His guardian Itard (played by Truffaut) comes up behind him and holds an apple over Victor's head. Victor tries to reach through the glass to seize the apple reflected there, finally navigating the space behind his head to grasp the actual apple.

What students note in this scene is that while Victor does use the mirror to orient himself and his actions in relation to other objects (Itard and the apple), nothing in the scene indicates that he in any way "recognizes" himself in his reflection. In contrast, the mirror scenes in the two films about Kaspar Hauser emphasize recognition and identification, though in different ways. In Herzog's film, which appears heavily influenced by existentialist philosophy, the actor playing Kaspar (Bruno S.) stands silently over a barrel of water in which his face is reflected.[7] He touches the surface of the water, causing waves to break up and distort his image, and the camera lingers on this wavering reflection until the end of the shot. Kaspar's self-identification is literally destabilized by the visual depiction, reinforcing the film's theme of social and psychological alienation. Sehr's film, which endeavors to be faithful to the primary documents of the Kaspar Hauser case, situates its mirror scene in a makeshift classroom in the home of the boy's guardian, Georg Daumer (Udo Samel). After a language lesson in which Kaspar learns the words "eye," "ear," "nose," and "mouth," Daumer places a small mirror in front of him. As if instructed to perform the very gesture Lacan assigns to his hypothetical infant, Kaspar (André Eisermann) leans forward in fascination and tries to reach behind the mirror to touch the person who appears to be there. "The boy isn't there," he says. "No," Daumer answers, "the boy isn't there. The boy *is* Kaspar."

These cinematic episodes stimulate student reflections on a number of critical issues, including the role of scenes of self-recognition in narratives of individual development. They also suggest the link between imaginary identifications and language, a connection central to Lacan's theory. Kaja Silverman, in an essay on Herzog's film, notes that "the mirror stage, and indeed the entire imaginary register, is always mediated through language, and can only be understood in terms of organized cultural representations" (85). Comparing the actual cases of Victor and Kaspar helps students grasp the critical role of this cultural and linguistic "organization" for the development of a coherent "self" and a personality capable of functioning in society. Unlike Victor, the historical Kaspar possessed the rudiments of speech when he was found, and subsequent research suggests that the boy was confined in an isolated room for many years, but had learned language before his incarceration.[8] As a developmental phase, the mirror stage occurs before the child learns to speak, but appears as a prerequisite for language acquisition, for the articulation of "I" as a pronoun referring to a self. The historical Victor never learned to speak more than a few words (Itard 86).

Viewed in terms of Lacan's theory, Truffaut's film suggests that without self-recognition, the human subject will fail to function as a social being. The films about Kaspar Hauser, on the other hand, offer a visual means of understanding the mirror stage in its ongoing, exemplary form, in which language—both the language we speak and the language we encounter in the social world—functions to reinforce our sense of ourselves as well as our alienation from our ideal self-images.

Sehr's staging of Kaspar's mirror encounter in a classroom setting allows the scene to function as a transition to the work of Louis Althusser, who is concerned about how the subject's self-identifications are conditioned by, and support, dominant ideologies. Lacan's notion of the mirror stage serves as a key element in Althusser's theory of how ideology interpellates subjects, maintaining the identity of the individual and the individual's relationship to the social world. For Althusser, ideology consists of "the imaginary relationship of individuals to their real conditions of existence" (162), a relationship that is established and reproduced in social institutions he calls "apparatuses." The Ideological State Apparatuses include the family, the church, the school, and other institutions of private and public life in which individuals are conditioned in socially acceptable beliefs and behaviors. For the protection of these institutions and the disciplining of individuals who do not conform, society sets up Repressive State Apparatuses such as the police, the army, and the judicial system.

Interpellation does not operate strictly on the level of conscious "learning." Like Lacan, Althusser is faced with the challenge of finding a means of visualizing what is essentially an invisible, unconscious event in an individual psyche. As Lacan dramatizes the infant before the mirror, Althusser, in what he calls a "little theoretical theatre," compares the function of interpellation to the experience of a pedestrian who turns around in response to a shout from behind. Why does the person turn around? "Because he [*sic*] has recognized that the hail was 'really' addressed to him and that 'it was *really him* who was hailed' (and not someone else)" (174). Dominant ideologies shape our consciousness because we identify ourselves as their addressees, and in this sense we recognize *ourselves* in them—as the infant recognizes itself in the virtual mirror of its mother's glance.

What Althusser calls his "theoretical theatre" is an extremely useful example of the difficulty of representing concepts visually. As soon as he presents his street drama, he notes a problem with the very structure of his example. As a narrative, his "little drama presents things . . . in the form of a temporal succession" (174). In actuality, however, we are at every moment interpellated by ideology: "The existence of ideology and the hailing or interpellation of individuals as subjects are one and the same thing" (175). Here we see Althusser performing a dialectical critical iconology of his own example, exposing the tensions between his concept and its visual representation. This moment of self-critique in Althusser exemplifies one of the most valuable contributions of visualization to theoretical work. As often as they capture the structure and dynamism of a concept, visual explanations offer thinkers—including students—the opportunity to step back and say "no, it isn't like that, exactly." The imperfection of a visual representation can lead theorists to refine their formulations and help students to deepen their critical understanding of a theory's strengths and limitations.

A political cartoon printed on 1994 in *Ka Leo O Hawai'i,* the campus newspaper at the University of Hawai'i at Manoa, restages Althusser's theoretical theater in the context of the neocolonial politics of Hawai'i (fig. 3.2). This cartoon by Grant Crowell appeared in *Ka Leo* shortly after the publication of *Light in the Crevice Never Seen,* a collection of poetry by Haunani-Kay Trask, a noted Hawaiian scholar and poet.[9] Its attack on Trask depends upon a set of assumptions that can be destabilized through an Althusserian analysis of the cartoon. The structure of the narrative conforms to the "shout in the street," with the role of the "hail" assumed here by Trask's reading aloud one of her poems, "Racist White Woman." The white female protagonist, hearing the poem's title, understands that it is *she* who is being addressed. Still assuming that the "you" of the poem refers directly to her, she runs in a panic to—who else?—an agent of the repressive state apparatus, the campus security guard, who in the third panel looks curiously like a French gendarme. The guard reassures her, with clumsy irony, that she is not under attack by a "crazy local," but that it's "just one of [the University of Hawaii's] distinguished professors reading from her published poetry book." His consolation is belied—and his irony presumably reinforced—by the appearance of a vampire-like Trask in the final frame.

In "citing" Trask, Crowell drastically condenses the phrases of her poem, dropping words willfully and deleting stanzas that situate the poem's threats in the context of colonial occupation and violence:

for all my people
under your feet

for all those years
lived smug and wealthy

off our land
parasite arrogant. (67)

Read in the context of a century of colonial rule, of ongoing discrimina-
tion against the Hawaiian people in all facets of society, and of the increasing political and cultural power of the Hawaiian sovereignty movement,
Trask's poem raises a battle cry against the occupiers of her country. Read

*TAKEN FROM HAUNANI TRASK'S POEM(?) "RACIST WHITE WOMAN," FROM
HER NEW BOOK, LIGHT IN THE CREVICE NEVER SEEN.

Fig. 3.2. Editorial cartoon by Grant Crowell, Ka Leo O Hawai'i. Reprinted
with permission of Ka Leo O Hawai'i, University of Hawai'i at Manoa.
Copyright 1994.

in terms of Althusser's model, however, Crowell's cartoon conveys a message that is diametrically opposed to its manifest meaning: that the consciousness of many white residents of Hawai'i, particularly in regard to Hawaiian claims for justice and self-determination, is indelibly marked by racism; that many white residents will enlist all the forces available to them, including state-sponsored violence, to defend their illegitimate claims to Hawaiian land. Within this context, students' curiosity about why the poem is addressed to a woman can open up discussions of the role of women in the ideological apparatuses that produce and perpetuate colonial relations, which range from the missionary project of the church to traditions of first-world feminism that overlook the specific conditions of women of color and women in colonial contexts. Insofar as it can flush out and expose the intersection of racism and violence, even in the supposedly innocent female college student in Crowell's cartoon, Trask's political poetry shows itself to be a powerful cultural and political force, undiminished by Crowell's jeering policeman and sniggering question mark.

In a sense, the minimalist narratives of political cartoons occupy a middle ground between the schematization of a diagram and the complexity of film; both cartoons and cinema can serve to contextualize and localize theoretical concepts. As the "mirror scenes" in the films of Truffaut, Herzog, and Sehr provide ways of visualizing Lacan's model of the mirror stage in human development, the opening sequences of Oliver Stone's 1989 film *Born on the Fourth of July* offer a complex visualization of the notion of interpellation. Based on Ron Kovic's 1976 autobiographical account of his experiences as a soldier in Vietnam and as a paraplegic veteran in the United States, *Born on the Fourth of July* opens with a series of micro-narratives that tell the story of Ronnie's development from boyhood to young adolescence.

The film opens with a group of boys playing war. A young Ronnie and a companion are ambushed and Ronnie is pinned to the ground. The scene cuts to a Fourth of July parade, then an evening of fireworks. In the following scene, Ronnie hits a home run in a little league baseball game. Next, his family gathers around the television to hear John F. Kennedy's inaugural address. A transition advancing the story several years shows us Ron (Tom Cruise) as a high school student training for a state wrestling match, in which he is defeated—again pinned down. Alternating these stories of personal failure and triumph with iconic images of American national consciousness, the film establishes the viewer's sense of Ron Kovic's Ideal-I, a self-image shaped by the dominant ISAs: the family, the church, and the school, all of which prepare him for his adult relationship with an elite branch of the repressive state apparatus: the Marines. The scene in which Ron listens to the Marine recruiter Sergeant Hayes (Tom Berenger) depicts a literal "recruitment" of the subject of Ron Kovic by the state apparatus of the armed forces.

The film's relentless display of ideological symbols (American flags and crucifixes, for example) suggests the total, all-encompassing scope of ideology and the permanent, ongoing function of interpellation that Althusser himself seeks to convey, but cannot adequately convey, with his own dramatization. The harrowing scene later in the film when Ron, in his wheelchair, arrives home drunk and repudiates all the values he has been taught—"there is no God," he cries, "there is no country"—serves as a powerful counterpoint to the earlier recruitment scene. Ron's rejection of his earlier beliefs suggests that a dominant ideology is not all-encompassing and that subjects can break away from the identifications nurtured by the ideological state apparatuses when contradictions within its ideology are exposed, as was the case for so many veterans of the Vietnam conflict. For Ron, this "falling out" with the ideology of patriotism is psychologically traumatic for himself and for his parents and siblings, indicating the profound intertwining of ideology and identity.

Born on the Fourth of July can also serve to link discussions of interpellation and identity formation with issues of gender; the opening sequence of the film is organized around an almost obsessive inventory of the markers of American adolescent masculinity such as prowess in sports, identification with male political leaders like Kennedy, sexual gratification through *Playboy* magazine, and bonding with other young men through verbal sparring. To counterbalance the gender focus of Stone's film, I turn to Todd Haynes's *Safe,* released in 1995, to address the applicability of Althusser's theory of interpellation in the context of a woman's experience.

Safe tells the story of Carol White (Julianne Moore), an upper-middle-class homemaker in suburban Los Angeles whose physical health mysteriously begins to deteriorate. To her husband's evident dismay and despite her physician's insistence that her problems are psychosomatic, Carol becomes convinced that her suffering is the result of environmental illness (EI), an acquired intolerance to common chemical substances that is not widely recognized by conventional medicine. One scene in particular seems to encapsulate the function of interpellation. At her health club, Carol finds herself too exhausted to continue her aerobics class. Leaving the club, she catches sign of a red flyer with the heading "Do You Smell Fumes?" tacked to the club's bulletin board. The camera zooms in on the flyer as Carol reaches out to take it, and we are able to read the other questions:

> Are you allergic to the twentieth century?
>
> Do you have trouble breathing?
>
> Is your drinking water pure?
>
> Do you suffer from skin irritations?
>
> Are you always tired?

As Carol tears the flier from the board, the film cuts to her first visit to a psychiatrist, whose initial question, "Do you work?" neatly juxtaposes the flyer's questions and their implications of a real physical ailment with the alternative, psychiatric possibility: that Carol's unfulfilling life has produced psychosomatic disorders. The following scene consists of a slow pan of Carol's family photographs and a voice-over representing the letter Carol is writing to an organization dedicated to environmental illness. Carol tells her life story in the letter, including her recent fatigue and illness, bringing her sense of identity into alignment with the language of the flyer. Because it remains ambivalent about Carol's identification with sufferers of environmental illness, Haynes's film raises compelling questions about epistemology and identity formation that are congruent with the questions Althusser explores in his essay on the ISAs. To what extent is our knowledge of our own experience the result of the preformed ideas our culture and society make available to us, ideas with which we identify and use to make sense of our lives?

Carol eventually takes temporary leave of her husband and stepson to join the community of EI patients at the Wrenwood Institute in the New Mexico desert. The film's ambivalence intensifies as it moves to the austere setting of Wrenwood, presenting the institute simultaneously as a haven for Carol, who needs an escape from the shallowness and tedium of her suburban existence, and as a tyrannical, paranoid subculture that is every bit as damaging to its inhabitants as the polluted world outside. *Safe* appears to suggest, like Althusser, that escape from ideological apparatuses is impossible. Even if we elect to resist a dominant ideology (the ideology of bourgeois materialism, for example, or of conventional medicine), the best we can do is exchange them for other ideological apparatuses which, despite their status as "alternative" or "oppositional," may be as fraught with disabling contradictions and hierarchies as those we have fled.

Trying to teach the concept of interpellation places the instructor in a paradoxical and not terribly comfortable position, for the experience of learning is itself a facet of the interpellation of the subject-as-student, with the instructors situated squarely within the ideological state apparatus of the school, themselves interpellated subjects-as-teachers. In asking my students to grasp the operations of Althusser's model of interpellation, I am asking them to engage in a kind of double consciousness: mastering "course material" on the one hand and, on the other, referring these new concepts to the experience of their own "material conditions of existence." I am asking them to understand the theory in its own terms and to test it against their prior understanding of the world. Out of the discrepancies that frequently arise between impressions of what the theory "says" and what life is "really like," we can collectively develop a way to approach the theory critically in its own terms, as well as in ours.

For many learners, the theory of interpellation just doesn't *feel right,* but how can this subjective resistance be channeled toward a rigorous critique? It is here that visual examples can serve to estrange the subjective response to a concept, displacing experience from the subject of the student to an Other who can be observed. Diagrams and illustrations can, in this sense, be thought of as passages from abstraction to the space-time of the material world, a transitional mid-range of phenomena between the theoretical concept and the intensely private, idiosyncratic phenomenal experiences of an individual reader.

In this respect, Todd Haynes's film *Safe* is particularly helpful insofar as it refuses to give a decisive interpretation of Carol White's experience. She may *in fact* be suffering from environmental illness, or she may be a late-twentieth-century version of Freud's hysterical patients who convert psychic distress into physical ailments, or she may as easily be a combination of both: really sensitive to a polluted environment *and* really incapacitated by psychic conflicts. The flyer on the bulletin board does not "produce" Carol's symptoms, but gives her a way to organize her experiences within a signifying system that invests them with meaning and identity. She recognizes herself in the "you" the flyer addresses, and this recognition fixes her into a pattern of subsequent social behaviors that reinforces her identity as a sufferer of EI. The film's final scene, in which Carol, enclosed in her igloo-shaped, porcelain-lined "safe place," confronts her own image in the mirror, gives students yet another opportunity to examine the explanatory power of Lacan's concept of the mirror stage. Optimistic readers might well take this scene as an indication of Carol's eventual triumph over the debilitating self-hatred that may underlie her physical anguish, but others might interpret the mantra she repeats—"I love you, I really love you," which has been suggested to her by the director of the Wrenwood facility—as an indication of Carol's imprisonment within the discursive frameworks of popular psychology and alternative medicine.

As narratives, *Born on the Fourth of July* and *Safe* allow us to explore the narrative dimensions of the theories that we might employ to understand them. Like all of the visual materials I enlist in my effort to engage students with theoretical concepts, film enters into a dialogue with the theory, resisting any instrumental "application" that would subordinate the film as a mere object to be "explained" or "illuminated" by the theory. By the same token, visual materials do not in any simple way "illuminate" the concepts of theory. Whatever light is generated in the encounter of the theoretical with the visual takes the form of sparks struck by that contact; insight comes from the encounter, emerging dialectically within a dialogue between different semiotic and conceptual registers.

Although we may be able to demonstrate that visual materials can be of great help in the teaching of theoretical concepts, can we really justify the teaching of theory itself, especially in the case of undergraduates, few of whom will go on to become specialists in literary or cultural studies? My own justification derives from the conviction that all students can benefit from the experience of grappling with abstract concepts, testing them through concrete applications, and debating their merits and limitations in face-to-face conversations and in writing. Students are free to select their own topics for their writing assignments; a significant part of the exercise lies in extending the concepts they have learned from the specific examples we treat in class to whatever texts and issues that they find compelling. In addition to research papers in which they explore a text or cultural production in terms of the theories they have been studying, students give in-class presentations based on written précis of a theoretical text of their choosing and are required to pose questions for class discussion. A class listserv allows us to continue these discussions outside of class times. Students who plan to enter the fields of medicine, law, or other professions that involve sets of complex concepts and specialized terminology generally appreciate the practice in careful reading afforded by the texts of philosophy and literary theory. I hope, too, that my own repeated efforts to show students how concepts are formed and how they work (and don't work) will serve as a rhetorical model for their own future explanations to patients, clients, colleagues, and other learners.

The element of narrative in films, and to a lesser extent in animations such as the one I have developed for the mirror stage, serve still another purpose in the classroom: offering stories that help us learn, they remind us that learning is part of history. Moments of theoretical insight, no less than any other moments of our lives, unfold in historical time. Each individual student grappling with a concept adds to the developing life of that concept; the "ah-ha" experience of every student comprises a moment of possible transformation. Learning the story of theory, both in the sense of the development of theoretical concepts and the implicit narratives that inhere in many of those concepts, students and teachers participate and contribute to intellectual history. Unrecorded, perhaps, but not insignificant, the everyday teaching of theory constitutes a major current in the history of ideas, an effective instance of ideas making their home in the world.

When Francis Bacon reworked the material on *memoria* from *The Advancement of Learning* in 1623, he expanded his remarks on how visual images contribute to a speaker's practical application of the theoretical canons of rhetoric and added more explicit examples of visualization:

> Emblem . . . reduces intellectual conceptions to sensible images; for an object of sense always strikes the memory more forcibly and is more easily impressed upon it than an object of the intellect; insomuch that even brutes have their memory excited by sensible impressions; never by intellectual ones. And therefore you will more easily remember the image of a hunter pursuing a hare, of an apothecary arranging his boxes, of a pedant making a speech, of a boy repeating verses from memory, of a player acting on the stage, than the mere notions of invention, disposition, elocution, memory, and action. (4:437)

"Theory," as we are often reminded, is etymologically connected with seeing. As Bacon suggested more than four centuries ago, and as the texts I have discussed demonstrate, theory depends upon the visual image not only to explain itself, but to constitute itself dialectically in a practice based on a set of concepts. "Ideas can only be associated as images," write Deleuze and Guattari, "and can only be ordered as abstractions; to arrive at the concept we must go beyond both of these and arrive as quickly as possible at mental objects determinable as real beings" (207). Images operate as means of connecting and elaborating ideas in the formation and reformation of what we call "theory." We might imagine the relationship between visual images and philosophy as a game of question-and-answer, with the image asking the philosopher "is this it?" and the philosopher answering "no, not quite," to which the image returns the question, "well, then, what *is* it?" If we risk the instrumental metaphor of the image as a "tool" of philosophy (and of pedagogy), the image might well appear as a cutting edge, continually moving at the forefront of active thinking rather than reposing as a static receptacle of already-formulated thought.

At their best, images that seek to help students understand ideas are able to perform two tasks: providing a clear representation of the concept *and* offering a way of testing, challenging, critiquing that concept. Popular books about philosophy and literary theory "for beginners" abound with diagrams and appealing visuals, but they almost never exploit the capacity of the image to question the concept it is supposed to convey.[10] Images employed to illustrate abstract concepts often turn out to be insubordinate employees. As many theorists of the relations between word and image have pointed out, visual representations stand in a dialectical relationship with the verbal representations of that concept. They rely on the verbal for their contours and contents, but they always turn back upon the verbal and force it to account for itself, its shortcomings, elisions, and omissions.

These points will be obvious to anyone who has explored the many philosophical treatments of the relationships among words and images such as those offered by Kress and van Leeuwen and by Mitchell; the challenge lies in integrating this dialectical tension between the verbal and visual representation of a concept into a pedagogical practice. As I hope the above examples have indicated, it is the rich particularity of visual materials, not their simplicity or universality, that make them useful vehicles for teaching theory. Diagrams, visual examples, and dramatizations function best as catalysts for dialogue and dialectical thinking. By not simply employing images of various kinds but by listening to them, admitting their disturbing questions into our attempts to explain, we can work towards turning the pleasurable experience of insight—for ourselves as much as for our students —into a no-less-pleasurable occasion for dialogue, critique, and struggle.

NOTES

1. I will use the expression "literary theory" throughout this essay to avoid repeating the cumbersome formulation "theories of literature and culture," but the concepts I am discussing are as central—perhaps even more so—to the diverse areas of inquiry organized under the rubric of "cultural studies" as they are to the theoretical foundations of contemporary literary studies. Teaching strategies involving visualization have proven useful to me in a range of courses in which "theory" is a significant component of course content, including undergraduate courses on research methods in English studies, literary theory and criticism, and the rhetorical tradition; as well as in graduate courses on the history of the profession of English studies, theories of poetics, and the rhetoric and aesthetics of electronic media. For undergraduate classes, I have used anthologies of literary theory that provide students with substantial excerpts of major theoretical texts, and I supplement the anthology with a course reader that contains articles I feel students should read in full. Most recently I have assigned Julie Rivkin and Michael Ryan's *Literary Theory: An Anthology,* which offers a fairly comprehensive survey of twentieth-century texts, carefully excerpted, and highly readable introductions to various critical approaches.

2. I will take up the diagrams of Saussure and Lacan in the following discussion. Lévi-Strauss's studies of the facial painting among the Caduveo appear in chapter 20 of *Tristes Tropiques* (186–231). *Desire in Language: A Semiotic Approach to Literature and Art,* a collection of essays by Julia Kristeva, includes "Giotto's Joy" (210–36) and "Motherhood According to Bellini" (237–70).

3. Saussure himself suggests the analogy of the molecule: rather than indulging the temptation to think of the signified-signifier relation in terms of "soul" and "body," he states that "a better choice would be a chemical compound like water, a combination of hydrogen and oxygen; taken separately, neither element has any of the properties of water" (103). The Saussurian sign appears as an excellent example of a "concept" in the terms of Deleuze and Guattari, who observe that "what is distinctive about the concept is that it renders components inseparable within itself. Components, or what defines the consistency of the concept, its endoconsistency, are distinct, heterogeneous, and yet not separable" (19). Saussure's representations of the sign, both visual and verbal, strive to make this very point.

4. See, for example, the published seminar notes on the "Ego-ideal and ideal ego," in which Lacan presents an elaborate optical diagram to demonstrate the "virtuality" of the ego (*Seminar I* 139–40).

5. For example, in the chapter "La Mystérique," Irigaray takes up the metaphor of the mother-as-mirror and turns it against Lacan's formulations: "Thus I have become your image in this nothingness that I am, and you gaze upon mine in your absence of being. . . . A living mirror, thus, am I (to) your resemblance as you are mine (197).

6. See Itard's own account of his work with Victor, *The Wild Boy of Aveyron,* 29–30.

7. A mirror appears earlier in Herzog's film, when a girl attempts to teach Kaspar the names of the parts of his body by holding a hand mirror in front of him. The scene does not, however, emphasize Kaspar's recognition of himself in the mirror; in fact, he seems to pay little attention to it. Sehr's film, which cites Herzog's in innumerable ways, also combines language-learning and an encounter with a mirror but, as I will describe, places a strong emphasis on Kaspar's reaction to his reflected image.

8. Jeffrey Massouieff Masson's *Lost Prince: The Unsolved Mystery of Kaspar Hauser* offers a translation of Anselm Ritter von Feuerbach's firsthand account of the Kaspar Hauser case.

9. Trask's scholarly work on colonialism in Hawai'i appears in *From a Native Daughter: Colonialism and Sovereignty in Hawai'i.* In the chapter "The Politics of Academic Freedom as the Politics of White Racism" (169–84), she offers an account of an earlier interaction with the student newspaper at the University of Hawai'i.

10. Following the appealing model of comic books and 'zines, texts such as *Introducing Lacan* by Darian Leader and Judy Groves (part of a series by Icon Books) or *Lacan for Beginners* by Philip Hill and David Leach (part of a series by Writers and Readers) do provide entertaining overviews of the thought of major theorists. Though they take up as much space page for page as the verbal texts, the inventive combinations of clip art and original drawings that illustrate these study guides remain ancillary to the text's didactic function. A similar problem arises with highly sophisticated "introductions" to theory such as Slavoj Zizek's *Looking Awry: An Introduction to Jacques Lacan through Popular Culture,* in which film and other forms of popular media are engaged in order to explore Lacanian concepts. Like their comic-book cousins, such works employ visual examples in order to validate and reproduce the theories they propose to teach, and spend less energy in engaging the visual materials in a critical dialogue with the theoretical concepts. The visual dimension serves as a medium for the presentation of theory but rarely as a means of complicating, challenging, or disrupting it.

WORKS CITED

Althusser, Louis. *Lenin and Philosophy and Other Essays.* Trans. Ben Brewster. New York: Monthly Review Press, 1971.

Bacon, Francis. *Of the Dignity and Advancement of Learning. The Works of Francis Bacon.* Ed. James Spedding. Vol. 4. New York: Garrett Press, 1968. 275–438.

———. *The Second Book of Francis Bacon of the Proficience and Advancement of Learning Divine and Human. The Works of Francis Bacon.* Ed. James Spedding. Vol. 3. New York: Garrett Press, 1968. 321–492.

Crowell, Grant. Cartoon. *Ka Leo O Hawai'i* 11 September 1994: 6.

Deleuze, Gilles, and Félix Guattari. *What Is Philosophy?* Trans. Hugh Tomlinson and Graham Burchell. New York: Columbia UP, 1994.

Grosz, Elizabeth. *Jacques Lacan: A Feminist Introduction.* London/New York: Routledge, 1990.

Haynes, Todd, dir. *Safe.* Perf. Julianne Moore. 1995. Videocassette. Columbia Tristar Home Video, 1995.

Herzog, Werner, dir. *Everyman for Himself and God Against All.* Perf. Bruno S. 1974. Videocassette. RCI/Columbia, 1975.

Hill, Philip, and David Leach. *Lacan for Beginners.* New York/London: Writers and Readers, 1999.

Irigaray, Luce. *Speculum of the Other Woman.* Trans. Gillian C. Gill. Ithaca: Cornell UP, 1985.

Itard, Jean-Marc-Gaspard. *The Wild Boy of Aveyron.* Trans. George Humphrey and Muriel Humphrey. New York: Appleton-Century Crofts, 1962.

Kress, Gunther, and Theo van Leeuwen. *Reading Images: The Grammar of Visual Design.* London: Routledge, 1996.

Kristeva, Julia. *Desire in Language: A Semiotic Approach to Literature and Art.* Ed. Leon S. Roudiez. Trans. Alice A. Jardine. New York: Columbia UP, 1980.

Lacan, Jacques. *Écrits: A Selection.* Trans. Alan Sheridan. New York: Norton, 1977.

———. *The Seminar of Jacques Lacan: Book I: Freud's Papers on Technique 1953–1954.* Ed. Jacques-Alain Miller. Trans. John Forrester. New York: Norton, 1988.

Leader, Darian, and Judy Groves. *Introducing Lacan.* Cambridge: Icon Books, 2000.

Lévi-Strauss, Claude. *Tristes Tropiques.* Trans. John Weightman and Doreen Weightman. New York: Pocket Books, 1973.

Masson, Jeffrey Massouieff. *Lost Prince: The Unsolved Mystery of Kaspar Hauser.* New York: Free Press, 1996.

Mitchell, W. J. T. *Picture Theory: Essays on Verbal and Visual Representation.* Chicago: U of Chicago P, 1994.

Rivkin, Julie, and Michael Ryan, eds. *Literary Theory: An Anthology.* Oxford: Blackwell, 1998.

Saussure, Ferdinand de. *Course in General Linguistics.* Ed. Charles Bally and Albert Sechehaye. Trans. Wade Baskin. New York: McGraw-Hill, 1966.

Sehr, Peter, dir. *Kaspar Hauser.* Perf. André Eisermann. 1994. Videocassette. Kino on Video, 1997.

Silverman, Kaja. "Kaspar Hauser's 'Terrible Fall' into Narrative." *New German Critique* 24/25 (fall/winter 1983): 73–93.

Stone, Oliver, dir. *Born on the Fourth of July.* Perf. Tom Cruise. 1989. Videocassette. MCA Home Video, 1990.

Trask, Haunani-Kay. *From a Native Daughter: Colonialism and Sovereignty in Hawai'i.* Rev. ed. Honolulu: U of Hawaii P, 1999.

———. *Light in the Crevice Never Seen.* Corvallis, OR: Calyx, 1994.

Truffaut, François, dir. *The Wild Child.* Perf. François Truffaut, Jean-Pierre Leaud. 1969. Videocassette. Warner HomeVideo, 1970.

Tufte, Edward. *Visual Explanations: Images and Quantities, Evidence and Narrative.* Cheshire, CT: Graphics Press, 1997.

Zizek, Slavoj. *Looking Awry: An Introduction to Jacques Lacan through Popular Culture.* Cambridge: MIT Press, 1991.

Simulation Machines, Media Boundaries, and the Re-expansion of Composition

JAMES W. MILES II

RECONCEIVING WRITING AS A SUBSET OF COMPOSING

Although our practices are slowly modulating and morphing, we can readily admit that the contemporary college or university experience, for the general student, is a profoundly verbal one. In the early grades, however, we allow our children to explore all sorts of communicative systems. Elementary school kids transmit messages and meanings by singing songs, painting with their fingers, speaking incessantly, and slowly learning to write. Likewise, they receive messages in a number of ways, rifling through books of pictures, browsing the Web, watching plays and videos, listening to stories, and of course learning to read. While it is true that we harness the powers of almost every medium for education as our students come up through the grades, we must nonetheless acknowledge a certain transition away from the near-synaesthesia of multiple-media classroom experiences into a more distinctly written and spoken practice as one nears high school and college. The older one grows in the academy, the more one lilts toward silent codex—the ultimate, perhaps, the emeritus professor reading Proust by fluorescent light in a concrete block office with no windows. Book reports and poems, research essays and short fiction, critical analyses and journals and even ethnographies—we ask students to inhabit written forms, to take up verbal conventions, and to produce, in the end, text.

And we certainly have important reasons for proceeding as we do, especially at the secondary level and beyond. The academy has had (and still has) fine uses for towering verbal structures, from articles to novels to grant proposals. It is in the written and read and spoken that we intend to locate our minds, to cultivate our deepest beliefs, to determine our values, to build and reform our societies, and to lay the foundations of what will come after us. And yet, and yet. Although we have convinced ourselves that the verbal is the one, true cyberspace—the best place of mental construction and convocation—I want to explore the notion that other sites for such construction also abound, though they lie essentially fallow in the contemporary college or university. Put differently, I am suggesting that even our finest practices may eventually crystallize into traditions which may or may not hold their value as rhetorical demands evolve through time and techno-social change.

In the university we favor writing as the real mark of understanding, the real sign of intellectual engagement; I come to you now in writing. But the rest of society—certainly in industrialized countries and increasingly other places as well—has grown fonder of many other kinds of media and media processes, which I will refer to generically as "mediation." Speed of access to textual purpose, ease of information transfer, invitation of eyes otherwise disposed to go elsewhere—all of these demands have created obvious media revolutions for about a century and a half now (since still photography, we could argue), taking us far beyond the black and white alphabetic page. In the humanities we have become aware of these shifts to the point of truism, and so this is not an essay which catalogs media revolutions. My question, and my real point of departure, is this: how should the academy be tapping into the ever-widening array of media that are around us, circulating in our senses, our minds, and our social structures? How might multiple mediation or alternating mediation make our students' work—and ours—vastly more effective, given the surging developments in communication outside of school?

Here's an example which has preoccupied me recently: college students are bored with their writing assignments. True, many college courses and writing assignments are compulsory, a situation that would suck the inspiration out of almost any writer, but if we as their teachers would come honest and say the truth, the writing assignments we give often don't resemble anything in their worlds. Many teachers of composition in recent years have tried to address this issue by radically opening up topic selection, allowing students to write about the exact things that attract or excite or agitate them. But even when the topics students choose do come "from their worlds," the written forms themselves still do not; this is a symptom of the media shifts occurring around us constantly. The freshman male might indeed be interested in steroid use or raves or the senatorial race in his state, but he's probably not so concerned about expressive essays, narratives, profiles, features, reviews, in-depth analyses, interview reports, research papers, and the like.

Of course, the consistent "disconnect" between our expectations as their instructors and their ability (or willingness) to fulfill them does not necessarily surprise us. The solution becomes a tenuous one; on the one hand, we should always expect our students to stretch and flex and move beyond their current abilities and desires. That, after all, is much of the value of education. If learning a given form teaches, then so be it. On the other hand, though, we should ask to what extent we—as their instructors—are failing to stretch and flex *ourselves* when we create assignments that look a lot more like us as verbally-entrenched academicians than our students as soon-to-be college-educated individuals who are deeply submerged in a culture with specific language expectations that are not merely verbal but actively, even aggressively mediated in manifold ways. Even those of us who happily profess the verbal still work and play extensively in a world of wider communicative practices.

Lest I mislead you, I am not necessarily arguing that we abandon the teaching of writing via forms (though I'll also acknowledge that many teachers have radically different, non-formal approaches). Considering textual conventions—how to describe and analyze and categorize and then achieve them in one's own works—is a powerful means of learning. Instead, I am suggesting that conventions themselves might be radically more pliant and dynamic than we are willing to accept. Furthermore, I'm not calling for a wholesale abandonment of the ways of our maturest and best scholars. A beautiful example is a senior colleague and teacher of mine, a well-known Shakespeare expert, who "came through" in a period when "the right way" to study Shakespeare was "on the page" and who now teaches Shakespeare almost exclusively as an interpretive performance phenomenon that happens onstage and on-screen. Incidentally, this is actually a media-based approach. Drama should indeed be considered one means of mediation, a particularly fascinating one in which the human body itself serves as the physical substrate and human action serves as the medium somewhere between fiction and rite.

I suppose I have accidentally raised an old question. That is, what exactly are we preparing students for? For academic success while they are with us? For instant, lucrative careers after college? For an expanded life of the mind no matter where they end up or when they get there? That tension is a delicious one, and we should strive to maintain it, but in the meantime, I propose that we begin to reclassify the concept of "composing" by re-broadening it to its actual scope, which goes far beyond the verbal, of course. Even today, when we hear of a "famous composer," none of us think of a great freshman comp student; we think of some arranger of music, Copland or Debussy or whomever. Likewise, photography courses normally begin by inculcating a set of conventions known as "photo composition," the positioning of subjects within the frame and the subtraction of distracting elements from the shot. Graphic design provides another good example in what the field calls "page composition." My guess is that all of us greatly respect these other forms of meaning-making, probably quite deeply, and so I return to the refrain; why not allow our students to explore media other than the purely verbal, to *compose* other ways?

I propose not the least diminution of writing but simply a more robust engagement of meaning-making in all its possible manifestations. In fact, I hold that exploring composition of various kinds will literally cause students to generate and reinforce crucial synaptic connections between meaning and any system for mediating it. Here is a simple example that is easy to introduce and use in the classroom, and one which encourages at least two methods of mediation—photography and writing. First, display a photograph (see fig. 4.1).

Then have the class attempt to duplicate the photograph verbally, in thirty-five words or so. Have a few students read their results, and then discuss how the verbal description and the photograph differ. Which does what? Do the written descriptions set up a virtual kind of vision? We often teach our freshman writers to produce "vivid sensory detail," so why not encourage them to explore the connections between the writing and the senses by actually using those senses? Eventually, ask the class to decide which is more descriptive and why, the writing or the photograph. At that point, it might be instructive to ask the class to do some writing to stand *with* the photo rather than in its place, asking their media to cooperate. What they'll essentially produce is a caption. You might even have them research

Fig. 4.1. *Leonardo da Vinci's Horse.* Photograph by James Miles.

the subject on their own. For example, this photograph is of *Leonardo da Vinci's Horse,* a twenty-four-foot rendition of da Vinci's *Il Cavallo,* by American sculptor Nina Akamu. This one stands in the Frederik Meijer Sculpture Garden in Grand Rapids, Michigan, and another was presented to the people of Milan, Italy, in September 1999. All such information comes to the aid of the photograph, spelling out details the picture can't, just as the image provides detail that words could reproduce in only a vague and cumbersome manner. One could even challenge the class to write a second, expressive, poetic caption about the warlike visage of the critter involved and what that means.

This sort of activity draws out relationships concerning description and detail and accuracy, highlighting the powers of the various sign systems at work, all in a much more direct and plain manner than a lecture about how to achieve more descriptive prose (which might now make a good lesson for the day after this one). Even so, the exercise still remains mostly verbal, as far as the student work is concerned. My call here is that we design far more potent mediation assignments. How do the media perform what they do, and how do they then interact, interoperate? And why is it important for us—teachers and students alike—to grasp such issues firmly in our increasingly media-saturated culture?

"MEDIA" ARE . . .

But *media* itself has become one of those catchall words (like *political* or *social* or *electronic*), deflated of real value by an inflationary process which has endowed it with too many meanings in too short a time. Therefore I'd like to clearly define the term before I employ it any further as it relates to the pedagogy of composition.

It is simple enough to begin with the notion that a medium carries something by embodying it in some way, by giving it a temporary body. From there it is a short leap to name off some more or less distinct media categories like print, radio, TV, and film, but even such a short list already contains the seeds of contention. For instance, TV and film share an obvious kinship, so perhaps they should be grouped under some other master heading like "moving pictures." Yet TV and film are stored and delivered on strikingly different vehicles, which begs another question regarding the physical substrates that carry our media, such as pulp paper, celluloid, or magnetic tape. And what of ink, silver halide emulsions, and metal oxides? And beyond that, how do we account, taxonomically, for broadcast? Even broadcast, which initially implied a transmission via airwaves, now also envelops delivery via fiber-optic and coaxial cable, as well as digitized delivery via all those same vehicles.

Obviously, categorization rapidly becomes tangled and difficult. We might try to work from the substrates in the other direction, but that approach also leads to troubles. Magnetic tape can carry both videography and recorded sound, which begs us to differentiate videotape from audiotape, not to mention data tape. Despite the hopeless confusion we've already achieved, we haven't even moved on to the finer gradations of mediation yet. For instance, think of all the arch-genres that go onto paper: broadsheet newspapers, codex books (and their magazine variants), posters, business cards, and so on. The fact that newspapers are not widely distributed on VHS cassettes strongly suggests that medium at least influences genre, if not controlling it deeply in some cases. Nonetheless, a single physical substrate can carry scores of genres; codex technology currently carries textbooks, novels, anthologies, self-help books, reference works, phonebooks, et al. The layers of material technology, delivery technology, aesthetic conventions, and even audience subdivisions become staggering in their absolute imbrication, converging and diverging differently depending on one's vantage. We tend to think of media as simple, discrete technologies, and mediation as simple, discrete processes, but it's radically more rhizomatous than that. Observe, for example, the inaccuracies involved in trying to create a simple media chart (see fig. 4.2). Study it for even a few moments, and contradictions and overlappings appear everywhere.

Perhaps not so surprisingly, McLuhan is extremely helpful in getting past this tangle by reconfiguring the entire question, reframing the syllogism. Early in *Understanding Media* he elucidates that "the content of any medium is always another medium. The content of writing is speech, just as the written word is the content of print, and print is the content of the telegraph" (23–24). Although I will argue below that the content of writing is in fact *not* speech, as others have noted, McLuhan's theory in its very generality and relativity is still more universally accurate than a top-down, Aristotelian chart. And so, simply, a medium is literally anything that can

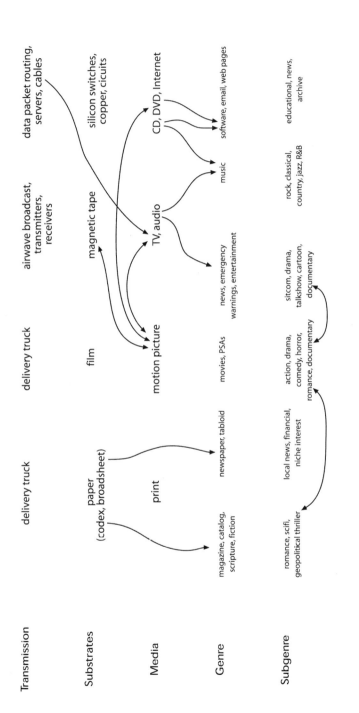

Fig. 4.2. Media imbrication chart. Designed by James Miles.

carry any other, which in turn will be able to carry some third thing, and so on into the infinitesimally imperceptible grain-resolution of meaning. It is something like a packet of serially nestled envelopes, one within the other. We should remember, however, that a given envelope can contain all sorts of others, not just a single one or even a specific set. The combinations hybridize at an astonishing rate, and what we end up with is a fantastically rich network of mutual media interdependence that can carry human meanings in literally infinitely variable ways. The system forms a fluid transcourse between the semiotic and the physical, an interface between the intellectual (the abstract, even the metaphysical) and the very mundanely material and technological. The tangible and the intangible meet in secret, out of our direct line of sight, and traffic between themselves.

Thinking of mediation this way seems to counsel against any straight-forward dichotomy between vessel and content, between carrier and carried. Better yet, perhaps it *is* valuable to try to discern such single-step relationships in the chain of mediation, as McLuhan suggested, but it is important to carry the process forward (or backward) by asking what the *next* nestled envelope is, including what it contains, and what *it* contains, and so forth. But even this model doesn't yet account for the way that one medium can branch off simultaneously to more than one other, forming not only chains but, alas, webs. For example, when Associated Press reporters write news items concerning events they have just witnessed, they are mediating many more than one source of content into a single story, a single container/carrier. One element encapsulated is of course some description of the event in its outer dressing, the people and places involved. But lurking in the naked facts will also be some human import, some reason that this is a story worth passing around. A third factor built into the message is the presumed audience, a world news consumer who is accustomed to a very specific set of conventions in news stories. Another intensely complex element that gets included to one extent or another is the judgment and bias and preference of the reporter. All of these elements eventually form the rhetorical complexity of almost any meaning-making moment, and we haven't even addressed the mechanical technology or the sign systems the reporter will use to actually transmit the story.

And we shouldn't ignore the interwoven nature of the technological and the rhetorical. Below I have labored to identify the actual passage of mediation from original sender to final consumer in the AP report example, presuming an eventual story for an Internet news site. What gets passed and how? Note the constant, furious intercourse between meaning and machines:

> event [people, location, probable political interaction] > observation [direct or secondhand? selection, discrimination, bias, assignment parameters] > recording [empirical data collection, reporter's inevitably subjective impressions, physical substrates] > composing [craft, convention, style, additional physical substrates] > transmission [telephone, fax, email/Internet, satellite > sound waves, digital or analog data (text, audio, video, photographs) > cables, routers, servers, desktop computers, software, transmitters] > reception [similar processes] > selection by an editor [bias, audience, criteria, "newsworthiness" competition with other stories] > copy/photo/audio/video editing [convention (length modification, cropping, emphasis, polish) > various machines] > layout and design [convention, space and size considerations > Macintosh hardware and software] > posting/publishing [UNIX hardware and software] > selection by user/reader [bias, special interest, visual acquisition] > retrieval [PC hardware, browser, transmission protocols] > absorption [skimming, selecting, reading (pixels, RGB colors, browser preference settings for typography)] > residual image [imagination, memory]

The really striking thing here is that we so instantly ignore all of that when we're on the receiving end. We court an intentional ignorance and posit that we are reading directly about the event itself, usually even bypassing any awareness of our own reading, as if the event itself, whatever it was, were unfolding directly before our own eyes. Scores of machines and people, as well as thousands of stylistic and editorial choices and policies, actually intervene. Amazingly, though, all of that, to a reader (and often to the composers, too), seems transparent. More on that below.

Each level both encodes and delivers; it's a passage between meaning and mechanical translators and carriers. It is neither pure semiotics (except inasmuch as semiotics accepts sign systems as technologies) nor a simple set of technologies, both of which are, to my observation, common misapprehensions about mediation. The digital, of course, comes with its own set of considerations, which is why we tend to refer to it as "the digital domain" or "the digital realm." However, to confer on the digital a "domain" status implies that mediation works fundamentally differently there, and I am not convinced that it does, given the definition of mediation I am advancing. Consider: the digital at first appears to collapse the distinction between meaning and machine, because media machines, in the digital, are built largely of code instead of paper and celluloid. Certainly, computers are made of metals, plastics, glass, and silicon, but they simulate other media themselves; the screen can simulate both print and television (as well as, increasingly, the movie theatre). The temptation is to think of these simulated media as being part of the encoded stories they deliver, and that is exactly what they are. The surprise is that it works the very same way in "traditional" media technologies. The substrate is not simply a delivery vehicle; it is a crucial part of the fabric of the meaning conveyed by the overall set of "nestled envelopes" it helps to carry. Medium and content blur into one another in an inextricable way. In one step, an "envelope" is the carrier, but in the very next step, it becomes part of meaning.

DEMYSTIFYING SIMULATION

Although my primary interest in this essay is not specifically computer-based mediation, the digital nonetheless offers a truly helpful opportunity for discussion. "Desubstantiation" is the term Richard Lanham applies to that process by which computers reduce their subjects to code (11)—images converted to pure, multi-bit data, forever released from canvas or photographic paper—sounds quantized at super-audible frequencies and laid down on CDs or MP3 servers—but we should take care not to forget that code itself (any code) is a perfect example of mediation. By nature, code both *is a machine* and *carries meaning*. That code has no physical body need not frighten us; it is still very much a machine. (Code *does* frighten some of us; Baudrillard, for example.) Digitization's primary technique shouldn't frighten us, either: dissolving an analog object and then simulating it back into virtual existence in some medium other than the one in which it originated, such as photos moving into pixels or letters moving into ASCII cipher. Most importantly, we should see that *all* mediation works this way, at least to some extent. News stories, for example, begin life in the minds of reporters, and we are not the least bit concerned when they make a transubstantial leap into a high-resolution imagesetter and ultimately end up as ink on a rubber blanket in a web press which gets "pressed" onto newsprint. All of this helps carry us even further from the confusing desire to separate media into categories like "substrate," "medium," and "genre," as discussed above. Meaning ripples through various carriers in an astoundingly complex manner on its way to wherever it ends up.

To take this even further, nearly all of the senses have been replicated by machines, as has everything perceived *by* those senses. That is, we have machines that can "see" (or at least register light and color and density), and we have also generated visual images with pure code. In other words, we have created both seeing agents and encoded versions of "the seen," as well. Digital images and sounds are now taken for granted, commonplaces, even though they couldn't have been thought so just twenty years ago, and touch and smell are also well on the way, with taste possibly to follow. Aldous Huxley prefigured the digital olfactory and tactile in *Brave New World* with his "scent organ" and its textural counterpart in the theatres in his novel, and science fiction has a way of coming true. In the 90s, for example, a company called DigiScents claimed to have developed working prototypes of a "personal scent synthesizer" call iSmell, "a technology for digitizing, broadcasting, and resynthesizing scent." Like a printer, the machine would sit by your desktop computer, supported by software called ScentStream. The company claimed to be ushering in a new age of "scentography." We smirk, but we should remember that we already use a more sophisticated semiotics of smell than we normally stop to acknowledge, and an olfactory medium would bring great development in that system, that "language." Why should we not mediate the work of the nose and simulate scent?

Nonetheless, simulation has been a spooky issue for theorists for quite some time. For instance, we have Plato's famous dialogue concerning imitation and reality in book 10 of *The Republic*. The notion of what we now call "Platonic forms" has everything to do with mediation; the "pure," for Plato, is the formal, the thoroughly bodiless, abstract idea, which is firstness, a purity attributed to God. Secondness derives from there: any bodily, physical manifestation of the form. Thirdness begins to drive too far away, presumably because of generational decay, such as in the case of a verbal or visual description of whatever is manifested in secondness. Thus Plato begins with the form of a table, moves on to a table built by a carpenter, and ends up disparaging a table in a painting, or rather a painting *of* a table, because the image relays appearances only, a single and potentially weak or incorrect human perspective. "Imitation is only a kind of play or sport," he says (46), and it allows us too easily to wander away from the truth, a full complexity that can only possibly be contained in the form, and not a copy of a copy.

I am suggesting, however, that the chain of mediation goes far deeper than three levels, as illustrated in the AP example above, and meaning-making, while certainly affected, does not necessarily suffer. Truth is the voice of God, but meaning is the voice of humanity. Of course an original gets altered as it gets passed from one medium to another, but the amazing thing is that it stays intact as well as it does. We should stop worrying, in other words, about the 3 percent of slippage and imprecision (the battle cry of the deconstructionist) and begin exploring the 97 percent of accuracy and success.

As hinted above, we should not miss Baudrillard's discussion of the four phases of the image at this juncture, as well. His use of "image" is intentionally generic; we could take it to be any representation at all, and not just a visual one (which seems to be the common sense we have now given to the word). The relationship of that image to a supposed original reality is his primary concern. He says,

Such would be the successive phases of the image:

[1] it is the reflection of a profound reality;
[2] it masks and denatures a profound reality;
[3] it masks the absence of a profound reality;
[and 4] it has no relation to any reality whatsoever; it is its own pure simulacrum. (6)

The first phase would indicate the simplest one-to-one, thing-to-image representation, something like the common assumption concerning representation before Wittgenstein or Saussure. The second phase Baudrillard identifies with our sense of evil and wrongness—images, in other words, that lie. The third, interestingly, Baudrillard connects to sorcery, the ability to conjure apparitions that literally have no connection to anything in our real, our reality, things that are totally other.

It is Baudrillard's fourth phase of the image, however, that most interests me in my discussion of the chain of mediation, because it highlights the work of simulation. Simulacrum emerges when there is no nod from a sign back toward some originating real, and yet *something* is happening, *something* is emerging. Somewhat like Plato in reverse, Baudrillard is troubled by the possibility of copies of copies themselves, copies not of anything real and original, but copies of other duplicates. Whereas Plato begins with pure abstraction, in form, and frets as we move toward the bodily and then the merely perceived, Baudrillard begins with the presumption of a real and frets as we move toward the unreflected, a simulation of something already simulated. "Simulation," he states, "corresponds to a short circuit of reality and its duplication through signs" (27).

The seduction of simulation is particularly problematic for Baudrillard, because it begins to generate its own field of possibilities, its own influences, its own system of order, and this makes it a particularly dangerous political weapon, for example. If a simulation is begun in stealth, and human perceivers don't realize it has begun, they begin to disconnect from their original reality and live—smoothly, unwittingly derailed and rerouted—in an artificial world, what becomes a functional hyperreal, for better or worse. Here Baudrillard tapped into or perhaps even helped to generate a reservoir of paranoia; we now have numerous pop culture explorations of just such hijacks by artificiality, and in them simulation is inevitably turned toward dystopian ends: *Neuromancer, Snow Crash, Tron, Star Trek Insurrection, The Truman Show,* and *The Matrix,* to cite a few. (Perhaps not so shockingly, all but one of these examples harness computer simulation technology.)

My concern with both Plato and Baudrillard is that they throw out the baby with the bathwater. As Baudrillard has it, the simulacrum is a copy without a real, but, we should ask, a copy of what, then? A copy of literally nothing is inconceivable, yielding only more nothing, and if we are discussing copies of copies, then one of those must at some point serve as a surrogate original (a bastardizer), and, reaching back via a chain of mediation, one of the copies must have been reflected from some "real" original. It all disintegrates into a true chasing of one's intellectual tail, and we may as well count the number of angels that fit on the head of a pin; so allow me to reframe the whole issue thusly. I see the two prominent cases in Baudrillard as the first and the fourth phases of the image. The first phase of the image is the actual site of reflection, just as Baudrillard says, and mediation is often reflection done to the best of our abilities. We observe an original and reflect it however we can. True, reflections inevitably under-represent and distort, as even the most perfect mirror flattens three dimensions to two. Just so with mediation; do not panic; we have lived with the shortcoming for a long time.

As for Baudrillard's fourth phase of the image, copying copies presumes an initially closed replicational circuit, in which no real representation is actually happening. Can we clone? Of course. Do we duplicate? Certainly. (A digital file can be duplicated a million times, creating a million and one twin files.) But neither replication nor cloning involves any representation. In other words, they gain no traction for the making of meaning. Representation requires *différance,* and cloning simply offers nothing but identicality. A language of one word is impossible; it takes a language with at least two words—like binary code, for example—for a meaningful pattern to emerge. What occurs in the fourth phase, then, is not duplication but pure *generation.* If with Baudrillard we say of the image in the fourth phase, "it has no relation to any reality whatsoever; it is its own pure simulacrum," we are really saying that you have just *built* something. Far from "copying nothing," you have instead *created something.* That's a much simpler way to go about describing it. And so reflection and generation are the primary output as well as benefits of mediation.

David Porush offers an extremely levelheaded redefinition of the practice of simulation, and he appropriately ties it to the issue of mediation, because that is at its heart. "To simulate," he says, "is to take one thing for another in a different medium" (9). For Porush, simulation is as old as we are. It is not a symptom or phenomenon of the postmodern condition only, as Baudrillard has it. "The hyperreal has always been with us. Indeed it is us, or at least the essential part of ourselves that lives in our brains, a compulsion of the nervous system" (Porush 10). All art, all thought, and all metaphor is simulation. Fiction, for example, is simply an elaborate convention of simulation via expansive verbal arrays, and every fiction—as a simulation—attempts to generate a hyperreality in which the mind of the reader can exist for a while. "The simulations that produce hyperreality are representations of one phenomenon in another medium, an essentially and basically fictive transformation. And like fiction, the allure of simulation is that it can seduce us because it is purer, more dramatic and more attractive than the thing it purports to re-present or tell the truth about" (Porush 11).

This approach fits squarely into the humanistic tradition of locating those attributes which best describe who we are. We glory in our artwork, we study our various histories, we map out and toy with our languages, we wrap ourselves in thought and wait to see what happens. All of these processes require simulation, either reflecting what we see in some sort of model or generating a fiery, new model that strikes out beyond what is already known, what it already understood and accepted, what is taken for granted. Jauss's horizon of expectations broadens continually because we push it and stretch it daily. We do so by hypothesizing, by speculating, by suggesting, by building dream-homes in our minds, by trying to imagine what a different career would be like. We simulate constantly.

That idea of modelling is crucial here. We construct models to try to understand what is around us, why something works or fails, how to do a given thing better. This inherently includes both reflecting *what reality already seems to be* and suggesting *what it might be,* beyond all current perception. Here is a compelling example which combines both. Combining high technologies available in 1945, Vannevar Bush *verbally modeled* a machine called the memex, an analog document system that could link information to other related information in what he styled "trails," allowing the human mind to access its material relationally (6–8). Lo, less than sixty years later, the human consciousness is experimenting with a new shell in the form of the Internet, full of the exact sort of associational, textual links that Bush foresaw. His written projection was both reflection of his contemporary technological realities and a contribution to the generation of a new system that has become monumentally, historically important.

Simulation-as-reflection is mimetic, and simulation-as-generation is heuristic. The difference between the two is often in the eye of the beholder. Imagine (that is, simulate in your mind) a NASA computer-generated wire frame animation that shows exactly how a flight engineer believes a Mars rover landing unit will pierce down through the planet's atmosphere and bounce-land on the surface. (Porush uses a NASA example, too.) In one sense, the simulation is generative, because no such lander may actually have ever done the maneuver, and so the simulation is heuristic; it creates all sorts of new ideas and questions and images. In another sense, though, the animation is only reflecting what has already been playing, over and over again, in the engineer's mind for the last few months of trajectory design. In this case, the very same bit of animation is mimetic, attempting to reproduce that original thought, probably falling short in some ways. In the first case, the simulation itself seems like pure content. In the second, it seems like a vessel, a carrier, which returns us to our caution about declaring precisely how a chain of mediation works. What is a vessel one moment will be content the next, and vice versa, in a sort of cascading and interlocking manner.

RECONCEIVING THE WHOLE ENCHILADA: SIMULATION VIA TEXTUAL MACHINERY

I have spent so much space developing this concept for a very specific reason. If simulation is really just a particularly seductive form of modelling, and modelling is such a powerful tool for our minds for either elucidating what we can see (reflection) or producing something we have not yet seen (generation), then simulation can be an extraordinarily powerful pedagogical tool. And, of course, it is. I want to suggest, in fact, that writing is simply one form of simulation, and we have used it in the academy so heavily precisely because of its benefits in mental construction. The technology of writing has been traditionally quite simple and cheap, too, so it has been an accessible and potent educational mainstay, and it should remain so, beyond doubt. But my call is additive: why stop there?

Writing can be reconceived as a fine means of simulation, and we should acknowledge, as we have not often done, that what one writes bears both of the sharp edges of mediation; it is both content and vessel, both meaning *and* machine. Our loftiest essays on epistemology, our subtlest haiku on the sad joy of watching rain fall, our most convoluted novels with roller-coaster plots, our grandest epics, our most secret journal entries, our floweriest letters of recommendation—all include a machine half, a device of code by which a perceiver can reconstruct the thing itself, the thing verbally simulated. For some reason we have a great distaste for this sort of honesty, as if recognizing the mechanics of this dearest activity will somehow debase it. Have you written a memoir of the Battle of the Bulge? Have you struggled in words to capture the sensation of impotence and loss at a funeral? Have you located adjectives to color the thrill of desire? You have been building machines.

We are more accustomed to referring to such machines as texts, and many of us are so invested in the verbal that we have even skewed the word such that we often mean only "a set of words" when we use it. Poststructuralism, however, has invited us to locate texts literally everywhere; anything can be "read." But sticking to reading in the traditional sense, even there we still have much to consider. Espen Aarseth's beautiful book *Cybertext* gets hold of the notion of textual machinery quite firmly, since the project is to investigate how different media for carrying words can affect the texts they carry in terms of how they are written and how they get read. The crucial element is the media machine between author and reader.

> Instead of defining *text* as a chain of signifiers, as linguists and semi-oticians do, I use the word for a whole range of phenomena, from short poems to complex computer programs and databases. As the *cyber* prefix indicates, the text is seen as a machine—not metaphorically but as a mechanical device for the production and consumption of verbal signs. Just as a film is useless without a projector and screen, so a text must consist of a material medium as well as a collection of words. (20–21)

Aarseth is acutely aware of the interdependence of author, textual medium, and reader, especially because he studies works that are strikingly different from traditional, read-through books on paper. His model for the structure/process is a classic Aristotelian triangle with operator, verbal sign, and medium on the corners and text/machine in the center. Aarseth correctly chooses the word "operator" where we might have otherwise chosen "reader," because the process occurring in that position is more than simply reading, in its narrower sense. The integration and comely fit of the reader/operator with the media chosen by the author, as well as signs, generates the textual machine at large. I think we could just as easily place an author/builder in the operator position and consider the whole system from the other side, the production side, and this would begin to round out a fuller description of the real work of composition, as explored below. Specifically, focusing on mediation technologies will allow us to do so. Although Aarseth is primarily interested in literary productions, and my message is broader than that, Aarseth nonetheless is using a similar approach: "Cybertext . . . is the wide range (or perspective) of possible textualities seen as a *typology of machines,* as various kinds of literary communication systems where the functional *differences among the mechanical parts* play a defining role in determining the aesthetic process" (22, emphasis mine).

The great cry of the humanist will of course be that we should be studying people and not machines. As Bruno Latour's *ARAMIS* or *The Love of Technology,* as well as most of McLuhan's work, makes abundantly clear, however, technology—its invention and its use—is a fundamentally human trait. The old theme of "man against machine" and humans being swallowed by our own creations is by now a particularly tired one, although we continue to fiddle with it in our depictions of maleficent artificial intelligence, a là *The Matrix,* again, or Kasparov's railings after his eventual defeat by Deep Blue. Our machines are as much an artifact of who we are as our artwork; they are a vital half of our artwork, not just in terms of tools for creating art, but the physical bodies of those same works themselves. As Porush declares, we cannot possibly separate our art from the process of simulation, and simulation presumes machinery.

THE VALUE OF CROSSING MEDIA BOUNDARIES

I hope that by re-seeing writing as one means of composition, and by re-seeing composition as a process of making simulation decisions within and among various media, we can reconceive the college writer as, simply, a human meaning-maker who can balance the needs of the simulation machine with what it is attempting to simulate, obviously a tremendously subtle and intricate undertaking. Learning to artificially separate the two for purposes of analysis and learning is an extreme difficulty, and for a somewhat straightforward reason, I think. In mediation, the vessel recedes before the content. The carrier is always present, but what it carries overshadows it, or rather outshines and outcolors it, attracting attention to itself. Look at a photograph, and you are unlikely to see design, shape, contrast, line, or tonal graduation, let alone emulsion layers and paper. You see "the picture" before you see a color print. Likewise, as we read, we read for content, looking through the textual machine to the message of the words. Harkening back to Havelock's study of the emergence of alphabets, Richard Lanham has enunciated this concept most clearly in *The Electronic Word,* recognizing that an alphabet that could support a high literate culture had to be simple enough to be learned easily in childhood. Thoroughly internalized at that time, it would become a transparent window into conceptual thought. The shape of the letters, the written surface, was not to be read aesthetically; that would only interfere with purely literate transparency. "Reading" would not, except in its learning stages, be a self-conscious, rule-governed, re-creative act but an intuitive skill, a literate compact exercised on the way to thought. (4)

We tend to think that this transparency is the greatest power of any medium, exactly why we mediate at all—to pass things along in an accessible manner. (Conversely, we even use the word "opaque" to describe works that are difficult to access.) Lanham describes looking *through* a text instead of *at* it, for example. But our habit of looking through a medium creates a heavy patina on its surface which keeps us from effectively looking at it, from noticing and analyzing the textual machine in addition to or instead of its content. McLuhan says that "it is only too typical that the content of any medium blinds us to the character of the medium" (24).

Transparency is a primary power of sign systems, to allow the machine to recede so that the content of thought can advance, and yet by nature it causes the imbalance of emphasis which shifts our attention away from the important work that our media are doing for us. Because we are so interested in the simulational work a medium can achieve, we forget to consider the needs and demands of the media themselves. In the worst cases, the imbalance toward transparency generates malaise because it rapidly degenerates the sign user's understanding of precisely *why* they are doing *what* they are doing. In a freshman writing class, for example, writing frequently dissolves into a drudgery of inculcating conventional stipulations at various levels, whether grammatical, stylistic, or even rhetorical—all of that despite instructors' very best efforts to show students the fine way writing can bring the mind to life, the way grammar and style are fine tools of support, the way rhetoric places the writing moment into its vital social context, filling it with purpose. Ironically, we are so interested in leading our students toward the *transparent* rewards of great writing that we forget they are likely not to understand the mechanical work involved; they have to build textual machines. A second phase of irony is that if we stop and focus too heavily on the mechanical level itself, momentarily tabling the transparent effects we want so badly to draw out, we compound the students' problems. Writing classes quickly dig their own ruts as teachers demonstrate mechanics at various levels, from forms and modes on the macro level to figures, usage, and grammatical strictures on the micro level. The letter of the law inevitably overtakes the spirit.

The problem, however, is not the mechanical issues themselves. All media make mechanical demands that stymie new and uninitiated practitioners; all media are radically complex machinery. The problem is the difficulty of keeping one's eyes on the prize, of gaining enough appreciation of a medium's transparent benefits to stay interested and engaged before and while one struggles through vagaries at the mechanical levels—of caring about writing at all while stumbling through sentence boundary training, even if that training occurs in the context of writing itself and not skills drills. It becomes a problem, to fall into cliché, of seeing the forest for the trees.

My suggestion, then, is that by occasionally but intentionally shifting media boundaries in a composition classroom, we can force students to see both levels anew and begin to field them simultaneously. If we foreground the *negotiation* of the various parameters of the act of composition, in other words, we keep meaning-making in plain view while openly acknowledging its difficulties, and students will see the value of slogging through the process and begin to compose with direction, intention, and investment. Moving across media boundaries keeps the ruts I mentioned above from forming, or at least from getting so deep.

"Crossing a media boundary" might be as simple as allowing (or requiring) students to mix words and photographs as in the *Il Cavallo* example above, which demands that they consider the talents of words as they differ from the talents of photographs, and these broodings demand that the student equally consider both meaning and mediation, both soul and body, both transparent content and machinery. The very moment of crossing from one medium to the other helps to dust and color what otherwise might remain hidden under the patina of transparency I have just described. Machinery suddenly becomes "visible," and students can begin to see both what they're doing and why, what they've actually been doing all along (even as they were writing). And by calling for us to "make the machinery visible," I am certainly not simply indicating that photography is a purely visual medium and written text a nonvisual one; both of those statements would require significant complication before they could stand as true. My point is that shifting between media in a composition classroom makes the process of meaning-making itself visible, tangible.

Note, however, that we have to shift from "writing classroom" to "composition classroom." To return to my opening remarks, composing includes far more than the verbal alone. We are probably familiar with the old etymology lesson; composition is *com* + *ponere,* literally "to put together," and we can put together meanings with absolutely any medium at all. Words are simply one option.

In such a classroom, an important part of each student's work is deciding which media best suit a given assignment, and suddenly a panorama of options encircles the composer's mind and generates a strong sense of possibilities, of enthusiasm for finding the most accurate way to represent the subject. The need-of-utterance becomes an imploring, contagious force that sets the meaning-making process into full motion, the excitement of toying with different kinds of media machinery melded with presumptions about nascent meanings, messages-emergent (again, both reflection and generation). What's the best approach? Photographs and words? A sound recording? A crisply edited video? Poetry? Dance? Storytelling? Storytelling with drawings? One of the beauties here is that there seem to be no hard and fast rules; one person, on a given task, might be most descriptive, for example, in writing, while another might be far more so in photographs. Change the subject, and those balances might shift.

Furthermore, as students move into assignments that allow open media selection, or even assignments that ask for use of specific media, they are faced ultimately with the reality that thoughts and their dress are one in function, even though they are two in form (medium and content, machinery and transparency). The logos, as some rhetoricians will say, is unified and not split; the logic (of a given utterance) and its execution are interdependent. The motion across media boundaries drives this home. A novel and its film adaptation, for instance, are not the same creature, cannot be, as Seymour Chatman so clearly sees in his essay "What Novels Can Do That Films Can't (And Vice Versa)." It might be a great experiment, however, to invite students to entertain the dichotomy between medium and content, to try to encode the same message into different textual machines so that they will (perhaps) see the hopelessness of the endeavor, running directly into the fact that composing is not simply dressing thought in words or images or sounds. Simulation is frequently a creative act, the thoughts born *as you compose*. One is not always coifing an idea for display, but giving it birth.

Modeling, simulation, and composition are, then, strikingly similar acts. The former two terms dominate scientific vocabulary, whereas in the humanities we prefer words like "write" or "create" or "compose." All, however, are constructions, acts of construction. All bring in selection or invention of components, juxtaposition and ordering, and massaging and polishing until rough edges are smooth enough to stay out of a reader/user/perceiver's way. Simulation, of course, brings with it a sense of the willful suspension of disbelief on the perceiver's part, during the act of consuming the eventual artifact, of encountering the textual machine. Porush notes that simulation is "pretty" and therefore seductive, and seduction implies some sort of duplicity (10). It is partially the possibility of a perceiver's *unwillful* or *unwitting* suspension of disbelief that so worried Baudrillard about simulation's potential dark side: that we could, either accidentally or at the hands of some oppressor, be misled into believing that a simulation was actually real. And yet what choice do we really have? The acts of modeling, simulation, and composition are the real house of the human mind, and we have little choice but to do our work there. The virtual worlds we can generate in these ways are exactly their own value, in fact; we specifically ask students to compose in order to expand their thinking and understanding. We should strive to demystify the entire process by demystifying its product, and that returns us to teaching the vital bodily half of meaning: mediation.

INTO THE CLASSROOM: EXAMPLES AND SUGGESTIONS

Let us strive to concretize. I am describing classes in which students specifically set out to build, if you will, simulation machines. In such classes, any juncture that begs a media decision is one that should be visited, because it is precisely at such crossings that composers at any level of proficiency consider how one medium will carry another, how the nestled envelopes get that way in the first place, and how meaning progresses from there. At any of these locations, students must decide whether or not they will cross a media boundary, how they will do it if so, and what happens when they do. Such choices will force them not outside but *through* and *beyond* the narrow and rigid demands of various conventions.

THE ORAL/WRITTEN CRASH-SITE RECONSTRUCTION

Here is an example which will undoubtedly be visiting all our writing class-rooms in coming years. Voice recognition and activation software for desk-top computers is already a technological reality and will quickly go mainstream, just as quickly as the Internet swept through the collective conscience in the 1990s (and probably much faster). To take one example, the Macintosh has had low-level, built-in voice recognition software for years, allowing users to administer voice commands for routine tasks. Reliance on the system initiates an evolutionary cycle in which detaching the user from the terminal's keyboard and mouse as input devices points up what's really going on: a new process of command mediation which relies on sound impulse rather than typing, pointing, clicking, and dragging. This, in turn, since the hands-free user might now be doing other things (thumbing a book, looking out the window, dusting the monitor . . .), will require the computer to respond to the user with an increasing dependence on sound, rather than the primarily visual feedback it now provides on-screen. The Mac OS also includes a speech synthesis component that allows the processor to pronounce any text selected by the user, including on-screen prompts, or even large documents like Web pages or essays, for that matter. Even beyond these relatively simple applications, far more powerful, multi-platform voice software is emerging, including IBM's ViaVoice (http://www-4.ibm.com/software/speech/) and ScanSoft's Dragon Naturally Speaking (http://www.scansoft.com/naturallyspeaking/). A consortium of telecommunication and computer companies has even developed a tagging system called VoiceXML (http://www.voicexml.org/ata_glance.html) that will allow users to navigate hypertext with voice commands, from auto-mated telephone menus to Web pages. (Such software/hardware solutions also promise continued improvements to existing interfaces for the visually impaired.)

These products are already creating an environment in which the voice, human and synthetic alike, will quickly become the composition tool of choice for at least some writing students, if not many. The result, of course, will be that they turn in essays in *writing* classes that were actually *spoken* into being. As if student writing were not already conversational and colloquial enough, it will suddenly become radically so, because it will consist purely of words composed by speech and not for written text. At least some of what they produce and hand in will be nearly unintelligible for the reader, because all of the live, para-verbal cues will suddenly be absent in the "written" document: the inflection, gestures and kinetics, tone, volume, speed, and other dynamics of the spoken word. (As Ong predicted, we are continually moving into secondary orality in the electronic age.) This whole imbroglio will cause a really nasty bump in the road for a number of composition teachers who have to mark such documents, even though we are now trained to strongly consider the writing process as it influences the product.

Instead of allowing the phenomenon to drive us to distraction, however, we should see the moment as a prime example of media shifting and embrace the chaos. The wreckage of the spoken/written collision will make for extremely valuable crash-site reconstructions in the classroom; why not take "spoken" essays and dissect them in class, comparing them directly to "written" ones to underscore the significant differences, while also recognizing and appreciating the undeniable kinship. The resulting environment is one in which we will be able to invite students to look down from above at both systems and begin to understand them, enabling students to make their own decisions at the oral/written juncture in the future. The unfortunate alternative would be to approach the whole issue inertly and demand that students observe the conventions of the written text "just because," a motion which obviates the context of their composing and stiffens them to treat it as an arbitrary task they would never consider doing unless required to. The approach we should foster, however, invites them to explore multiple systems as increasing options, increasing opportunities.

Any such transaction that allows students to escape mere rule-following and enter active decision-making is welcome. Furthermore, everybody in the contemporary academy already lives in a world of radically multiple media, from entertainment to news to education, and it seems straightforward to me that constantly consuming such an array provides us with some level of familiarity with how they work, even if we haven't fully (or even partially) articulated the intricacies of the mechanics for ourselves. Orality is a striking example: something the non-expert does constantly and never studies. The composition class should be directly about learning to make media decisions by first recognizing media themselves, controlling them across several options on a horizontal plane in addition to mastering any given medium in a vertical plane.

SOME PRACTICAL MEDIA CONVERSION ASSIGNMENTS

Here's a sample of the flexibility I am suggesting. Whereas my introductory example concerning *Il Cavallo* asked students to compare their own verbal output to an existing photograph in order to beg a fuller engagement of the creation of so-called "sensory detail," this assignment goes a step further into a full demand for media decisions from the student. Instead of showing a photograph and asking students to replicate it verbally, ask them to choose some object (like a car, for example) and describe it in as many ways as they can: with words, with photographs, perhaps even with sound recording. With disposable cameras cheap and ubiquitous, it's easy to turn around such an assignment between two class sessions. Polaroids and digital cameras, though more expensive, can even provide instant photography so that you might be able to do such a lesson in a single class session, on the fly, putting the tools into the students' hands and letting them work.

Wrangling up the equipment obviously takes time and at least some money, but the results are easily worth the trouble. The composers will very quickly locate radical differences in the output of their various attempts, and that acknowledgment of diversity is exactly the benefit of the assignment. At this point, when students have words and images and various recordings in hand, it's vital that they stop to analyze what they have done. Display a student's results and take some time to discuss them, comparing and contrasting, listing positive and negative effects of the various means of mediation. Could words ever have *really* captured the particular contour of the hood of the car? Or the precise color? Likewise, could a photo *really* show the student's sentimental attachments to the car or provide any sense of how that sentiment was generated? The answers to either set of questions might not be as obvious as they initially seem, and sharp students will push the discussion into some instructive grey areas. If they tried audio recording, for example, what does the ambient noise in the recording say? Something other than the sounds of the car itself? Likewise, in the verbal description, is there any background noise? Should it be trimmed away, or does it add some second layer of meaning to the piece?

Describing real-world objects makes photography and sound recording or videography possible, sticking to the reflective side of simulation. It's just as easy, however, to ask the students to mediate an imaginary object, an assignment which allows them to explore the generational side of simulation, modeling something into existence, which is an equally descriptive task. Here it should become quickly apparent just how convenient writing is; one can plop down and describe an imaginary object in words with relative ease and speed. This will yield something very like the fibre of fiction. Let's take an imagined house as the subject: "The house was oblong and pompous, covered with cedar shakes, squatting at the end of the street like a crocodile." While the adjectives and the simile bear that sort of literary implication that so many of us relish, we must admit that the written line doesn't yet get us very close to a tight, detailed description. In fact, that's part of the power of the line; we get to imagine, to visualize for ourselves exactly what sort of house might seem pompous to us, exactly how a house might squat like a crocodile. In this regard, written description carries within itself a kind of media crossing, a motion from the verbal to the visual or other sensory imagination.

Obviously, the author could continue to write into finer and finer detail about the house, expanding the description verbally, but might some other medium be more appropriate, especially if the writing student isn't attempting fiction? Since many of our institutions have been sinking hundreds of thousands of dollars into advanced computer labs, why not explore some of the inexpensive 3D modeling programs that specialize in architectural projections? Relatively detailed color images of houses spring up in minutes. I can hear the cry: why demolish the tasty ambiguity of the written line by dragging it into physical minutia and literalist, visual description in the form of an image, which robs the reader of the opportunity to visualize? That sort of question underscores my point exactly: the two media objects—the written line and the image, the two simulation machines—are indeed different, and it's the very fact that we have at least two of them for comparison that will enable students to suddenly notice things like a literary quality that invites the mind's eye to do the seeing. The differences beg all sorts of instructive contrasts: what's literary, what's journalistic, what's commercial? The student must suddenly confront questions concerning both purpose and audience and determine what's to be done. The presence of competing textual machines demands a choice. It might be nice to stick with the ambiguity of the written version in a short story, and yet it might be much more effective to go with the 3D rendering in a report on American residential design. Even better, in many cases, the student might well find a way to allow both machines to cooperate in one document.

Moving beyond description, what other parts of traditional writing classroom assignments might get converted to other media? If students are attempting to set scenes for narratives, could photographs assist? The classic assignment to describe one's hometown could thus quickly turn into a weekend home for photography or videography or sketching into a drawing pad. "New media," however, can even go significantly outside the sensory arenas in which we are accustomed to composing. For instance, in setting a scene, could a DigiScents scentscape help? (My own hometown, for example, has a tarry, mineral smell, thanks to a major shingle plant that sits at its heart.)

Radically new simulation machines can mediate in radically new ways, carrying messages in ways we simply don't yet add to our repertoires. A great example would be QuickTime Virtual Reality images. A QTVR panorama is a computer-mediated, 2D image that can be manipulated and "turned" or spun in 360 degrees of yaw and often a few degrees of pitch (http://www.apple.com/quicktime/overview/qtvr.html). The result is the simulation of both vision and motion, of turning around in a real or virtual space and seeing what's all around you. Why not create a QTVR panorama to visually set a scene? QTVR can also work in the other direction, looking in at an object from a spherical exterior viewing space, creating a virtually real, manipulatable item either from photographs of a real-world object or a computer-generated 3D model, meaning that the student's work could still be either mimetic or heuristic. In all such considerations, we should certainly remind the composers that they are still in a rhetorical situation. What if the audience has no computer, for example? Then print technology mediation might be more suitable than artificial scentscapes and virtual panoramas.

The choice is the thing, and choice implies options, which suggest the importance of juxtaposition of multiple media in such a class. Put another way, any medium will eventually go transparent if it is the sole object of attention. Photography will get transparent in the photography classroom (pardon the pun concerning slides), just as writing gets transparent in the writing lab. QTVR models would get transparent to students who did nothing else, and so on.

As an important aside, I realize that a number of these ideas require the presence of computer equipment to be feasible, and not every institution has decided to create such environments, which is an extremely important and complicated subject in itself. Nonetheless, the conversion to the digital realm does make the work of mediation extremely convenient and relatively inexpensive. While we thought we were building "writing labs" in most of our major universities, we were actually installing somewhat full-featured media labs, by a default which relies on the multiple talents of the desktop computer. Media convergence is greatly simplified and thereby accelerated in the presence of computers. One medium is rarely replaced or supplanted by another. Instead, they coexist and supplement each other, and the computer happens to be a central technology by which they conjoin. But I am suggesting—with mountains of other current articles, of course—that their presence in our writing programs means far more than a quick way to hop on the Internet to gather sources for research papers. In this case, their presence means a rapid way to explore media boundaries and conversions.

HYPERTEXTUAL RESEARCH REPORT

I have tried to emphasize that I am arguing not for an abandonment of the verbal, but a broader contextualization of the same. We should remember that the verbal can be mediated in a number of ways, spanning almost all substrates and genres. Hypertext systems have gathered massive attention for the way they can mediate in analogy to human cognition itself, developing a given idea and then linking it to another, and so on into giant webs of intertextuality and interconnected meaning. If most of our students spend far more of their personal time, and increasingly their academic time as well, negotiating hypertext documents than they do paperbound ones, why shouldn't we ask them to compose in hypertext?

As I have just suggested, we are awkwardly straddling media eras when it comes to research writing. We rush into our computer labs and teach our students how to effectively search out and evaluate Web-based sources for research *papers,* documents that cobble together articles from the digital realm so that they can be committed to paper to be turned in. The transaction grows particularly reverberant when we stop to consider that many of the sources located on the Web, especially via academic search indexes like Masterfile or Infoseek, began their lives on some writer's computer, were published in a print journal or magazine, and then were archived back to the Internet for researchers, who will again pull them out and put them down on paper. In this scheme, the computer has been reduced to an extraordinarily quick and expensive card catalogue system, as well as shelving. I think we should begin to discuss the several ironies of this practice with our students and then reconceive the traditional research paper, reconfiguring it as the research hypertext.

This is certainly not a new idea, and certainly not original to me, yet I still find it particularly rare at the university level, perhaps owing to the psychological barrier of learning about the technologies involved in producing hypertext, a barrier for many students as well as many instructors. HTML editing software, however, has now made such an assignment completely conscionable; it's simply not that hard to do basic hypertext any more. Staying within the hypertextual, as opposed to punting text back to paper print, allows writers to think quite differently about the meaning of research and how to present it. Many Web sites, search indexes and publications alike, feature full-text articles, right online. Why not take those texts and hyperlink them right into one's essay, right there, foregoing antiquated pointer systems like parenthetical references and endnote markers? This allows the reader to instantly visit and peruse the other source at will, instead of facing an inert set of works cited which may or may not be readily available.

The convenience to the reader, though, is for our purposes secondary to the new field of considerations the composer encounters. Suddenly, the traditional form of the research essay comes into question. In the traditional, paper-based research essay, the author holds the hand of the readers, carefully leading them from summary to paraphrase to quotation, putting on the sometimes helpful and sometimes simply false guise of linear exposition, of outlined care and organization. In hypertext, however, one has a new set of demands to consider, and they aren't as simple as dropping all notions of sequential order. To some extent, for example, the hyperlink becomes one's mode of transition, at least part of one's connective tissue, and thus the media technology invades and alters the fabric of accepted form itself. Transitions are extremely important in a paper-based essay; the reader presumes to be lost and eventually perturbed if the material gets too disconnected. The reader's presumption upon following a hyperlink, however, is that a transition is occurring; the tour has become self-guided, in other words.

That a reader gets to select a path through a text places new considerations before the author. Should my introduction now be longer, so that I can set up a firmer direction for my material before letting go of directorial control of the reader? Or should it be shorter, presuming that the reader will chafe at a long textual passage? And how do I appropriately set up and tag a quotation? When should I abandon quoting and simply link to the other document? And what happens if the reader decides to read that other document instead of coming back to mine? The media technologies invite a reconsideration of a very old rhetorical reality: to whom am I writing, and why should they be interested in what I have to say? The hypertext research project will undoubtedly generate its own set of difficult questions, each of which is an opportunity for learning, of course.

THE PHOTO ESSAY

Intentionally turning from the digital, I want to discuss an assignment idea that does not require computers but still foregrounds mediation. The photo essay can prove successful and deeply engaging for comp students as a first assignment. We're far more familiar with this visual form than we might think; it populates all sorts of magazines, like *Time* and *Life* and especially *National Geographic*. A photo essay, like its written counterpart, is simply an attempt at expression, exposition, and comment, but it is made predominantly of still photographs, often accompanied by brief captions and sometimes a short piece of explanatory writing. The point is to try to say something specific with pictures, and we're frequently amazed at just how eloquent they can be. The bonus in the comp classroom is that it lays out so many composition issues so nicely: topic selection, drafting, technical difficulties, editing, and revision.

Begin by having the students determine some theme, some subject: a person? a place? an event? an issue? an idea? You might also discuss various kinds of photographs, such as establishing shots, which provide some sort of introduction of the photographic subject, whether it be a wide-angle shot of a city street (if the subject is the city), or a relative close-up of a person (if the subject is that person). The possible establishing shots are as infinite as the possible introductions for a written essay; the subject and purpose and audience will help determine which one to use. Beyond the establishing shot, discuss character shots, extreme close-up detail shots, and action shots. Also, discuss the photographer's choices of vantage points. How can you say something more starkly meaningful by experimental decisions concerning where to stand to get a certain photo?

Then, send the class out with cameras and at least twenty-four exposures of film, preferably more. (As above, disposables can fit this assignment nicely.) Give them a day or two, and get the shots developed quickly. Then have a student volunteer spread all his or her prints out on a table and have the class gather around to see what's there. Ask the student what the specific theme or subject is, and begin looking for six or seven photos out of the set that best carry and deliver that meaning. This process is the first stage of photo editing, and it serves as a very clear example of building a simulation machine; you actually choose the shots you feel best represent what you're trying to say. The photos don't magically form a complete statement on their own; the statement is composed as the photographer decides which shots say the most, which shots articulate. In this sense, as Barthes perhaps first taught us, photographs don't "record reality." They say what we make them say; representation is something that humans do, not cameras.

Classes can get quite animated during a photo editing session. Once the student and the rest of the group have agreed on a limited set of communicative shots, move to the second stage of photo editing and consider which ones could be cropped to become more effective. Which ones should be enlarged? And what sequence best serves the photographer's purpose? The order in which the images were made isn't necessarily the most provocative. Once the shots are selected, have the student write captions as desired, which will demand that the student think about how a reader/viewer who has never seen the images before will react to them, since they will not have had the benefit of working through the process of making and editing the shots as the class did. The resulting photo essay will partly simulate what was really "out there" and partly model what the student was trying to say and show. The teacher's job during the entire process is to point out how the real work of composing is being done, the fact that a machine is being built (a set of images on paper technology) by a human builder for the purpose of mediating a meaning to some other person. Some shots will be scene setters, some will be describers, some will be event narrators, and so on.

THE CALL FOR COLLABORATION AND A RESPONSIVE INSTITUTIONAL TECTONICS

In all, the kinds of assignments I've been explaining visit the boundaries between various media as often as possible. Eventually, those boundaries blur, and what we begin to see is not writing or photographing or digitally manipulating, but composing. None of my argument is really pure theorization. Rather, it derives from a frank look around us at the way people mediate between themselves outside the university, and it asks why we don't expand our practices to embrace the wide range that is actually available. I'll be the very first to admit, however, that the media practices I've discussed here are themselves not a complete list. Instructors with expertise in other areas could very quickly add dance, performance, sculpture, music, graphic design, industrial design, and others, to be sure.

And the very diversity of those specialists brings me to my final comment. I am perfectly aware that I must stop to write ourselves a reality check. Obviously, it takes multifarious expertise to teach in the manner I have been describing, some fluency in all sorts of media. Few of us can hope for the luxury of receiving ample media training to achieve such expertise, even if we were to focus only on the most pervasive, culturally dominant forms of mediation, and even determining that list would require argument. But the fact remains: most writing teachers are trained as exactly that, and not as specialists in graphic design, HTML, video editing, and sound production.

Two comments. The first is that at least some of the suggestions I've made don't necessarily require advanced skill; one may dabble, and that may be enough. For example, the photography-related assignments and ideas concern a technique and technology that many of us can at least struggle through, without having to channel Ansel Adams. Photographic processing is cheap and ubiquitous, and digital cameras become cheaper and more powerful every month. The second comment is that at least some students will arrive in class on the very first day already having acquired significant skills in different forms of mediation: acting, singing, Web site creation, sound recording, photography, and possibly even video production, among others. And, just as we don't expect our writing students to instantly become E. B. White or Maya Angelou, we should likewise not expect them to be able to bypass the various phases of learning when it comes to mediation. Fumbling is part of the package.

Moving beyond these concessions, however, we should also remember that our schools, no matter what educational level, brim with people of radically varied talents, and collaborative teaching is a particularly attractive solution for a cross-mediation class. Some of the samples shown above were created in an experimental course that I team-taught with two other instructors, and each of us brought various backgrounds and skill sets with us, allowing us to constantly defer to one another on issues both theoretical and practical, from tracing the arc of media history to effectively using PowerPoint. The result was actually not a dilution away from but a concentration into our various specialties.

We also have a number of models upon which to draw. Journalism and communication departments, for example, are already way ahead of the rest of us when it comes to composing in multiple media. Why? They are forced to prepare students for the infamous "real world" of journalism after graduation, and that real world is and has been for some time a thoroughly multiple-media place. Journalism departments commonly house experts in writing, photography, layout and design, typography, digital imaging, and online media production. Communication departments often focus on radio, television, and sometimes film production, also covering extremely broad ground. Why not invite specialists from these areas to at least visit a composing class, if not to co-teach for a semester?

The professionals housed in any university department will normally be hired as experts, meaning that they will teach primarily in a vertical way: all writing or all photography or all video editing. And as I have argued above, any significant work done in a single medium will tend to veneer it with transparency, a force that causes students—again, sometimes quite helpfully—to work in a vertical plane, learning the complexities of a single set of media conventions. Asking both students and teachers to work across some of their normal boundaries, then, would still be a very healthy thing, yielding a combination of both the horizontal coverage and vertical altitude that begin to flesh out a really full and solid education.

Moving up yet another organizational level, however, eventually we must begin to question, as is healthy, the very structure of our institutions, especially at the departmental layer. Lanham, for example, has long since foreseen the institutional effects of moving the word out of the printed realm and into the electronic. Even that specific a move of mediation, he says, will reverberate throughout our universities:

> Electronic text creates not only a new writing space but a new educational space as well. Not only the humanities curriculum, but school and university structures, administrative and physical, are affected at every point, as of course is the whole cultural repository and information system we call a library. In the university world, it is disciplinarity and its departmental shadow that will be most transformed. (xii)

In the meantime, let us begin to think of combinations. How might we collaborate across disciplines? What would happen in a classroom inhabited by both a writing and a photography teacher? A literature and a film teacher? A design expert and an HTML wizard? A writer and a videographer? Every institution already houses its own, unique set of human resources that will allow it to explore cross-mediation while incurring a relatively low tectonic impact.

WORKS CITED

Aarseth, Espen J. *Cybertext: Perspectives on Ergodic Literature.* Baltimore: Johns Hopkins UP, 1997.

Baudrillard, Jean. *Simulacra and Simulation.* Trans. Sheila Faria Glaser. Ann Arbor: U of Michigan P, 1994.

Bush, Vannevar. "As We May Think." *Atlantic Monthly* (July 1945). 17 April 2000 <http://www.ps.uni-sb.de/~duchier/pub/vbush/vbush.shtml>.

Chatman, Seymour. "What Novels Can Do That Films Can't (And Vice Versa)." *Film Theory and Criticism.* 5th ed. New York: Oxford UP, 1999. 435–51.

DigiScents. "DigiScents FAQs." 15 April 2000
    <http://www.digiscents.com/insidedigiscents/faqs/>.

Lanham, Richard A. *The Electronic Word: Democracy, Technology, and the Arts.* Chicago:
    U of Chicago P, 1993.

McLuhan, Marshall. *Understanding Media, the Extensions of Man.* 1964. New York:
    Mentor, 1964.

Plato. *The Republic. Criticism: The Major Texts.* Ed. Walter Jackson Bate. San Diego:
    Harcourt, 1970. 43–48.

Porush, David. "The Rise of Cyborg Culture, or The Bomb Was a Cyborg." *Surfaces*
    (1994). 5 September 1997 <http://www.elias.ens.fr/surfaces/vol4/porush.html>.

The Guises of Martin Guerre

Pedagogical Applications

JOONNA SMITHERMAN TRAPP

B y the end of a course focused on argumentative writing, students have studied and practiced using forms of persuasion. They have learned how to read and craft various appeals, to analyze an argument presented in verbal or visual form, to defend and to present an argument in oral form, and to recognize and avoid ineffective arguments. What is needed at the end of the semester is a project that pulls the course together, allowing the student enough room to analyze, debate, and then write within the full range of options learned during the semester. The project also needs to lend itself to oral, written, and visual discourse since the course spends time on all three types. The most successful projects I have designed to fulfill these needs are centered on film and a source text.

In early experiments using film to teach argument, my students and I read Shakespeare's *Richard III,* stopping after each act to talk, debate, watch multiple film versions of the act, and write. While I deemed this a worthy project, the real problem was getting at the historic Richard. With limited time allotted for such a project (after all, it is a writing class and not a literature or European history class), trying to understand why Shakespeare's portrayal of Richard functioned as argument necessarily means understanding the rather complex political context of the age. Since *Richard III* is a creative work, it is already an interpretation of complicated historical events. The film versions are then rich re-interpretations of an already complicated vision of a much-debated historical subject. I needed a text which explained itself, which included a discussion of the historical and social context. I found such a text in Natalie Zemon Davis's *The Return of Martin Guerre.* Because it is not a "creative" work, but is rather a historical text which discusses in detail the social trends and historical context of the story, my students are relieved of most of the historical entanglements of my original version of the project.

The story of the real Martin Guerre—who left his wife and family in sixteenth-century France, returned suddenly, and then was discovered to be an imposter several years later—is fascinating and complex in its own right, as told by historian Natalie Zemon Davis in her accessible *The Return of Martin Guerre* (1983). The French film version with the same title by director Daniel Vigne is similar to the Davis text, since she was an advisor during production, and adds subtlety and depth through the work of the actors and the questions left unanswered by the narrator. But in the American film version *Sommersby,* produced ten years later, text, subtext, and cultural placement are altered by updating the story to the American South immediately after the Civil War, giving new directions of interpretation for the social questions posed by the Davis text. Using the Zemon Davis text and the two film versions based on the historic and unusual story of Martin Guerre, teachers of composition can encourage students to think more profoundly than they have before about both social and aesthetic issues. Because these texts are grounded in a variety of historical times and social contexts, students have the opportunity to trace changes in important social issues, thus providing topics for writing and evidence for arguing. And since these texts are aesthetically successful works, they also provide topics for discussion and writing about art and its interpretation.

WHY AUGMENT WRITING INSTRUCTION WITH FILM?

As James Monaco has suggested, almost anyone can "apprehend" a film, but the comprehension of film as art and its relation to the other arts is a more difficult process (17). Since the art of film representation and the art of writing share a number of similarities, the combining of the two in a classroom is both appropriate and useful. Many of the same characteristics Monaco assigns to film can just as easily be attributed to writing. Both arts are mediums of communication; both arts require technological understanding; both arts can be properly termed *art* in that they appeal to the intellect and the passions and, in spite of their uses of technology, cannot be subject to scientific method without loss of something vital (Monaco

17–18). Many teachers assume that because students are frequent viewers of film they will, in turn, be good readers of film. Though the screening of a film within a class can excite student interest, this excitement does not necessarily lead to thorough understanding or articulate interpretation. Because a film and a written text are similar, they still present for the student the same problems in rhetorical understanding and interpretation.

To be effective writers and readers, students have to become careful students of rhetoric—learning to think of the intricate relationships between the text, its purpose, and the impact on the audience. In the same manner, students can learn to use their rhetorical skills to read a film as a rhetorical text—a text with a purpose and a social context. Even when the students innately recognize that a film has persuasive content, often they have difficulty expressing the reason for their attitudes toward the film in any terms other than matters of personal taste. One of the first lessons learned in an argument class is that matters of personal taste do not constitute the basis for good argument (Fahnestock 14–15). Because most conversations about film as popular culture begin with personal taste—"I liked that movie," or "I hated that movie"—the study of film in a writing class becomes an excellent vehicle for testing, expanding, or even discarding previously held notions of personal taste. Timothy Corrigan begins his guide for students learning to write about film with this same focus, noting that "movies are a part of a cultural life we generally take for granted" and that "we all understand the movies, but how do we explain them?" (1). He continues by pointing out how "analytical thinking and reading about an 'entertainment' invigorate and enrich" the experience of watching the film (2). While this is true, an awareness of the rhetorical impulse of the media, its sources, and its transformations create more than just enrichment. The student viewer learns to treat the film not as a mere entertainment, but as a text needing interpretation, contextualizing, criticizing, and rebuttal. No longer is the viewer an open receptacle into which ideas pass without pause; now the viewer functions as an educated member of a culture, selecting information from the flood surrounding her, sifting out the insignificant from the valuable, and reflecting on both.

Students also learn to employ their newly found reading abilities as a spur for invention—one of the primary goals in teaching writing. Films, perhaps because they operate on such a variety of levels (pictorial, oral, discursive, narrative, among others), generally provide many threads of discussion for writing. According to the groundbreaking essay on rhetoric "Looking for an Argument," one of the primary goals of a composition teacher (or any teacher using writing) is "to help students to find relevant and effective arguments" for writing; the teacher must provide opportunities for invention or "the discovery of content—of relative supporting material" (Bilsky 14). Film provides such a wealth of spaces for the invention of writing topics that no list of possibilities is complete: the dynamic of *mise en scène,* the role of the close-up, the use of the cinematic space, the mutability of time, the participation of the viewer, the physical work of the actors, the interaction of the voice-over/narrator, the interplay of alienation and identification, the battle between aesthetic production and the representation of realism, the role of the camerawork, the rhetoric of the musical score, the point of view, the role of editing, and the use of metaphor, analogy, and symbolism. Even though this list is incomplete, it provides a sense of the imaginative breadth of writing options for the student. No unit within a class can touch on all these topics. Teachers will discover that the particular interests of the students, the students' perceptions gained from the viewing of the film, and the film itself will guide the direction of class discussion and the production of writing topics.

As a tool to unpack some of the valuable ideas found in the three works under consideration, I will use a three-part rhetorical construct to help view the works in a fresh and productive manner suitable to writing classes. Since the Davis text is a historical account of the real Martin Guerre and his place, time, and culture, the text lends itself to an examination of historical narrative as *logos.* Additionally, the Vigne film provides opportunity to study the various depictions of moral character or, in other words, the *ethos* of the story's presentation. *Sommersby,* causing a high level of emotional response in its viewers, makes the application of *pathos* evident in argument and persuasion. Finally, in light of the possible readings of these texts, I will consider the benefits of this approach to the students.

THE DAVIS TEXT—*LOGOS* AND HISTORY

Natalie Zemon Davis sets us up for something unique in the preface to *The Return of Martin Guerre.* Her opening sentence reads, "This book grew out of a historian's adventure with a different way of telling about the past" (vii). She claims that the story had a "perfect narrative structure" and that she knew it must become a film. When she discovered that Daniel Vigne was in fact directing such a film, she began collaboration on the project. Working on the film with its many constraints of narrative, audience, and time prompted her to write the history that became *The Return of Martin Guerre.* She wanted to be faithful to the historical record and especially the time and cultural events surrounding the story (viii-ix). In an interview with Pat Aufderheide, Davis claims that her work on the film included going "over every word" to "make sure that it was all within the frame-work of reference of the characters, and to see that it was probable within the discourse of the sixteenth century." She also "met with all the actors," "brought in pictures, lithographs, sketches," and used Brueghel's period paintings as means of insuring historical accuracy in the film (137). Davis's own journey as a writer and researcher of history is, as a result, tinged with the experience of working with actors who were learning dialogue and scriptwriters who were rewriting both story and dialog to suit a purpose quite different from that of a historical treatise.

Because of the book's dialogic quality and because Davis utilizes and manipulates evidence in unusual ways to present a portrait of Martin and Bertrande as a man and woman within a particular time, country, province, town, family, religious heritage, and society, her book's faithfulness to the historical record has been questioned by other scholars in her discipline. Robert Finlay's challenge came in the "Forum" of *American Historical Review* (June 1988), and in the same issue Davis responded. Finlay, although admiring Davis's work in general, faults her assigning to Bertrande the general view of peasant women during the time period. He further calls her evidence for Bertrande's imposture regarding Pansette's real identity "flimsy" and merely an "opinion" of a "modern historian who apparently believes that unsubstantiated insight can itself be taken "as evidence" (559). But Edward Benson had aptly supported Davis's work and the film several years earlier in *Radical History Review* (1984), claiming that Davis's research and insight allow the reader "to see the lives of early modern peasants" and noting the richness of her prose (134). To what can we attribute the differences of scholarly opinion regarding the quality of Davis's book?

What Finlay and other opposing scholars are wondering, from a rhetorical standpoint, is whether *logos,* which is the keystone of historical research, is present in Davis's book. Aristotle's rhetorical system defines *logoi* as the arguments that "show the truth or the apparent truth from whatever is persuasive in each case" (1.2.6). Though historians traditionally define truth as historical accuracy, Davis, part of a newer generation of historians, has defined truth as something that can be, in part, an "invention" which is "held tightly in check by the voices of the past" (*RMG* viii-ix, 5). Finlay attributes these innovative qualities to her incorporation of research methodologies from "anthropology, ethnography, and literary criticism" (554). These methodologies allow her to tell the "truth" of the story without knowing exactly what happened or what a character was thinking. She relies on the manner in which people acted during the period, other accounts of similar situations, and of a "sense of possibility, of options," as she puts it (Aufderheide 138). In her rebuttal to Finlay, Davis says that her book intended to make the reader question where "reconstruction" stopped and "invention" began ("Lame" 572).[1] She further shows her attitude about historical writing by noting the differences between her approach and Finlay's. She says, "I see complexities and ambivalences everywhere; I am willing to settle, until I can get something better, for conjectural knowledge and possible truth." About Finlay's approach she says, "He wants absolute truth, established with no ambiguity by literal and explicit words" (574). Though her painstaking research methods and careful documentation of sources demonstrate her commitment to historical accuracy, she does not think the tendency toward seeking absolute truth in history either obtainable or particularly valuable.

Clearly, her perceptive ideas about "possible truth" are important to an understanding of the nature of argument. Reading her history, students can begin to practically apply and understand their own recently acquired knowledge of proofs. Aristotle writes of two kinds of proofs (*pisteis*) used in argumentation: nonartistic or atechnic proofs can be imported using eyewitnesses, contracts, and other forms of "preexisting" kinds of evidence; artistic or entechnic proofs are invented or discovered[2] by the rhetor to convince his audience when the atechnic proofs do not satisfy or are nonexistent. Artistic proofs often deal with probability but can stand up to reason and are convincing, at least in Aristotle's system (1.2.2). The fact that artistic proofs are invented does no damage to the argument in rhetorical thinking; in fact, rhetoricians often point to the valid use of invented proofs and artistic arguments in scientific writing. When data and facts end, a good scientist will use judgment and probability to determine an outcome. But others besides rhetoricians recognize the validity of these inventions. For example, UCLA's respected Renaissance scholar Carlo Ginzburg says about Davis and her book, "the term 'invention' is intentionally provocative but, on the whole, misleading. Davis's research (and her narrative) does not hinge on the opposition of 'true' and 'invented' but upon integration—always indicated, point-by-point—of 'realities' and 'possibilities'" (116).

While often students will balk at the notion of valid proofs other than "hard" evidence, they can quickly be shown how argumentation necessarily depends heavily on these structures. Davis's book and her presentation of history through the use of artistic proofs instructs students in the deft handling of sources, both obvious and unusual, to present a valid case. An excellent example of an artistic proof is found in chapter 9 of the book. Martin Guerre decides unpredictably to journey across the Pyrenees and return home in the nick of time for an amazing appearance at Pansette's trial—and all this on a wooden leg. Davis admits that evidence is lacking for a clear rationale behind the journey. Her sources do not provide a conclusive answer, and they often differ in their opinions. She considers and weighs various possibilities—was it mere chance, or was the journey motivated by other factors? Based on her knowledge of the time and culture as well as her familiarity with the characters acting in this incredible story, Davis proposes a possibility. She says,

> More likely, I think, is that he heard of the trial before his return. Pierre Guerre would certainly have hoped to get news to him, if he were still alive. The case was being discussed in villages throughout Languedoc, and the judge of the Rieux had sent investigators as far as Spain to check the testimony of the new Martin about his visit there. . . . Word also might have been passed to the original Martin Guerre through the order of Saint John of Jerusalem. . . . Who am I, Martin Guerre might have asked himself, if another man has lived out the life I left behind and is in the process of being declared the heir of my father Sanxi, the husband of my wife, and the father of my son? The original Martin Guerre may have come back to repossess his identity, his persona, before it was too late. (83–84)

Davis uses freely what she knows about the actual facts of the case, the situation surrounding the events, and her own sense of how these characters

might have acted and thought to create a convincing case, a probable rationale with which the reader can agree.

Additionally, the quality of her writing—the liveliness of the prose,
the density of detail, and the pure excitement arising from the narrative—
gives students an excellent model for quality nonfiction writing and
inspires with the depth of the research and questions, rather than the often
pat answers that students think research produces. Since one of Davis's primary sources of information is found in the writings of Coras, one of the
judges in the case of Martin Guerre, we might expect her to find concrete
answers in his works. Instead, Davis points frequently to the contradictions in his works, and even more interestingly to the ambivalence he
demonstrates in his attitude to the impostor Pansette. In one of her notes
she finds an example of strangeness in Coras's account: "Either Coras is
misrepresenting what happened, or we have here another example of the
mixed feelings of the judges toward the extraordinary Arnaud du Tilh"
(91). Appreciating a source while remaining critical of it is a valuable skill
students can learn from Davis's writing. Since students have been looking
at models all semester and studying the sorts of research a writer can do,
they are often impressed by the level of accomplishment in Davis's work
and the ingenuity of her evidence and arguments.

Students can benefit from an examination of the obvious quality of the
narrative as well. Though the book opens with a chapter which describes
the geography, society, and people of sixteenth-century France, the remaining chapters lead the reader through the events of the story. The engagement of the narrative does not come by way of surprise or the revealing of
the stranger's identity as it does in the film versions. Rather it comes from
the kinds of evidence Davis draws upon and the manner in which she draws
conclusions, makes general statements, and even ponders unanswerable
questions. Her chapter entitled "Quarrels" is especially interesting. After
describing the various accusations against Arnaud, she slips into a loving
description of his return from his first imprisonment at Toulouse: "Bertrande
received him with tenderness, washing his feet and taking him into her bed.
Very early the next morning, Pierre and his sons-in-law, all armed, seized
him in Bertrande's name and had him bundled off to prison in Rieux" (59).
She cites in her footnote that this information came from Coras, but her presentation of the narrative sounds as if she herself were there watching the

events as they happen. This is an amazing way to present historical testimony and evidence, but she further enhances the narrative with the following: "Let us pause here a moment and ask whether such a situation was inevitable. To put it another way, if the real Martin Guerre had never come back, could Arnaud du Tilh have gotten away with it?" After describing the opinions of "fellow historians" and current day residents of Artigat, she disagrees with the historians. "I think the people in Artigat are closer to the mark. . . . [A] big lie, a whopper—especially one imposed by a single person on others—has troublesome consequences both for personal feelings and for social relationships" (59). Because she talked personally to living people in Artigat, Davis is able to ponder situations intelligently and draw conclusions which are convincing and make for a compelling story. Her enthusiasm for getting at the real Martin Guerre as a man of his time is infectious.

Students will often be motivated to talk about the nature of truth—does Davis present the truth or the truth as it seems to her? Given her humorous admission of scholarly doubt at the end of the book, the students begin to fruitfully question the nature of argumentation and the presentation of evidence. How are facts manipulated to tell a certain story? Is this a manipulation that we can accept without damaging the presentation of the *logos* of an argument? How can knowledge of a cultural milieu convince a reader of the accuracy of a narrative? Is it possible to know the "real" story when most of the evidence comes from witnesses and statements encumbered by their own particular agendas? How does this sort of evidence compare to the evidence delivered in legal courts, which we all readily accept?

Reading and discussing give the students the background necessary for understanding and writing about the narrative—its social context, historical context, cultural milieu, and even its religious setting. All of this is accomplished in an accessible book that is both engaging and challenging. While grasping the background they need to interpret the films, the students also read fine prose and analyze a complicated argument with unique but solid *logoi*.

THE FRENCH FILM VERSION— *ETHOS* AND THE COMMUNITY

While the Davis book allows the students to engage in careful consideration of the nature of truth and how argumentation actually shapes the presentation of "truth," the Vigne film provides an excellent training ground for discussions and applications of the rhetorical concept *ethos*. Turning once again to Aristotle, *ethos* is a term which describes "character" or "moral character."[3] The story of Martin Guerre is already morally complicated, as Davis points out, by many problems in the recounting of the trial by one of her primary sources, the judge Coras. Coras chose not to use the format of an "official document," but to rather use narrative and commentary, neither of which have much to do with actual law (Davis 106). Davis even admits that Coras "exaggerates," "omits," and "lies a little" for the sake of his narrative (108). In addition, Coras shows a sneaking regard for the argumentative prowess of the false Martin and presents Bertrande as both "duped wife" and an aware woman fashioning for herself a better life (112).

The Vigne film, *The Return of Martin Guerre,* adds to these already existent moral complications within the story by the creation of *ethos*. Ethos is a concept that students seem to readily grasp, at least in part. A speaker must convince the audience to trust her; her character is all-important as a tool of persuasion. However, this level of understanding, though important, is insufficient for good writing and reading. Films, such as the version by Vigne, assist the students in visualizing what actually can happen in good writing.

The young Martin should command a measure of respect in the community as an inheriting part of a landholding family, but since he and Bertrande fail to produce a child, he is subject to ridicule and open mockery. Faced with communal rejection, he plans to leave the village and is caught stealing in his effort to gather money for his journey. His father severely chastises him, saying, "Our family doesn't steal!" The young Martin had already damaged his own standing in the community by failing in his sexual role, but his theft endangers the entire family's place in the social and economic fabric of Artigat. This scene begins a series of comments on the moral character of this family throughout the film. As students progress through the film, they begin to understand the way *ethos* is ultimately intertwined with social ideals and familial relationships.

Relations between the Rols family (Bertrande's family) and the Guerres are naturally strained by Martin's departure. Martin's uncle Pierre (most likely to ease this strain, to help Bertrande and her widowed mother, and to increase the economic holdings of the family) marries Bertrande's mother. For many years after Martin reappears in the village, Pierre is content, apparently fully believing that his nephew has indeed come to help the family work the land. Pierre's concern with economic matters is increasingly demonstrated in the film, culminating in a confrontation with the returned Martin. When Martin demands a restitution of monies owed to him by Pierre for the years he profited from Martin's holdings, Pierre is furious. At this point he begins to question Martin's identity, securing witnesses to testify against him. Did Pierre ever really believe that the stranger was his nephew? Does this family truly hold to the value of not stealing as Martin's father said? Who is the thief here—Martin for asking or Pierre for refusing? Pierre is certainly not above attempting to kill Martin by enlisting the aid of others. The Guerres are much more concerned about the fate of the holdings and monies of the family than they are about religious infraction or moral character. Pierre's plea to the court is that the imposter "wants to deprive me of my name and all my property!" The matter of concern, then, is money and status and not whether the imposter defiled the sacrament of marriage or used witchcraft to deceive the village. Students must decipher this presentation of character in the film. Does it naturally fit with Davis's outline of the society in her book, or is this adaptation significantly different?

Above all the characters in the film, Bertrande's depiction is most beguiling and the most challenging for students to decode. Many critics noticed that the actress, Nathalie Baye, plays the part without much emotion. In his article in *National Review,* film critic John Simon claims that Baye is too "unsensual" and does not show enough "headstrong pawkiness" or "jovial lasciviousness" for a peasant girl (952). This evaluation fails to recognize how important the work of the actress is in the deliberate avoidance of common stereotypical film portrayals of peasant women. In fact, in an interview Davis reveals that the only thing saving the film from having too much of a romantic feel and look was the work of Baye. Davis claims that Baye "realized the Bertrande of the film script had more of the nineteenth-century romantic in her than was realistic. And she put some of the sixteenth-century woman back into the role" (qtd. in Aufderheide 139). Other critics more correctly assess Baye's work. Daniel Ansen says that Baye "invests" the role "with a luminous and mysterious stillness" (80). Stanley Kauffmann admires Baye for her understated acting which hides "many secrets" and "few smiles" (25).

Edward Benson finds Bertrande the most believable character in the film because "she acknowledges and resists our desire to see and know the most intimate part of her life" (133–34).

Baye's Bertrande is beautiful, delicate, and quiet outwardly, but her eyes sparkle and flash and weep, enticing the viewer into the emotion behind them. Bertrande is amazingly silent. The viewer never really knows what she thinks about Martin—if she believes him to be her husband or not. Only in the final scene with Coras after the ordeal is over does she seem to confess that she suspected Martin of deception. The silence of the character, the deep, knowing eyes, the "confession," and the act of near self-sacrifice to save Martin from death at Pierre's hands, all prevent us from knowing Bertrande's heart. Does she manipulate the arrival of the new Martin in order to satisfy real sexual, family, and community needs? Is she merely a stupid peasant woman who does not recognize her own husband when she sees him? These are questions with which students must wrestle as they attempt to understand the presentation of character in the film.

The real Martin voices his own solution to the riddle. He thinks Bertrande is at fault. "You alone are to blame," he says when the trial is over. But even this statement does not tell us if Bertrande was merely duped or acting craftily. Students often recognize that in hiding her real intentions and emotions behind a mask, Bertrande represents the moral uncertainty and moral duplicity that resides in the whole community. The cruelty shown to the young Martin, the fickleness of the village during the trial, and the willingness of Pierre's recruits to lie and plot all betray a corrupt community. This community externally maintains a set of moral values regarding economic trade, religious observances, and moral integrity, but in truth, the community is willing to live by a set of situational ethics suited to their own selfish interests. The *ethos* of the village is corrupt, and individuals within the community seem to reflect that corruption in their own personal characters.

The two returns of Martin in the film, the first of the false Martin and the second of the true, bring students to consider a crucial issue revolving around *ethos*—the nature of identity. In the history of rhetoric, identity and ethos are constantly wedded ideas. As the students try to decide, along with the villagers and the judges, who the real Martin Guerre actually is, they can work their way through Platonic and Aristotelian ideas of the importance of character. Plato argues throughout the *Gorgias* that virtue must reside in the individual for rhetoric to contribute to moral good.[4] Aristotle, always more "relativistic" than Plato, argues that the individual anticipates the sort of character that the audience will respect, inspiring "confidence" in the individual's "good sense, moral character, and good will" (Johnson 243). Students consider then the nature of identity—which Martin carries the *ethos* of husband, father, and reliable member of the community?

The young husband, ridiculed by a section of the village, experiences a disintegration of his social identity when he is unable to live up the expectations of the community. His theft further causes him to lose a certain amount of identity as a trusted member of the family. Leaving the village and his wife is an act of rebellion against social and moral constraints. Does he forfeit any right he has to his social identity as a result of the desertion? When he comes to accuse the imposter, he is upheld by the courts, but the false Martin, Pansette, accuses him with "the blame" for all the trouble. Pansette feels that desertion of wife and responsibilities means social death—loss of identity. In taking up Martin's responsibilities as husband, family procreator, father, family businessman, and community participant, Pansette assumes Martin's identity. He becomes Martin, actually playing out and fulfilling every role which had been the original Martin's obligation—so much so that Bertrande accepts him for her own husband. Pansette, in Martin's social role, carries an *ethos* which fits the Aristotelian model. He inspires confidence in those around him.

Additionally, part of Pansette's appeal to the audience and to everyone in the village is through his gifts of written and oral communication—the mark of a good orator in the Aristotelian sense. Even though the original Martin never displayed these abilities, Pansette's remarkable talents create an atmosphere of ready acceptance for the stranger. He is able, through the telling of his adventures, his writing, his teaching of writing to Bertrande, and his development of convincing arguments, to create such a "character" as Aristotle pictures.

> [There is persuasion] through character whenever the speech is spoken in such a way as to make the speaker worthy of credence; for we believe fair-minded people to a greater extent and more quickly [than we do others] on all subjects in general and completely so in cases

where there is not exact knowledge but room for doubt. And this should result from the speech, not from a previous opinion that the speaker is a certain kind of person. (1.2.4)

Pansette, in this light, does not merely take on the persona of the previous Martin Guerre; he creates a new, improved Martin Guerre through his impressive gifts of oratory and communication. The citizens of Artigat are dazzled by his exploits as a soldier and cultural explorer. The new Martin is experienced, confident, knowledgeable, and willing to share all he knows with his community. This Martin is more acceptable, more believable, and much more desirable than the one who left after destroying all of his credibility. Even Coras is amazed by the defense Pansette gives in court, but what lawyer would not appreciate the effective deployment of such a powerful rhetorical device as *ethos*? When Pansette is tried, the whole village is in effect tried—the character of the new Martin is interwoven completely with the character of those who had believed him. Why else would most of the community travel from place to place, live in courtyards and streets during the trials as depicted in the movie, if not because they had a deeply vested interest in the identity of this man they identified as Martin Guerre?

Further complicating the notion that the village may be implicated in Pansette's deception, Davis briefly mentions an unpublished report which came out of a graduate seminar at the University of Iowa ("Lame" 600, n. 108). This report, called the "Hawkeye Propositions," claims that a legal examination of the Martin Guerre proceedings suggests the entire village of Artigat knew that the returned Martin was not the real Martin. Davis lends much credence to this notion, and the film seems to suggest that the village did accept Pansette in spite of their knowledge to the contrary. When Pansette arrives in the village, he fails to recognize some of the women and Nickolae, his former tormentor. He fails to remember where the family keeps the candles. The local cobbler tells him that his feet are no longer the same size. All of these signs are quickly ignored by the village, along with the testimony of the vagabonds, in favor of believing and accepting the stranger. The village recognizes that the new Martin is the true Martin in the sense that he has fulfilled the village's expectations of him. He contributes to the economic vitality of the community; he fathers children, securing the longevity of the community; he supports his family as a husband should do; but most of all, he remains in the village and shows no sign of deserting. He then truly becomes the real Martin for them. Only when he angers Pierre do any of the villagers doubt his role or identity. Even then, the film depicts the women of the village as primarily supporting him. They recognize him as a good husband and father—just what women would expect of Martin Guerre, the husband. Identity, to the people of Artigat, resides in the fulfillment of expectations and social role, not on an accident of birth.

Even though the people of Artigat accept this presentation of *ethos,* the judges at Pansette's trial are seeking truth. Students often express regret over the death of Pansette and sympathy for this man who fulfilled his social role so well. In doing so, they must come to terms with Platonic notions of the just individual as intrinsically good. Pansette is a con artist, a liar. He is not truthful. As a result, neither his eloquence nor his actions can be considered right or just in the Platonic sense. This conflict provides excellent opportunities for both discussion and writing. Beyond these benefits, students have a model in the film to help them think through one of the most debated issues in rhetorical performance—the ethics of character invention.

THE AMERICAN FILM VERSION—
PATHOS AND THE COMMUNITY

Identity is as much a central theme of *Sommersby* as it is of *The Return of Martin Guerre*; however, the theme is not presented for the same purpose in both films. The French film reflects the historical time of its setting. Identity connects with status, society, and community and revolves closely around responsibility. In *Sommersby,* the question of identity is more associated with *pathos,* reflecting perhaps either the southern sentimentalism of the mid-1800s or, more likely, the romanticism of Hollywood films in general. Whatever the cause, the film effectively manipulates the pathetic appeal for rhetorical purposes and provides students good opportunities to write and talk about the way *pathos* operates in argumentation.

Aristotle writes that persuasion also occurs by the creation of strong emotions in the hearers. The rhetor must aid the listeners to "clarify" these emotions. Aristotle's system, according to Kennedy, recognizes that "among human beings judgment is not entirely a rational act."[5] *Sommersby* is fraught with an over-abundance of emotional responses which need clarifying. In fact, set in the period of southern reconstruction in which southerners are beaten, poor, and confused, and in which southern society is in total upheaval, the primary responses which arise from the characters of the film are emotional ones. Hatred, hope, despair, suspicion, fear, and love flood the scenes of *Sommersby* to create a picture of the aftermath of war which convinces the viewer of the film's messages. The students obviously experience the emotional appeals during their viewing of the film, but trying to articulate how and why those appeals either are or are not effective is a more difficult task. Their careful consideration of key scenes leads to insight, however.

Sommersby opens with a shadowy figure burying someone in a lonely spot. We, as viewers, know immediately something is not as it should be— a mystery waits to be unraveled. Unlike Martin, who enters a peaceful, pastoral world and adapts himself to it, the new Jack Sommersby enters a world of violence and injustice. Jack must not only refashion himself from the con artist he has been, he also has to become an agent of change and betterment in this war-torn world. Early in the film he is shown with blood on his hands from the burial. He journeys in the dark, the cold, and the snow. He walks past a graveyard, groups of rag-tag Civil War soldiers, and a particularly chilling scene of a vigilante hanging of a young black man. When he finally arrives at the Sommersby plantation in Tennessee, he is given a hero's welcome, and even the preacher exclaims, "Thank the Lord for bringing you back!" This journey as depicted in the opening sequence of the film foretells the movement and the emotional journey of this hero. He changes from a bloodstained stranger to a loved and respected individual acting on the behalf of others rather than himself. As students watch this change in Jack, they also experience a shift in their own emotional response from suspicion to trust. This shift is exactly the kind of change an orator would want to evoke in an audience.

Even though Jack shows some of the same uncertainty that Martin shows, he is readily accepted into the community. The trouble begins because he treats his black tenant farmers with the same respect and dignity he shows to whites. The gradual revealing of the imposture results not from greed, but from "racial bigotry" (Canby C8). The educated con artist who becomes Jack Sommersby sees an opportunity in the town for improvement and advancement. The viewer is not certain why he concocts the notion of planting tobacco and making the planting and harvesting an effort of the entire community. Does he plan to leave with everyone's valuables and never return? Does he really intend to return? As the town and even his own wife begin to doubt him, the student viewers also experience that emotion. Whatever his original intent, Jack does return with enough tobacco seed to plant all of his land. The overwhelming release of tension signals the growth of trust and love for this once con artist. The viewer is drawn into the feelings and made to believe in the possibility of hope. For the first time, everyone—black and white, male and female—all work together on the crop to save their town and their individual dignity. Whatever the con artist was before coming to town, he becomes a community binder, a healer, a prophet of sorts, seeing into the possible future and preaching a message of rebuilding the city.

This message of hope overcomes the prejudice, fear, distrust, and hate to enable the people to act as a unit, side by side in the fields. The film contains wonderful glimpses of men, women, children, blacks, and whites, working together. One scene even shows a reversal of the traditional southern societal roles. Needing to get the fields plowed, Jack shoulders the harness of the mules and pulls the plow while the black field hand, Joseph, joyfully encourages the "mule" (Jack). Jack has created a new society built on need and hope in which the ultimate ends of a successful crop are more important than any imposed social structure of worker and master. We, as viewers, believe completely in this new society because of the emotional building of the film.

The hope growing in each member of the community is seen nowhere as clearly as in the case of Joseph. He endures a night of terror at the hands of the Ku Klux Klan and still maintains hope for his family. Everything he has is tied up in the promise of land ownership which Jack has extended to him. His hope is threatened, however, when Jack is accused of murder. As Jack is pressured during the trial to renounce the name of Sommersby and live, the camera pans the audience. Each face—the white faces on the lower floor and the black faces gathered in the upper decks—shows anxiety. When the camera focuses on Joseph, he leans forward, body tense, hands gripping the railing, and eyes full of fear, replacing the hope we have seen so often before. Jack sees his friend's fear and argues that if he is not Jack Sommersby, then the contract which everyone signed and to which everyone pinned their hopes and dreams would not be worth "the paper it was printed on. They wouldn't own anything." His wife Laurel under cross-examination answers that at least he wouldn't hang. Jack replies that, emotionally "I'd be dead already." Are these scenes really believable? If the students answer that they are, they will find themselves using language to talk about the scenes that lead the discussion toward the use of emotion in argumentation.

Students often quickly recognize that characters in the film use emotional appeals to great rhetorical effect as well. The person that Jack has become is tied up in the fulfillment of his promises. Just minutes before his hanging, he hears from Laurel that the tobacco crop has sold for an astounding figure, raising over 10,000 dollars for the community. His joyous pride over this victory is only part of this new identity, however. "Being your husband," he tells Laurel, "is the only thing I've ever done that I'm proud of." When she presses him for information regarding Horace Townsend, the con artist, he finally admits to knowing him. "I remember Horace Townsend—very well. Everything they said about him in the courtroom was true. I hated the bastard. The only piece of luck he ever had was being locked up with a man that looked just like him. Could've been brothers. . . . Anyways, he's dead now." When Laurel asks if he killed him, he says no, but he does admit to burying him—"I buried Horace for good." Laurel pleads with him, asking him to remember his pledge of love for her. He becomes angry, exclaiming, "I will not be Horace Townsend again! If you can find some way for Jack Sommersby to walk out of here, I'd be glad to do it." Both of them use *pathos* in their arguments very effectively, but Jack's argument benefits more than just Laurel. He sees a way to maintain dignity and respect for himself, his family, and his entire community— but that way requires that he keep his name and identity and be hanged as Jack Sommersby.

As the sentence is passed on Jack, the crowd of people in the courtroom are quiet and still. The camera reveals their faces; they realize the emotional power of the sacrifice Jack is making for them. Later, as he is led to the gallows, the crowd is respectful, holding themselves aright as he enters into view. One man yells out, "God bless you, Jack!" Women are seen crying or turning their heads into their husbands' chests to hide their tears. Once again, white and black stand together in awe at the price this man is paying for their sakes. The community is whole again. As Jack's face is covered with a white bag, the scene fades to white and then blue as we hear the sound of the trapdoor dropping open. The blue becomes a gentle blue sky filled with white clouds. The camera pans down. We expect to see the scaffold and a scene of horror, but instead, we hear hammers and see another kind of scaffolding. The men of the town are standing on a scaffolding surrounding the church building, endeavoring to repair the steeple. Earlier, the destroyed steeple was a symbol of the destruction of the sense of community after the ravages of the war and of the prejudice found in southern society. With the rebuilding of the steeple, we experience the emotion of hope along with this community. The camera continues around the town: men are busy painting the white columns of the plantation house; another man repairs a fence around a house; the trees and landscape exude lovely and fresh newness; and Laurel, rather spryly, walks to the graveyard with a bouquet of flowers. These she places on Jack's gravestone, clearly marked with his name. The rejuvenation and healing of the town is thus associated with the identity literally inscribed on the tombstone.

The emotional pull of the film is remarkable. Is *Sommersby* merely a "chick flick," as some of my male students have suggested, which uses emotion to make a buck by drawing in a large female audience? I often ask students to compare Bertrande's expression of sorrow over the loss of Pansette to Laurel's over Jack. Bertrande's restraint and composure is diametrically opposed to the overt and frequent emotional swings that Laurel's character undergoes. One way to look at the excessive emotional outpouring in *Sommersby* is to think of it as a product of Hollywood. Hollywood's audience wants a love story, a romance which overcomes obstacles, a restoration of order and stability, and a world without racial problems. So, this film offers all of that in a tight, convenient package and makes it palatable and believable through the excitement of our emotions. In this heightened state, the viewer can accept a post–Civil War South where black and white work together, where con artists will sacrifice themselves for others, and where true love will, in fact, change an entire community—the Hollywood version of the American dream.

This view of the film lends itself to discussion of Platonic notions about the dangers of rhetoric. Students can explore the negative tensions in the use of the emotional appeal. An orator who was unscrupulous might inflame an audience to act hastily and in rage, as Anthony does in Shakespeare's *Julius Caesar*. Emotional appeals might be so strong as to blind an audience to acting with proper forethought and reason. The manipulative power of *pathos* needs to be recognized, and the film can assist with that. Equally, however, pathetic appeals can be used by good individuals for just purposes. Rhetorician Gerard Hauser has said that "a responsible rhetoric does not separate our thoughts from our feelings; it unites them by addressing the whole person in terms of that person's experiences and the judgments they support" (119). In most rhetorical treatises, emotional appeals are important to audience understanding and adherence. Another way to look at *Sommersby* is through its effective use of emotion.

This emotional tug—a tug on all the students watching, whether they are male or female and whether or not they find themselves actually shedding tears—could have been intended by the filmmaker for a purpose other than merely manipulating a Hollywood convention. How does the emotional appeal connect with the subject of the film? As students begin to formulate the main ideas of the film—the fruitlessness of prejudice, the importance of honor and commitment, and the value of community—they realize that these intangible themes are brought home in quite tangible ways through the emotional appeal to the viewer. This question can lead the discussion to the ways in which abolitionists used emotional appeals before the Civil War. Looking at a sample speech from that time period and pairing it with a speech from Martin Luther King Jr. can demonstrate the usefulness of an appeal to *pathos* in terms of race relations.

Aristotle views emotion as one of the primary ingredients in any effective conclusion. The speaker must move "the hearer into emotional reactions" for the sake of his or her argument (3.19.1). The conclusion of *Sommersby,* as we have seen, effectively moves its audience into "emotional reactions." Canby argues, however, that the film has a "near vacuum at the center of the film" (C8). He may be right, for the film opens with intense emotions. Laurel's reuniting with a man whom she in her heart knows is not her husband, but whom she grows to love and respect, is full of emotional difficulties. More than one critic has been struck by the power of the shaving scene and the layering of emotions built into it. As Laurel shaves the man who claims to be her husband, there is a certain uneasiness in Jack.

Laurel delights in the new power she seems to have standing over him with a razor in her hand.

She asks, "Are you sure, hmm?" He replies, "Am I home?" Jack's unease is clear as she turns a mirror around for him to see his new face, his new identity. We can tell that he is more interested in her reaction than his own face. When he asks her what she thinks, she replies, "I'm thinking, who is this man sitting in my kitchen?" Even the atmosphere of the scene is ambiguous and dark. The lighting comes from candles, causing shadows to play on faces and walls. The ambiguity works so well on the viewers' emotions that we find ourselves caught up in the mystery. Caryn James claims that this scene is the exception rather than the rule—"too little of the film suggests this emotional depth and mystery" (17). The middle of the film is quite different from the ending and the beginning, but it is so to heighten the appeal to *pathos* at the end of the film, to make the argument stronger. If the entire film was maintained at the emotional depth of the beginning and ending, the viewer would be wrung dry before the final point is made. The hanging and its connection to the rebuilding of the town is crucial to the film and has to be emphasized.

Another reason for the middle of the film to lack emotional depth is to provide for the playing out of smaller vignettes. Most students, for example, recognize the powerful suggestiveness of the death of the dog, Jethro. The boy loves Jethro, but the dog, not recognizing Jack upon his return, growls and snarls at the soldier. Later the boy discovers the dead dog. This upsets the boy terribly, so when Jack travels to buy tobacco seed, he brings the boy back a new puppy. Upon seeing Jethro dead, the viewer begins to wonder about this man who calls himself Jack Sommersby. Did he kill the dog? If so, is he evil and only seeking to make a fortune? Even Orin confronts Jack later, accusing him of killing the dog to hush him up. But the sight of the new puppy soothes the viewer's concerns. Jack seems genuinely concerned about the boy's feeling and welfare. All of these feelings about Jack on the part of the viewer come as a result of the viewer's intimate connection with the boy and his feelings. The middle of the film is full of this sort of identification between character and viewer, and the connection is accomplished almost entirely through emotional appeals.

Richard Corliss, a *New York Times* film critic, has written, "Is Sommersby a great movie, or even an honorably affecting one? Not quite;

there are too many reaction shots of sweet young cheeks stained with big wet tears" (70). He is right about the amount of emotion-revealing shots in the film; however, Corliss has missed the value of those shots and the role they can be said to play in developing themes and ideas about the evil nature of prejudice and the value of true community. The film is suasive, and largely so because of the emotional appeals which connect so powerfully with the view. Just as the Vigne film provides fruitful ground for examining the conflicting views of *ethos, Sommersby* exemplifies for students conflicting attitudes toward the use of *pathos* in argumentation.

BENEFITS TO STUDENTS—INVENTION AND EVIDENCE

Of course, consideration of the three texts— Davis's history, the French film, and the Americanized version—should not be restricted individually to persuasion by *logos, ethos,* and *pathos.* In fact, evidence of all three types of persuasion is present in each version. Students should be encouraged to see the strains and threads of persuasive tactics running throughout all three. But the value of familiarity with three such different texts goes beyond even a discussion of argumentation. By reading, discussing, and writing on the three texts, students find they can invent topics and strategies for considering difficult subjects which will lead to intriguing thinking, speaking, and writing. Since the responses of Bertrande and Laurel are so different in their respective situations, what role do women have in these worlds and how does that change in each text? The physical and moral journey of the main characters can cause reflection on the Ulysses theme resonating in these works. What does it mean to construct your own identity, and what ethical problems does this raise? The combining of a historical text with imaginative interpretations calls up questions of the nature of reality and truth and how they might be altered. These texts become the evidence the students draw upon as they develop their arguments. Concrete verbal and visual examples strengthen writing that, more often than not, is weak and unsupported when dealing with large philosophical issues. Student thinking and communication improves remarkably as they learn how to properly use evidence in conjunction with their own developing ideas. Also, working through the films using rhetorical analysis gives the students a new lexicon which will be useful to them in thinking about any text they may study or encounter.

Although I have developed this teaching strategy for use in an argument class, other teachers of humanities courses could creatively use the same texts (or alternate texts) for their own particular purposes. History teachers will find a wealth of criticism available on the relationship of history and cinematic representations. Natalie Zemon Davis, in an interview, encourages filmmakers and students of film to "experiment with cinematic strategies to suggest ambiguity and contradiction" (qtd. in Aufderheide 138). What does this position do to historians' ideas about facts, evidence, and truth?[6] French language and culture teachers might choose to use the French documents upon which Davis bases her account.[7] Literature teachers might use the novel written by Vigne and his collaborator, which is based on the movie, as a way to discuss art adaptation and transformation.[8] The interest in adaptation of this particular work continues with a modern musical version. The music is available to provide students with yet another version of *Martin Guerre*.[9]

Using film in the classroom creates a common ground for talking to students. Film's accessibility is part of the attraction but, beyond this, film's popularity within our culture means that images, words, and motifs can be recognized over a wide segment of the population. Arthur M. Schlesinger has said that "the very nature of film as supremely popular art guarantees that it is the carrier of deep if enigmatic truth" (ix). Further, he argues that since film is a "mass undertaking" and not really the work of a single individual, the film, more than any other art form or expression is "intimately interwoven with the *mentalité* of the society" (x). Our students can approach films, such as *The Return of Martin Guerre* and *Sommersby,* with previous knowledge that runs deep from their own culture. This richness of thought, of cultural expression, of various "truths," gives impetus to strong, original thinking and writing—the goal of any course in the humanities.

NOTES

1. Davis's work goes beyond mere reconstruction of the facts, and in fact, the quality of her work asserts that good historical writing invents dialogue and happenings based not on fancy, but on research of the culture and society around the events in question. She playfully structures her book around the indefinite line between historical reconstruction and invention by opening her book with an acknowledgment to her "authentic husband," who helped her make the history of the "imposter-spouse" (x). Also, as a final gesture towards the subject of inventing a history, she says at the close of the book, "I

think I have uncovered the true face of the past—or has Pansette done it again?" (125). She perfectly realizes how she has manipulated historical reconstruction and relishes in its delights.

· 2. "Discovered" is from the Greek *heurein* meaning "to find out," according to Kennedy's note 39 on page 37 of Aristotle's *On Rhetoric*.

3. For Aristotle's definition of *ethos*, see 1.2.3. Kennedy's note on the text appears on page 39, in note 40.

4. For a good brief description of Plato's and Aristotle's ideas and how they are altered and used in the history of rhetoric, see Nan Johnson's entry under *"Ethos"* in Theresa Enos's *Encyclopedia of Rhetoric and Communication*.

5. Aristotle's description of *pathos* is found at 1.2.5. Kennedy's note appears on page 39, note 45.

6. Natalie Zemon Davis has published an article ("'Any Resemblance to Persons Living or Dead': Film and the Challenge of Authenticity") on the subject of film and its presentation of history in the *Historical Journal of Film, Radio, and Television* 8.3 (1988): 269–83. The journal *Film and History* is devoted entirely to the subject as well. *The Oxford Guide to Film Studies* (ed. John Hill) contains an article by Andrew Dudley, "Film and History" (1998).

7. See Davis's bibliography, pp. 127–31.

8. An interesting work on adaptation of film is the practical *The Art of Adaptation: Turning Fact and Fiction into Film* by Linda Seger, published by Henry Holt and Company, 1992. Lorne M. Buchman's *Still in Movement: Shakespeare on Screen*, though focused on Shakespearean adaptations, is an excellent study of the art of film adaptation (Oxford, 1991).

9. This musical opened on the London stage but closed after a few months even though it won four prestigious Oliver awards. Then the production was revamped for a Broadway production by the same team responsible for *Les Miserables* and *Miss Saigon* in 1999. The musical had a hard time finding a suitable theater on Broadway and received mixed reviews in its pre-Broadway U.S. run. Currently, the show is closed.

WORKS CITED

Ansen, David. "Great Pretender?" Rev. of *The Return of Martin Guerre*. *Newsweek* 27 June 1983: 80.

Aristotle. *Aristotle on Rhetoric: A Theory of Civic Discourse*. Trans. and ed. by George A. Kennedy. New York: Oxford UP, 1991.

Aufderheide, Pat. "Interview with Natalie Davis." *Radical History Review* 28–30 (1984): 136–39.

Benson, Edward. "The Look of the Past: *Le Retour de Martin Guerre*." Dir. by Daniel Vigne. *Radical History Review* 28–30 (1984): 125–35.

Bilsky, Manuel, McCrea Hazlett, Robert E. Streeter, and Richard M. Weaver. "Looking for an Argument." *Landmark Essays on Rhetorical Invention in Writing*. Ed. Richard E. Young and Yameng Liu. Davis, CA: Hermagoras Press, 1994. 13–19.

Canby, Vincent. "Husband Back from War: Too Good to Be True?" Rev. of *Sommersby*, dir. Jon Amiel. *New York Times* 5 February 1993: C8.

Corliss, Richard. "Remade the American Way." Rev. of *Sommersby,* dir. Jon Amiel. *Time* 22 February 1993: 69–70.

Corrigan, Timothy. *A Short Guide to Writing about Film.* 4th ed. New York: Longman, 2001.

Davis, Natalie Zemon. "On the Lame." *American Historical Review* 93.3 (June 1988): 572–603.

———. *The Return of Martin Guerre.* Cambridge: Harvard UP, 1983.

Fahnestock, Jeanne, and Marie Secor. *The Rhetoric of Argument.* New York: Random House, 1982.

Finlay, Robert. "The Refashioning of Martin Guerre." *American Historical Review* 93.3 (June 1988): 553–71.

Ginzburg, Carlo. "Proofs and Possibilities: In the Margins of Natalie Zemon Davis's *The Return of Martin Guerre*." Trans. Anthony Gureratne. *Yearbook of Comparative and General Literature* 37 (1988): 113–27.

Hauser, Gerard A. *Introduction to Rhetorical Theory.* Prospect Heights, IL: Waveland, 1991.

James, Caryn. "A Mystery Haunts the Ages." Rev. of *Sommersby,* dir. Jon Amiel. *New York Times* 21 February 1993: 17.

Johnson, Nan. "Ethos." *Encyclopedia of Rhetoric and Composition: Communication from Ancient Times to the Information Age.* Ed. Theresa Enos. New York: Garland, 1996. 243–45.

Kauffmann, Stanley. "Stanley Kauffmann on Films." Rev. of *The Return of Martin Guerre.* Dir. by Daniel Vigne. *New Republic* 2 May 1983: 24–25.

Le Retour de Martin Guerre. Dir. Daniel Vigne. Perf. Gerard Depardieu, Nathalie Baye, Roger Planchon. French release, 1982; U.S. release, European International Distribution, 1983. Dussault.

Monaco, James. *How to Read a Film: The World of Movies, Media, and Multimedia.* 3rd ed. New York: Oxford UP, 2000.

Plato. *Gorgias. Readings from Classical Rhetoric.* Ed. Patricia P. Matsen, Philip Rollinson, and Marion Sousa. Carbondale: Southern Illinois UP, 1990. 59–74.

Schlesinger, Arthur M., Jr. Foreword. *American History/American Film: Interpreting the Hollywood Image.* Ed. by John E. O'Conner and Martin A. Jackson. New York: Frederick Ungar, 1979.

Simon, John. "Surfaces Mostly." Rev. of *The Return of Martin Guerre,* dir. Daniel Vigne. *National Review* 5 August 1983: 950–52.

Sommersby. Dir. Jon Amiel. Perf. Richard Gere, Jodi Foster. Warner Brothers, 1993.

Staiger, Janet. "Securing the Fictional Narrative As a Tale of the Historical Real." *South Atlantic Quarterly* 88.2 (1989): 393–413.

"Strange Prisoners"
Plato Goes to Pleasantville

MARIA BACHMAN

Despite the proliferation and variety of English composition readers, we are hard pressed to find a table of contents that does not include Plato's "Allegory of the Cave." But while Plato persists into modernity, attempting to teach the dialogue of Socrates and Glaucon to college freshmen is often dismissed by English instructors as little more than an exercise in futility. A few idealists among us, however, persevere, insisting on the importance of the allegory as a vital pedagogical tool for teaching critical thinking. We want students to understand that knowledge cannot simply be transferred from teacher to student; rather, education consists in directing students' minds toward a questioning of the institutional and larger social contexts of their "learning" and ultimately enabling them, through reflective and skillful thinking, to learn for themselves. I would argue that the real value in teaching the allegory derives mainly in getting students to notice context, period, for many of them assume that course content is a self-revealing entity with no contextual strings attached; and Plato's dialogue, at the very least, reveals the existence of puppet masters, and allegorizes received, unquestioned "wisdom" as the show of ideological shadows that wisdom often is.

Plato's main conceptual scheme of the cave reveals that people understand "the truth" (also, "the good" and "justice") to be only the visible (i.e., most readily apparent) world before them, when the real, "higher" knowledge ("the intellectual world," according to Socrates, and the space of "divine contemplation") in fact is much more complicated than that, and even *not readily visible*. While Plato's use of visual perception as an analogue for perceiving knowledge in the proper way is provocative, it is partly inscrutable for students because they are initially unable to *see* the resemblance between their position in the classroom *viz.* the teacher and her blackboard and Plato's chained prisoners who think reality consists of the passing shadows cast onto the wall by the fire that blazes behind them. *Pleasantville,* the recent "blast from the past" film, offers a visual analogue to Plato's essay that students can enthusiastically apprehend, and provides a unique opportunity for the instructor to combine classical and contemporary texts in order to teach critical thinking. More specifically, *Pleasantville* shows students how the acquisition of "higher knowledge" (intellectual, sexual, social, academic, and practical—the prisoner's "journey upwards," according to Socrates) has the power to literally change the way the world looks.

The most important philosophical and practical component of my composition class, and, I would argue, of the discipline of English, is critical thinking. Admittedly, assigning Plato's allegory at the beginning of the semester in a freshman composition class in order to begin to acquaint students with strategies for argumentation can be an ambitious, if not foolhardy adventure. My purpose in doing so, however, is not only to inculcate the value of particular classical rhetorical skills, but also to emphasize to students the importance of their role as investigators in their own education, as well as the larger "real life" importance of critical questioning. Specifically, I encourage an ongoing process of self-critique that necessitates a careful and vigilant examination of the beliefs, values, and judgments students will bring with them into the classroom and out into the larger world. I also want students to know that the freedom to think for themselves— the freedom to present and defend their views—is not only a fundamental *right* of the individual, but also a democratic *skill* and *obligation* that must be properly developed, nurtured, and protected; and this necessitates, as well, the development of a keen attention to, and even empathy for, other viewpoints. I have found that a most fruitful place to get students critically engaged with questions about the relationship between knowledge and social values is with Socrates' classic argument about the potential of the educated to lead citizens out of the darkness of the complacency engendered by a certain comfort in superficial appearances, and with *Pleasantville,* a modern cinematic rendering of the problematic relationship between appearances and reality, as well as a plea for the importance of education (in all its myriad forms, formal and informal) in lifting society out of its conformist, and even bigoted, ignorance. The film translates Plato's allegory into a modern idiom that helps students to identify a question from Plato that serves as a touchstone for the rest of the course: To what extent can we let go of our preconceived opinions and beliefs about the world around us in order to perceive that world more clearly?

Socrates begins his lesson by telling a story of a group of people who have been, without being fully aware of it, imprisoned in an underground cave for their entire lives, and where they have assumed that the shadows projected onto the unchanging surface of the cavern wall in front of them are more real than the persons casting those shadows, of whose existence the prisoners are wholly unaware. Above and behind the prisoners a fire blazes, and between the fire and the prisoners there is a low walkway where some are carrying objects; these make up the "puppet show" which the prisoners watch daily, unaware of the wide mouth of the cave behind them, open to the light of the sun. Because the prisoners are bound and chained, they are unable to distinguish between the distorted reflections, in much the same way that they cannot distinguish between the cacophony of voices inside the cave and the echoes. "The truth," for them, is "literally nothing but the shadows of the images."[1] Glaucon's response to the introduction of the analogy is important: "It is a strange image, and they are strange prisoners" ("Allegory" 2:377).

Like Plato's allegory, *Pleasantville* opens with a suggestive picture of the pathetic condition of the average citizen. The movie's conceit is the teenaged David's obsession with television and, in particular, his enthrallment with the utopian 1950s sitcom "Pleasantville," an indiscriminate anodyne which enables him to escape from his own trouble-plagued reality, a world described by his teachers as under the catastrophic threat of AIDS, ozone depletion, massive famine, and dismal job prospects. Adding to these global misfortunes is the fact that David's parents are divorced and his mother appears to be deeply unhappy with her situation as a single mother. Delighted at the prospect of chaining himself to the television for a 24-hour marathon, David lives *for* and *in* the alternative virtual reality of Pleasantville, a brightly-lit black-and-white world of sublime suburban bliss. My students are initially perplexed by my directive to consider this image of David in front of the TV as an exemplary postmodern paradigm for the scheme of the cave. Further, I ask them to examine the extent to which David's reification of a fictive place might be analogous to Plato's prisoners who watch shadows dance upon the wall of their cave and take them for reality. After all, Pleasantville—a place where life is simple and predictable, where people are perfect and change is nonexistent—cannot be anything but an obviously false construct. Most students will accept this connection, but then I pose another question: How can the prisoners and David not know the difference between reality and illusion? Some students are quick to point out that since the prisoners have spent their whole lives in the cave, they cannot be faulted for believing that the projected shadows of people walking behind them are not merely images of real things, but reality itself. An astute reader will go one step further and explain that the cave dwellers have been *conditioned* to accept what has been placed before them, and ultimately, they know no other world. Then we consider why it is that David, who *is* aware of the difference, and who can come and go in and out of the living room as he pleases, nonetheless willfully invests more of himself in the illusory televised world than in the real world (as opposed to his sister, Jennifer, whose interest in television—specifically a live concert on MTV—is merely a means to the end of "scoring" with the current object of her desire, Mark Davis, a verbally challenged high school version of Stanley Kowalski). The answer is simple: for David, it is a choice between pleasant and unpleasant (at least, as he perceives them).

I then ask students to consider the media through which the images are cast for the cave dwellers and for David (fire and television, respectively), and whether there are any similarities. This is a difficult question—students are initially compelled to point out what they see as a fundamental difference—fire is natural, television is technological—but when pressed to consider the *nature* of the images that are projected, students see that both mediums are powerfully mimetic. That is, they begin to understand that the images that are presented before the viewers, although lifelike and powerfully *real,* are artificial representations, and do not truly exist outside the means of their construction. Students will concede, rather sheepishly, that in our electronically saturated age, our culture's addiction to (or perhaps, worship of) television makes us similar to Plato's chained slaves, who, through sheer inertia (and even resistance to change) choose to live in an underground den, dumbly watching shadows dance on the cavern wall in front of them.[2] I can then begin to guide them to discern one of the initial arguments that the film's director, Gary Ross, advances through the metaphor of television: The members of contemporary society are willfully ignorant of and even indifferent toward the messy social complexities of their own world.[3]

Just as Plato presents the case in which one of the prisoners is, by some unknown agency, released from his chains and disabused, with some reluctance, of his former errors of sight (a painful awakening, according to Socrates), likewise, through the agency of a mysterious TV repairman, David and his sister undergo, also with reluctance and even outright resistance, their own individual "steep and rugged ascents" into enlightenment. Brother and sister, in their struggle with each other for control of the remote (which is ultimately a battle over their choice of what is pleasurable, i.e., "pleasant"—for David, the sexless suburban idylls of Pleasantville reruns and for Jennifer, the aphrodisiac of MTV), are zapped back into the black-and-white world of *Pleasantville* where they are transformed into the pasty, yet "swell," Parker family cast members "Bud" and "Mary Sue." Trapped in a radically different dimension of sight, their initial reactions to their predicament are completely different: David/Bud pleads with Jennifer/Mary Sue to "just play along," to peacefully assimilate into *Pleasantville,* taking care not to "alter their whole universe" (and therefore, David does not want to "alter the script"). Mary Sue, however, is disgusted, defiant, and determined to shake things up. She recognizes from the start that there is something terribly wrong in a place where everything is always "pleasant." The weather report, for instance, is never mercurial: every day is a sunny 72 degrees, and umbrellas exist only as dramatic props for the school play. The basketball team never loses a game, leaving the men at the barbershop to contemplate the origins of the saying, "You can't win 'em all." There are no fires in Pleasantville, and firemen serve only to rescue cute kittens from trees. Sex, toilets, and profanity are all nonexistent in Pleasantville, and so too are passion, intellect, curiosity, creativity, confrontation, and change. It is a world couched in convention and entrenched in the comforts of blissful ignorance.

The movie chronicles what happens to the "strange prisoners" of Pleasantville as "Bud" unwittingly, and "Mary Sue" deliberately, introduce the inhabitants to "radical" new ideas. On her first day of school at Pleasantville High, Mary Sue sits through a class lecture on "the Geography of Main Street." Clearly somewhat perplexed by the teacher's concentration on such a small area (and, one would think, so familiar to all it does not warrant a "lesson"), Mary Sue asks, "What's outside of Pleasantville?" This query is met with unabashed bewilderment. "Why what do you mean, Mary Sue?" the teacher responds incredulously, to which Mary Sue responds, "You know, what's beyond Main Street?"

Chuckling, the teacher dismisses such foolishness: "Oh, Mary Sue. We all know that the end of Main Street is just the beginning again." One does not question the lie behind the tautological loop that defines Pleasantville.

When Mary Sue, at the soda shop on a first date with Skip, the captain of the basketball team, and clearly bored, provocatively suggests that they continue their evening at Lovers' Lane, he's beside himself with excitement at the prospect of holding her hand. Skip gets more than he could possibly wish for, however, when they reach their destination and Mary Sue jumps him, assuring him in hands-on fashion that the hard-on he is horrified to find himself afflicted with is *not* evidence of a fatal illness. When Skip drives Mary Sue home later that night, he is jolted out of his blissful post-coital stupor by the first image of the change brought to Pleasantville via Mary Sue's frank and open sexuality: a rose, in contrast to the gray, monochrome world surrounding it, has turned a deep, vivid red. Soon kids are making out in the soda shop while "Lawdy Miss Clawdy" blasts out of the jukebox.

I invite students to compare the initial responses to the gradual emergence of color in Pleasantville and to the blinding light which greets Plato's released prisoner after he is "dragged up a steep and rugged ascent" ("Allegory" 2:377). Socrates suggests that we might be inclined to believe that if only the prisoners were released from their chains, they would cease to mistake shadows for realities and would happily throw off the chains of their former ignorance:

> . . . conceive someone saying to him, that what he saw before was an illusion, but that now, when he is approaching nearer to being and his eye is turned toward more real existence, he has a clearer vision— what will be his reply? And you may further imagine that his instructor is pointing to the objects as they pass and requiring him to name them—will he not be perplexed? Will he not fancy that the shadows which he formerly saw are truer than the objects which are now shown to him? ("Allegory" 2:377)

Bud wants to cling to the shadows, and he is none too pleased at the changes that have come to Pleasantville due to Mary Sue's rewriting of the standard script. He warns Mary Sue again, "You can't do this. I warned you. You're messing with their whole goddamned universe." "Maybe it needs to be messed with," Mary Sue responds, "Did *that* ever occur to you?" Bud continues, "You can't do this to these people," while Mary Sue snaps, "If *I* don't do it, who will?" "But they're happy like this," Bud moans. Mary Sue, however, refuses to concede such limitations: "These people have a lot of potential," she argues, "they just don't know any better."

I ask students to consider why Bud is so vehemently opposed to change. Has he successfully followed his own directive? Students are usually torn on this point. Some contend that Bud works diligently to preserve the Pleasantville status quo because of his own personal investment in *things remaining pleasantly the same,* while others point out that although Bud does not realize it, he has already set things in motion himself. In one scene he arrives late for work at the soda shop and finds a nearly comatose Bill Johnson wearing down a section of the counter with a cleaning rag. Mr. Johnson explains his routine: after he wipes down the counters each day, Bud sets out the napkins, and then he can begin making the french fries. But since Bud was late in arriving at the soda shop, Mr. Johnson was thrown into a state of paralysis and rendered incapable of independently moving from one task to another. While Bud seems to offer a reasonable solution to this situation—"If this ever happens again, you can make the fries even if I haven't put out the napkins"—I ask students to consider the repercussions of liberating Mr. Johnson from his routine. Bud's words seem well intended and certainly innocent, but it is not until the next soda shop scene that students understand that Bud has unwittingly unleashed a host of repressed desires and impulses. In this scene, Bud arrives to find a despondent Bill Johnson slumped on the floor. The soda jerk informs him that "there are no cheeseburgers." Bud is incredulous. "What do you mean, no cheeseburgers?" demands Bud. Wallowing in a kind of existential despair, Mr. Johnson explains, "What's the point? It's always the same. . . . Nothing ever changes. . . . It never gets any better or any worse." He confesses to Bud that he only really looks forward to the Christmas season because it is the one time of year that he is permitted to decorate the storefront window and every year it is something *different.* Mr. Johnson, in fact, so looks forward to this event every year that he begins to think that once a year is an "awfully long time to wait for just one moment." Bud advises him to "try not to *think* about that anymore," but that is just what is beginning to happen in Pleasantville: people are beginning to question their existence, and with that comes existential despair—the price of knowledge—which is why Socrates informs

Glaucon that "the bewilderments of the eyes" can be caused as much from going into the light as coming out of it ("Allegory" 2:380). Knowledge, therefore, necessitates a certain amount of confusion and even suffering.

In one scene, Betty Parker, Mary Sue's "Mom," wonders why all the kids have been spending so much more time than usual at Lovers' Lane. "What are they doing there?" she wants to know. "Sex," Mary Sue whispers emphatically. "Oh," Betty responds thoughtfully. Pause. "What's sex?" Another pause. "Do you really want to know?" Mary Sue asks. Betty's subsequent response to Mary Sue's sanitized version of the birds and the bees ("Well, Mom, when two people love each other very much, they want to share that love . . .") is hardly met with shock or horror, but rather with disappointment. "Oh, Mary Sue . . . your father would never do anything like *that*." Without skipping a beat, Mary Sue assures her that "fortunately, there are alternatives." Cut to the next scene where Betty, apparently taking Mary Sue's advice, prepares her bath and we witness her awakening to sexual pleasure, while husband George drifts blissfully off to sleep, alone, in his single bed.[4] As the music and Betty swell to a climax, bursts of color appear on her toes and cheeks, on the walls, and outside the window, culminating significantly, at the moment of orgasm, in the tree on the front lawn bursting into flames. As I query students about the emergence of color in this key scene, they initially note clichéd metaphors: color=sex, or more particularly, red is the color of passion, danger, etc. However, when Mary Sue laments later that she's still in black and white, despite the fact that she's "had ten times more sex than anyone else [in Pleasantville]," Bud (who is also still black and white) assures her that the process of colorization is a bit more complicated: "I think maybe there's more to it [than just sex]." And it is Bud's suggestion that "it's not all about sex" that sparks a lively and inquisitive discussion among students. After all, if we are to believe that Bud and Mary Sue are the instruments of change, why is it that they remain in monochrome? What feats of fury must they perform before they can also burst into color?

The transition from black and white to color, students begin to see, is not so much about carnal knowledge as it is about various forms of enlightenment—emotional, sexual, intellectual, and social. As the citizens of Pleasantville (mostly, at first, teenagers) open their eyes to a fuller spectrum of human actions, and as the contours of their imagination begin to extend beyond the town limits, things and people bloom from the monochromes of

black and white into full color. Color starts breaking out on cars and shrub-
bery (at first, reds and greens to herald the passion and verdant vitality that
have come to Pleasantville). Each new discovery—sex, literature, and art—
adds a splash of color to the people and their town. The possibilities that exist
on the outskirts of Pleasantville's continually re-running (and therefore
"looping") script are further exemplified in Bill, the cheeseburger-flipping-
guy-turned-avante-garde-artist. When Bud checks out a coffee-table art
book from the library for Bill, the awestruck soda-jerk's own creative (and
dangerous) energies are unleashed, and, in no time at all, he transforms the
soda shop into a Van Gogh-esque gallery and site of radical energy, painting the town not only purple, but red, blue, chartreuse, and magenta. It is
only fitting, therefore, that later in the film, when the town is divided against
itself on the issue of "colorization," that Bill's soda shop will serve as the official headquarters of the "underground."

Change actually makes Pleasantville *more* beautiful, not only for the
viewers of the film, but also for those who have been trapped there all
along. In one scene, Bud has a date with the school's cute cheerleader (who,
according to the original "script," should only be interested in Whitey) and
he drives her to the Edenic Lovers' Lane while pink cherry blossoms swirl
seductively around their black-and-white car and Etta James's "At Last"
plays on the radio. Like the other kids, Bud's girlfriend is curious about
what lies outside of Pleasantville, and, in fact, it is her very curiosity that
first turns her away from an interest in Whitey and towards an interest in
Bud, who has now gained a reputation for knowing what's "outside" of
Pleasantville. Hence, her question to Bud at Lovers' Lane (where, finally,
knowledge is as erotically intoxicating as sex once was, and the camera
pans the lake to show students lying next to each other, not passionately
kissing and coupling as in earlier scenes, but reading to each other):

> "What's it like . . . out *there*?"
> "Louder . . . scarier . . . more dangerous. . . ."
> "It sounds *fantastic*," [Bud's girlfriend] replies, before offering him a
> bite of the apple she has just picked.

In a reversal of the Garden of Eden myth, curiosity and knowledge (carnal and intellectual) transform this dystopia into a virtual paradise. At this
point, I ask students to return to the scene where the heat of Betty's sexual

self-discovery literally creates fire—specifically, a burning tree. Usually a few students will note that the scene is suggestive of the scene in Exodus where God speaks to Moses through the burning bush.[5] We discuss how for Moses, stumbling into the burning bush while he was watching his flock of sheep was a *transformative* event. God commanded Moses to go back to Egypt to lead the people of Israel out of captivity. The people, however, were not able to fully comprehend the revelation given to Moses and so he spent his life persuading the Israelites (sometimes futilely) to adopt the code of life that was revealed to him. I ask students whether they can make any connection between the Bible and Plato's allegory and they generally have little difficulty in noting how distinctly similar the allegory is in its portrayal of the man who has found divine truth. Though he will be misunderstood, like Moses, and will, in all likelihood, meet with resistance, having found the "truth," he has a responsibility to lead the less enlightened masses—out of Egypt, out of the cave, and out of darkness.

In his review of the film, "Exile in Pleasantville," Charles Taylor notes that the film's director, Gary Ross, understands that open sexuality and music and books all interrogate society's assumptions.[6] Indeed, on her first day at school, Mary Sue gets lost and ends up (to David's surprise) in the library. She is shocked to learn that all the books in the library have titles, but the pages are blank; encouraged by her classmates, Mary Sue ends up recounting what she remembers of the *Adventures of Huckleberry Finn* and magically, as she reads, the text begins to appear on the pages. Fortunately, Bud, being the better student, remembers the novel in its entirety and picks up where Mary Sue left off, filling in the pages for the captive soda-shop audience. It is certainly no coincidence that the first work of literature the kids of Pleasantville are introduced to is a novel that pointedly interrogates the nature of freedom and democracy, and illustrates the need of the individual to break through society's oppressive shield of conformity. Bud's overly simplistic distillation of Twain's novel—"Huck and the slave were going up the river trying to get free, and in trying to get free, they see they're sort of free already"—is particularly salient to the theme of the film, as is the musical backdrop to this scene, Dave Brubeck Quartet's "Take Five," a jazz tune that could boast (for 1959) one of the most innovative and defiant time-signatures (5/4). The disruption of harmony in Pleasantville is underscored as "Take Five" segues meaningfully into Miles Davis's "So What," an innovative jazz composition that is distinguished by its polytonality and chromatization. Not surprisingly, following this scene, things really begin to swing in Pleasantville.

The very next scene shows kids lining up at the library and walking with piles of novels clutched to their chests with thrilled expressions on their faces. Lovers' Lane is soon in full technicolor and oddly enough color isn't the only evidence of change. The kids are no longer groping each other in the back seats of cars. Instead, they're reading! In fact, Mary Sue's eventual transformation to color occurs only after she decides (uncharacteristically so) to stay home and read, rather than have another hot date with Skip Martin, who himself can still not even say the word, "sex":

> "Hey, Mary Sue, c'mon . . . aren't you ready to go . . . to uh, go uh . . . you know . . . ?"
> "No, I'm busy."
> "Doing what?" Skip asks incredulously.
> "Busy studying," replies Mary Sue emphatically as she closes her bedroom window.

Thoughtfully, the hitherto-slut-turned-bookworm glides back to her desk where she puts on a pair of geeky glasses and, with slightly furrowed brow, proceeds to read the night away—*Lady Chatterley's Lover*—until color literally comes to *her* cheeks. (The implication here is of course that D. H. Lawrence is far more satisfying than Skip Martin.)

As we interrogate Plato's allegory further in relation to the film, students begin to understand that no simple deliverance from ignorance is possible. Socrates notes that initially the freed prisoner will have difficulty adjusting to the outside light and he will even persist in maintaining the reality of the shadows. He will "have a pain in his eyes which will make him turn away to take refuge in the objects of vision which he can see, and which he will conceive to be in reality clearer than the things which are being shown to him" ("Allegory" 2:377). And just as the cave dweller's initial response (to the excess of light) is disbelief, discomfort, and resistance, so too when change (an excess of color) comes to Pleasantville, things become distinctly *un*pleasant. Indeed, Pleasantville finds it has a "color" problem—the black-and-white folk against the so-called "coloreds"—and it is a conflict that very quickly becomes ugly and violent as placards declaring "No Coloreds" are posted in every Pleasantville storefront. Students can see that the film is suddenly a provocative parable about racism as they make the connection between the historical Jim Crow laws and the sinister movement towards segregation in Pleasantville. The riot scene in which the black-and-white townspeople destroy the soda shop is, in fact, a haunting reenactment of the intimidation and violence that the nonviolent civil rights demonstrators were met with during the 1960s when they challenged the "whites only" policies at restaurants and other places of public accommodation throughout the South.

The fears of those who remain in Plato's cave and are unwilling to be enlightened are echoed in one scene by the three town honchos incredulously watching the parade of readers. Disgustedly, one remarks, "Going to a library. What's next?" Learning in Pleasantville—expanding one's intellectual, psychological, and physical horizons—is perceived as an unequivocal and dangerous rebellion against the established *pleasant* order. These narrow-minded bigots are among those who, resistant to change, have remained black and white. Like Plato's prisoners who, even when dragged from the cave by force, feel absolutely repulsed by the light, they want to remain entrenched in the comfort of convention:

> And suppose once more, that he is reluctantly dragged up a steep and rugged ascent, and held fast until he is forced into the presence of the sun himself, is he not likely to be pained and irritated? When he approaches the light his eyes will be dazzled, and he will not be able to see anything of what are now called realities. ("Allegory" 2:377)

Like Plato's prisoners of darkness who choose to remain below conferring ridiculous honors upon one another ("Allegory" 2:378), the Pleasantville cronies induct each other into the Rotary Club and have a murderous disposition toward the newly enlightened that is undeniable. They want to maintain conformist decency and, in an effort to do so, they enact a Pleasantville Code of Conduct—rules of civic behavior which prohibit anything and everything "unpleasant." Both the library and Lovers' Lane are closed; all music that is not of a "pleasant and temperate nature" (excepting, of course, Perry Como, Johnny Mathis, John Philip Sousa, and "The Star-Spangled Banner") is banned; books are burned (a sinister reminder of Nazism); and the only paint colors permitted are black, white, and gray ("despite the recent availability of other choices"). They even go so far as to decree that "all elementary and high school curricula will teach the non-changeist view of history, emphasizing continuity over alteration." But just as Socrates posits that if the released prisoner were to go back to the cave, it would be impossible to revert back to his old world, so too has Pandora's box already been opened in Pleasantville, and the film cleverly works toward demonstrating that ultimately, despite the mayor's fascist edicts, knowledge *is* power.

What is left deliberately ambiguous in Plato's allegory is the way in which the prisoners might be set free—would it be some external agent or non-cave-dweller, or some other force? *Pleasantville* enables students to see that while the chains are physical in the cave, they are, in reality, mental shackles, and can only be unhinged through a strenuous process of willed self-enlightenment. I guide my students to see that if the chains are psychological rather than physical, then Plato's newly released prisoner must have at some point had the temerity and self-prepossession to wonder if there was anything else beyond the surface of the cave and the shadows that danced on it. *Pleasantville* helps students to see that when they are unwilling to examine and question the status quo, when they indifferently refuse to acknowledge the possibility of innovation and change, they willfully give up their freedom, not only as students, but as citizens of a polis. For Plato, understanding the Forms and not merely their shadows in the physical world is a goal that all people should strive for (if, that is, they are striving for the "good" and the "just"—for that is what creates the posture of "leaning toward the light"). They see only the outward structures of social forms and thus become the architects of their own "prison-house." When, however, we consciously identify our predispositions and how and where we have acquired those views, we can begin to make an approach toward open-mindedness.

In defiance of the town's Code of Conduct, and, in a larger sense, in a challenge to the established government, Bill, the soda-jerk-turned-artist, paints a massive allegorical mural on the brick wall of the police station. Though the graffiti is a hybrid of artistic forms, it derives some of its inspiration from Diego Rivera's famous "Man at the Crossroads mural"[7] to depict all the changes that have come to this seemingly changeless town. We see the burned books with angel wings flying up to heaven—*Moby Dick, Catcher in the Rye, Lady Chatterley's Lover*—books, of course, which serve as our own cultural markers of once-forbidden knowledge. The camera slowly pans the mural, but the one image that is especially provocative and one that the camera catches three times (albeit quickly), is what appears to be a group of people, not being led, but leading themselves out of a dark hole.

The film ends with a courtroom scene (Bud and Bill are on trial for willfully propagandizing in violation of the Code of Conduct) where Bud, as part of his defense, forces his father, George, and the Mayor to realize the transformative power of their own creative potential. As they acknowledge their own emotional capacities and complex connections to other people (as they give way, respectively, to their feelings of love and rage), they change into color. Case closed. The doors of the courthouse burst open and the townspeople joyously spill out into Technicolor streets that are now peppered with signs pointing in the direction of places *outside* of Pleasantville: "Springfield 12." Bud is jubilant, but then his attention is caught by something the viewer does not yet see. Indeed, he seems to be lured by some strange force as he makes his way deliberately against the surge of the crowds thronging Main Street. He stops in front of the display window of Norm's TV and Radio, which now features a vast array of color televisions, each showing a different image of hitherto unheard-of faraway places. A beatific expression comes over Bud as the camera scans a placard which boasts, "What a difference color can make in your life." I stop the film. What's going on here? I ask students. Has the director lost sight of his opening claim about the ill effects of television? Surely, his attack wasn't simply on nostalgic television reruns? Is Ross ultimately saying something about the seduction of television or its potential? Students are perplexed. Of course, Ross may just need a quick, economic way to show "the world" coming to Pleasantville, and the TVs in the store window are an easy way to do that; nevertheless, this is a problematic undercutting of a larger point made in the film—the banality of TV.

We return to the final sequence, a juxtaposition of Bill and Betty on a park bench, and then George and Betty on a park bench, with each man asking, "What is going to happen now?" Their response is liberating in its absolute uncertainty. The film closes to Fiona Apple's quiet and carefree rendering of the Beatles's "Across the Universe," a peculiar choice given the song's refrain, "Nothing's gonna change my world." Are we to interpret this song literally or ironically? Students generally consider this an irony that Gary Ross wants them to recognize. After all, most students will recognize that Apple's performance is a remake of a Beatles classic, and this is another instance of Ross putting formal musical elements to significant thematic use. That is, Apple's performance, like Bill Johnson's artistic style, is interpretive, improvisational, impressionistic—just as human experience should be. But what has the film really *taught* us? Do we accept its many arguments and buy into the knowledge of human experience that the film so diligently promotes? Can a movie—indeed, *this* movie—really teach us to question what we are shown? After all, I contend, isn't film just another a powerful illusionistic medium (a human invention)—much like television and the shadows in the cave—that possesses the ability to manipulate and mold our beliefs, desires, and fears, and in some ways, even our very identities in accordance with its images? Ultimately, the question is whether the film's interventions into our experience are morally and socially beneficial or dangerous. And it is by now that students are equipped with skills with which to adjudicate this question, as well as to adjudicate between the real and the copy, between fact and fiction, between what they apprehend as social goods and social ills. They realize that questions are as important as the answers. They see that while the film and television directors are no different, to a certain extent, than the puppet-handlers in their ability to cast images on the screen or wall, ultimately they do not possess the power to insure that everyone in the audience will see in the same way. Images can educate as well as corrupt. Imitation of reality is not a limitation, but what is limiting is wholesale acceptance of the copy without an understanding of its artifice. The power of interpretation, or revision, I want students to realize, lies solely with the viewer.[8] Following Irving Singer's argument for the "transformative power" of film, I want students to realize that the power of interpretation or revision lies, ultimately, with the viewer: "The flickering photographic images are realities in themselves, but their capacity to transform other kinds of reality gives them their place as an intermediary between the audience and the world that is being represented." Irving explains further that "the new meanings that arise out of cinema exist only in relation to its audience."[9] So, finally, knowledge is not only transformative, but also transactive.

Socrates tells Glaucon at the end of his story that the path of the prisoner who escapes the cave parallels the soul's ascent to knowledge or enlightenment. Like the "Allegory of the Cave," *Pleasantville* is an exemplary allegory about education (and a perfect "fit" for the writing classroom) that calls on students to interrogate their own beliefs about what constitutes not only knowledge, but also authentic experience. Ultimately, I want students to come to the realization that they do have the power and the ability to see, in their own world, the shadow-objects and those who hold them before the artificial light of the cave's fire. Our escape from the cave (ignorance) is only possible when we begin to challenge the status quo—when we begin to question authority and established beliefs, when we begin to think for ourselves, rather than relying on others to think for us . . . or, like David/Bud, when we become actors, rather than just spectators:

> . . . in the world of knowledge the Idea of good appears last of all, and is seen only with an effort; although when seen, it is inferred to be the universal author of all things beautiful and right, parent of light and of the lord of light in the visible world, and the immediate and supreme source of reason and truth in the intellectual; and that this is the power upon which he who would act rationally either in public or private life must have his eye fixed. ("Allegory" 2:379)

And thus, perhaps most important, I remind students that Plato's motivations and goals were very much political—he himself made fun of the "philosopher" who fell into a ditch while looking at the stars. That is, I want students to understand that Plato's allegory doesn't end with the freed prisoner reaching the top of the hill and contemplating the sun, but continues with his return into the cave where he (like Bud and Mary Sue) tries to enlighten his fellow prisoners at the risk of his own life. As Socrates reminds Glaucon, "the intention of our law . . . seeks rather to spread happiness over the whole State, and to hold the citizens together by persuasion and necessity, making each share with others any benefits which he can confer upon the state and the law aimed at producing such citizens, not that they may be left to please themselves, but that they may serve in binding the State together" ("Allegory" 2:382). For he who escapes from the shadows of the cave/Pleasantville must return to help rescue those in darkness or, in the case of Pleasantville, those in black and white, for this is ultimately the message that *Pleasantville* so cleverly trumpets: the individual can make a difference.

NOTES

1. *The Dialogues of Plato,* trans. B. Jowett. 4th ed. 4 vols. Oxford: Clarendon Press, 1953), 2:377. Hereafter cited in the text as "Allegory."

2. Students will go so far as to admit that their own television viewing practices are primarily escapist. When they tune into a program, they tune out all outside cares. In a recent study of the personality and imagination of television addicts, Robert D. McIllwraith finds that self-acknowledged television addicts use television to distract themselves from "unpleasant" thoughts: "TV viewers who described themselves addicted to or dependent on TV reported that they used television for its mood-altering effects, [and] as a coping mechanism to distract them from unpleasant rumination" ("'I, Addicted to Television': The Personality, Imagination, and TV Watching Patterns of Self-Identified TV Addicts," *Journal of Broadcasting and Electronic Media* 42.3 [summer 1998]: 371–87).

3. Indeed, Gary Ross's claim that television viewing can be detrimental to the social body has been substantiated by scientific studies. Most recently, *Scientific American* explored the "allure" that television has on the viewers and the ways in which viewers, trapped in this technological lair, unwittingly give up control over their lives. Authors Robert Kubey and Mihaly Csikszentmihalyi cited studies which measured brain wave production during television viewing. Not surprisingly, study participants "showed less mental stimulation" while watching television, but what was more alarming was that "feelings of passivity and lowered alertness" continued in individuals long after the television had been turned off: "Survey participants commonly reflect that television has somehow absorbed or sucked out their energy, leaving them depleted" ("Television Addiction Is No Mere Metaphor," *Scientific American* [February 2002]: 74–81).

4. Well, George is initially disturbed by his wife's lingering in the tub because this is the beginning of his "end," so to speak.

5. "Now Moses was tending the flock of Jethro his father-in-law, the priest of Midian, and he led the flock to the far side of the desert and came to Horeb, the mountain of God. There the angel of the LORD appeared to him in flames of fire from within a bush. Moses saw that though the bush was on fire it did not burn up. So Moses thought, 'I will go over and see this strange sight—why the bush does not burn up.' When the LORD saw that he had gone over to look, God called to him from within the bush, 'Moses! Moses!' And Moses said, 'Here I am.' 'Do not come any closer,' God said. 'Take off your sandals, for the place where you are standing is holy ground.' Then he said, 'I am the God of your father, the God of Abraham, the God of Isaac and the God of Jacob.' At this, Moses hid his face, because he was afraid to look at God. The LORD said, 'I have indeed seen the misery of my people in Egypt. I have heard them crying out because of their slave drivers, and I am concerned about their suffering. So I have come down to rescue them from the hand of the Egyptians and to bring them up out of that land into a good and spacious land, a land flowing with milk and honey—the home of the Canaanites, Hittites, Amorites, Perizzites, Hivites and Jebusites. And now the cry of the Israelites has reached me, and I have seen the way the Egyptians are oppressing them. So now, go. I am sending you to Pharaoh to bring my people the Israelites out of Egypt'" (Exodus 3: 1–10).

6. Charles Taylor, "Exile in *Pleasantville,*" *Salon* [online magazine], 23 October 1998 (cited 8 December 2000); available from <http://www.salonmag.com/ent/movies/reviews/1998/10/23reviewsb.html>.

7. Diego Rivera was a Mexican artist and devout Marxist and was noted for making ordinary people—peasants and laborers—the heroes of his art. The "Man at the Crossroads" mural was commissioned in 1934 by Nelson Rockefeller for Rockefeller Center in New York City. Its subject was intended to be "human intelligence in control of the forces of nature." The massive mural (sixty-three feet by seventeen feet), unbeknownst to Rockefeller, featured a picture of Lenin. When Rockefeller asked Diego to replace the image of Lenin with another face, the artist refused. Charged with willful propaganda, Diego declared defiantly, "All art is propaganda." Rockefeller paid Diego $14,000 for his work and then had the mural destroyed.

8. In his preface to *The Picture of Dorian Gray,* Oscar Wilde provocatively declared, "It is the spectator, and not life that art really imitates."

9. Irving Singer, *Reality Transformed* (Chicago: U of Chicago P, 1999), 28.

WORKS CITED

The Dave Brubeck Quartet. *Time Out.* Compact disk 40585. Columbia Records, 1959.

Jowett, B., trans. *The Dialogues of Plato.* Vol. 2. 4th ed. Oxford: Clarendon Press, 1953.

Kubey, Robert, and Mihaly Csikszentmihaly. "Television Addiction Is No Mere Metaphor." *Scientific American* (February 2002): 74–81.

McIllwraith, Robert D. "'I, Addicted to Television': The Personality, Imagination, and TV Watching Patterns of Self-Identified TV Addicts." *Journal of Broadcasting and Electronic Media* 42.3 (summer 1998): 371–87.

Pleasantville. Written and directed by Gary Ross. Videocassette. 122 min. New Line Studies, 1998.

Singer, Irving. *Reality Transformed: Film As Meaning and Technique.* Cambridge: MIT Press, 1998.

Taylor, Charles. "Exile in Pleasantville." *Salon* [online magazine] 23 October 1998 (cited 8 December 2000); available from <http://www.salonmag.com/ent/movies/reviews/1998/10/23reviewsb.html>.

"Where Can I Get a Camera?"

Documentary Film, Visual Literacy, and the Teaching of Writing

DALE JACOBS

The last time I was at my parents' house, I came across a faded color photograph of me, aged four or five, sitting in front of the television set. I am seated on a tiny wooden chair, clad in overalls and red running shoes, feet pressed firmly to the floor, palms flush against my thighs. I am rapt, completely engrossed in what must be *Sesame Street,* a program that I failed to miss for my first conscious years of childhood. Like many others of my generation, I learned my alphabet and numbers, plus some elementary reading and counting, those mornings in front of my parents' television set. That is, I began to enter the worlds of literacy and numeracy through the content of the show. However, my entry into the literate world through *Sesame Street* was not restricted to its content, the words and numbers that are usually associated with the teaching mission of the program. Rather, the form of those lessons had as much impact on me (and, I suspect, most children) as did the content. When I watched, I learned not only that the letter "A" was the first letter in "apple," "ant," and "airplane," but also how to connect the images and words that flashed across the screen, how to read and create meaning from the visual information presented to me.

Unlike alphabet books, with their static images and physical presence, the word lessons on the television were fleeting, seemingly disconnected, requiring a very different set of skills to interpret. As a child of four, I was learning to make sense of the transitions between images that television editing provided; I quickly understood that a series of quick cuts from apple to ant to airplane implied that these items were related and that the centrally framed capital letter "A" was the common denominator. Of course, I could not tell you how I knew to create those meanings and associations, no more than I could tell you why "B" followed "A." I was moving towards more and more literate behaviors, but did not achieve any kind of self-reflectiveness about these processes until much later. However, through these simple acts of making meaning in a variety of contexts, I was becoming literate.

This story of the dual processes of learning to make meaning through written and visual cues is not unique; I was no prodigy in my abilities to read either of these kinds of texts. In fact, I think that I am fairly typical of those who grew up since the early 1960s in both my ability to move between different kinds of literate practices and in the learned blurring of those practices. The unfortunate situation is that what I learned in front of that television set on those countless mornings—the rudiments of visual literacy, or how to read and make meaning from moving visual images—is often discounted or devalued within the school environment. However, as Kathleen Welch argues in *Electric Rhetoric,* "Television is so heavily implicated in children's acquisition of language that they require school training in how to be effective decoders of television. Adults as well need training in the grammar, vocabulary, and ideology of this pervasive symbol system" (134). If we take the pervasiveness of television—part of what Welch terms "electric rhetoric"—seriously, then we need to consider how to help students be critical and self-reflective as they read *both* the texts and the images that surround them. In other words, we need to reconsider such visual literacy as one among many literate practices in which all of us, including students, engage in our daily lives. It is through the exercise of these various kinds of literacy that we make and re-make our sense of the world; in doing so, we construct and are constructed by the world and the ways that we are multiply situated within our cultures.

But what exactly do I mean by literacy, a term that has traditionally been linked with print culture. Here it will be useful to begin with Welch's definition of literacy:

> [literacy] constitutes an intersubjective activity in encoding and
> decoding screen and alphabetic texts within specific cultural practices
> and recognizes the inevitable deployment of power and the control
> that larger entities have over these media. Literacy in this sense resists
> widespread devotion to individualism and recognizes how individu-

alism operates to maintain a particular Enlightenment ideology; collaboration then becomes primary. (135)

Literacy thus involves not only encoding and decoding screen and print texts (both of which may use visual and alphabetic sign systems, often in various combinations)[1]—what might be called functional literacy—but also thinking critically about the ways in which such texts situate us and the ways in which we can situate ourselves in these texts. Such a conception of literacy relies heavily on the concept of articulation—making knowledge—both in terms of reading and writing. Articulation occurs not just in terms of subject, but also in terms of form; form and content cannot thus be separated in this conception of literacy as one always affects the other. This idea of literacy can also be seen to be aligned with a Sophistic conception of rhetoric in which knowledge is seen as contingent, contextual, partial, and socially constructed through language and, I will argue, through the visual. Literacy and rhetoric are thus wrapped together as active ways of engaging with the world through language and image in "a kind of consciousness partly conditioned by technology but not fully determined by it [which] requires attending to these screens that are as graphic as they are verbal" (Welch 195). Rhetoric and literacy involve the ways in which we create meaning—which is always provisional, contextual, and negotiated socially through language and image—in the world, as well as the ways in which we communicate those meanings to an audience, itself a negotiation of meaning. Reading and writing are not simply technical matters of decoding and encoding, then, but are implicated in the ways in which we live our lives. Such is the case not only in reading a novel or writing a letter, but also in watching a film or taking a photograph; all imply various kinds of literacy, various ways of reading the world, all of which are important within the lives of human beings. Paulo Freire expands on this idea of the relationship between literacy and living in *Literacy: Reading the Word and the World*:

> Reading the world always precedes reading the word, and reading the word implies continually reading the world. As I suggested earlier, this movement from the word to the world is always present; even the spoken word flows from our reading of the world. In a way, however, we can go further and say that reading the word is not preceded merely by reading the world, but by a certain form of *writing*

it or *rewriting* it, that is, of transforming it by means of conscious, practical work. For me, this dynamic movement is central to the literacy process. (35)

This quotation applies equally well to the visual and its relationship to the world. That is, we read the world before we read the image and our reading of images is done within the context of our continual reading of the world. We do not engage in any literate practice in a vacuum, detached from the way we live in the world or from the way we engage in other literate practices. We write and are written by the world and this relationship is continually enacted in both alphabetic and visual literacies. Literacy, then, is much more than a tool for communication, but instead must be seen as one of the primary ways that we exist in and make sense of the world.

Literate practices, then, are a way of creating meaning from varied and multiple contexts and our relations to them, of becoming, as Deborah Brandt argues, involved in our worlds. In *Literacy As Involvement: The Acts of Writers, Readers, and Texts,* Brandt writes that

> literacy learning requires intensifying—not subordinating—reliance on social involvement as a basis of interpretation in reading and writing. It requires heightening of understanding of how human beings create reality together.... Writing and reading are pure acts of human involvement.... Learning to read requires learning to maintain—in fact, intensify—reliance on social context even under new and precarious circumstances. Literacy failures are not failures of separation but rather failures of involvement. They arise not from an overdependence on context but from the lack of access to a viable context.... (6–7)

In this passage, Brandt is referring to reading and writing, but it seems to me that her comments apply equally well to visual literacies, for, as Welch writes, "[t]he polis of our time exists on the screens of television and computers" (195). In other words, rhetorical engagement with the world through the practice of literacy must involve not only the verbal, but the visual as well. Through an involvement in the social contexts of visual literacy we can intervene in our situations, acting on the world as it in turn acts upon us. As I sat in front of the television, for example, I was immersed in the shared context created by the television, one which included talk with my parents and with my friends about what appeared on the screen.

I was making meaning—learning to read the world—based not only on my cognitive interaction with the information of the screen, but based also on the community of discourse created by the show and its multiple kinds of literacy. Through our talk, we engaged in a shared discourse, both about the subject matter of the show and also about the ways in which that subject matter was conveyed; meaning was formed collaboratively through dialogue in a common language created through both verbal and visual means on the screen. What I want to argue, then, is that if we pay attention to students' visual literacies, the ways in which they make sense of visual texts such as films, television, music videos, and so on, we can help them to move towards using that knowledge of visual rhetoric to make meaning and intervene in their worlds.

I have come to believe that we can use this kind of literacy as a point of contact with students and a bridge between visual and written rhetoric/discourse. Such a "contact zone" is, as Joseph Harris re-visions it, "something more like a process or event than a physical space—and thus it needs to be theorized . . . as a local and shifting series of interactions among perspectives and individuals" (122). This "series of interactions among perspectives and individuals" forms the core of the courses I teach, a process which begins where students are and progresses through a multi-sided dialogue towards an increasingly self-reflective use and awareness of discourse. In a 1997 article entitled "Beginning Where They Are: A Re-vision of Critical Pedagogy," I described my teaching as an attempt to help students "to think about their locations in the cultures and discourses in which they reside" and "to recognize and negotiate their own uses of language and the uses of language around them within specific contexts" (43). When I wrote that piece, I was thinking mainly about reading and writing, or what we think of as traditional literacy, especially within the composition classrooms. As I thought more about literacy as plural and contextual, however, I began to see the need to spread the net wider, embracing visual literacies and their connections to reading and writing.

In the months before that article appeared in *Composition Studies,* I was planning a summer course in intermediate composition, a class for sophomores and juniors, at the University of Nebraska. In revising that essay, I was thinking a lot about what it means to begin with students' knowledge as a starting point and to work from there. In my courses students were already choosing their own topics and genres, getting feedback from peers in writing groups and from me in conference, and exploring alternatives through the process of revision. By having students begin with familiar subjects, I hoped we could move towards an examination of how our languages and identities are socially constructed, while simultaneously using that knowledge to make critical strides towards writing those worlds. As I planned, I realized that my emphasis on traditional written literacies did not go far enough, that many students instead read the world through visual, in addition to written means. To live in today's world is to engage not only with print, but with the visual as well. To quote Welch once more, for intellectuals to not acknowledge or to disdain "video texts as untouchable means that we have lost contact with our students and our public. It means we have become the priests of Dead Culture, an Arnoldian world that replicates much of the worst that has been thought and said and that can offer up, as a feeble justification, only the bromide that it has always been this way" (109).

In order to enact my emerging theories, then, it seemed to me that I needed to expand my definition of literacy into a concept that was plural, encompassing the multiple literate practices in which all of us are engaged every day. But what would this expanded theoretical definition mean for my classroom practice? How could I combine a theory of visual literacy with a pedagogical practice? What would happen if I brought visual literacy into the classroom, initially through discussions of how we read visual texts, but then by pushing towards student creation of their own visual texts?

This idea evolved into an assignment that I have come to call the mock documentary. In using the term mock documentary, I do not refer to fictional parodies of the documentary film, such as *This Is Spinal Tap* or *Fear of a Black Hat,* nor do I use this term to denigrate the efforts of the students by implying that their efforts are somehow inauthentic. Rather, I derive the term from the usage of mock, or "mock-up," in the production or process of making a film or magazine. Thus, I use the term mock documentary to imply process within the development of the projects. While the final product is important (some of them are fascinating, as will be seen in the following pages), I also want to emphasize the collaborative process through which meaning is created and the provisionality of those meanings. In other words, I see this exercise as rhetorical, emphasizing both the creation of meaning and the communication of that meaning. By emphasizing process, this assignment acts as a bridge between visual and written literacies, helping students to see that they are continually reading the world and creating meaning from their social involvement in the world.

The mock documentary, then, is a collaborative undertaking in which several students decide on a topic, research it, and make a presentation to the class. I realize that such a description doesn't sound very new or innovative; many readers are probably asking how this is any different from a standard group research project. The difference, I think, lies in the way that I try to tie such a project into the visual rhetoric of documentary film. I usually introduce the idea of visual rhetoric by showing clips of a number of documentaries such as *Roger and Me, Hoop Dreams, Troublesome Creek, Baseball,* and *A Brief History of Time.* These films offer an assortment of compositional styles, editing techniques, uses of lighting, narrative/informational structures, and subject matters. As such, they represent a range of ways to think about visual texts and the ways in which they can be composed; they offer a variety of ways to see how "a director writes in film" (Bazin 39). In addition, these films, in the tradition of the feature-length documentary film, are both connected to and outside of students' experiences with documentaries, which usually include television biographies, nature shows, and news pieces. In showing clips from films such as these, we can begin with a shared sense of visual texts, but also move beyond them into different uses than students have previously known.

After I have shown these clips, we talk about the meanings that we constructed from them and the ways in which these visual texts act as points of mediation between filmmaker and film viewer. In other words, we talk not only about how we read these films, but also about how these films have been "written," visually encoded by the filmmakers; the film as an artifact is both the medium of communication and the medium of meaning-making. In these discussions, students demonstrate a visual literacy which is usually devalued within their classroom experiences. They do so not only through their ability to read these texts, but in their ability to examine how filmmakers have attempted to create meaning through visuals. I am not saying that all students are immediately able to critique documentary films and perform sophisticated analyses of them, but rather that students have an implicit knowledge of the grammar of film that can be tapped into through dialogue.[2] For example, students understand how to read a freeze frame within a moving picture, knowing from a lifetime of watching film and television that they are meant to linger on that static image, to contemplate its relation to the moving images that surround it. Through dialogue, however, they see that these relationships differ between viewers and that meanings are created through social interaction, including the interaction between filmmaker and film viewer as mediated by the film itself.

An example will help to illustrate this point. From Ken Burns's *Baseball,* I often show the first ten minutes of "The Third Inning (1910–1920): The Faith of Fifty Million People." The first part of this section of the film is comprised of a series of still images from the period, accompanied by an instrumental version of "The Star Spangled Banner." As a class, we discuss the cumulative effect that these images have and the relationship between the music and the visuals. Some students focus on the order of the images and how they are related to each other, while others focus on the composition of individual shots. Various readings of this section of the film are offered and, through the discussion, we see how different people go about constructing meanings from visual cues. We come to see that not only are our readings influenced by the talk in the classroom, but they are conditioned by our individual histories, including our past experiences with visual literacy. The next section of the film introduces more elements so that our discussion encompasses still images, moving images, voice-over narration, music, and interviews. Having started with a small number of elements, we gain practice in thinking about our visual thinking and in being self-reflective about our processes so that students are able to deal with the increasing complexity demanded by this section of the film. Through dialogue, students can thus move towards a more critical understanding of how the filmmaker uses various aspects of the language of film to create meaning and how their readings of the film are created within a social context that includes the film as a device of mediated communication. In other words, by focusing on visual literacy, I hope to move from implicit ways of reading towards a kind of critical literacy. More than that, however, I hope to help students move from merely reading the world through the visual towards writing it as well.

Here is where the mock documentary project and its differences from other forms of collaborative research projects come into play. After students have chosen topics and researched their projects in multiple ways, they are asked to present their material—to make meaning out of it—in ways that mimic the rhetorical strategies of documentary films. In other words, students move from creating meaning through reading visual texts to creating meaning through writing visual texts; the emphasis is thus on articulation and on active involvement in the creation of shared meaning that is not absolute, but is partial and contextual. Just as topics and research methods are negotiated collaboratively within the group, so too are the methods of presentation, the visual rhetorics that students use to create meaning. I ask students to think about the strategies that documentary filmmakers use to make meaning from their material and then to communicate those meanings, which will be negotiated with the viewers as they watch the film. Of course, the ways in which they choose to present their material will also affect the kinds of research they do and the ways they conceive of their material; the process is recursive, just as the process of writing is recursive. Past presentations have ranged from the familiar oral reports, to poster boards, collages, skits, demonstrations, photographs, overhead transparencies, maps, and—in a large number of cases—video footage that comprises part or all of the presentation. Any presentation method is acceptable and I encourage students to explore all of these options as possibilities in order to see how different rhetorical media allow them to construct meanings for their topics. One of the interesting results is a kind of hybridization, a blurring of the media as students try on a number of different options. The assignment encourages such transgression because it emphasizes process and the provisionality of meaning. Allow me to describe a few of these projects and attempt to unpack some of the ways in which this assignment creates an important contact zone between the literacies expected of students in the university and students' other literacies, which are often devalued within the university.

I first introduced the mock documentary in an intermediate composition class at the University of Nebraska at Lincoln. There were thirteen students in that class who, after some initial thinking and exploration of topics, divided themselves into five groups according to shared interests. The small number of students allowed us to have smaller groups, including pairs; logistically, groups of this size would be impossible in a larger class. Without going into great detail about the logistics of collaborative groups, let me just say that groups of this size have distinct advantages and disadvantages. On one hand, it is much easier to coordinate the schedules and ideas of two people and so the collaborative experience is often more intense. On the other hand, fewer people also means fewer perspectives and fewer contributors to the dialogue and creative energy of the group. That summer, I think that the two most interesting projects came from the two pairs—their processes were intensely collaborative and their presentations were fascinating examples of visual rhetoric—but whether this was a result of the smaller groups or of the particular participants, I cannot say. As you will see, this same kind of intense collaboration and innovative use of visual rhetoric also occurred in larger classes and with groups of four and five. The underlying factor, it seems to me, is not group size, but rather a commitment to dialogue and a willingness to experiment with and reflect on the process of making meaning through visual rhetoric.

While a couple of groups that summer did venture out with video camera in hand, one of the most interesting projects did not involve videotape, but was instead a hybridization of other forms of visual rhetoric. The two young men who undertook that project shared a mutual interest in the military and in military history; early on, they decided that they were interested in doing their research into Wounded Knee. Both successful juniors, these students took advantage of the library holdings, as well as material at the Nebraska Historical Society and the Nebraska State Archives. In creating meaning from their research, however, these students were faced with using a different medium than the academic writing they had previously been rewarded for using. In other words, they knew how to research the material and synthesize it into a thesis statement with supporting evidence; they already knew how to create meaning in a way that is valued by teachers. The mock documentary project, however, asked them to utilize a different kind of literacy and to create meaning in a new way. It was in seeing Ken Burns's *Baseball* that they found their form, a kind of documentary that they could mimic in class without any need for videotape. Burns utilizes archival photographs, interviews, voice-over narration, and music to create documentaries that weave meaning together from a number of different textual fabrics. That is, Burns's work is itself a hybrid of film styles, drawing as it does upon a variety of strategies in the making and communicating of meaning, strategies that could be adapted to their project on Wounded Knee.

The visual portion of their presentation involved a series of still photographs and maps projected onto the wall, carefully arranged with accompanying voices and music. As we saw a map of the battle site projected on
the wall, we heard one of them reading a transcript of one of the army survivors describing their movement towards the site of Wounded Knee. As
we saw a picture of a family of Native Americans, we heard the other reading a transcript of one of the Native American survivors. In both cases, they
used source quotations read without outside comment; the participants'
words were allowed to speak for themselves. Between these uses of archival
material, there was enough narration of the events at Wounded Knee for
the audience to make sense of what had happened. Throughout, Native and
military music intermingled in the background. In the presentation, then,
three major elements came together to create and communicate meaning—
visuals, speech, and music. They made choices about which photographs
and maps to use, in what order they should be projected, for what period of
time each should be on the screen, what balance to have between source quotation and narration, when to use Native music and when to use military
music, and what the relationship should be between all of these visual, oral,
and musical elements. The presentation ended in silence, a solemn backdrop
to the list projected onto the screen of all the Native Americans who lost
their lives that day. This ending was also a choice that the pair made as they
used the rhetoric of silence to create and communicate solemnity and intro-
spection. In this project, these two students bridged the gap between different literacies, creating complex meanings that went beyond a simple thesis
statement and supporting evidence and moved them into a more critical, yet
provisional creation of meaning.

The second pair of students that summer chose to make a documentary film about weightlifting and the culture of the gym. Both of these students were scholarship athletes at Nebraska and this project connected to
the worlds they inhabited outside the classroom. Like the pair described
above, these students combined visuals with oral discourse and music to
bring the culture of the gym into the classroom. Unlike the pair described
above, they used videotape exclusively in the creation of their project,
experimenting with an entirely new form and its uses in the generation
and presentation of their existing and emergent knowledge. Throughout
the film, they intercut interviews with weightlifters about the sport and

their reasons for lifting with shots taken in gyms of workouts in progress. During these action sequences, the sound of voices is replaced by a high energy, non-diegetic soundtrack of contemporary music, which is effective in creating/conveying the atmosphere of the gym. In the course of the entire film, there is no narration or comment from the filmmakers. Instead we, the audience, are immersed in this culture by the interviews that are conducted through our agents, the filmmakers, but also by the combination of visuals and music used to evoke the setting of this culture. In talking to the two of them, it became apparent that this approach to their subject was a conscious choice and represented for them a commitment to the worth of this activity; they felt that the audience could best understand weightlifters' motivations through the lifters' own words, rather than through the presumed authority of a narrator's voice. In making this rhetorical choice, they were also making decisions about how they would think about and present their material in much the same ways that writers make rhetorical choices. Though they made different choices about how to combine the visual and the verbal than the previous pair, these students were also exercising their visual literacies in ways that were connected to the literacies demanded in school. In both form and content, this pair began with their own knowledge and linked their external lives with the demands of the classroom. By making rhetorical choices and thinking about those choices, these students invested the assignment with consequences both inside and outside the classroom.

Of course, not every group that summer was able or committed to producing projects of the caliber I have just described. However, a brief look at one of these groups will allow me to further analyze the mock documentary assignment. The first group was comprised of three young men who were all interested in the National Basketball Association. From this shared interest, they decided that they wanted to focus their project on the history of the NBA, including a look at the top teams and players, as well as its changing business environment. Their research went smoothly in that they were able to find all the information that they needed. However, their presentation involved little more than simple oral recitation of that information interspersed with long clips of a pre-existing video history of the NBA. To make things worse, it was nearly impossible to see the relationship between the words they spoke and the images that they showed. As I thought about that group after the class ended, I realized that I had failed to help them see the purpose behind the mock documentary exercise. Rather than using their multiple literacies to think through their topic in a variety of ways and to then synthesize these different ways of reading and writing into a presentation, this group tried to adapt the mock documentary to research and presentation methods that were already familiar to them from years of schooling. In doing so, they approached literacy as a functional skill that involved finding information and then transmitting it in an almost completely unaltered form. In previous school situations, they had been rewarded for displaying these skills and, in my interactions with them, I failed to help them understand what the mock documentary project was instead asking of them. Such misunderstanding accounts, I think, for the disjunction between the oral and video portions of their presentation; no attempt was made to merge their own ideas with or to comment on the prepackaged video that they showed. The mock documentary project was not successful for this group because it failed to help them think in a variety of ways about their topic or to help them see the links between their various literacies. Not only did this group learn little about visual literacies, I would say that they learned little new about research or writing. In their case, the mock documentary had simply become another piece of busy work.[3]

The next time I used the mock documentary was in an introductory composition class at East Carolina University. The projects again were of the students' own choosing, ranging from a mixed media presentation on services for students with disabilities at ECU to a look at hurricanes and how they affect eastern North Carolina. These projects combined several different ways of thinking about and presenting the material, including poster boards, classroom demonstration, speeches, and use of videotape. The group that chose to work on services for students with disabilities handed out cards with the Braille alphabet, did a demonstration of signing, played a videotape which introduced the equipment available at ECU for students with disabilities and explained how it is used, and explicated a poster board which detailed local services. The group whose project was on severe weather combined a videotape of a staged emergency weather broadcast with overheads, posters, and oral explanation. These various methods allowed the two groups to conceptualize and present their ideas in a variety of ways. Without doubt, these diverse presentation methods were beneficial in more effectively conveying the groups' ideas to the audience because people take in information in different ways and are less likely to lose interest in the presentation when a variety of media are used. These in themselves are valuable lessons to learn about communication, but beyond that, these students also learned that the knowledge they created (and then communicated) changed depending on the medium that was used. Creation and communication of meaning are thus fused in the mock documentary assignment.

Another group of first-year students created a documentary about a local landmark known as Acid Park, a huge sculpture garden that is covered in reflectors. Teens often go there at night to see their friends and watch the patterns of light and shadow. The group initially wanted to present an informative look at the site, including its history and the reasons for its popularity. They all knew the myth of its creation: a young girl and her boyfriend die in a car wreck on prom night while tripping on acid and so the despondent father erects Acid Park as a tribute to his daughter. However, as they began to do their research, these students discovered that what is known as Acid Park is simply the sculpture garden of a well-known folk artist named Wallace Simpson. Their project, a twenty-minute filmed documentary entitled *The Truth About Acid Park,* included interviews with visitors to the site, footage of the sculptures in daylight and at night, and an extensive interview with the usually private sculptor. One of the interviews was with a folk art dealer who described Simpson's importance as an artist; between that interview and Simpson's description of his work, it became clear that what they thought they knew about Acid Park was inaccurate. In very tangible ways, then, the mock documentary assignment helped these students to create new knowledge and think differently about something they thought they already knew, thus creating negotiated and contextual knowledge. In communicating that knowledge through their documentary, they helped to contextualize various versions of Acid Park's history for the rest of the class; as their film demonstrates, the legends remain part of the "truth" about Acid Park, but also show the ways in which truths are multiple, partial, contingent, and constantly negotiated. But the impact of their documentary went beyond the class: the folklorists in the department were so impressed that the film is now shown regularly in upper-level folklore courses as a way to begin to talk about multiple ways of looking at the world. *The Truth About Acid Park* has significance beyond the class in which it was created and demonstrates that assignments can connect to the lived experiences of students and to the world outside of the classroom.

Let me end this essay by describing two projects from my first year at East Carolina University. The first of these projects was undertaken in the fall of 1997 by a group of four young women who decided almost immediately that they wanted to do their project on Princess Diana, who had died only days before. Diana was everywhere in the popular media at the time, but I admit that I was at first leery of this idea because I didn't really see what Princess Diana had to do with them and their lives. It seemed to me that they would have a hard time connecting to the subject and creating any new knowledge for themselves or anyone else about Diana and her life. After all, there had been endless coverage of her death and countless retrospectives about her life. What else was there to say about her? In looking back, however, I can see that I was wrong and that I needed to trust those students. I could see from the beginning that their interest in her was tangible, but it was not until after seeing their presentation that I realized how her story connected in important ways to these women. What they came up with was a twenty-minute documentary film that utilized a similar style to the presentation on Wounded Knee that I described earlier. The four of them managed to gain access to a scanner and slideshow computer program. They scanned hundreds of photos of Diana and then used Photoshop to create a slideshow, complete with editing effects such as dissolves. Using their research into her life, they wrote a biography for their script. They then used a video camera to film the slideshow while one of the group members read the script and Elton John's "Candle in the Wind" played in the background. From a lifetime of watching movies and television, they instinctively knew that editing was important and that transitions between images could be used to create meanings and emphasize relationships; through our explicit discussions in class and through viewing other visual texts with a critical eye, they were able to make conscious choices in the creation of their own visual text. They also knew that through the arrangement of words, images, and music, they could create a complex picture as all of the elements commented on one another. In other words, they came to the class with an implicit visual literacy and the mock documentary project forced them to reflect on these nascent ideas.

Through the arrangement of photos and accompanying text these four students created a picture of a woman trapped by societal expectations of her, a woman constructed in ways that were ultimately damaging to her. The meaning that arose for these four women as they researched and composed their project involved the ways in which a woman's identity and self-image are circumscribed by the society in which she lives. In Diana's case, this social construction of identity was compounded by her very public position, but nonetheless, through the project, these women began to think about the expectations their cultures placed on each of them. Throughout the film, there was a definite focus on body image and eating disorders and an implicit argument that it would have been nearly impossible for Diana to avoid such problems. I am not saying that all or any of these women were dealing with eating disorders, but through this project each of them came to think in more critical ways about the relationship between self/body image and the larger culture. I was wrong in my initial assumption that this topic was not relevant to their lives; their film showed me that they could create and communicate important knowledge about Princess Diana. Visual rhetoric allowed these students to write through their own worlds and through the creation of shared meaning about a woman who is both removed and not removed from them, about a problem that directly concerns them and the worlds they inhabit. Such meaning must be seen as partial, provisional, contextual, and negotiated, as are all meanings, created through a specific articulation, an active attempt to situate themselves within the world. By engaging in such articulation *and* being self-reflective and critical about the process, students can thus learn to more actively engage in their worlds.

Finally, let me describe a group of young men who were far from engaged with the class for the better part of the semester, who actively resisted writing as a means of creating meaning in their lives. All three were student athletes, highly recruited for their ability to play basketball or football. Throughout the semester, however, each of them expressed frustration at the expectations and limitations placed on them as student athletes, at the lack of choices they now had about their own lives, at the ways they felt they were exploited by the school because of their athletic talents. Throughout the semester I encouraged them to try to write about their experiences, to name their situations as a way to start rewriting their worlds. I hoped that in writing they might recapture some of the agency they felt had been stripped from them by the school. All three resisted, likely seeing me and the course as simply another part of the oppressive structures that surrounded them. When the mock documentary project came up, however, the three of them asked if they could make a video about the life of a student athlete. They wanted to show the rest of the students what it was like to be a student athlete, to talk back to the voices that say they are on an easy ride through college. In other words, each of them saw writing as a kind of busy work, another academic requirement with little correspondence to their own lives, but they saw the mock documentary as a way to reach their classmates, to persuade them through visual rhetoric. This project had consequence in the world and was thus valuable to them. And it was not an academic writing project, involving literacies which they did not value and with which they were not comfortable, but a project that involved visual literacy, a way to make meaning which all three felt was possible. What resulted was a film that combined interviews with athletes, coaches, and teachers with footage of practices and study hall. That film made sense of being a student athlete for them in ways not accessible through their writing. Through this project, they were able to begin to claim agency in a world in which they felt used, thus moving from simply reading their situations, to intervening in them through the visual equivalent of writing. Through the mock documentary project, these students, along with the others I have described and many whom space has forced me to omit, moved towards a kind of critical literacy, making sense of their multiple places in the world through visual literacy.

A photograph. Me, aged four or five, sitting in front of a television set watching *Sesame Street*. In this picture, I am immersed in words and images, enveloped by a culture of multiple literacies in which I learn to make sense of the world. I, like the students I teach, am a product of and am engaged in the process of the many kinds of literacy that this photograph suggests. My immersion in these literate worlds sustains me and enables me to understand and have agency in the world around me; it also helps me to connect and move between various kinds and communities of literacies. I hope that through the experience of my classroom, students will be able to say the same thing.

NOTES

1. For more on this idea, see Scott McLoud's *Understanding Comics.*

2. For more on the grammar of film, see Bazin's *What is Cinema?,* especially the essay "The Evolution of the Language of Cinema," as well as Welch's *Electric Rhetoric.*

3. Students are asked to write reflectively about their experiences and learning in the mock documentary project and to explain the choices that they made in terms of both form and content. Such reflective writing forms part of their grade; in effect, such writing helps me see into the process of creating meaning so that I can determine level of engagement, critical thinking, and self-reflection. They are also graded on the effectiveness of their presentation in terms of thinking about audience, purpose, and context. While I emphasize the creation of meaning, I also pay attention to communication.

WORKS CITED

Baseball. Dir. Ken Burns. Florentine Films, 1994.

Bazin, Andre. *What Is Cinema?* Vol. 1. Trans. Hugh Gray. Berkeley: U of California P, 1967.

Brandt, Deborah. *Literacy As Involvement: The Acts of Writers, Readers, and Texts.* Carbondale: Southern Illinois UP, 1990.

A Brief History of Time. Dir. Errol Morris. Channel Four Films, 1992.

Fear of a Black Hat. Dir. Rusty Cundieff. Incorporated Television Company, 1993.

Freire, Paulo, and Donaldo Macedo. *Literacy: Reading the Word and the World.* South Hadley, MA: Bergin and Garvey, 1987.

Harris, Joseph. *A Teaching Subject: Composition since 1966.* Upper Saddle River, NJ: Prentice Hall, 1997.

Hoop Dreams. Dir. Steve James. Kartemquin Films, 1994.

Jacobs, Dale. "Beginning Where They Are: A Re-vision of Critical Pedagogy." *Composition Studies* 25.2 (fall 1997): 39–62.

McLoud, Scott. *Understanding Comics.* New York: HarperCollins, 1993.

Roger and Me. Dir. Michael Moore. Warner Brothers, 1989.

Sesame Street. Children's Television Workshop.

This Is Spinal Tap. Dir. Rob Reiner. Criterion Pictures, 1983.

Troublesome Creek. Dir. Steven Ascher and Jeanne Jordan. West City Films, 1995.

Welch, Kathleen. *Electric Rhetoric.* Cambridge: MIT Press, 1999.

My Tribe outside the Global Village

RAI PETERSON

I f you are nearing middle age, you probably remember the early days of televised instruction. Promptly at 10:00 A.M. two days a week, seven of us (including our teacher) who'd never heard of the Latin Quarter or the Champs Élysées, let alone the Tuileries, and seemed hopelessly land-locked by the seas of waving grain in central Iowa, tuned in to "educational TV" for French language classes. Minutes after our teacher adjusted the antenna and volume on the Setchell-Carlson set in the corner of the class-room, it crackled to life, and a prim woman in an unadorned studio melo-diously inquired, "Bonjour, élèves. Quelle heure est'il?"

We would respond in unison to the indifferent picture tube, our flat Iowa accents as close to Anglo-Saxon as was still spoken anywhere, "Bone jore Madam. Ill ay dicks airs."

"Très bien, étudiants," she would enthusiastically reply, although we were more than our physical three thousand miles from eating snails and quaffing champagne along the Seine.

Since 1873 when Scottish scientist James Clerk Maxwell hypothesized about electromagnetic waves capable of broadcasting sound and pictures to multiple receivers, humankind has dreamed that television would live up to its tremendous potential as an educational medium. Sometimes I think the tragedy of being human is that we can yearn for and aspire to a level of perfection that our limited ability cannot match. My associations with televised instruction convince me that: 1) we can make televised instruction better, and 2) we can never make it as good as we want it to be. Televised courses have great, but limited, potential—even in this age of two-way audio and video connections and bit-stream technology.

A lot of people around the state of Indiana sort of know me. Some of them think I am enormously tall. Others see that my hair is entirely turned gray or silver; more believe it is brown. Quite a few think I have brown or black eyes; not many know they are very pale blue. Almost no one realizes that I walk with assistance. A good number think I should always dress in black because I look best in that color in my surroundings. Every last one of them, I feel certain, has scrutinized the cowlicks in my hair, my prominent overbite, and my formidable nose. Not one of them has ever glimpsed my shoes.

For each of the past nine years, I have taught a composition course in writing about literature in the distance education program at Ball State University. The class is the second in our required composition sequence, and the master syllabus mandates the teaching of literature as part of it. As happens when one aims at two birds with a single stone, one fowl is struck squarely and the other suffers an oblique hit. In my class, the literature is prevalent, but students also must write a research paper, and for that, they choose their own subjects (usually current events revolving around the legalization of drugs, control of guns, protection of animals, and fear of cloning). I choose to teach about poetry because it is easily made episodic to fit our fifty-minute program length, the students tend to know less about it than any other genre (which is a great leveler when students range in age from 16 to 70), and I know more about it (and who wouldn't teach to her strengths in a televised class?). Generally, I assign 5–8 poems to be read for each class meeting, then let the students choose which one or two we will discuss in detail during class. In all, students write four short reaction papers about selected poems, usually incorporating the critical skills and language we have used in class. We use two poetry anthologies: a standard loaded with "chestnuts," and a very contemporary collection; many of our readings are available online and linked to the course Web site, which enables earnest lurkers to prepare for class as well.

The course is delivered on video monitors in real time, via satellite, to students at designated sites with one-way video and a cumbersome two-way audio connection. It is also transmitted to, essentially, correspondence students who register with the university and receive broadcasts via local television stations at home in real time and asynchronous, tape-delay, transmissions; those students cannot communicate directly with the studio during class time. There are also half a dozen or so live, real-time, on-campus students in the studio from which the course emanates, who are enrolled in the class, and they do, of course, have full view of class proceedings (including the instructor's footwear) and participate at will as most college students do. Additionally, hundreds, possibly thousands, of casual viewers who are not registered at least occasionally watch the class on cable stations in towns around the state where it is aired at various hours of the day or middle of the night.

You might think it would be weirdly anonymous to teach a broadcast class, where most of the "participants" give little or no sign of their presence all semester. Instead of the nods, raised eyebrows, sighs of boredom, wrinkled foreheads, smiles, chuckles, buried faces, and snores that most of us teachers have learned to decipher expertly, I must assume the agreement, understanding, amusement, even the attendance, of many of my students as a leap of faith. Years of producing "Must See TV" on the subjects of iambic pentameter, sentence fragments, introductions and conclusions, traditional sonnet schemes, and MLA documentation formats has convinced me, however, that there is indeed an audience for *everything*. Moreover, I have learned that there are few truly anonymous or invisible students, and most are quite tenacious about making themselves known.

On the very first day that I taught a televised course, I arrived at the studio expecting twenty-five fellow participants to help populate the room (which seats eighty) and carry the class discussion. Instead, I discovered that the university computer had kicked out the televised course during registration because of its unorthodox section number. As a result, I was literally locked in a large, very brightly (and hotly) lit room with one inarticulate student who had petitioned back into the university after academic dismissal. "Paris" (not his real name) said he had made the calculated mistake of telling his parents during a family vacation in Hawaii that he'd flunked out of college. They left him in the Aloha State, and he spent three years living on the beaches, selling Tai Stick, and apparently consuming much of his product. After tangling with Hawaiian law enforcement, he was repatriated to his parents' basement. They sent him back to the university, where the registrar found enough pulse in him to assign him to the otherwise unpopulated televised section of English composition.

My carefully developed, ninety-minute, summer school lesson plan, written with the help of telecommunications instructional planners, said I would ask "all of the students present" to tell a little something about themselves and their previous composition and literature courses. Somehow, I sustained an hour and one-half of the verbal equivalent of treading water,

occasionally thrown the deflated life buoys of Paris's range of three possible utterances: "Uh uh," "Uh huh," and "I dunno." I was drowning, and
anyone who might save me was safely distanced, watching on TV with
neither means nor responsibility to act heroically.

I later learned that one of our campus fraternities found a practical use
for Paris's linguistic limitations. They partitioned their living room into
three equal sections, and assigned seating for the evening rebroadcast of
the class on the local cable channel. Each team was loyal to one of Paris's
cryptic communicative comments, and each time that signature statement
was uttered, everyone in those chairs was required to chug a beer. I worry
about the brain and liver cells of those assigned to the "I dunno" section.

At the end of my first televised class session with Paris, I staggered
back to my office and drew the shades. Not only my department colleagues,
but much of the whole eager university and Indiana state legislature had
tuned in to witness the launching of the Indiana Higher Education Telecommunications System's educational initiative. If I had been tenured at
the time, I'd have refused to ever darken the doorstep of the campus
"Teleplex" again. When the phone on my desk rang, I answered weakly.
It was a thoughtful and gracious member of the university's board of
trustees, calling to say that, although the situation was less than ideal, she
was certain that I, with my enthusiasm for the subject matter and bound-
less energy, could carry this off with style. I hoped she was clairvoyant.

Then the building custodian entered my darkened office. "Hey, Rai,"
she said with an air of superiority. "I just saw you on television." I allowed
as how I would prefer not to discuss it. "I was just going to say," she continued, "that it's true what they say about you." Hoping she was about to
offer more encouragement, I asked what that was. Without a hint of irony,
she said, "TV does add ten pounds." That was my introduction to working in the public gaze.

Although Paris was the only student in the studio, there were, ostensibly, four other enrollees in that first televised English 104 course. Three
were R.N. completion students who gathered in a hospital conference
room in Fort Wayne on Saturday mornings for continuous satellite
rebroadcasts. Fortified with carryout cuisine and a back-up VCR, they
watched a full week's offerings of summer school classes (seven and one-
half hours in all) for five consecutive weekends. By modern academic stan-

dards, they were martyrs, but it's hard to say who suffered most from our initial attempt at televised distance education. The remaining student was Carol, an Indianapolis resident who commuted into the city each weekday, hoping to participate long-distance via satellite hook-up established at a local technical school's campus. However, technical difficulties thwarted her attempts to engage Paris and me in classroom repartee.

About two and one-half weeks into the five-week course, Carol's audio connection to the studio was tenuously established. I spoke with her frequently by phone from my office during those frustrating weeks when she could see and hear Paris and me but not contribute to the questions he let slide right off his plate. One day Carol volunteered over the phone that she "just loved this distance education thing." Given the problems, I was surprised, and I asked what she liked about it. "Well," she said, "when I walk into class, can't nobody write me off 'mediately as a big, ole black woman with four kids on ADC."

Touched by the trust implicit in that revelation, I replied, "Your secret's safe with me, Sister."

The day Carol's audio connection finally reached out to touch someone, Paris and I were going to read Tim Seibles's poem "For Brothers Everywhere." It is about pick-up basketball games, and written in the fluid rhythms and metaphors of street language. Jeff, an R.N. completion student from Fort Wayne, had been assigned to write an introduction to the poem. I read his remarks, which included reminiscences of playground basketball games and a rundown of the poetry prizes Mr. Seibles had garnered. At the end of Jeff's commentary, he had appended a question. It said, "Although I didn't find this anywhere, I just have a feeling that Tim Seibles is African-American. Am I right about that?" I started to say that we would look at linguistic clues in the text and discuss that point after we'd read the poem.

Suddenly the heavens in the studio were parted by a crackling in the overhead speakers, and Carol's voice descended on us like a savior. I asked her to read "For Brothers Everywhere," and she eagerly began her recitation. As Carol's mellifluous voice spoke of "finger-rollin'," "cockin' the rock," and "throwin' it down," my face remained full screen on the monitors (and therefore on television screens around the state and state house), broadcasting my contentment. But at the poem's conclusion, Carol did not release the red button on her phone that would relinquish control of our audio broadcast back to me. I wanted to thank her for her charming reading, but instead, the audio that went out over my visage was Carol's answer to Jeff's question. "Whoooeeeeee; that boy shore enuf is a Nigga!"

Immediately the light went out on our TR-90 system monitor (meaning Carol had relinquished the audio to me), and it was incumbent upon me to say something redeeming. "It would behoove me to point out," I began in the deadpan monotones of shock, "that Carol herself is African-American and knows of where she speaks." Already I had betrayed Carol's confidences.

Paris, Carol, the nurses, and I survived that initial summer session, although Paris, sadly, was drummed out of the university again at the conclusion of our experiment. During the following school year, Indiana's foray into televised distance education proved successful. The second semester that the class was offered, in the spring semester of 1994, nearly one hundred participants at remote sites enrolled. I had the equivalent of a full teaching load in a single class meeting in rooms scattered all over the state at times all around the clock. The World Wide Web was not yet a household *world,* and few students had access to personal computers or e-mail. The university assigned me a teaching assistant to help with the mountain of correspondence the class generated.

I soon learned that there are no invisible students, only ones that are unvisible to the television audience. Extraneous correspondence poured in, addressed "Confidential to Dr. Peterson." My phone at work and at home rang constantly. At first, the distant students wanted to explain their unperceived absences; and a litany of minor surgeries, after-school soccer games, work-related crises, childhood illnesses, and car troubles dominated their discourse.

One day an on-campus student in the studio said, "It's not fair that they can see us, and we can't see them. Make all of them out there send us their pictures." We received an album full of family snapshots—pictures of our distant peers with their spouses, children, and pets; one crossing the finish line in a marathon; one at the altar during her recent wedding; one dancing with her husband wearing pasteboard hats on New Year's Eve; and one in surgical garb, totally obscured except for shining eyes. The course director and audio engineer surmised that it was everyone's promised "fifteen minutes of fame," and that the students had chosen photographs depicting the characters they wanted to play on TV. While there was probably some truth in that, I think the pictures represented a kind of empathetic risk-taking. Whenever the satellite dishes filled up with snow, or heavy rain or fog prevented clear transmission, and the day's lesson plan had to be junked or amended, the studio students and I were out there as our true selves, without scripts or coherent lesson plans, making do on the airwaves. The distant students, many of whom worked in business and could have dispatched sterile head-and-shoulders professional photographs of themselves, chose to reveal something of their lives outside of the classroom through their pictures.

The course I teach on television is concerned with writing about poetry, and eventually, a fair number of the distant students (but so far none of the on-campus participants) sent me unsolicited parodies and responses to the poems we discuss in class, often revealing intimate details of their lives, dreams, and desires. With the increased popularity of email, I find that I am often in daily contact with distant students outside of the classroom. They tell me about their jobs (only fair, since they have to observe me at mine), their frustration and delight with returning to college after years in the work force, or their anxiety at the prospect of graduating from high school and going to college away from home next year; their aspirations and epiphanies; their children, marriages, divorces, and the deaths of loved ones. I try to remember the less private details about each correspondent, so that I can give assurance that I do *know* them when the system crackles and they "appear" in class. Some feel the need to travel to campus and meet their counterparts face to face; others prefer to keep the screen between confessor and listener.

I often think about Deborah, so beset by agoraphobia that hearing her name spoken during a tape delay rebroadcast made her tune out for a week; or Mark, who owned a small business and didn't want his employees to know he hadn't yet completed a bachelor's degree. I still wonder what happened to Valerie, who was recovering her memory and movement after a terrible car accident; or Katie, whose parents made her move back home and take distance courses after she became pregnant during her first semester away at college. I know that Jeff received his Bachelor of Science in Nursing in time to retire with full benefits, and Michelle left her policeman husband and quit her dead-end job as a security guard to go to another university as a full-time chemistry major. Of course, I am privy to similarly various, dramatic, and poignant stories among my on-campus students, but I see them everyday. I *know* them.

Who else knows me as a result of my televised classes? When I began this phase of my career, the administrators responsible for distance education at my university assured me that I would have "complete control" over my image: where it was aired, how it was marketed, and when the master copies of the tapes would be destroyed. The school produced complicated contracts in triplicate, and I was given time to read each thoroughly and to specify the modes of delivery allowed. After careful cogitation, I decided that the course could be aired at the designated satellite reception sites around the state and on a local cable channel. On the television station, it was broadcast live in the afternoons and again from videotape in the early evening so that students who worked all day could simultaneously cook for their latch-key kids and earn composition credit before dinner. Each week's class meetings were broadcast again on the weekends to enable more working students to participate. I specified that videotapes could be loaned to enrolled students who missed class, either for their own reasons or because of transmission problems (which were frequent when site coordinators were less skilled at adjusting satellite dishes and removing snow and ice from them). And I decreed that no tapes could be shown or circulated after the semester in which they were made, and that all should be destroyed at the completion of the term in which the course was originally offered.

This was all sort of exciting and flattering. One day I was an English teacher as anonymous as anyone else in a car at a stoplight on the edge of campus, and the next semester I had an image which I "owned" and could "assign" and "protect." That is heady stuff for someone who is used to differentiating between schemes and tropes for a small group of semi-attentive students in a windowless classroom. I believed, as I hope everyone does, that the subject matter I taught was interesting, even important; and, frankly, I looked forward to the start-up of our local college channel, where academic lectures would provide an alternative to standard television fare.

I was given some instruction on adapting my classroom teaching materials to television, but as a host of other tele-education instructors have revealed in print elsewhere, nothing can adequately prepare you to take an unscripted classroom discussion onto live television, aired throughout the town where you live. Every successful televised instructor eventually learns to adapt to the medium uniquely. I have confronted on-air expressions of racism, sexism, homophobia, and most other forms of prejudice and hatred, with the acute awareness that the affronted group is well represented in the television audience and closely monitoring my response— along with my colleagues, supervisors, neighbors, and viewers in general.

Let me stress that most of the unregistered audience for my televised class is highly supportive. If you've ever felt out-numbered by students and wished you could have some seasoned, tax-paying, self-actualized people who enjoy learning for its own sake on your side, televised distance education is a good venue for you to try. When correspondence started rolling in from Indianapolis, Vincennes, and South Bend—all authored by "viewers" who were not registered in the class—I discovered that vague wording in the contract I'd originally signed allowed the university to release the course to television stations in *any* broadcast area where students were enrolled or *recruited*, not just the local channel. In several regions, the course was re-aired once a week between 2:00 and 5:00 A.M., so that asynchronous participants could set their VCRs to record the week's lessons and view them at their own convenience. In the Indianapolis region, the courses are aired on public television; anyone with a bent coat hanger antenna can "attend" my class. So much for control of my "image" and the programmed destruction of course tapes.

While giving an uncharacteristically well-attended poetry reading in a southernmost corner of the state, I learned that many of the folks who'd turned out had come to see the "TV teacher" in person. During an asthma attack in a hospital emergency room, I was recognized by a respiratory therapist who shouted into my blue-ish face, "Hey! You're the metaphor lady!" A family shopping trip to an Indianapolis mall was frequently interrupted by strangers who wanted to know, among other things, the name of Sharon Old's book about her father (*The Father*), what I would call E. E. Cummings's poems that are very much like sonnets (sonnets), and the name of the book with MLA guidelines for writers of research papers (*MLA Handbook for Writers of Research Papers*).

At a distance education conference, I was amused to meet a fellow Indiana tele-education instructor who told me that she insists that course

tapes loaned to absent students be returned within one week, in order to
maintain "control" of her "copyrighted course materials." I have to admit
that I laughed in the face of that. Once an image is broadcast on the public airwaves or distributed on videotape, it is among the simplest matters
in the world to duplicate it. Few people have photocopiers, or the means
to reproduce a book at home, but nearly every middle-class American
household has at least one VCR and can copy whatever they like from their
television sets. Once I'd faced up to that, I knew that the restrictions in my
tele-education contract were illusions of control. Images of me are owned,
even altered, by people I will never know. I have seen clips of my class in
an art film produced by a student at a different university from the one
where I work. Some of my former students showed me a segment of one
of my classes, re-engineered by dubbing in audio featuring Beavis and
Butthead critiquing a Brittany Spears video; it was, admittedly, hilarious.
An English education major recently confided that it is a goal of many of
her peers to graduate from Ball State with a full year of composition
courses on videotape as a reference tool for their first years of teaching.

My widespread picture and persona are ones I did not reckon upon
when I decided to be a scholar and teacher. Every other day, an hour of my
life at work is broadcast. The burden of being a public figure, a representative, not only of my own institution, but of higher education in general,
is crushing if I think about it too much. The studio where my class meets
is lined with television monitors. Surrounding me in various shades of
brightness and hues are multiple likenesses of the picture being instanta-
neously transmitted from that room. It is always too late to recall a cumbersome sentence, a revealing expression, or to comb my hair, straighten
my collar, or better prepare the lesson going out on the airwaves. So I focus
instead upon teaching the students who are enrolled in the course—
communicating with them across physical distance and time. I reach out
to those for whom distance education is salvation—the opportunity to
attend college after all, the chance for professional advancement, the
promise of intellectual stimulation (and therefore sanity) amid stifling circumstances. And I shut out the voyeurs. As teachers, all of us have learned
to leave our personal problems outside the classroom—and the unautho-
rized uses of my image are a personal problem. I have convinced myself
that my televised image is not my *self*—in spite of what others may believe.

Just last week an investment banker, to whom I had just introduced myself, kept saying, "You don't seem like you; you're so much quieter in person than on TV." I assured her that the person in her office was the real me.

I live near campus, and I walk to work. My daily routine is reasonably predictable. One day, when I was not quite a block from my house, a car door slammed loudly near me, and an angry woman approached me on the sidewalk. She began shouting, but fell into step beside me and started talking in a menacing tone. A couple of days before, my students and I had discussed Gwendolyn Brooks's poem "The Mother," written in the voice of a woman who had had multiple abortions. The poem's speaker "remember[s] the children [she] got that [she] did not get," telling them, in the lyric's emotional crescendo, "Believe me, I loved you all." My incensed walking companion was demanding a retraction. "Go on the air and say that that woman did not love those children. Say she's a murderer." Her demands escalated and turned to accusations and personal attacks. (You can imagine them well enough.) As calmly as possible, I proceeded to my office, and locked myself in it; my ardent critic eventually went away, and I never heard from her again.

The studio where I teach is generally kept locked, even during class meetings. That is mostly out of concern for the very expensive equipment there, but it also prevents anyone from entering the room while class is in session—for any reason. I am assiduously careful about protecting my students' last names, telephone numbers, e-mail addresses, and so forth from being aired. The studio students' faces are shown on camera daily, and they tell me that other students and townspeople who have seen them on television frequently recognize them. Those interactions that my students report to me have been, without exception, pleasant. A few students enjoy being televised in class, and they have learned to recognize tele-education section numbers and deliberately seek out those courses.

My own identity is impossible to protect. Frequently, I must tell students on the air how to contact me immediately after class and throughout the day. As you can imagine, this leads to some uninvited interactions as well. One afternoon last spring, I returned to my office after teaching a lesson on traditional sonnet forms, to find an English sonnet written by a man who identified himself as "an unofficial student." I was amused, but I did not respond. It is my policy never to encourage correspondence with casual viewers of the class—partly because keeping up with the demands of the enrolled students is time-consuming enough. My class focuses upon reading and explicating poems, and I receive enough unsolicited manuscripts from viewers to start a small press (and may I say "terrible"?) magazine. As Somerset Maugham observed, "They come to me for criticism, but all they want is praise," and I cannot afford to engage in either with them.

The sonneteer, however, was persistent. Following several class meetings after that, I would find a perfectly executed English sonnet in my email within minutes of dismissal. Each was obviously composed during the hour, as it contained details of my dress, monologue, and mannerisms during the preceding class meeting. I found this rather creepy. Then the writer, who always signed his name, told me, "You may think you're just teaching poetry, but there is more going on here" (Young). I forwarded some of the sonnets to the dean of distance education at my university, who deemed them "harmless . . . a tribute." When I mentioned them to the statewide director of the Indiana Higher Education Telecommunications System, he assured me that specific federal laws have been enacted in response to the 1989 stalking and shooting of television actress Rebecca Shaeffer. He said that the FCC would step in and immediately handle the situation if a viewer said or did anything truly threatening. A former student who has become an attorney (don't we all need some of those?) tells me there is no such specific law. There is a federal criminal law against stalking (U.S. Code 47USC230), and it has been updated to protect people from stalking or harassment carried out by computer, but there are no special provisions protecting people in the media. Meanwhile, the sonnet writer became frustrated by my silence and emailed the graduate assistant for the class, asking him why I did not respond to his messages. The graduate student replied that I uniformly do not respond to unsolicited correspondence regarding the class. Subsequently, I received an email from the sonneteer, telling me that I am boring, and he would not be watching my classes any longer. Touché.

A weirder but less persistent viewer mailed me a pre-paid long distance phone card and asked that I call him at home some time. That was pure profit for the phone company. The card went unused.

The bulk of my "viewer mail," however, is charming and encouraging. A third grade teacher wrote to say that my class is her students' favorite "show," and she sent along poems the students were writing in response to some we had discussed in class (Drill). (My students and I responded directly to the third graders on the air.) An Indiana family that moved to New York sent a Christmas card from their new home with a note that said that they missed "sitting in front of the television, eating popcorn in pajamas, pondering the life of Sylvia Plath" (Clearczyk). A fellow shopper in a grocery store told me that she watches the class with her daughter because she hopes she will go to college some day. The checker at a home improvement warehouse asked me if William Carlos Williams wrote "anything besides 'The Red Wheel Barrow.'" Three workers at the car wash told me they watch the class everyday because they always learn something and I'm their "most famousest customer." A woman my mother's age wrote to say that she acquiesces and watches the class with her eighty-year-old mother, who often weeps at what she missed by not going to school (Doe).

I became a college professor because I wanted to increase appreciation for modern and contemporary poetry. Doubtlessly, the televised class helps me meet that goal exponentially. I have no way of knowing how many people actually watch the class regularly, how many linger on the station for a few moments while channel surfing. Scarcely a day goes by that a stranger doesn't tell me he or she has watched the class. The age, education, and socio-economic diversity among those viewers is amazing. Nearly every semester a newly enrolled nontraditional student makes the pilgrimage to my office to tell me about finding the courage to attend college after watching the university channel. As anyone involved in distance education can tell you, the students enrolled in the classes are enormously grateful for the opportunity and tremendously deserving of it.

I have spent a significant part of my teaching career honing pedagogical methods for televised distance classes, but I hope to soon see those skills become obsolete. Televised classes are the iron lung of distance and continuing education; they are cumbersome, costly, and inadequate—but the best we can do in many circumstances currently. I hope that the World Wide Web will continue to develop rapidly, that personal computers will get less and less expensive, and that options for connecting to the Internet at high speeds will become affordable and available to everyone. The computer is a far more efficient and cost-effective medium for education than is the television. It will require much less hardware and no specialized reception sites. It is as effective in asynchronous modes as in real-time instruction. It already includes the security measures that will provide different levels of access for enrolled and non-matriculated students.

As of last spring my televised English class has included an Internet component, accessible only to students enrolled in the course. This year additional coursework will be conducted in the slightly more secure environment of cyberspace. Eventually, I hope to abandon the television studio and conduct the course from the variety of computers at my disposal. I regret that I am plotting a retreat behind the ivory-dished microwave towers of the modern university. Televised classes have proven to be a very effective public relations tool for the schools that sponsor them. They can recruit students; educate citizens without the time, money, or courage to officially enroll; provide a model of teaching for education students and colleagues; and put human faces on the brick-and-mortar public facade of the academy. Frankly, I will miss the persona that my public image has adopted: "the metaphor lady," the kindly professor who will answer questions about literature in the shopping mall or grocery store. Because of its benefits and its flaws, televised education is a noble experiment.

However, televised courses require studio time, production personnel, satellite coordination, air time on multiple channels, site administrators, and multiple pieces of expensive reception hardware—the cost of which must be borne by higher education institutions and passed on to all students. A distance education journal reported that in 1997, it cost the state of Wisconsin about $2,000 per month to maintain each of its remote instructional television sites (Lozada 24). For the same money, each distant student probably could have been given a personal computer to use during and beyond his or her distance education. That is a lot of money. And that is only the monetary cost of televised education.

WORKS CITED

Brooks, Gwendolyn. "The Mother." *Blacks*. Chicago: David, 1987.

Clearczyk, B. Personal Correspondence. 23 December 1998.

Doe, Jane. Personal Correspondence. 10 May 1998.

Drill, K. Personal Correspondence. 17 April 1996.

Lozada, Marlene. "Looking Out for Distance Learning." *Techniques: Making Education and Career Choices* 72 (October 1997): 7, 24.

U.S. Code 47USC230.

Young, C. Personal Correspondence. 22 February 1998.

The Televised Interview as Focus Group Research Text

Students Analyze Reactions to Monica Lewinsky's Interview with Barbara Walters

BARBRA MORRIS

When I talk with pre-college and college teachers about using newscasts as classroom subject matter in order to teach critical thinking and analytic writing about media, they often say that television news does offer intriguing instructional possibilities, but complain that there are problems with asking students to analyze the subject matter. On the one hand, daily news programs tend to provide a lineup of eight to ten encapsulated reports, summarized rapidly in half an hour. Most students haven't acquired sufficient background knowledge about issues being raised to ask penetrating questions about them.

On the other hand, there are some subjects dealt with thoroughly over time in the media, meaning there are extended debates, in-depth interviews and expert evaluations. In such cases, students do accumulate a great deal of contextual information. However, in these instances, continuous coverage of a topic raises many complicated issues, some of which may be uncomfortable to deal with in class. Quantity and quality of extensive material is difficult to sort through.

In responding to the former question about how to teach critical thinking about television using brief news stories, students can resist simply accepting brief news stories that are not sufficiently informative. We can ask students to monitor the news for several nights: keep track of who is not heard from or interviewed and what points of view are not being considered; identify limitations of simple spins or one-dimensional perspectives applied to complex problems, while taking notes on what is missing from the content; list questions that need to be asked about each subject; and pay attention to what is being dismissed or ignored.[1]

However, there are times when a great deal of information is available about a subject over a long period of time. In this instance, how can students sift through news coverage that is elaborated, extensive, and exhaustive? A case in point here would be the long-term coverage of White House intern Monica Lewinsky's relationship with President Bill Clinton; it sustained a high level of newsworthiness, partly attributable, of course, to its culminating in the rare spectacle of impeachment hearings.

Roughly beginning late in 1997, on the heels of numerous other independent investigative counsel claims about executive office wrongdoing, the public began to hear the name Monica Lewinsky associated with Bill Clinton. On 27 January 1998, Hillary Rodham Clinton appeared on the *Today* television show saying that her husband absolutely had not had an intimate relationship with Lewinsky. This did not head off further speculations. Thereafter, reporters combed through leaks each day from Special Prosecutor Starr's inquiries, relaying to the public new claims of improprieties with a combination of gravity, enthusiasm, and shock.

Actually, the circumstances of the Lewinsky/Clinton meetings were comparable to other claims by women regarding his conduct in the workplace, though he admitted nothing. From the White House, cycles of denial, deception, and limited disclosure continued. Relentless mass media reporting, followed by rehashing of possible consequences for Clinton, occurred concurrently.[2] As time passed, it seemed clear to the public that until everything finally was out in the open, and a Senate impeachment trial concluded, final unraveling of legal, political, human, and ethical questions would be impossible.

Several troubling issues intersected within this story. Following Lewinsky's disclosure of numerous White House meetings with Clinton, there arose questions of inappropriate gender/power relations in the workplace, as well as about Clinton's evasive, untruthful testimony under oath about their relationship.[3] Staggering amounts of national time and money were required to extract a "true" picture of what actually happened and, then, what should be done about it.[4]

Throughout the long discovery period, continuous speculation absorbed public attention. With impeachment hearings looming ahead, various possible scenarios merged together into what rhetorician Kenneth Burke would have characterized as the unfolding "plot."[5] Indeed, the Clinton/Lewinsky story had problem-solving aspects not unlike those found in a novel or play. Although Lewinsky and Clinton were caught in a calamitous narrative of their own making, the story fueled public debate about the cultural hypocrisy of singling out their behavior from the rest of the citizenry. Though fool-hardy and unseemly, this kind of relationship was hardly unheard-of, either within the general public or among world leaders. This realization raised questions about whether full disclosure or an individual's right to privacy should prevail, and, moreover, what constitutes realistic public expectations about the conduct of elected officials in their own lives.

Obviously, the scope and significance of this ongoing national conversation produced a fascinating teaching opportunity. But how best to examine this kind of controversial and complicated subject matter within the framework of a productive academic lesson? Apparently, this is a perfect example of the public dilemma of experiencing a huge volume of coverage. The public has to sort through a blizzard of information about people involved in an event, as well as weigh experts' perspectives on larger societal issues being raised. All the while, ongoing polling data tracks evolving citizen opinions, lumping them into hundreds or thousands. What is reported in polls about mass public opinion, however, tells us nothing about how or why individuals choose to arrive at particular conclusions.

In class, we can fill this gap by inquiring into the realm of individual decision-making about the news, using television focus group research. This means turning students' attention toward differences in viewers' interpretive strategies. Audience response researchers consider what viewers hear that matters to them about a consequential mass media text, and what aspects of it influence their opinions.[6]

Ordinarily, teachers of media content analysis help students become alert to and circumspect about media representations of people, events, and ideas. At the same time, however, we ought to demonstrate to students that even when people are receiving roughly the same media content, they are unlikely to arrive at the same conclusions about its intentions, implications, and meanings. In other words, readers or viewers or listeners bring different histories, points of view, and preferences to texts. Straightforwardly tackling television audience analysis allows us to address the question:

How do individuals regard evidence, make distinctions, and draw conclusions? Focus group researchers collect and compare differing viewer responses to text in order to better understand the analytic process.

Certainly, most classroom teachers already talk with students about stories that appear in current news; ignoring world events makes little sense if schooling is meant to encourage thoughtful approaches to life outside classrooms. In a basic television focus group project, students attempt two-dimensional inquiry: (1) What important issues does the text raise? and (2) What does a sampling of viewers think about them? In a sense, the assignment is analogous to work we regularly do as teachers. We read and compare students' papers, all the while reconsidering how and why different student writers respond as they do to one and the same body of information.

To collect and compare a range of responses by a television focus group, students learn to think like researchers and employ a basic research approach. The idea here is that students set aside, for the time being, their own opinions or viewpoints, which ordinarily they are asked to concentrate upon for argumentation assignments. Instead, they are to focus on soliciting and analyzing what others say about television text.

SELECTING A MODEL TELEVISION TEXT

From time to time, as mentioned earlier, television rivets public attention upon thought-provoking and multi-faceted dilemmas that are likely to be disturbing in their ethical or cultural or criminal implications. They grip and hold public attention, while triggering profoundly contrasting reactions. For example, Watergate, the Iran/Contra hearings featuring Oliver North, Anita Hill's testimony regarding Clarence Thomas's pending appointment to the Supreme Court, the O. J. Simpson trial, the custody battle over Elian Gonzalez, and President Clinton's impeachment all fit into the distinctive category of compelling mass media narratives.[7] In such instances, television, alongside other mass media, saturates audiences with commentary from diverse points of view, presumably to keep people apprised of important and as yet unresolved matters. This process of providing up-to-date information while raising more and more questions about an emerging situation occurs through many communication outlets, such as daily or editorial news coverage, television, newsmagazines, talk shows, the Internet, and interviews. Despite frequent repetitions of details and complaints of information exhaustion, the public remains vigilant. Citizens' attention to debatable points is fueled by thick descriptions, alternate versions of events, and competing, conflicting claims.

Whenever a media topic achieves a high incidence of topic concentration and public conversation, students, too, are far better informed than when an incident appears once, or just occasionally, in the news. With so much debate in the air, students are also primed by the attentive and vibrant social climate around them to wonder about the reasons behind personal opinions. Here is a summary of the process that television focus group researchers follow: (1) decide upon and tape a significant text and analyze its controversial elements, (2) prepare pre-screening and post-screening questionnaires, (3) arrange to show the tape to a selected focus group, (4) collect the written responses, and then (5) hold a general discussion about the content with participants.

When employing this research procedure, students have to pay attention to factors and kinds of reasoning that shape diverse opinions. Viewer response research combines curiosity with tolerance; it means putting one's own opinion aside, at least for the time being, in order to gather and weigh viewpoints and beliefs that may not be congruent with one's own.

CONTEXTUAL FACTORS REGARDING
THIS MODEL CLASSROOM EXPERIENCE

I want now to detail how focus group research proceeded in my classroom using the televised Monica Lewinsky interview; students looked especially into the question of whether her explanations were regarded differently by females or males. A group of four undergraduate women formed a research team, wrote pre- and post-screening questionnaires, held a screening session, collected written responses from viewers, and conducted an audience discussion. The model text was the two-hour interview by Barbara Walters on the ABC network (9:00–11:00 P.M., 3 March 1999) of Monica Lewinsky. This particular television program was highly anticipated by a vast viewing public, probably because their involvement eventually resulted in Clinton facing impeachment hearings. Heretofore, the public had never heard Lewinsky directly recount her recollections about the relationship, though there had been secondhand reports of her testimony to official investigative panels.[8] However, the media reported she was preparing herself for a televised, in-depth interview scheduled March 3.[9] The Lewinsky interview was an internationally anticipated television event, which drew an estimated audience of seventy million people worldwide.[10]

Once the focus group session was held and completed, each of the four student-researchers had a sizeable packet of completed questionnaire responses to use as basic quantitative and qualitative data. Each researcher then wrote a separate analysis of data they acquired together. With the completed questionnaires in hand, they each compared and interpreted differing viewer reactions to Monica Lewinsky's televised testimony about her involvement with Clinton. During a lengthy trial-like interview by ABC's reporter Barbara Walters, Lewinsky was asked to describe her side of the relationship with Clinton.[11] Students who led the Lewinsky focus group research project wanted to know in what ways their classmates' reactions to her account might differ, and, especially, if opinions about her might change after hearing her first-person rendition of events; most media accounts predicted an ominous outcome.[12]

MY CLASSROOM ENVIRONMENT

I want to describe the context for this particular class project in television analysis because it was atypical. At the exact time the Lewinsky interview was broadcast to the American public on 3 March 1999, I was a faculty member in the University of Michigan/University of Wisconsin/Duke University Study Abroad Program sited in Florence, Italy. Everyone involved in this college-level cross-cultural educational program shared living/learning housing in a villa during the entire winter term (January–April) 1999. In order to be eligible for this study abroad opportunity, students must have acquired junior or senior level academic standing in their home institutions in the United States. Before arriving in Europe, the fifty or so participants were concentrators in a wide range of fields (no communication majors; two English majors). While abroad in Florence, however, they all enrolled in similar courses, essentially to learn more about Italian life, language, literature, and arts. Since my teaching interests and specialties center upon contemporary media (primarily print, film, and television), my own seminars in Florence asked students to examine aspects of Italian popular culture, arts, and society.

In Ann Arbor, Michigan, when I was preparing media-related assignments for the Florence campus, I imagined that American students might become local television researchers on-site, studying Italian program content and documenting various genres of Italian telecasts: news, sports, commercials, and entertainment, in order to evaluate their visual/verbal content. However, once I arrived in Italy and examined closely the country's telecasts for the first time, I realized that most students probably did not have sufficient everyday cultural background to unpack and assess meanings of the broadcasts as the actual Italian viewing public would. A likely outcome of students having so little time and too brief a history to evaluate Italian television would be my receiving unnervingly superficial and negative observational critiques. Therefore, I rethought my television analysis assignment. Instead of asking students to judge unfamiliar broadcast content, I decided to veer from the original subject matter, but keep the objective of television response research intact.

I took advantage of my son having sent me from the United States a taped copy of Barbara Walters's much-anticipated interview of Monica Lewinsky. Indeed, while we were in Italy, it was not as though we lost sight of the prospect of her television appearance. The ubiquitous *USA Today* was available everywhere in English and, along with other American newspapers, was quoted regularly by European wire services; the Lewinsky/Clinton story was often front-page news. Almost from the time we arrived in Italy, stories appeared every day regarding the outcome of Clinton's impeachment and of Monica Lewinsky's revelations. All of us in the villa had been discussing questions raised by European newscasters, so instead of an assignment to describe and analyze Italian television, I suggested students try focus group television analysis about Lewinsky, with all students in the villa program invited to respond to her actual interview.

The idea proved intriguing to four women who had been meeting together with me in a small seminar.[13] First, we watched the videotape together, with all of us taking notes on quotes and impressions from the entire two hours of questions and answers. Then, we devised numerous questions based upon Lewinsky's responses to Walters, and discussed our reactions to what she said. Afterward, students developed two brief questionnaires, one for before and one for after the screening. All students living in the villa were asked to meet for a focus group session, watch the videotape of Lewinsky's interview in its entirety, and, both before the screening and after seeing the videotape, answer questions about their attitudes toward Lewinsky and her performance.

Granted, this setting for focus group research was unusual. My students were living outside their own country, and were therefore seeing American television from a considerable geographical distance; strangely enough, I think the distantiation may have made us more, not less, curious about the impact of Lewinsky's story on differing populations comprising the immense worldwide audience. Of course, living in another culture, we were among people who were not likely to be interpreting Lewinsky's story as Americans would. Most importantly, while in Italy, my students were not witnessing continuous American media coverage of the White House intern's relationship with the president. We observed that European response to the affair seemed, overall, distinctly less inclined to be condemnatory or outraged. Although Clinton's attempts to avoid blame were regarded as problematic by the European press because he first denied everything, only later admitting the truth, their coverage often suggested that telecasting the Lewinsky version of events was primarily a media money-making scheme. From this skeptical cross-cultural vantage point, America was indulging in hypocrisy about sexual matters, while the media was exploiting the scandal for profit.

As for the student focus group, they had arrived in Italy already knowing something about Monica Lewinsky's story. Before the study abroad program began in January, Lewinsky's emotional drama was disclosed through Linda Tripp's audiotaped phone conversations with her. My study abroad students wondered about long-term effects that her revelations about Clinton might have on the United States' world stature and international credibility.

At this point, villa students were hungry for American television, for sportscasts, but also for direct news. They especially wanted news about Clinton's future from the United States. At the same time we were living in Florence, European allies were receiving military support via American aircraft sited in Italy; students wondered about the impact of impeachment hearings on Clinton's leadership in delicate conflict negotiations.

By and large, then, we reconsidered more concerns than is typical of people abroad who wonder what is happening back home. In any case, we were eager to analyze the Lewinsky interview and discuss its meaning and likely ramifications. While the geographical distance from the actual broadcast undoubtedly impacted upon the teaching/learning situation, I want also to note that students, when I offer them a chance for focus group television analysis in Michigan classes, say afterward that they come to understand the complexity of critical thinking about media far better once they become audience researchers. Typically, they say that they never realized individual viewers could react so differently to the same text. My closing remark here would be that focus group research is a useful model for student-centered collaborative inquiry and is educationally feasible and thought provoking for students no matter where it takes place.

PRE-SCREENING AND POST-SCREENING FOCUS GROUP QUESTIONNAIRES

To determine whether the text of the televised interview made a difference in viewers' perceptions of Monica Lewinsky and Bill Clinton, students sandwiched the videotape screening between two questionnaires. The four student-researchers raised matters of her motivation, situation, responsibility for conduct, and credibility. In addition, they identified a particular Lewinsky quote from the interview for focus group response. The two blank questionnaires appear below. As you see, pre-screening and post-screening questionnaires elicit both quantitative and qualitative data.

Name (optional) _____

Gender   M   F   (Please circle one)

Age _____

1) Do you consider yourself (circle one):
   a) Liberal   b) Conservative
   c) Neither (Please provide a descriptor)

2) Do you consider yourself (circle one):
   a) a feminist   b) not a feminist

   Please provide your definition of feminism:

3) Before viewing this tape, what words would you use to describe Monica Lewinsky and her relationship with Bill Clinton?

4) Before viewing this tape, what words would you use to describe Bill Clinton and his relationship with Monica Lewinsky?

5) What have been your sources of information about Lewinsky prior to today? Be specific.

6) Do you think she has been unfairly portrayed by the media? (Please circle one)
   a) YES   b) NO   c) UNCERTAIN

Post-screening Questionnaire

1) Now that you have seen Barbara Walters's interview of Monica Lewinsky, what words would you use to describe Lewinsky?

2) What words would you use to describe Clinton?

3) If your opinion of Lewinsky changed, to what would you ascribe your change of attitude?

4) Do you believe Lewinsky has done harm to the American culture? (Please circle one)
   a) YES   b) NO   c) UNSURE

5) Do you believe the Lewinsky interview clarified any social issues? Please explain.

6) After seeing this interview, do you believe Lewinsky is being honest? (Please circle one)
   a) YES   b) NO   c) UNDECIDED

7) What question would you now want Lewinsky to answer?

8) What question would you now want Clinton to answer?

9) In your opinion, what does Lewinsky intend by her answer to Walters's question of what she will tell her children; the answer was "Mommy made a big mistake"? Please add any additional comments you wish to make below.

FOCUS GROUP COMPOSITION AND SELECTED QUESTIONNAIRE RESULTS

In total, 27 students formed the actual focus group: 24 females and 3 males, ranging in ages between 20 and 22 years old. Although we had not had much time to anticipate the results of the two questionnaires, all four researchers believed that attitudes of males and females toward Lewinsky would differ, and they did. In this regard, their hypothesis was confirmed. We needed preliminary background on existing points of view; focus group respondents self-identified themselves in two categories:

Liberal 13 (two males)   Conservative 4 (one male)   Neither 10
Feminist 17 (one male)   Not Feminist 9 (two males)   Neither 1

Below is a gender-differentiated sampling of answers to two questions that were clearly gender-divided in post-screening results:

Is Monica honest?
    Yes 17   No 6 (includes all three males)   Unsure 4

Did she harm U.S. culture?
    Yes 5   No 13 (includes all three males)   Unsure 9

Four Student-Researchers Interpret Focus Group Responses

Student-researcher #1, Jessica, began her essay by describing observations from what was her first experience with focus group research (one additional male returned his questionnaire after the others had been tabulated):

> As they gathered for the screening, many students were laughing and making jokes. Before they saw the program, words used to describe Lewinsky were pretty negative: naive, immoral, power hungry, and manipulative. Yet, when it came to a post-viewing response, the women used a much more serious tone, and many described her as genuine, lonely, intelligent, and sensitive.

Jessica later identified a research outcome:

> Sympathy for Lewinsky was reported only by females. All four males said she was not honest. Three of the four males went beyond what was asked, one male circling no to the question of her honesty and adding an exclamation point! Another male wrote that Lewinsky was not honest with herself or the public. A third male drew several excessively heavy circles around no, presumably to emphasize dislike of her.

After summarizing questionnaire results, Jessica described her own reaction to the Lewinsky interview:

Personally, I found Lewinsky sympathetic; she turned her story into an innocent crush, typical of someone our age. She talked about her relationship with Clinton as any twenty-two year old might. I think a comparable age bond touched women of my age in this focus group and drew Lewinsky into a personal space with us. Here is one female student, who reacted to questions of Lewinsky's clandestine affair: "I see Monica more now as a young person deeply hurt by a powerful man that she cared a lot about, as well as her being hurt by the media. I see her as a victim of her age, circumstances, and media cruelty now."

In the concluding section of her paper, Jessica considers future research she would like to pursue:

I find the male's beliefs fascinating. I would want to create a new focus group of males from a wide range of ages. My questions would especially explore their perceptions of female appearance to look into how their idea of a physically ideal woman influences their attitudes toward her credibility.

If Monica had lived up to their super model standards, would their perceptions of her behavior change? Are females more swayed by her emotional intensity than males? I need to have an equally mixed gender focus group to investigate that. Males may see her testimony in a way that females cannot. Is this an area of overwhelming gender identification, regardless of other factors?

Student-researcher #2 was Amy, whose essay extended the theme of possible connections between Lewinsky's appearance and her believability for males:

I think Lewinsky's being overweight is a key factor in media and male attacks upon her. Her failure to look good was focused on by journalists, comedians, and tabloid reporters. A viewer unfamiliar with the Presidential angle of the scandal might believe that it was all about her weight. In the Barbara Walters' interview, Lewinsky's lack of self-esteem and self-worth emerged and somehow provided female viewers with a possible ameliorating reason for her actions and reactions during her ill-fated affair with Clinton. In the end, many people (including all the males in our group) said she had not harmed the culture. Withholding responsibility for societal harm can be interpreted in many ways, but I sense that males regard Lewinsky as just another unattractive and needy female, rather than thinking that her attempts at candor could lessen public derision.

In making a comparison of Lewinsky with a literary figure, Amy ended her paper this way:

> Daisy, in the Fitzgerald novel *The Great Gatsby,* is controlled by her environment, pretty things, and power. Monica Lewinsky seems to be similar to Daisy. She cherished presents given to her by Clinton, and she seemed thrilled by his power. The thrill of their affair was rooted in his absolute power but also was a danger to their relationship. This is a setup for a dependent relationship. Person A (Lewinsky), having no sense of personal value, latches onto Person B (Clinton). Person B might boost A's self-esteem at first but totally controls access to their relationship (Lewinsky had to wait for his attentions and phone calls), causing A to be constantly subservient and unhappy. In the long run, subservience and invisibility harms A, so that her original sense of self-worth is gradually eroded and erased. Subservience is ultimately harmful when it is essential to a relationship. Sometimes the outcome leaves A more harmed than in the original state, before becoming involved with B. This is a moral issue but, perhaps more importantly, an example of a clearly unhealthy human condition.

Student-researcher #3, Kristie, in analyzing both her own and others' responses to the questions, observed how her own opinion had altered:

> After viewing the interview and reading all the responses, some of my feelings about Monica and the meaning of the situation changed.
> I described her in the end as being powerful, intelligent, young, and sensitive. The program made my feelings toward Clinton more negative. I wrote words about him like: pathetic, pitiful, sick, and unprofessional. Monica made me see that her feelings toward him in the relationship were similar to those that some of my friends and I have known in our dating. I feel she has done harm to the American public, though certainly with Bill's help. I also feel that she had an affair with a married man and he got away with it more than she did; he has probably caused infidelity to seem more OK to men. Still, both of them seemed to believe extra-marital affairs were acceptable from the beginning, and that fact may make people reassess their ideas about what marriage is. I would like to do future research with people of different ages, with equal numbers of males and females, to see whether there are significant differences in what people learned by watching this entire disclosure process evolve.

Finally, student-researcher #4 was Wendy. She began her paper by observing that the name Monica had become a household word and recounted analysis of questionnaire responses in the following way:

> I feel that people are concerned about unanswered moral questions behind this scandal involving the now famous intern Monica and the President. Some respondents said that our country has a moral ideal about marriage, and our attitude toward religious contracts dates back probably to our Puritan heritage, but that history is essentially an illusion today. Other people blamed the media for callous superficial treatment of the matter and behaving as though it was just a soap opera. They said that there is a preference in the media for sensationalizing issues and sneering at people who are hurt by being involved in human errors. This means a large percentage of people begin to treat human weaknesses merely as shallow entertainment.
>
> One magazine article we read, for instance, published an article about the Lewinsky interview that emphasized not her experience but only how she looked. They had a sidebar dealing exclusively with what's wrong with her appearance. Another article only discussed her weight problem. If the public is not urged by the media and journalists to take her predicament and her life seriously, how can we fault Monica for what she did, for not taking what she did more seriously?

CONCLUSIONS

We see each of the four women writers taking a somewhat different approach to assessing the same data. Jessica reacted to the differing tones of research responses by females and males. The males' strong uniform rejections of Lewinsky led her to wonder whether their decision was determined by her girth, not her guilt. Extending the theme of Lewinsky's fragile self-esteem, Amy spoke of the destructive psychology of the relationship and used her literary background to determine how the arrangement undermined Lewinsky's shaky confidence; her power in the situation was limited to occasional admittance into Clinton's presence, always at his convenience.

Kristie turned to re-evaluating her own assumptions about Lewinsky, in light of their similar ages. She emphasized the disparity between what Clinton should have known and what Lewinsky had to learn, feeling that he would, nonetheless, escape with less scorn and psychic damage. Also, she felt that public attitudes toward lifelong commitment, bonds of extended trust, were not holding up well to public scrutiny, because of Clinton's infidelity and denials. In a similar way, Wendy expressed concern about how the media treat human flaws as freakish entertainment, with analysis of personal and social causes for problems taking a backseat to ridiculing participants and their failures.

All in all, student-researchers expanded their thinking beyond the telecast to raise questions about personal psychology, professional ethics, and researcher objectivity, as well as issues of media reportage turning into exercises in punitive mockery and public humiliation. Therefore, when the four women presented their research results to students who had participated in the study, once again, we noted how their analyses differed, even though all researcher interpretations were based upon the same set of viewer responses.

Questions of Clinton's character, responsibility, and conduct, as well as Lewinsky's intentionality, responsibility, and vulnerability, arose in our full focus group discussion. Later, as we continued through the semester, we sometimes returned to reflect about differing cultural standards and assumptions that lead to attributions of cause or blame. Focus group research, as I hope to have demonstrated here, is a way to engage students in thoughtful reflection about individual reactions to television texts. Students first design questionnaires about the content based upon their own perspectives and observations of news coverage, but, by the end, they are led to critique how and why beliefs are formed, in light of a surprising range of textual interpretations. In focus group research, students work collaboratively, together reconsidering the bases for beliefs in relation to the prevailing cultural norms and context.

EPILOGUE

Since we engaged in this 1999 classroom assignment, things have changed for Monica Lewinsky and for Bill Clinton. In his case, though he was roundly chastised by other politicians and the general public, events that once seemed would result in his immediate removal from office faded from the national agenda. At this writing, Clinton is scheduled to leave office on 21 January 2001, at the end of his second full term as president; polls indicate he has a high public approval rating for his leadership but not for his character. This seeming contradiction notwithstanding, and although the media often made a case that he could not serve effectively as president with a record that cast doubt on his good judgment and truthfulness, the public apparently weighed his weaknesses and strengths and preferred to have him soldier on.

As for Lewinsky, she has been able to capitalize on her media identity. Popular magazines with follow-up stories about her post-Bill life brought her into the arena of marketing products, promoting such items as scarves, handbags, and makeup, employing name and face recognition in advertisements. She is a player in the lucrative consumer niche of self-help and self-improvement; her public admission of low self-esteem about her appearance translated into a Jenny Craig business contract for weight loss. She has retained a degree of media momentum.

The names of Clinton and Lewinsky are forever linked on the pages of American political and media history. Despite Kristie's earlier prediction, as a researcher, that Clinton would be held less accountable and be less harmed than Lewinsky, a newspaper article dated 11 April 2000 (more than two years after the Lewinsky involvement was unequivocally denied) imagined indictments in his future, after the presidency. Robert W. Ray, who replaced Starr as the government's independent legal counsel, claimed that Clinton's evasions had not been dealt with adequately and "there is a principle to be vindicated, and that principle is that no person is above the law, even the president of the United States."[14]

This essay has examined a very small percentage of viewer reactions to a single news-magazine interview within an enormous onslaught of coverage. Nonetheless, despite the limited scope of this study, what can be observed are factors reported to be significant by viewers and researchers as they developed interpretations and beliefs about the affair: personal experience, proximity in age, gender, literary education, analysis of approach and tone of press spokespersons, and intuitions about the psychological and human parameters of the encounter. It would be interesting to develop a profile of types of major stories and then try to determine similar or differing audience effects.

In time, other points of departure for media and cultural studies researchers may well lead toward examination of this story's long-term consequences on the public consciousness, including looking into what kinds of character traits that voters subsequently appeared to value in presidential races. The Clinton/Lewinsky media narrative, with which many viewers found themselves for so long engaged in deciphering, may well have left in its wake a far deeper sense of betrayal and reorientation than people realized at the time the events actually took place.

NOTES

1. Barbra S. Morris, "New Knockoff News: Commentator Attitudes in Newsmagazine Stories," *Arizona English Bulletin* 37.3 (1995): 32–35.

2. "Too Much Information?" *USA Today* 8 February 1999: 1A.

3. Carol Morelio, "Poll Reflects Disapproval of Bill Clinton, the Man," *USA Today* 23 February 1999: 5A.

4. Robert Dreyfuss, "Collateral Damage: The Personal Costs of Starr's Investigation," *Nation* 27 July/3 August 1998: 11–18.

5. Kenneth Burke, *A Grammar of Motives* (Berkeley: U of California P, 1969) 14.

6. Barbra S. Morris, "Toward Creating a Television Research Community in Your Classroom," *Trends and Issues in Secondary Education* (Urbana, IL: NCTE, 1999): 7–17.

7. Diane McWorter, "Weighing Monica's Long-Term Effect on Society," *USA Today* 4 March 1999: 7A.

8. Kathy Kiely, "Lewinsky Very Sorry about Affair," *USA Today* 4 March 1999: 1A.

9. Kathy Kiely, "Sad, Giggly Lewinsky Tells Story on 2 Continents," *USA Today* 5–7 March 1999: 7A.

10. Mark Hosenball and Barbara Kantrowitz, "Ready for Her Close-Up," *Newsweek* 15 March 1999: 30–31.

11. "Lewinsky Tells All, and Tells and Tells," *New York Times* 4 March 1999: 5A.

12. Robert Blanco, "No News Is Good News for This Affair's End," *USA Today* 5 March 1999: 8B.

13. The four students whose work appears in this essay are Jessica Falbo, Amy Elliott, Kristie Bosart, and Wendy Ascione.

14. David A. Vise, "Investigation of Clinton Still 'Open,'" *Ann Arbor News* 11 April 2000: A3.

WORKS CITED

Bakhtin, M. M. *The Dialogic Imagination. Four Essays.* Ed. Micheal Holquist. Austin: U of Texas P, 1981.

Burke, Kenneth. *A Grammar of Motives.* Berkeley: U of California P, 1969.

Butler, Judith. *Gender Trouble.* New York: Routledge, 1999.

Converse, Philip E. "The Nature of Belief Systems in Mass Publics." *Ideology and Discontent.* Ed. David E. Apter. London: Collier-Macmillan, 1964. 206–61.

Hawkins, Robert P., and Suzanne Pingree. "Television's Influence on Social Reality." *Technical Reviews.* Vol. 2 of *National Institute of Mental Health. Television and Behavior. Ten Years of Scientific Progress and Implications for the Eighties.* Ed. David Pearl, Lorraine Bouthilet, Joyce Lazar. Rockville, MD: National Institute of Mental Health, 1982. 224–47.

Iyengar, Shanto. "How Citizens Think about National Issues: A Matter of Responsibility." *American Journal of Political Science* 33.4 (November 1989): 878–900.

Morris, Barbra S. "Toward Creating a Television Research Community in Your Classroom." *English Journal* 87.1 (January 1998): 38–42. Also in *National Council of Teachers of English Annual Collection: Trends and Issues in Secondary Education.* Urbana, IL: NCTE, 1999. 1–17.

Morris, Barbra S. "Two Dimensions of Teaching Television Literacy: Analyzing Television Content and Analyzing Television Viewing." *Canadian Journal of Educational Communication* 22.1 (spring 1993): 37–45.

Turner, J. C. "Towards a Cognitive Redefinition of the Social Group." *Social Identity and Intergroup Relations.* Ed. H. Taijfel. Cambridge: Cambridge UP, 1994. 52–63.

An Imitation of Life

Deconstructing Racial Stereotypes in Popular Culture

STEPHANIE THOMPSON

Despite Danzy Senna's satiric assertion in "The Mulatto Millennium" that "hybridity is in" (18), I continue to find myself teaching in classrooms that are predominately populated by white students. This lack of diversity, coupled with the fact that students who grew up in the eighties and nineties cannot fathom the legacy that fosters such antagonism when states like South Carolina refuse to stop flying the Confederate flag, often creates tension or a complete shutdown in participation when I try to raise the issue of race in my classroom. Many of my students, who are mostly from the South, insist that racism is far behind us, despite the evidence to the contrary when a man is dragged to death in Texas simply because of his skin color. As Patricia Williams reminds us,

> It seems to me that the ability to talk about diversity (now synonymous with balkanization) depends, therefore, on a constant clarification of terms, a determination to leave nothing to presupposition, and a renewed insistence upon the incorporation of multiple connotative histories into our curricula, our social lives, our politics, and our law. Our hardest job in these times is not to forget why we are where we are at this historical intersection. We cannot forget the sacrifice that went into our presence in the social world. (75)

The need to look at the past in order to understand the present, coupled with my agreement with Tessa Perkins that films "play an important role in forming ideas about, and attitudes to, the world, in setting agendas, in enabling (or not) other ways of envisaging the world, in alleviating anxiety and even in defusing conflict" (76), prompted my decision to study Fannie Hurst's novel *Imitation of Life* and its 1934 and 1959 film adaptations in introductory composition and women's studies courses, for these texts utilize the racial stereotypes that still trouble so many African Americans today. Popular culture can tell us much about our past and future, and examining the same text in various forms—a novel, a film, a remake—can allow us to see subtle permutations in ideology over time and thus force us to evaluate where America has been and where it is going.

The once-famous and prolific Fannie Hurst is now a footnote in literary history, remembered more for her patronage of Zora Neale Hurston than her writing despite the fact that she published over twenty-five novels and short story collections, an autobiography, and numerous stories in periodicals; in addition, her work served as the source for over thirty films, among them *Humoresque,* two adaptations of *Imitation of Life,* and three versions of *Back Street.*[1] While *Imitation of Life* has long been out of print, the film versions, particularly Douglas Sirk's 1959 adaptation, have enjoyed serious critical attention. The 1934 film, directed by John Stahl, starred Claudette Colbert and Louise Beavers in the roles of Bea and Delilah; the 1959 remake cast Lana Turner and Juanita Moore in these roles, although the characters' names and much of the plot were altered significantly. Rainer Werner Fassbinder's description of the significance of Sirk's lavish, Technicolor version of the narrative encapsulates well *Imitation of Life's* "meaning":

> A great crazy movie about life and about death. And about America. The first great moment: Annie tells Lana Turner that Sarah Jane is her daughter. Annie is black and Sarah Jane is almost white. Lana Turner hesitates, then understands, hesitates again and then quickly pretends that it is the most natural thing in the world that a black woman should have a white daughter. But nothing is natural. Ever. Not in the whole film. And yet they are all trying desperately to make their thoughts and desires their own. It's not because white is a prettier colour than black that Sarah Jane wants to pass for white, but because life is better when you're white. Lana Turner doesn't want to be an actress because she enjoys it, but because if you're successful you get a better deal in this world. And Annie doesn't want a spectacular funeral because she'd get anything out of it, she's dead by then, but because she wants to give herself value in the eyes of the world retrospectively, which she was denied during her lifetime. None of the protagonists come to see that everything, thoughts, desires, dreams arise directly from social reality or are manipulated by it. (244)

Sirk's films have come to enjoy a privileged status, as critics like Fassbinder and Thomas Elsaesser articulated the potential of his melo-dramas "to act as a revolutionary form during times of cultural struggle" (Klinger xii). The 1950s melodramas by Sirk, Nicholas Ray, and Vincent Minnelli, often criticized upon their release for pandering to the tastes of a mass audience, are now praised for "at once celebrating and severely questioning the basic values and attitudes of the mass audience" (Schatz 150). While melodrama as a genre often struggles to gain critical accep-tance, as Fannie Hurst's erasure from the canon attests, it can and does offer poignant social commentary from a unique perspective—the char-acters are usually completely unaware of the social reality which constructs their desires, their "imitation of life," as Hurst terms it.

At times, Fannie Hurst herself seems to suffer from this blindness about the ideological framework of her fiction. In her autobiography and elsewhere, she claims that she experienced a new "consciousness" about race after World War I, a period of "war residuum" characterized by "labor unrest, strikes, displacements, economic crises, race relations, plunging morale and morals" (338). Yet, despite her stated concerns for combating gender and race stereotypes, her treatment of racial otherness in *Imitation of Life* garnered criticism from the African American community, in par-ticular Sterling Brown's charge in *Opportunity* that the novel perpetuated racist stereotypes. The debates about the novel and the film versions' char-acterizations of race offer students a compelling example of the power of cultural images to influence social reality, and examining varied responses to the novel and its film adaptations encourages students to see the impor-tance of historical circumstances in determining what a text "means." As Geoffrey Nowell-Smith reminds us, meaning is "the result of a process whereby people 'make sense' of something with which they are confronted" (10); while I would not go so far as to say that texts have no "intrinsic mean-ing," that they are "historical chameleons with shifting identities" (Klinger xvi), I do agree that culture leaves its ineffable stamp on the reception of a text like *Imitation of Life*. While Hurst may not have recognized the racism coloring her representation of African American characters, a closer inter-pretation of *Imitation of Life* suggests that her exploration of the desires of characters who attempt to transcend racial boundaries is more complex than critics presumed.

The novel opens with a description of Bea Chipley, a recent high school graduate forced into adult responsibilities after her mother's death from cancer.[2] Bea must take over her mother's role in the household, caring for her meticulous salesman father and their tenant, Benjamin Pullman, who has been living with them for over a decade. The two men decide that it is indecorous for Pullman to continue living there after Mrs. Chipley's death unless Bea marries him, which she does without hesitation despite the fact that she is not in love. She merely desires the comfort and security that she believes marriage will bring, although the shock of the more intimate side of marriage briefly obscures her naive conception of domesticity. She quickly becomes pregnant, but soon after this, her father suffers a debilitating stroke. Mr. Chipley is confined to a wheelchair, but his impotent rage at his condition causes him to lash out at his pregnant daughter, even hitting her with a rolling pin. Bea's security is dealt a final blow when Mr. Pullman is killed in a railroad accident; left with little except a paltry settlement from the railroad company, Bea is forced to seek work despite the fact that she has no connections, job training, or education.

The luck of her shared first initial with her husband, who merely placed "B. Pullman" on his business cards, allows Bea to carry on his mail-order syrup trade; however, she needs someone to stay at home with her newborn daughter Jessie and her now child-like father. Enter Delilah, a widowed black woman with an infant herself. The woman needs food and shelter and offers to work for Bea for little pay in return for these creature comforts; as it turns out, Delilah also holds the key to Bea's future success as the operator of a chain of waffle houses. Delilah's talent as a cook—combined with Bea's intuitive business acumen—creates first "Delilah's Delights," candy made from the syrup, and next the "B. Pullman" waffle-house chain. Bea devotes her life to ensuring her makeshift family's security, postponing the pursuit of a romantic relationship and the cultivation of her bond with Jessie. While she believes that economic stability will allow her to have a personal life eventually, the final chapters of the novel depict a woman emerging from the fog of her fantasy life, realizing that her daughter is grown, Delilah's daughter Peola has left home so that she can pass as white, and Delilah is dead from a cancerous growth that, along with her heartbreak over Peola's desertion, has slowly eaten away at her. Bea does not even have love to sustain her, for the young manager of her company whom she hoped to marry instead falls in love with her daughter; Jessie, then, enjoys the life which Bea spent her entire existence making possible.

As this plot synopsis indicates, one reason that the novel endured harsh criticism is its reliance upon the melodramatic themes of maternal sacrifice and thwarted desire. While in the nineteenth century, as Jane Tompkins reminds us, "the aesthetic and the didactic, the serious and the sentimental were not opposed by overlapping designations" (17), our contemporary suspicion of melodrama makes it difficult for us to see novels like *Imitation of Life* as anything other than sob-inducing soap opera. Hurst in many ways belongs to the nineteenth-century tradition of which Tompkins speaks: she hoped to infuse her popular narratives with social messages, and furthermore, she aimed to create "Art" in the process. In an unpublished essay entitled "Whither Fiction?," Hurst claims that most fiction does not "live up to its requirements as an art. Art, in its highest forms, is not a mere imitation of life. It is rather a reaction and protest against it" (ts. 10).[3] This comment aligns her with the directors of 1950s film melodramas; her choice of *Imitation of Life* as the title for the novel first published in serial form as *Sugar House* indicates her desire to emphasize the very lack of self-awareness that Fassbinder identifies as a central motif of the Sirk adaptation. She exposes the impact of racial prejudice on individuals by focusing upon the consciousness of a single character, Bea Pullman, who certainly does not perceive herself as a "racist." Along with Bea's inability to fuse her maternal and domestic impulses with her more "masculine" drives for success and even fulfillment in the business world, we can see her lack of perception concerning issues of racial and sexual identity. The fact that a reader can perceive Bea's blindness to the fact that society (and often, Bea herself) defines Delilah and Peola solely upon the basis of their race indicates that Hurst deliberately chose this narrative perspective for the ironic commentary on racism that it would provide. This awareness of the complex intersections between aesthetics and identity politics aligns Hurst with female writers of the Harlem Renaissance like Nella Larsen.[4]

However, Hurst's contemporaries did not see the novel as a step forward in the contemplation of racial identity. Jane Caputi explores the controversies surrounding the reception of *Imitation of Life* by the African American community, including the Sterling Brown review of the 1934

film in *Opportunity*. Despite the complex sexual and racial issues which
structure the novel (the 1934 film dilutes the sexual tensions, possibly due
to Hays Code restrictions), critics attacked the portrayals of Delilah and
Peola, characterizations which Brown felt perpetuated the "contented
Mammy" and "tragic mulatto" stereotypes so common during this period.
While the review focuses upon the film adaptation, he notes that the film's
"characterization and ideas . . . are little changed" from the novel, and he
goes on to berate the portrayal of Delilah:

> Delilah is straight out of southern fiction. Less abject than in the
> novel, she is still more concerned with the white Jessie than with
> Peola. She has little faith in Peola's capacities: "We all starts out smart;
> we don't get dumb till later on." Resignation to injustice is her creed;
> God knows best, we can't be telling Him his business; mixed bloods
> who want to be white must learn to take it, must not beat their fists
> against life; she doesn't rightly know where the blame lies. (88)

Brown's condemnation of the film's racist depictions drew a response
from Hurst herself; she defended the film in an editorial letter published
in *Opportunity*. Here, she chooses to ignore his criticisms of her novel, suggesting instead that the racist stereotypes he condemned were only evident
in the alterations that John Stahl's 1934 film made to her work:

> As the author of the novel from which this picture is made, there are
> many aspects of it that fall short or deviate or even malign my origi-
> nal theme. But for purposes of what I have to say, that is beside the
> point. I do think, however, that instead of the carping, petty angles
> of criticism presented by your reviewer, there is a much larger view
> of this picture which he has overlooked. In other words, he did not
> see the woods for the trees. The important social value of this picture
> is that it practically inaugurates into the important medium of the
> motion-picture, a consideration of the Negro as part of the social pat-
> tern of American life. (121)

Her failure to mention his charges against the novel itself may be calculated, but her correspondence with Zora Neale Hurston suggests that the
two women believed that the novel did have value as social commentary.
Perhaps Hurston felt compelled to praise the novel because of Hurst's various favors for her, but in a 1940 letter to her former employer, she defends
the novel against Brown's charges:

> You have a grand set of admirers in this part of the world [Durham,
> N.C.] because of *Imitation of Life*. So it seems that Sterling Brown is
> not in the majority. He picks on me all the time now. He tells people
> that he wants to riddle me, and otherwise deflate me because he says
> that I stand convicted of having furnished you with the material of
> "IMITATION." I let it stand without contradiction because I feel he does
> me honor. In so saying, he pays you an unconscious tribute because
> he is admitting the truth of the work. What he and his kind resent is
> just that. It is too accurate to be comfortable. . . . (6 Feb. 1940)

Hurston rather coyly avoids the question of whether or not she *did* furnish
the material for Delilah, but the fact that these two women are discussing
Brown's distaste for the novel years after its publication clearly indicates
Hurst's continued obsession with defending the "truthfulness" of her
novel's representation of race relations. Of course, their use of the term
"truth" seems suspicious to those of us trained to cast a postmodernist, pes-
simistic eye on anyone who claims that an absolute truth or meaning can
be determined, but their belief that the novel does express a "truth" is
telling in and of itself. Neither expresses what they perceive as "true" about
the text, so we can only assume that they are referring to the accuracy of
the character portrayals. What, then, might be so uncomfortable about
these representations?

Jane Caputi argues that a number of authors, including Hurston herself, were so unsettled by the novel's portrayal of race that they parodied
the text. Langston Hughes and Hurston, both of whom praised the novel
to Hurst's face, "specified" on *Imitation of Life,* writing texts that either
overtly parodied the race roles of the novel or indirectly critiqued the racial
types. Hughes's "Limitations of Life" (1938) is, as its title indicates, the most
direct parody of the novel and film, but Caputi also argues that Hurston's
Their Eyes Were Watching God (1937) is a reconstruction of the "folk" which
Delilah's character represented to the white audience of *Imitation of Life*.
Extending the novel's impact to later generations of writers, Caputi also
believes that Toni Morrison's *The Bluest Eye* "specifies" on *Imitation of Life,*
serving as a critique of the ideals of beauty that Peola adopts by rejecting
her mother and choosing to pass. She argues that Pecola Breedlove's name
is a play on "Peola," and, in fact, a scene in *The Bluest Eye* which describes
the narrator's hatred of the "big, blue-eyed Baby Doll" she received at
Christmas does revise the scene in the 1959 film when Sarah Jane (Peola's

name in this version) rejects a doll because it is black (Morrison 305).[5] Such
a scene, however, is not in the novel; Peola's awareness of her difference
from Jessie occurs in two crucial instances: During a fight, Jessie calls Peola
a "nigger" (179), and later, Peola's attempt to pass is undermined by her
mother's appearance in her classroom (224).

Such mergings of the novel and its film versions continue today; in
fact, discussions of *Imitation of Life* are so deeply influenced by the two film
versions that critics discuss the various texts interchangeably.[6] Lauren
Berlant's insightful analysis of the three versions of the text, while drawing distinctions among their various plot devices and characterizations,
essentially reads them as one super-text by purposefully conflating their
social function:

> In this complex *text* the women fight for dignity and pleasure by
> mutually exploiting the structures of commodity capitalism and
> American mass culture. As we trace the various embodiments of
> *Imitation of Life*, we will see its "stars" transformed into trademarks
> and corporate logos, prosthetic bodies that ideally replace the body of
> pain with the projected image of safety and satisfaction commodities
> represent. From some angles these commercial hieroglyphs look like
> vehicles of corporeal enfranchisement; but we will also see the fail-
> ure of the erotic utopia of the female commodity, as the success mon-
> tage of one American generation can not reframe the bodies of the
> next. (114, emphasis mine)

Unlike critics who seem to confuse the narrative strands of the three versions, her conflation is purposeful; she seems to suggest that after reading
the novel and viewing the films, one cannot consider the texts apart from
one another, for "they collectively imagine the American body politic from
the points of view of the overembodied women who serve it" (115). In
essence, her materialist approach demands that the texts overlap, for their
similarities highlight the repetition of the dilemmas that confront the protagonists. Despite a twenty-five-year gap between the two films, the
African American characters are no less subject to racism in the 1959 version than they were in the 1934 adaptation. Berlant's materialist analysis
of the three versions of *Imitation of Life* highlights the means by which
characters negotiate the complex influences of commodity capitalism, especially its impact on the female and African American body and con-

sciousness. Hurst attempts to create a female utopia, a quasi-nuclear family in which Bea and Delilah achieve solidarity and financial security, but ultimately, they cannot maintain their maternal bonds due to the complications of the family romance and passing plots which overtake Bea and Delilah's economic "success" narrative.

However, by focusing her analysis on the success montages and visual representations of the female body, Berlant tends to emphasize the cinematic versions of this "text." I argue, instead, that the novel's point of view, an element essentially ignored by critics of the novel, foregrounds Hurst's awareness of the very inability of commodity capitalism to ensure the (emotional) security that Berlant highlights in her analysis. While the film versions may have fulfilled a kind of national popular fantasy, as Berlant suggests, through the "positivity of difference: of female households and workplaces that protect the hyper-embodied frame; of an unalienated capitalist public sphere; and an identity in labor that eases the psychic burdens of gender and race" (123), the symbiotic structure of the white woman and her Other created by the film versions is much less comforting in Hurst's rendition of the relationship. We should not perceive this novel (or the films) as an endorsement of the kinds of racial stereotypes that Americans would have seen as comforting during an era when *Gone with the Wind* saturated the market—a belief that the mammies of America would protect white womanhood and that nurturance, not hostility, undergirded race relations. Thus, a better understanding of the complications raised by Hurst's narrative technique can help us to see the film versions in a new light.

An early moment in the novel marks Bea as someone who lacks racial awareness. On her wedding night, she finds a pornographic picture propped on her dresser, one of her husband's possessions that has just been moved into the room that day. Unable to recognize the staid (and much older) Mr. Pullman as someone who has ever experienced sexual desire, a misconception soon unraveled by the experience of her wedding night when he becomes a "panther . . . breathing in the dark" (53), she blames the girl who, "with what seemed actual malice," had placed the photo in plain view. "Those darkies . . ." is her response, the only way she can make sense of the character of the man with whom she is about to share her wedding night, absolving him of eroticism while displacing it onto the Other (50). Berlant's reading of this passage focuses on the image in the photograph, a woman (her race is not specified) gazing at herself in a mirror, wearing stockings and a hat like Abraham Lincoln's; Berlant wonders if the photo provides a parodic moment, a reminder that "the nation holds out a promise of emancipation and a pornographic culture both" (135). Such a "promise" would indeed be a difficult schism for women to negotiate, as Bea's confusion about her own sexuality makes clear. However, Bea's response to the photo is much less complex than Berlant's; even after she is faced with the shock of recognizing her husband's sexuality, she cannot recognize her own: "It seemed a lot to be able, through just the volition of being herself, to bring to him what seemed to be almost intolerable ecstasies of the flesh which, through the calm unruffled curtain of her own unawakened flesh, she could regard with almost clinical detachment" (58). Her assertion of "clinical detachment" is evasive, for the claim that her flesh is "unawakened" indicates an awareness that something is missing from her relationship with Pullman; however, we cannot untangle what Bea herself recognizes and what Hurst's narrative voice is revealing to the reader.

In the novel, the characterization of Bea Pullman deeply influences the way we perceive the other characters. Hurst's decision to render the entire narrative through Bea Pullman's consciousness (but not in the first person) problematizes the reader's ability to comprehend Delilah—her housekeeper, caretaker for her daughter and father (who outlives Delilah), and the inspiration for her waffle business—because Bea herself is incapable of perceiving anything about this woman beyond the functions she performs for Bea's family. The narrative voice reflects Bea's inability to grasp the significance of anything around her except her business: her sexual desires, her overidealization of her daughter Jessie, and, of course, the racist implications of her perception of Delilah.[7] A potent example of this is when the adolescent Jessie, who leaves for boarding school in Switzerland at the age of thirteen, visits her mother during one of her school vacations. Bea is upset by her daughter's emotional distance; Jessie is clearly in awe of her successful mother, and her schoolmates' perception of the famous "B. Pullman" has supplanted any maternal image she had of Bea. Thus, she takes to calling her mother "B. Pullman," a nickname which Bea sees as "delightful," but which we see as a sign of her daughter's inability to perceive Bea as anything other than the icon she has become to the masses (210).

Likewise, Bea can only perceive Delilah in an abstracted, stereotyped manner. For the most part, Delilah's sexuality is displaced onto her love of

food and her wish, the only one Bea can ever draw from her, for an elaborate funeral; the grotesque conflation of her massive body and the desire to
have that body celebrated after her death do make her a caricature. However,
Delilah is turned into this caricature by Bea herself; this state is not a "natural" one. The "mammy" icon Bea creates to advertise her waffle business
is, of course, the target of Brown and other critics; that is, they argue that
Hurst has reiterated racist stereotypes by presenting Delilah as an Aunt
Jemima figure.[8] But this very representation is part of Hurst's critique, for
Delilah is an icon to Bea herself—she cannot "see" the real Delilah any more
than the hordes who troop to the B. Pullmans, allured by the vision of the
reassuring "mammy" in the window. Bea is so self-absorbed, mostly out of
the necessity to survive, that she sees only those aspects of Delilah which suit
her needs: the good cook, the maternal figure who will protect her family,
and the "mammy" who will sell the waffles, the profits of which art will
make them secure.

A potent example of Bea's tunnel vision occurs when she has the idea of
putting Delilah's face on the box of candy and we see her constructing the
image that will prove so lucrative: "Delilah's Hearts! Why not Delilah's photograph, in her great fluted white cap, and her great fluted white smile on
each box? Delilah, who, though actually in no more than her late thirties,
looked mammy to the world. . . . Delilah beaming and beckoning from the
lid . . ." (103). Delilah actually protests this self-presentation, wishing to have
a more "proper" photograph taken as a record for her daughter, but Bea
believes that the effect of the first photo is perfect: "The heavy cheeks, shel-
lacked eyes, right, round, and crammed with vitality, huge upholstery of lips
that caught you like a pair of divans into the luxury of laughter, Delilah to
the life beamed out of that photograph with sun power!" (105). Bea's former
attention to budgets and basic survival shifts to shaping Delilah into the icon
which will assure them of economic security. Bea even spends her spare time
constructing slogans for her company, ones which further place Delilah in
the realm of the unreal: "One of her favorite and most successful feature
pages was a catalogic summary of those reasons [why Delilah delights].
1. Delilah is the most indulgent hostess in the world. 2. Delilah loves to spoil
you. 3. Delilah has a mother-complex. 4. Delilah cares" (175).

Unlike Delilah, who seemingly succumbs to the personification Bea
and the racist stereotypes of black womanhood in America at that time
construct for her, Peola rebels against the constraints of her era. Peola's

color, according to Delilah, is a matter of "'Accident, honey. And style. Her
pap jes' had style mixed in, I guess, wid a teaspoonful of white blood back
somewheres, an' it got him through life an' three wives widout ever turnin'
them lily-pink palms of his'" (143). Revolting against her mother's plan
that she attend Howard University and pursue a teaching career, she moves
to Seattle at the age of seventeen to work as a librarian, eventually meeting a white man whom she decides to marry. In the final confrontation
with her mother, Peola insists that she cannot live with being black:

> "I've cried myself dry. Cried myself out with self-loathing and self-
> pity and self-consciousness. I tell you I've prayed same as you, for the
> strength to be proud of being black under my white. I've tried to glory
> in my people. I've drenched myself in the life of Toussaint
> L'Ouverture, Booker Washington, and Frederick Douglass. I've tried
> to catch some of their spark. But I'm not that stuff. I haven't pride of
> race, or love of race. There's nothing grand or of-the-stuff-martyrs-
> are-made about me. I can't learn to endure being black in a white
> world." (297)

Thus, she decides to recreate herself, opting to imitate the life of a white
woman.

Peola willingly sterilizes herself so that she can protect her secret from
her husband, but perhaps she feels less guilty about her deceit because he,
too, is "maimed"—he has lost part of his hand and suffers from his having
been gassed during the war. South America is Peola's "Promised Land," but
in order for her to make it to this land, she must ensure that she will not pro-
create, for her child could look more like Delilah than herself. "Passing" is,
then, a tenuous proposition, and Peola's self-destruction is a palpable
reminder of her overwhelming desire to have all that Bea had wanted when
she first married: "Security! Her own curtains to select and hem. Her own
place in the life of a man" (33). While Bea's naive vision of domesticity is
deconstructed as her life unravels and she is forced to create an alternative
domestic arrangement, Peola, too, yearns for the same fantasy, telling her
mother, "I want my happiness. I want my man. I want my life" (300). Her
mother's religious fervor and self-effacement are responses to a world that
will not allow her to have the life that she might choose for herself, and Peola
cannot imagine following in her mother's footsteps. While her husband's
physical disabilities and his lack of knowledge about Peola's origins insinu-

ate that this model of domesticity is no more tenable than Bea's had been, she does leave for South America never to return, prompting the reader to assume that she succeeds in her endeavor. Her sterilization and exile ensure that she will never have to reclaim her mother, in life or death, but this complex "solution" to the problem of otherness is not one that could be acknowledged by the film industry, for it is too unsettling and it fails to endorse the fantasy of racial harmony that the two film versions inadvertently promote. Instead, the films depict a guilt-ridden daughter returning to claim her mother publicly (but only in death); the daughter takes her mother's place in order to atone for the "sin" of passing.

Despite Hurst's emphasis on Bea's complete lack of comprehension about the obstacles imposed on Delilah's and Peola's lives because of race and the horror of Peola's "solution" to her problem, both film versions erase the complications posed by the novel's construction of Bea's consciousness, turning her first into a sophisticated socialite and then into a famous actress; both Claudette Colbert (Bea in the 1934 film) and Lana Turner (Lora Meredith in the 1959 film) project a glamour and self-confidence which bears little resemblance to the novel's characterization of Bea Pullman. In the novel, we only see Delilah through Bea's eyes, and Hurst repeatedly reminds the reader of the insufficiency of this point of view. Yet, without this point of view to structure the characterization of Delilah, the films' depictions of her—as an Aunt Jemima figure in the 1934 film and as a self-effacing housemaid, Annie, in the 1959 version—*are* often essentialist and racist, characters pulled from cultural stereotypes which do not force us to question those stereotypes and do not ask the audience to question *why* Bea/Lora accepts Delilah/Annie's self-sacrifices without any qualms about her positioning of Delilah/Annie.

There are, however, moments in each film where the ruptures exposed in Hurst's narrative threaten to break forth, and these are the moments I examine in my classes in order to convey to my students the importance of film as a medium for exploring the fissures beneath a society's seemingly smooth surface. The 1934 John Stahl film, written by William Hurlbut, relies much more heavily on Hurst's source material than does Douglas Sirk's 1959 adaptation; the primary differences come in the closing third of the film, where Hurlbut rewrites the most troubling aspects of the novel, Peola's marriage to a white man and Jessie's marriage to her mother's would-be lover; instead, the ending of this "woman's film" reinforces mother-daughter bonds. While the film's ending highlights the cementing of the Bea-Jessie bond, the Delilah-Peola relationship often manages to usurp the central pair. As Thomas Cripps points out in his survey of African Americans in film, Fredi Washington and Louise Beavers's portrayals of Peola and Delilah are the most powerful aspects of the film, but he insists that the actresses cannot overcome the script, which contained "weaknesses . . . hidden beneath the liberal surface" (303). Like Sterling Brown, Cripps is frustrated by Beavers's "urge to be lovable" which can only be achieved by claiming, over and over, that one must submit to the color line because it is tantamount to submitting to God's will (303). The character's resemblance to the Aunt Jemima logo along with her dialect-laden voice conforms to the "mammy" stereotype so prevalent at that time. However, in key moments in the film, we can see that here, too, Delilah is constructed by Bea and the conventions of a racist culture.

When the harried widow Bea Pullman finds a vacant store to open her pancake business, she uses her feminine charm to procure furniture and kitchen supplies on credit. As she comes up with an idea for a sign to draw in customers, she asks Delilah to "smile." Delilah immediately responds in a moment drawn from a minstrel act, proffering her employer an artificially wide grin that is a clear invocation of the Aunt Jemima logo and which then transmutes into the newly painted sign on the window. While the scene cannot provide the troubling thoughts of Bea as she ruminates over the photo taken for "Delilah's Delights" and it eliminates Delilah's protest that she wants a more "proper" photograph taken, the visual impact of the scene invokes a discomfort similar to the novel's.[9]

In a later scene, Bea asks for Delilah's signature so that they can incorporate their booming business and Delilah can receive her 20 percent share. Delilah worries that this means that Bea is going to send her away and tells Bea, "I make you a present of it." Bea puts the money in the bank for Delilah, bemused by her lack of ambition and unaware of her fear, but her business adviser Elmer mocks, "Once a pancake, always a pancake." This line is both a slur, a racial epithet at this time, and an intimation that there is something unnatural about Delilah's self-effacing manner (while said manner is seen as a racial trait); this moment shows the film's struggle to offer a message of racial harmony when such bitterness about racist constructions of identity rages beneath its surface. The fact that, according to Sterling Brown's unfavorable review, many moviegoers and critics disagreed with him because they felt that the film *was* a "breaking away from old patterns of the [motion] picture" indicates both the entrenched racism of Hollywood at this moment in history and the ways in which the film manages to disrupt the "old stereotype of the contented Mammy, and the tragic mulatto; and the ancient ideas about the mixture of the races" (Brown 87–88).

Another subversive moment deals more specifically with the "tragic mulatto" theme. Lifted almost directly from the novel, this scene occurs on a rainy day when the ever-concerned mother Delilah takes a raincoat and rubbers to Peola at school, fearful that her daughter will catch a cold on her way home. However, Peola has been passing at her school, and the appearance of the very-black Delilah shatters the illusion she has so carefully constructed. Her rage when her mother insists to the teacher that Peola is her daughter, despite her initial insistence that she does not know the black woman, is palpable—her fury betrays her need to be white. Most interesting, however, is a detail incorporated by the director: when Delilah appears, the teacher is reading *Little Women* to them. A number of feminist critics have explored the potentially subversive messages in Alcott's novel, but in the 1930s, the novel still would have been seen as a message about the "proper" way that girls should grow up, shedding childhood whims and influencing men's lives from the appropriate domestic sphere.[10] Here, Peola is ingesting the very ideals about home, family, and womanhood that her novel counterpart so clearly longs to emulate when she tells her mother: "I want my happiness. I want my man. I want my life" (300). However, Peola feels that she can achieve this life only if she is white—the "cult of true womanhood" applies only to white womanhood, and Delilah's inability to have her own man and domestic space can only reinforce Peola's belief in this ideology. While Bea has also failed to achieve the model of domesticity described in *Little Women,* for she focuses on her career, in some ways she is like the Jo March of the first part of the novel, a woman who rejects convention in order to pursue economic security, albeit so that she can care for her family. Peola longs for the final, domesticated tableau of *Little Women,* but more than that, she longs for the choices that she thinks Bea and Jessie have because of their skin color.

Ironically, in this film adaptation, none of the women gets their man; the final shot focuses upon Bea and Jessie as they remember the moment right before Delilah entered their lives, a moment with Jessie playing with her "quack, quack" in the bathtub while her mother looks on adoringly. While the novel emphasizes the tensions imposed on the mother-daughter bond by romantic entanglements, the Stahl film seems to strip away these complications, leaving us with the image of a "simple" moment of connection between mother and child. Such a resolution reminds us that at this moment in history, maternal sacrifice triumphed over sexual desire; while this may have been comforting to 1930s audiences, we find it troubling today. In addition to this transformation, Peola, who marries a white man in the novel, never pursues a romance in the 1934 film. Not only is she stripped of sexual desire, but she also agrees to pursue the life her mother wanted for her, not the life she would have chosen for herself.

Douglas Sirk's 1959 adaptation chooses not only to resurrect the sexual themes absent from the 1934 version, but he makes them the focal point of his film. While this later film version of *Imitation of Life* indicates a desire to revisit the novel's story of potential harmony between the white woman and the Other, the restructuring of Delilah and Peola's characters in Sirk's adaptation makes them almost unrecognizable to readers of Hurst's novel. In fact, their new names, Annie and Sarah Jane, are more distinctly Anglicized and even more ironically, a white actress portrays Sarah Jane. At the onset of the Civil Rights era, the national fantasy that Sirk's characters act out is premised upon degradation and self-erasure. In this adaptation, Sarah Jane becomes an exotic dancer, seemingly choosing sexual objectification as an assurance that she is a desirable (hence, "white") woman, while her mother Annie is repeatedly forced into a masochistic position, searching for her daughter to bring her home, only to watch Sarah Jane enact the worst sexual stereotypes of black womanhood on stage.

The revisions in the Sirk film can be understood in relationship to his stated goals for filmmaking; according to Barbara Klinger, "the director consistently compared his aims with those of authors (such as Euripides, Shakespeare, Calderon, and Lope de Vega) who worked ingeniously within genres to present critiques of their own societies" (8). The resurging interest in Sirk's oeuvre, including *Imitation of Life,* is rooted in the belief that these melodramas encoded darker messages; as Laura Mulvey states,

> ... the interest in Hollywood 50s melodrama lies primarily in the way
> that fissures and contradictions can be shown, by means of textual
> analysis, to be undermining the films' ideological coherence, contra-
> dictions of a kind, whether on the level of form or of narrative inci-
> dent, that seem to save the films from belonging blindly to the
> bourgeois ideology which produced them. (75)

In other words, only the belief that these films are saying more (and other)
than what they *seem* to say validates our return to these films. Jon Halliday's
interviews with Douglas Sirk (published in 1974) allowed the filmmaker
himself to shape the perception of his work; in his introduction to these
interviews, Halliday describes the "world of pretense" in Sirkian melodrama, a cinematic landscape which entraps its characters "by the multi-
plication of intermediate objects" such as mirrors, a central motif in
Imitation of Life (12). More importantly, however, the valorization of Sirk
as an auteur capable of using melodrama as an ironic commentary on
bourgeois American life means that critics generally perceive his film adaptation of Hurst's novel as an ironic commentary on *that* text as well.

Sirk transforms Bea Pullman into Lora Meredith, an actress portrayed
by no other than Lana Turner (in the midst of scandal at the time of the
film's release due to her lover's being murdered by her daughter), and casts
a white actress, Susan Kohner, to portray Sarah Jane, turning her into a
"performer" in the narrative as well, highlighting her desire to emulate
Lora. Such casting choices, combined with the drastic changes to the
novel's plot structure, do indicate a purposeful distancing from Hurst's narrative. Hurst's biographer Brooke Kroeger is unsure "whether or not
Fannie liked [this] latter-day remake" as much as she did the film version
which appeared on the heels of her novel's original publication (338).
However, her autobiography (which appeared shortly before the film's
release and enjoyed a sales boost because of the film) indicates a favorable
response: she attended numerous Hollywood promotional events for the
film, and her endorsement appeared on film advertisements. Hurst may
have sensed that Sirk was manipulating certain themes of her original
work in ways that would reshape its meaning, but as with Stahl's version,
particular moments in the film evoke the discomfort created by the perspective used in Hurst's novel; in short, he uses the evolving conventions
of 1950s melodrama to reinvent Hurst's message about race.

While Bea Pullman's naiveté may have been forgivable in the 1930s, Sirk restructures Bea into the worldly Lora Meredith, a woman who is more aware of her desires than Bea could have imagined possible. Unlike Bea, who longed for domestic security, Lora rejects a marriage proposal by Steve Archer, insisting that marriage means giving up "something I've wanted all my life" (Griffin and Scott 83). Archer berates her for chasing after a fantasy when he offers her a reality, an essential theme of the film that in many ways is drawn directly from Hurst's novel. Bea often imagines a "reality" quite different from the one that actually exists, and characters in the novel often construct alternatives to replace unsatisfactory realities—Delilah's vision of heaven, Peola's passing as white. Sirk develops this theme by using the motif of acting and performance to expose the futility of believing in the romances constructed both in our minds and by the silver screen. Fassbinder's comment about the film's "unnaturalness" and the inability of the characters to perceive the ways that "social reality" manipulates their desires could equally apply to the novel; and it is Sirk's development of this theme, rooted in the novel's title, that provides insights into the horrors of racism during America's supposed "golden age."[11]

In many ways, Lora Meredith is only a foil in the film, a reminder that white Americans have no idea what occurs in the "back rooms" of their houses or in the lives of their domestic servants. After a frustrated Sarah Jane delivers Lora and her guests hors d'oeuvres while balancing a platter on her head and speaking in a thick "slave" dialect, an infuriated Lora asks her, "Have I ever treated you as if you were different? Has Susie? Has anyone here?" (Griffin and Scott 117). And while Sarah Jane admits, "You've been wonderful," we have seen numerous moments where Sarah Jane and her mother proceeded to the back room or stayed in the kitchen while others went to the front of the house, palpable reminders that they were, indeed, "different."

Her inability to understand that she has treated Annie and Sarah Jane as "different" is reiterated in a later scene, as Lora and Annie discuss the funeral of Annie's dreams: "I really want it elegant. Got it all written down the way I want it to be and all the friends I'd like to have there." Lora replies, "It never occurred to me that you had so many friends," and softly Annie replies, "You never asked" (120–21). These moments, along with the film's use of door frames to separate the characters, and mirrors to show their reliance on reflections of reality, underscore the fact that while Lora "performs" the role of a woman liberated from the constraints of gender and race boundaries, she ultimately conforms to the expectations of her culture. Like Annie, she encourages Sarah Jane to take on roles "appropriate" to her station in life, and ultimately, she finds her film career unfulfilling, just as Steve told her she would. Sirk most devastatingly reminds us of the difficulty of playing roles when Sarah Jane's white boyfriend finds out her true racial identity and mercilessly beats her in an alley. When she insists to him, "I'm as white as you!," we only see her reflection in a dirty store window (119). The three scenes just described are juxtaposed together to underscore the dangers of passing, the humiliation of playing the role expected of a black woman, and the white woman's inability to understand the complicated lives of the black women who have inhabited her life and house for many years.

While Sirk's film uses the funeral scene as its capstone—causing many to remember most vividly the tear-inducing moment when Sarah Jane throws herself on Annie's coffin, at last proclaiming to the world that Annie is her mother—an earlier scene in which Annie actually helps her daughter to disavow her is the more powerful exclamation on the power of the maternal bond. After Annie yet again finds her daughter performing in a nightclub (although the latest incarnation is more Moulin Rouge than seedy bar), she follows her daughter to her hotel. Sarah Jane fears another exposure of her identity and subsequent job loss, but Annie seems resigned to the life her daughter has chosen and introduces herself to Sarah Jane's friends as her "mammy." One of the friends jokes, "Well—get you! So, honey child, you had a Mammy!" and her mournful reply, "Yes—all my life" foreshadows her inability to throw off her past (141). Annie's willingness to eradicate herself so that her daughter can pursue her chosen life contrasts with Lora's selfish pursuit of success on the stage at the expense of nurturing her relationship with Susie, implying that sacrifice is the more viable portrait of maternity, much like the maternal melodramas of the 1930s and 1940s. This message is underscored by the fact that while Steve and Susie repeatedly tell Lora to "stop acting," as if her every reaction to others was only a constructed response meant to achieve the desired effect—a suspicion which seems founded in light of a number of scenes in the film in which Lora does "perform" in order to get what she wants—

every emotion Annie expresses seems genuine. Annie's sadness and self-denial finally begin to affect Sarah Jane in the very scene in which the audience knows that a dying Annie has come to say good-bye to her daughter.

Perhaps as expected, my female students always react most strongly to the scenes of mother-daughter melodrama provided in each film; but particularly in Sirk's version, they find the scenes between Lora and Susie rather false, while the scenes between Annie and Sarah Jane, layered with racial complexities most of us can't even begin to fathom, come across as more convincing to them. If nothing else, these films force them to confront and identify with characters far outside their own realm of experience. But hopefully, students raised in a culture which emphasizes the value of individuality will see that for characters like Delilah/Annie and Peola/Sarah Jane, the choices which most of us take for granted were not possible for them. By exploring the ways that these characters traversed the rocky terrain of race in mid-twentieth-century America, perhaps they can better understand the legacy such lack of choice leaves for us today.

As Spike Lee's recent film *Bamboozled* suggests, negative stereotypes of African Americans still abound in American popular culture. I encourage my students to consider the lingering use of "Uncle Tom" figures in films like *The Green Mile* and *The Legend of Bagger Vance,* the "Mammy" characterizations in films like *Fried Green Tomatoes,* and the discomfort provoked (both within the narrative and by the audiences) by interracial relationships in films like *The Bodyguard, Save the Last Dance,* and *The Pelican Brief.* While television shows such as *Homicide* and *NYPD Blue* and the occasional film such as *Eve's Bayou* do offer realistic explorations of racial conflict and depict the lives of "ordinary" African Americans without resorting to stereotype, such instances are still rare. Tessa Perkins reminds us of the need to study the aesthetic function of stereotypes (77), and *Imitation of Life*'s complex use of point of view to structure our response to the race stereotypes and the films' elaborations on the "mammy" and "tragic mulatto" types provide a useful starting point for a classroom discussion of the perpetuation of racist ideology and the capacity of popular culture either to uphold or undermine such images.

NOTES

1. Refer to Brooke Kroeger's *Fannie: The Talent for Success of Writer Fannie Hurst* (1999) for a complete bibliography. Kroeger's work is the only full-length biography on Hurst, and, in addition to Hurst's autobiography, *Anatomy of Me* (1958), it offers the most detailed information about Hurst's life. However, she focuses more upon Hurst's social and political life, particularly her friendship with Eleanor Roosevelt and her unconventional marriage to pianist Jacques Danielson (the two inhabited separate apartments for over fifteen years of their marriage) than she does upon Hurst's fiction. As for the relationship between Hurst and Zora Neale Hurston, refer to Hurston's own account of the relationship in *Dust Tracks on a Road.* Virginia Burke and Gay Wilentz have written excellent essays about their friendship and correspondence; both authors offer some reasons for the total exclusion of Hurston from Hurst's autobiography, including the charge of statutory rape leveled at Hurston around 1949 (which was later dropped).

2. Unfortunately, *Imitation of Life* is out of print. Except for a brief republication in the 1990s as part of the Perennial Library's Literary Film Classics series, the novel has become increasingly difficult to find. A Web site devoted to finding out-of-print books, www.sbebooks.com, usually lists available copies, and some public and college libraries still have copies. There are portions of the novel included in the Rutgers University Press film casebook for *Imitation of Life,* edited by Lucy Fischer (1991), and these excerpts do focus on the Bea-Delilah relationship. When I have used this text, I copy several chapters for my students. I would suggest chapters 17 (Bea comes up with the idea for the "Delilah's Delights" campaign), 26 (Peola's attempt to pass at school), and 39 (Peola tells her mother that she is marrying a white man and plans to sterilize herself).

3. This essay, along with Hurst's manuscripts and other unpublished works, are housed at the Harry Ransom Humanities Research Center at the University of Texas, Austin. "Whither Fiction?" is not available in print.

4. I taught Nella Larsen's *Passing* along with *Imitation of Life*; comparing the two portrayals of the "passing" issue raises interesting questions about how an author's life experiences influence her work.

5. See Jane Caputi's "Specifying Fannie Hurst: Langston Hughes's 'Limitations of Life,' Zora Neale Hurston's *Their Eyes Were Watching God,* and Toni Morrison's *The Bluest Eye* As 'Answers' to Hurst's *Imitation of Life*" (*Black American Literature Forum* 24.4 [1990]: 697–715).

6. Mary Rose Shaughnessy's synopsis of *Imitation of Life* particularly shows the extent of this confusion. Supposedly writing about the novel, she instead describes the plot of the 1934 film, in which Frank Flake's character is named Stephen Archer, and the ending of the novel, according to her, finds a repentant Peola at her mother's funeral and a maternal Bea banishing Stephen so that her daughter will not have to suffer his rejection. These are the narrative strands of John Stahl's film, not the novel.

7. For example, the novel, and more particularly the manuscript version, indicates that Bea only believes she needs "man-lovin'" because Delilah and her peers like Virginia Eden repeatedly tell her that she does. Her professed but unconsummated passion for Frank Flake seems odd in light of her lack of passion in her marriage and the many years during which she focused on her business.

8. Another discussion about Delilah as an icon can be found in M. M. Manring's *Slave in a Box: The Strange Career of Aunt Jemima* (1998). This analysis of the Aunt Jemima advertising phenomenon surveys the use of the "mammy" stereotype in literature, and Manring claims that *Imitation of Life* "shaped the popular image of the mammy as black matriarch as much as any single work of this century" (34). While Manring acknowledges Delilah's role as a figure of Christ-like suffering, he blames Hurst for representing her as "a spokeswoman for an old racial and gender order, particularly concerning the place of white womanhood" (37).

9. The novel's and films' original white audience probably did not experience this discomfort, but today's viewers (including my students) find the representation distasteful. I ask them to think about why such a scene is uncomfortable and if they can find similar scenes in today's cinematic representations of African Americans.

10. The "images of women" criticism of second-wave feminist theorists especially focused upon questions concerning how a novel's depiction of women influenced its readers and the society at large, and the critical discussions of *Little Women* repeatedly return to this issue. Frances Armstrong insists that the novel "was indeed a contributor to the ideology of women's littleness which had been developing for at least two centuries" (453), while Catharine Stimpson replies that "much of the joy of *Little Women* exists because one part of the text encourages rebellion" (969). Beverly Lyon Clark believes that Alcott wrote out of a sense of familial duty, not as a creative outlet, and thus, while Alcott "gives some play to subversive ideas of self-expression, her overt message is that girls should subordinate themselves and their language to others" (81). Elizabeth Lennox Keyser offers an extended analysis of the subversive elements in *Little Women*, arguing that her "sensational" fiction should prompt us to reread the message of her famous domestic novel.

11. See Stephanie Coontz's *The Way We Never Were: American Families and the Nostalgia Trap* (1992) for a discussion about the stereotype of the 1950s as America's "golden age."

WORKS CITED

Armstrong, Frances. "'Here Little, and Hereafter Bliss': *Little Women* and the Deferral of Greatness." *American Literature* 64.3 (1992): 453–74.

Berlant, Lauren. "National Brands/National Body: Imitation of Life." *Comparative American Identities: Race, Sex & Nationality in the Modern Text.* Ed. Hortense Spillers. New York: Routledge, 1991. 110–40.

Brown, Sterling. "*Imitation of Life*: Once a Pancake." *Opportunity: A Journal of Negro Life* (March 1935): 87–88.

Burke, Virginia M. "Zora Neale Hurston and Fannie Hurst As They Saw Each Other." *CLA Journal* 20.4 (1977): 435–47.

Caputi, Jane. "'Specifying' Fannie Hurst: Langston Hughes's 'Limitations of Life,' Zora Neale Hurston's *Their Eyes Were Watching God,* and Toni Morrison's *The Bluest Eye* As 'Answers' to Hurst's *Imitation of Life*." *Black American Literature Forum* 24.4 (1990): 697–715.

Clark, Beverly Lyon. "A Portrait of the Artist As a Little Woman." *Children's Literature* 17 (1989): 81–97.

Coontz, Stephanie. *The Way We Never Were: American Families and the Nostalgia Trap.* New York: Basic Books, 1992.

Cripps, Thomas. *Slow Fade to Black: The Negro in American Film, 1900–1942.* 1977. Oxford: Oxford UP, 1993.

Elsaesser, Thomas. "Tales of Sound and Fury: Observations on the Family Melodrama." *Imitations of Life: A Reader on Film & Television Melodrama.* Ed. Marcia Landy. Detroit: Wayne UP, 1991. 68–91.

Fassbinder, Rainer Werner. "Six Films by Douglas Sirk." *Imitation of Life.* Rutgers Films in Print. Ed. Lucy Fischer. New Brunswick, NJ: Rutgers UP, 1991. 244–46. Originally published in *Fernschen und Film* (February 1971).

Griffin, Eleanore, and Allan Scott. Continuity script for *Imitation of Life. Imitation of Life.* Rutgers Films in Print. Ed. Lucy Fischer. Rutgers, NJ: Rutgers UP, 1991. 43–156.

Halliday, Jon. *Sirk on Sirk: Interviews with Jon Halliday.* New York: Viking, 1972.

Hurst, Fannie. *Anatomy of Me: A Wanderer in Search of Herself.* Garden City, NY: Doubleday, 1958.

———. Editorial letter. *Opportunity: A Journal of Negro Life* (April 1935): 121.

———. *Imitation of Life.* New York: P. F. Collier and Son, 1933.

———. "Whither Fiction?" Box 63, folder 5, ts. Fannie Hurst Papers. Harry Ransom Humanities Research Center, University of Texas, Austin.

Hurston, Zora Neale. *Dust Tracks on a Road.* 1942. New York: HarperPerennial, 1996.

———. Letter to Fannie Hurst. 6 February 1940. Fannie Hurst Papers. Harry Ransom Humanities Research Center, University of Texas, Austin.

Imitation of Life. Dir. Douglas Sirk. Writ. Eleanore Griffin and Allan Scott. Perf. Lana Turner, John Gavin, and Juanita Moore. Universal-International, 1959.

Imitation of Life. Dir. John M. Stahl. Writ. William Hurlbut. Perf. Claudette Colbert and Louise Beavers. Universal, 1934.

Keyser, Elizabeth Lennox. *Whispers in the Dark: The Fiction of Louisa May Alcott.* Knoxville: U of Tennessee P, 1993.

Klinger, Barbara. *Melodrama and Meaning: History, Culture, and the Films of Douglas Sirk.* Bloomington: Indiana UP, 1994.

Kroeger, Brooke. *Fannie: The Talent for Success of Writer Fannie Hurst.* New York: Times Books, 1999.

Manring, M. M. *Slave in a Box: The Strange Career of Aunt Jemima.* Charlottesville: U of Virginia P, 1998.

Morrison, Toni. *The Bluest Eye.* 1970. *Seven Contemporary Short Novels.* 3rd ed. Ed. Charles Clerc and Louis Leiter. Glenview, IL: Scott, Foresman, 1982. 293–429.

Mulvey, Laura. "Notes on Sirk and Melodrama." *Home Is Where the Heart Is: Studies in Melodrama and the Woman's Film.* Ed. Christine Gledhill. London: BFI Publishing, 1987. 75–82.

Nowell-Smith, Geoffrey. "How Films Mean, or, From Aesthetics to Semiotics and Half-Way Back Again." *Reinventing Film Studies.* Ed. Christine Gledhill and Linda Williams. London: Arnold, 2000. 8–17.

Perkins, Tessa. "Who (and What) Is It For?" *Reinventing Film Studies.* Ed. Christine Gledhill and Linda Williams. London: Arnold, 2000. 76–95.

Schatz, Thomas. "The Family Melodrama." *Imitations of Life: A Reader on Film & Television Melodrama.* Ed. Marcia Landy. Detroit: Wayne UP, 1991. 148–67.

Senna, Danzy. "The Mulatto Millennium." *Ourselves among Others: Readings from Home and Abroad.* 4th ed. Ed. Carol J. Verberg. Boston: Bedford/St. Martin's, 2000. 18–23.

Shaughnessy, Mary Rose. *Myths about Love & Woman: The Fiction of Fannie Hurst.* New York: Gordon Press, 1980.

Stimpson, Catharine. "Reading for Love: Canons, Paracanons, and Whistling Jo March." *New Literary History* 21 (1990): 957–76.

Tompkins, Jane. *Sensational Designs: The Cultural Work of American Fiction, 1790–1860.* New York: Oxford UP, 1985.

Wilentz, Gay. "White Patron and Black Artist: The Correspondence of Fannie Hurst and Zora Neale Hurston." *Library Chronicle of the University of Texas at Austin* 35 (1986): 20–43.

Williams, Patricia. "Talking about Race, Talking about Gender, Talking about How We Talk." *Antifeminism in the Academy.* Ed. V. V. Clark, Shirley Nelson Garner, Margaret Higonnet, et al. New York: Routledge, 1996. 69–94.

The Gumpification of Academia? Teaching the Ideological Analysis of Popular Film and Television

DIANE NEGRA AND
WALTER METZ

O n any typical evening in homes and at local multiplex movie theaters, a large number of Americans are watching film and television. In contrast to the great deal of time invested in viewing,
however, most audience members seldom speak in critical terms about
what they watch, participating instead in a code of silence which is remarkably comprehensive despite the fact that it constrains only a certain kind
of talk about the media: Americans are used to articulating codes of pleasure, but not codes of meaning, in their media texts.

As moviegoers, we are culturally conditioned to confine ourselves to
a certain category of straightforward and generally apolitical questions
when we walk out of the theater. Did it hold our interest? How was the
acting? Did we enjoy it? Teaching film and television in the United States
requires a response to this phenomenon, which should be of greater complexity than merely the recognition that our intellectual responses to media
tend to be unspoken. Why is it that when we walk out of the cinema or
turn off the television, we generally find ourselves with so little to say?

In this essay we discuss an introductory college course on media,
appropriate for literature, media studies, and communication departments,
designed as an intervention into this proscribed silence about the issues that
subtend any engagement with mass media. Teaching the ideological analysis of film and television is difficult and yet crucially necessary. We argue
that younger college students can master the complex theoretical vocabulary associated with academic investigations of media when this material
is presented to them in a carefully designed pedagogical program. In large

part, this discussion takes shape in response to a predominant assumption within the academy that theories of radical politics[1] have little place on the syllabi of lower division survey courses.[2] We have experienced this assumption first hand in trying to construct an agenda for teaching ideology within the confines of an introductory media studies course.

In this article, we consider the challenge of teaching students not just what has been said about canonized film and television, but a larger task, that of teaching a mode of critical engagement which will empower students as media consumers. We argue that it makes pedagogical sense to communicate complex political goals using accessible and familiar means of expression. Too often those of us who teach media studies have relied on "approved" texts (that is, canonical texts, such as *Citizen Kane*) as a means of legitimizing our status as workers within a discipline.

We cite the example of "Narrative Strategies," a course we taught at the University of Texas at Austin, which effectively combined analysis of films by Alfred Hitchcock and John Ford with "blaxploitation" films and teenpics, and the study of classical sitcoms with reality television and the Weather Channel.[3] At a time when departments devoted to the study of media are increasingly called upon to justify their existence, courses of this kind provide an indispensable means of heightening awareness of the cultural and political import of our media environment.

In a class on media, under the aegis of asking how and why we are entertained, we can begin to pose crucial questions about ideology. When we confine our teaching to those works deemed most meaningful by canonical consensus, we tend to impose a rigid frame of reference that students do not then transpose to their own viewing of an action film or the nightly news. Often, students learn the sound of politically engaged criticism, but not the spirit. This article stresses the importance of timeliness, of teaching texts that are relevant to the students' experience.

The course was intended to serve as an introduction to film and television aesthetics. The significant difference between our course and the way such courses are traditionally taught involves the weight we place on critical theory and the ideological analysis of media texts. The belief that critical theory is a subject for only upper-division students is a surprisingly common one. This position, we might add, is not one taken solely by cultural conservatives, but also by those who are generally supportive of and

participatory in the goals of radical politics. Generally, those responsible
for curriculum development in media studies departments maintain the
position that lower-division courses are the place for introductory "content,"[4] and that the students will have the opportunity to learn more sophisticated theory later, in their upper-division classes.

There are two fundamental problems with such a bifurcation in the curriculum. The separation of content from theory implies both that content is
free from ideological considerations and also that theory is something that
one merely lays over content. In our initial encounter with them, our students constantly tell us that aggressive theoretical analyses are "reading into"
the texts unfairly, that the ideological implications of the films are not "really
there." The students' position cannot merely be explained away as the ideas
of novices. Instead, students are socialized to such ways of thinking by
assumptions about the relationship between cultural artifacts and their ideological significance. To think that the curriculum is free of such ideological positioning is also to be naive about the effects of ideology.

The acceptance of the enforced split between the content of media
studies and its theories leads to the avoidance of teaching, and our students'
learning of, contestatory material within our anti-intellectual culture.[5]
Forrest Gump (1994), the most widely seen film in America at the time we
were teaching this course, serves as an instructive example of this kind of
anti-intellectual vision of culture. The film suggests that people would be
better off not thinking and trying to "just" be happy, rather than worrying about the complexities of recent political events. As a model for our
citizenry, Forrest treats each incident—be it the Vietnam War or the deseg-
regation of the University of Alabama—as an event to be experienced but
not contemplated. To delay the teaching of critical theory to our undergraduates is, then, to Gump-ify academia.

Accordingly, we engage in a form of affective comparison with our students in discussing films like *Forrest Gump*. In his essay "Critical Theory
and Media Production," Stan W. Denski theorizes the necessity of forming
this intellectual bridge between teachers and students. Denski argues that
instructors who teach film and video suffer from a schizophrenia, a conflicting identity between their roles as teachers and scholars. The cure for
this schizophrenia, argues Denski, is to break down the binary oppositions
that define the academic: teacher/student, teaching/research, and real

world/ivory tower. We must connect scholarship and teaching to demonstrate the relevance of our "ivory tower" pursuits to the students' "real world." One way to do so is to teach popular texts, removing the academic barrier between students and their ability to understand critical theory.

Rick Worland addresses the problems of overly canonical pedagogical approaches in a similar vein. In his essay "Politics, Film Studies, and the Academy," he concludes his discussion of the mediation between theory and activism in the academy by arguing, "To the degree professors convey to students that we are above them intellectually, morally, and politically, that we are detached from the general culture they know, and indeed hold it in utter contempt, we will seldom reach them. For better or worse, this culture is our culture" (54).

Our classroom discussions of *Forrest Gump* bear out both Denski's and Worland's arguments. In our initial exchanges with students about the films with which they were most familiar, *Forrest Gump* surfaced repeatedly. Many students expressed a profound identification with Forrest and a general emotional engagement with the film. To then directly mount an ideological assault on a film that matters to a large number of students would position us as experts, and students as passive vessels whose opinions do not matter.

Avoiding the tendency to instruct students in the "correct" interpretation, we use *Forrest Gump* to activate a discussion of the multiple possible responses to a film. We enable the students to use their emotional engagement with the film as a point of departure for pursuing the wider political significance of the film's representational strategies. Very often, a minority of students in the class who share a suspicion of the film's politics will begin the conversation, allowing a germ of discontent to grow. After all, these are largely eighteen- and nineteen-year olds, teenagers notorious for their critical skills to determine what "sucks" and "rocks." The key is to harness such teenage discontent into productive, analytical directions. We provide an environment in which an affective consideration of *Forrest Gump* leads the class to an understanding that there are other emotional engagements with the film beyond its "feel good" manipulations, including outright anger at its ideological positions.

Paul Willis mounts such a defense of the popular as a useful mechanism for forwarding a politically engaged pedagogy. In his book *Common Culture,* Willis argues:

> The field of education is likely to come under even more intense pressure. It will be further marginalized in most people's experience by common culture. In so far as educational practices are still predicated on traditional liberal humanist lines and on the assumed superiority of high art, they will become almost totally irrelevant to the real energies and interests of most young people and have no part in their identity formation. Common culture will, increasingly, undertake in its own ways the roles that education has vacated. (10)

Willis theorizes the ways in which popular culture "educates" the students before they ever enter our classrooms. Our role as instructors of popular culture is thus twofold: to validate the identities which popular culture has created while at the same time to empower the students to understand what is problematic about this "real-life" education. This is quite a departure from a traditional Marxist view on popular culture, which would theorize the students as cultural dupes to the power of the media. Instead, following Willis, we hypothesize that the way to engage theoretically with the students is to employ popular culture as both a pedagogical device and a site for analysis.

In what follows, we discuss the rationale for the organization of the course, present both lecture and discussion strategies, and explain the design of essay assignments. We also analyze student writing about film and television, offering examples that serve to illustrate the scope and variety of critical questions that can be asked when students are encouraged to consider timely, vital texts using the tools which they find most useful and productive.[6] The course encompasses the media texts most likely to be watched by the students themselves.[7] The students are therefore more likely to come to terms with their own viewing assumptions, and the classroom becomes a space that catalyzes personal inquiry that continues beyond the limits of a single course. Teaching popular media has one other great benefit: students tend to have and to more readily share opinions about these "low-brow" texts. The pedagogical task we discuss is the conversion of these opinions into critical analysis. Because academics have too often offered students what they perceive to be a closed history of ideas couched in jargon, teachers need to strive to open the critical conversation, even to those who are only beginning to master the vocabulary.

TEACHING POPULAR FILM

The validation of the students' engagement with popular culture, and the subsequent process of challenging them to engage critically with such texts, must begin on the very first day of classes. We therefore typically chose to begin with a film text recently released, which many of the students were bound to have already seen in the multiplex. In the spring semester of 1995, we chose James Cameron's *True Lies,* starring Arnold Schwarzenegger, a summer blockbuster from the year before.

Beginning the course with a popular film immediately suggests to the students that the assumptions about popular culture that they have internalized are most limited. They arrive in the course believing that most films are purely entertainment. What they do not consider upon arrival is that there is an ideological vision of the Hollywood cinema that necessitates the exploration of critical theory. Beginning the course with a popular summer blockbuster permits us to intervene in the distinction students make between those films we enjoy and those we study.

Our job from the start, therefore, is to motivate the students' discovery and experimentation with a different way of watching the movies that they otherwise would find merely viscerally entertaining. Before the first screening that constitutes the first class meeting, we theorize the differences between pleasure in entertainment and a critical pleasure. We tell the students that the class will ask them to look at films with both aspects of pleasure in mind. Whereas when they saw *True Lies* for the first time in the multiplex they thought solely of its entertainment pleasure, now they will be asked to discover what critical pleasures it contains.

At this early stage in the course, it is difficult to get the students to articulate the political pleasures in analyzing a film like *True Lies.* Yet, the class discussion provided some provocative insights. The students quickly linked a discontent with the film to criteria of believability. This analytical strategy started with one student vaguely arguing that she did not like the film because it was too "unrealistic." This is a common early response by students, because realism is one of the sanctioned critical apparatuses which popular culture gives to media consumers.

However, another student quickly politicized this debate.[8] The student commented upon a scene in which a nuclear bomb detonates off the coast of Florida while Harry Tasker (played by Arnold Schwarzenegger) kisses his wife Helen (played by Jamie Lee Curtis) in the foreground. The student performed a subtle analysis of this moment as an example of the Hollywood romance's happy ending, but duly noted the irony that in the real world they would have been completely immolated by radiation in the process. At this point, we attempted to elicit a trajectory in the discussion that would lead to a political interpretation of the film. However, the students remained hesitant at doing so this early in the semester.

At this point, it is the instructor's job to take up the slack, modeling critical confidence and methods of argumentation. We offered students examples of risk-taking while demonstrating the power of theory to develop ideological critiques of the American cinema. Carefully using the students' observations about the nuclear bomb scene, we presented a brief lecture on relevant tropes in the history of representation. In the film, Arab terrorists hijack nuclear bombs and bring them to the United States. Harry, and later Helen, are charged with stopping the terrorists. The film not-so-subtly represents the Arab characters as totally incompetent with technology, the female characters as using technology accidentally, and the white men as employing it perfectly. We connected this representational strategy to nineteenth-century social Darwinists who attempted to use scientific discourses to justify men's superiority over women, and white people's superiority over people of color. We argued that *True Lies* participates in this seemingly discredited scientific project, and engaged a discussion with the students as to why it would do so, given that such nineteenth-century discourses of race seem to them to have been thoroughly discredited in the wake of the Civil Rights movement. This is of course a fallacy, as evidenced by the resurgence of such discourses in books like *The Bell Curve,* a point that we used to suggest the importance of knowing history.[9]

The students' lack of knowledge about the history of science is a concern they immediately address. In class, many students argue, "I didn't see it that way because I've never been taught social Darwinism." The students' courage in challenging the instructors allowed us to present various methods for analyzing media texts. Soon, we argue, the students will have a vast array of intellectual tools to perform criticism of this sort.

Stan Denski argues the importance of engaging the students' interests in critical theory. He invokes Stanley Hauerwas, who, in "The Morality of

Teaching," states: "Our task is to give students the confidence, to empower them to take themselves seriously as people who would rather know than not know" (6). The most effective strategy we have discovered to get our students interested in knowing—in fighting the anti-intellectualism of our culture—is to model for them the ways in which critical theory can be useful for a fuller understanding of popular texts with which they will be dealing for the rest of their lives. In this way, we actively position ourselves against the impulse to "not know" that is rewarded and revered in a film like *Forrest Gump*.

In forwarding such an analysis of *True Lies,* we follow the pedagogical approach that Lawrence Grossberg theorizes as "a pedagogy of articulation and risk" (18). The goal is to get the students to take risks in making connections between their own experiences and the texts we are studying. Students thus do the following: listen to our applications of theory to film criticism in lecture, look at the writing we are doing as media scholars,[10] read various approaches to film analysis as homework, and listen to other students' interpretations of media texts in class.

At this early point in the course, "the pedagogy of articulation and risk" is primarily concerned with the teacher taking the risks and doing a lot of the articulation. However, Grossberg warns of the dangers of the teacher positioning him or herself as the expert. Such a hierarchical relationship establishing the teacher's power over the students potentially forestalls their ability to learn to be empowered critics of their culture. Yet in Grossberg's progressive pedagogical approach "an ethical model of authority" is replaced by a "model of thoughtfulness" (19). Our course attempts to teach students to be thoughtful about the media texts they consume; we model what such thoughtfulness can look and feel like.

As we envision it, our political analysis of *True Lies* offers the students a model of a viewer different from the friends with whom they go to the movies. Rather than seeking entertainment pleasure from the film, we seek a critical pleasure in coming to terms with the film's representational strategies. In the case of our discussion of *True Lies,* we used our mutual discussion of the atom bomb explosion to talk about the ways in which the Arabs' use of the technology failed while the bomb's ill effects were not even noticed by the film's white heroes. In this way, we engaged a learning experience for the students about representational strategies without being the traditional "experts."[11]

Self-consciously, we demonstrate to the students that political issues (questions of identity politics, stances on nationalism and patriotism, beliefs about human nature, etc.) are a vital aspect of film criticism. While most of our culture tells them not to think politically, especially about cultural artifacts, our course attempts to do little else. As Peter McLaren argues about critical thinking in the American academy, "Both neoconservatives and liberals have removed from the term 'critical' its political and cultural dimensions (resulting in an under-theorized meaning as 'thinking skills')" (6). To counter such a trend, we constantly attend to the fact that we are forwarding critical theory as a political act, one that attempts to get the students thinking about the implications and meanings of the texts we are studying.

We have discovered that students become increasingly empowered as the course progresses. In the case of *True Lies,* a tragic event served to crystallize for the students the importance of our discussion of systematic racism against Arab peoples. The day after the Oklahoma City bombing, we began talking before class about the news coverage of the event. One of our students who watched the coverage as the bombing occurred observed that the newscasters immediately assumed that the bombers were Arab terrorists. Another student added that the president's news conference also subtextually made that assumption. We spent the better part of that hour talking about the ways in which *True Lies'* depiction of Arab terrorists fit together with the assumptions of the discourse surrounding the bombing. What on the first week of class had been a teachers' intervention therefore became later in the semester a site for dialectical exchange between peers in the classroom.

Beyond such incidental linkages between critical theory and the texts under study, we also organize the course around issues in critical theory we feel are vital to an introductory media studies course. For example, psychoanalysis is a notoriously difficult theoretical apparatus to teach to undergraduates. Students feel validated to ridicule Freudian theory because of the dominant culture's reduction of it into inanities. Having heard the theory of the Oedipus complex in its most simplistic form, students laugh at the absurdity of literally marrying one's mother and killing one's father.[12] Factoring in the students' repression of the unconscious drives which Freudian theory itself hypothesizes, teachers are left with a seemingly insurmountable barrier to presenting psychoanalysis as a useful critical tool for analyzing the sexual politics of popular culture. Despite its typical absence on undergraduate syllabi, we have had success using psychoanalytic frameworks to discuss the filmic representation of familial and gender issues. We found that by addressing students' reservations from the start, many will be willing to entertain psychoanalytic readings of texts. In "Narrative Strategies," we introduce psychoanalysis via Alfred Hitchcock's *Shadow of a Doubt* (1943). This film concerns Young Charlie, a suburban teenager with a crush on her Uncle Charlie, who turns out to be a murderer. Read psychoanalytically, the film presents a family romance scenario that requires Charlie to give up her incestuous love-object, the murderous uncle, in order to couple with her "proper" mate, the young detective investigating the murder.

We found that introducing Lacanian revisions to Freudian theory, while seemingly even more complicated for undergraduates, actually establishes a relevance that the abstractions of Freudian theory cloud from view. In Lacanian terms, the passage through the Oedipal trajectory involves the move from the Imaginary to the Symbolic state. Lacan combines the psychic trajectory with linguistics, such that the entry into the Symbolic—learning "the Law of the Father"—is coincident with the mastery of language. In this way, the abstractions of the Freudian trajectory are rendered politically, establishing a cultural explanation for patriarchy. We thus use a lecture on Lacanian theory to help explain how *Shadow of a Doubt* interrogates Young Charlie's position within the patriarchal nuclear family.

In response to our first essay assignment, which requires students to construct an ideological analysis of a classical Hollywood film, one of the students demonstrated that psychoanalysis is by no means too complicated for lower-division undergraduates. For her paper, the student performed a psychoanalytic reading of *The Wizard of Oz*.[13] Predicting Julia Kristeva's revisions of Freudian and Lacanian theory (which were not covered in class), the student noticed the parallel character development between Glinda the Good Witch and the Wicked Witch of the West as good and bad mothers: Since Auntie Em is unable to provide Dorothy with love and support, Dorothy cannot wish harm to her in the waking state, and it must be repressed through her dream. Therefore, her dream splits into two mothers: Miss Gulch who turns into the Wicked Witch, or bad mother, and Glinda the Good Witch of the North, a fairy-tale mother. These two women are the only symbols of power in a film about the powerless.

In this way, the student combined our class discussions of psychoanalysis about dreams and repression with our discussions of feminist analyses of power and patriarchy. The student continues her connections between psychoanalysis and *The Wizard of Oz* by studying the *mise-en-scéne* of the film:

> The Wicked Witch grows down or melts into nothingness, therefore Dorothy grows up and is able to fill her slippers. Dorothy has defeated the Wicked Witch, therefore she can now return home. Well, she must first return to the Wizard with the witch's broomstick. The broomstick is parallel to the phallic tornado.[14] This can be seen at the film's climax when Dorothy confronts the Wicked Witch and acquires her broomstick. Once this has been accomplished, the phallus can be returned to its proper and parental owner, the Wizard. Dorothy has thus been initiated into the phallic state.

While the student effectively applied Freudian theory with respect to *Shadow of a Doubt,* the paper continues by exploring the usefulness of psychoanalysis for other aspects of *The Wizard of Oz.* Employing the Lacanian concern with possession of the symbolic phallus, the student traces the passage of the broomstick from the phallic mother, the Wicked Witch, to its "rightful" owner, the Wizard. The student never quite argues the gender politics of these psychic dimensions effectively. Why does the film ridicule the Wizard's power? Is Dorothy really empowered by the recovery of the broomstick? However, the student more than makes up for this in the paper's conclusion, in which she analyzes the imagery of the film's ending:

> The entire epilogue is spatially compressed into a small corner of Dorothy's bedroom. All the characters are gathered around Dorothy's bed, creating an overtone of a maternity setting. There is hardly any movement within the scene, suggesting no visual tension, only peace and tranquillity. The unity of the characters' heads form a circle suggesting completeness. This helps create forceful pacing in the narrative. In a sense, Dorothy is now complete since her adulthood comes about by her being treated like a proud young mother.

In this way, the student concludes the paper with a sparkling analysis of the conservative co-optation of Dorothy's maturation—she lies post-partum, encircled by admirers—into the traditional role of mother and caregiver.[15]

Our experience with *The Wizard of Oz* suggests that examining popular culture reduces barriers to student understanding of critical theory.
In this rough yet elegant paper, the student took a film that she saw on television many times, and looked at it anew through the filter of critical theory. She demonstrates that even lower-division undergraduates, given the
opportunity, possess the needed skills to master the techniques of psychoanalytic criticism. Many students are more than willing to work through
the most complicated material to produce a piece of work of which they
can be proud.[16] As Grossberg argues, "People are uninterested, not because
they can't do the work—in most cases the so-called jargon is in the
dictionary—but because they don't see any reason to; they don't care about
the questions we ask" (20). In our case, the student might not necessarily
have cared about our questions when applied to *Shadow of a Doubt,* but
she was interested enough to work through that material in order to come
to an understanding of a text that did matter to her. In the paper, she frames
her own questions about *The Wizard of Oz* and answers them intelligently
and maturely using Freudian and Lacanian principles. Given the chance
to work on films that matter to them, students will grapple with the intricacies of critical theory. They quickly discover that this work rewards their
deep engagement with the films in ways beyond their experience of them
as apolitical entertainment.

We are not arguing that all students will be won over by our methods.
Clearly, many students will outwardly resist or just not care to make the
effort to do this difficult critical work. However, it has been our experience that enough students will do this work so as to make the effort on our
parts as teachers of radical thinking more than worthwhile. We offer no
prescriptive measures for winning over resistant students, other than to be
open and self-conscious in offering interpretations, as well as in listening
to and respecting contrary views.

TEACHING POPULAR TELEVISION

At the beginning of the semester, we ask each student to complete an index
card that lists basic information such as the number of media courses the
student has taken, the extent of their writing experience, etc. We also invite
students to list any films or television shows they know well, specifically

avoiding the propensity to have students list "favorites." Problems with that strategy are self-evident; students will not always choose to report their actual favorite films and television programs when they feel that this index card is the instructor's litmus test designed to evaluate their taste. Asking students to jot down favorite films and television shows assumes instant recall of the many thousands of films and television shows experienced by the average college sophomore. Many students, of course, cannot immediately produce an accurate list of favorite media texts even when they are inclined to do so. These difficulties are moderated when the assignment is re-formulated in terms of familiarity rather than preference. The information generated from students can indeed be valuable to the instructor who is supplied with a ready-made list of examples that will be pertinent to the students' viewing experiences.

One of the most consistent trends in students' self-reporting on these index cards is the tendency to disavow any exposure to television. In the set of index cards completed by our students in the spring 1995 semester, for example, were such characteristic responses as "TV?," "don't watch it," and "never watch it." Other responses acknowledged familiarity with the "low" texts of television but in ways that suggested a defensive awareness of the connotations of knowing television. One student wrote, for instance, "[*Beverly Hills*] *90210* (yes, I admit it!)." Other students declined to specify any television shows they watch as if differentiation of the separate texts of television was unnecessary. One student, rather than citing specific programs, noted only that he was familiar with "the usual TV reruns of all young Americans."

Comments such as these presuppose an equally shared participation in the ideological "community" sponsored by television (a notion which our course is designed to question) and yet simultaneously bespeak not only disdain for the medium, but an initial unwillingness to consider the viewing of television as productive time. Our course introduces critical theory to students as a means of revising this widely-shared early judgment of television, in part working against the impulse students feel to deny their own investment in the medium, because these students do watch television and they know many of its programs very well.

Accordingly, when we teach television in the latter half of "Narrative Strategies," we begin by discussing how it is talked about in our culture. We

note the significance of the various pejorative terms we employ for television, such as the "boob tube," the "idiot box," etc. Students volunteer how
frequently they talk about television viewing in ways that suggest they are
doing nothing when they watch (frequently saying that they are "just watching television," for example) and in ways that forestall any serious appraisal
of the medium. The first television screening is especially illuminating, as
students perceive that television, unlike film, is a medium not intended for
consumption with strangers. Students also chafe under the restriction that
they watch most of the television programs with the commercials intact; they
find it torturous to "sit through" these especially disposable segments of the
television text. On this basis, we initiate a discussion of television as a "domestic appliance" and begin a conversation about television's gendered status.
Such a strategy plants the possibility that watching television may be associated with a passivity understood to be feminine. We begin to investigate
why the domestic consumption of television fare is such a devalued activity
although it is one in which we all engage. We question whether the impulse
to deny our own viewing (to say or suggest that we are doing nothing when
we watch) may be related to the maintenance of social systems such as patriarchy and capitalism.

Of course, within television itself there are higher and lower status
genres. In the mid-1990s, some of the most distinct trends in television
include the tendency toward hybrid and recombinant genres, an increased
emphasis on spectacle, and a proliferation of programs that hinge on reality, inviting questions about the representational status of reenactment and
real-life "performance." Reality programming is generally considered to
be one of the most dismissible of television genres (despite the fact that its
aesthetic strategies have been infiltrating such "quality" television hits as
ER) and is spoken of in the same breath as "tabloid TV." Shows in the reality genre such as *Unsolved Mysteries* (NBC), *America's Most Wanted* (Fox),
Rescue 911 (CBS), and *COPS* (Fox) increasingly co-opt our ability as spectators to maintain a distinction between the fictional and the real.[17] By making explicit connections to reality, these programs necessitate an active
political response on the part of the spectator who does not wish to have
her politics dictated to her by the program's implied ideological stance.
That stance, in very general terms, typically stresses the sanctity and centrality of the family, the necessity and glorification of an armed police force,
and the inhumanity of those who break the law.

In the television section of "Narrative Strategies," we tend to organize the material generically. Thus, we discuss the sitcom, the soap opera, the hour-long drama, etc. In the fall 1994 version of the course we specifically neglected to discuss the emergent genre of reality programming, so that students could investigate it in an essay assignment, thus providing an excellent opportunity to engage with a television genre relevant to their experience. Since reality shows per se did not exist before the late 1980s, these students have been witness to the entire trajectory of the genre's existence. In keeping with what we knew about many students' attitudes toward television, we selected this genre in part due to its association with an emotional, and frequently uninformed, public rhetoric. It was important for students not to see shows like *COPS* and *Rescue 911* as easy objects of attack, but to consider them from an informed, critical perspective.

In designing an essay question for students in which the object of analysis is one of two selected episodes of two reality shows (*COPS* and *Rescue 911*), we tried to craft an assignment that was sufficiently open to lead students to think about their own politics. This assignment was designed in keeping with the mode of pedagogy delineated by Grossberg—a pedagogy that he describes as aiming "not to predefine its outcome (even in terms of some imagined value of emancipation or democracy) but to empower its students to begin to reconstruct their world in new ways" (18). It seemed inappropriate therefore to tightly structure the essay assignment, possibly conveying the impression to students that a single, particular "reading" of these shows was sought. Instead, the question was written expressly as an invitation for students to reflect on the various critical methodologies we had discussed and employed up to that point in the class and to decide which of these methodologies they found the most productive. The essay assignment's specific wording was, "Since by this point in our course, you have accumulated considerable information about various methods of critical investigation, I leave the specific choice of methodology up to you." This sort of open essay question can be tricky in a variety of ways. Some students feel anxious without a clear blueprint instructing them how to proceed, or suspect that there is some "code" to the assignment that it is their job to crack. These potential problems need to be addressed by the instructor when distributing the assignment. We have found that a positive emphasis on students' discernment conveyed by the instructor with a sense of respect for the students' abilities tends to neutralize fears of there being a disguised assignment within the assignment. Of course, a paper of this kind can only be written by students at a late stage in the course, once they have had time to consider a range of critical methodologies. It works well as a last take-home assignment before a final exam because it prompts students to review their readings and class notes, synthesizing and processing the material of the course.

Given that it would be inappropriate and counter-productive to dictate the terms of politicized engagement with reality programming, this assignment offered students a short list of questions they might opt to take up in their essays: What specific claims to realism are made by these narratives? What sort of narrational approach is employed? Do these modes of programming constitute 'alternatives' (either aesthetically or ideologically) to more established TV genres? A case study of student responses to this assignment demonstrates some students' potential to analytically apply critical theory to the texts they experience in their everyday lives, an experience which would not necessarily be replicated by attention to the "great texts" of film and/or television theory.

At this point in the course, having extensively discussed conventions of editing, sound, *mise en scène,* and other aspects of aesthetics, the students were well equipped to critique the aesthetic manipulation in these shows. In this assignment, they were able to selectively draw from their repertoire of modes of aesthetic investigation in order to support their analysis of issues of race, class, and gender.

One student analyzed the segment in regard to its narrative form, considering the ways in which "false closure" served to impose superficial solutions to complicated social problems:

> There is a beginning, middle, and end as we move from equilibrium, police cruising their beat, to disruption, the call from dispatch, and back to equilibrium, the officers deal with the problem to the extent of their abilities under the law and the man eventually gets his car back.[18] These people's problems will continue, but we, as viewers, have experienced a closure typical of fictitious dramas.

Camera angles, camera proximity, and framing were scrutinized by another student as a means of analyzing the typical strategies of spatial organization in reality programming:

The framing of the shots helps illustrate the cops' role in the program and the relationship of the cops to the suspects. The suspects are almost always framed with a frontal shot. The shots of the suspects (or non-cops) are mostly medium shots, almost always from the waist up. The suspects are only shown in close-ups when in close proximity to an officer.

Students were thus able to support an argument about power relationships and spectator identification in the shows by building on their aesthetic analysis. For example, another student argued:

The names of the suspects are never given (perhaps for legal reasons, but nevertheless, the suspects' identity and importance is greatly downplayed by this). The suspects are not allowed to speak to the camera except as seen through the perspective of the cops. The techniques described serve to distance the viewer from the suspect. The suspect is looked at and analyzed (or pitied, or scorned), but not identified with.

Other students responded to the fabricated realism of shows like *COPS* and *Rescue 911* by placing emphasis on what we do not see in shows that are meant to be viewed as comprehensive accounts of police officers on duty or emergency situations. Of *COPS* one student noted:

Probably for every ten-minute action-packed segment of COPS with car chases and gunfights there are thousands of minutes of paper work, of waiting in the car for something to happen, or of fake calls. If this is true, then COPS is not showing what the reality of a police officer's life is at all, if there is one, but is instead a high entertainment construction of what the audience wants to see, or at least what the makers think we want.

Still other students focused on the perpetuation of class and ethnic stereotypes in the content of reality programming, demonstrating attentiveness to the ways in which programs like *COPS* focus almost exclusively on blue collar and urban crime, naturalizing a particular image of the criminal as a person of color and/or low income. In one student's words:

If news and entertainment media depict marginalized perspectives according to popular stereotypes and preconceptions, such representations serve effectively to reconfirm those beliefs. With the example of *COPS*, such problems rise as interventions shown involve minorities and lower income individuals almost exclusively.

A different student took a feminist position, noting, for example, the inherent gender politics of many of the *Rescue 911* scenarios:

> [While the segment] humanizes the police officer onto a sympathetic level with the audience, it is also an emotional reaction by an authority that sets off Shatner's more formal, rational, authoritative stance, and, of course, it also serves to hold the audience's attention through an attempt at dramatization and suspense. In this way we are presented with two pleasing constructions of the law as the "great protector": the humanized, sympathetic, and protective (paternal) grounded in the rational, firm and defensive.

Some students made provocative comparisons between reality programming and other television genres. In an essay entitled "*COPS*: The Male Soap Opera" one writer observed that soap opera and reality shows (both modes of daytime programming, since shows such as *COPS* are often broadcast in the late afternoon) share many of the same textual features and gendered narrative styles:

> Soap operas are said to be feminine narratives because of the way their characters, male or female, often verbalize their emotion (generalized as a female trait). . . . Soap operas have no closure to them. They continue day to day. In its own way, it can be said that *COPS*' characters display their emotions through emphatically masculine ways, specifically physical aggression.

Taken as a whole, these essays were characterized by rhetorical sophistication, strong argumentation, and insightful ideological analysis, all predicated on a willingness to take one of the "low" genres of television seriously. We attribute this dramatic shift to the students' willingness to treat television texts in serious ways, and not merely to the fact that this was assigned work. Students developed fluency in critical language via an exposure to challenging methods of analysis. The students were willing and able to seriously appraise the aesthetic and narrative strategies being employed by shows in the reality genre when given the tools to do so. Furthermore, when given a certain amount of freedom in the kind of approach they selected, students' engagement tended to be driven by their own convictions and articulated in the terms of their own politics.

The range of student responses to this essay assignment exemplifies an exchange process that is the heart of our course. This exchange involves the modeling of a thoughtful, politically engaged mode of criticism by the instructor early on in the course, a demonstration of "risk" in that the instructor does not disguise or deny his/her own political commitment. The exchange takes place when the instructor, having modeled this kind of critical endeavor, steps aside somewhat to permit students to pursue their own applications of critical theory. We believe that supporting students in their critical risk-taking leads to higher caliber analysis reflective of students' personal politics. Giving loosely structured assignments that center on popular media encourages students to break new ground, sometimes producing analysis of these forms that is of a higher quality than anything we have discovered in print. Sharing these insights with one another in a discussion that takes place when essays are returned provides students with the excitement of knowing that they have become part of a sophisticated interpretive community. This builds a feeling of mutual respect and tolerance that we see as central to the critical endeavor.

The results of this one essay assignment are by no means anomalous. For each area of critical theory we teach in "Narrative Strategies," we can point to a group of papers that work through the theory in order to produce an effective analysis of a text of their choosing. As just one more example, we presented various theories of postmodernism, and discussed postmodern television shows like *Mystery Science Theater 3000* and *The Simpsons*. In another final paper assignment, we asked students to use these theories of postmodernism to talk about a television show of their choice. One of the better papers responded by comparing *Beavis and Butthead,* the MTV cartoon, with Anthony Burgess's novel *A Clockwork Orange*. This student, an English major, was concurrently taking a course on modernist literature, in which he read the Burgess novel. The student combined his knowledge from the English class and "Narrative Strategies" to produce a paper which effectively argued against the notion of high art canons. The paper argues that *Beavis and Butthead,* a postmodern television show, and *A Clockwork Orange,* a modernist novel, both achieve a critique of violent teenage angst using their own aesthetic principles. In a writing conference,

we discussed with the student a passage from the paper in which he analyzes a moment from *Beavis and Butthead* in which Butthead takes a jar of
poison and looks at the label. Beavis asks him what he is reading. Butthead
replies, "words, words, words." The student connected this linguistic min-
imalism to Burgess's use of language in *Clockwork* to demonstrate the emotional and moral depravity of the teenagers. We suggested to the student
that his was a tremendous reading, but that there was another one he had
not considered, that Butthead's citation was also an intertextual reference
to *Hamlet*'s first act, where Hamlet feigns his madness to Polonius.[19] We
discussed how this *Hamlet* reference could orient his paper toward assessing the comparative ideological positions of *Beavis and Butthead* and *A
Clockwork Orange*. The student ended up concluding that both Hamlet
and Butthead were figures rebelling against a corrupt adult culture, but
that Butthead's comments also engaged the pathetic school system that produces a teenager incapable of reading the warning label on poison.

We believe this student's bravura connection between *A Clockwork
Orange* and *Beavis and Butthead* was, if not enabled, then at least encouraged, by our particular pedagogical method. We begin the course by completely rejecting the cultural hierarchy of texts implicit in the current
university curriculum. Since we had already discussed as wide a range of
audiovisual texts as possible,[20] this student felt validated in connecting a
well-respected high modernist novel to the lowest form of denigrated television culture. This elegant analysis of the politics of representation of
teenage angst would have been foreshortened by a traditional curriculum
separating high art from television. This student's paper typifies the benefits of Grossberg's pedagogy of articulation and risk. Unlike our application of the history of science to *True Lies* early in the course, the articulation
and risks are here being taken completely by the student who feels empowered in his ability as a critic.

Kobena Mercer argues that a critical pedagogy would seek not to "save
the world" but to "multiply connections between things that have apparently nothing to do with each other" (18). Grossberg's pedagogical method
also emphasizes such rhizomatic connection-making processes:

> Refusing to assume ahead of time that it knows the appropriate
> knowledge, language, or skills, it is a contextual practice which is will-
> ing to take the risk of making connections, drawing lines, mapping

articulations, between different domains, discourses, and practices, to see what will work, both theoretically and politically. (18)

The student's *Beavis and Butthead* paper refuses to accept high culture's intrinsic value and low culture's status as detritus. Instead, making a risky connection, he concludes that both of the texts under study have a political contribution to make to the analysis of teenage angst. By the end of the course, the students feel empowered to make their own interventions into debates over television, the canon, and cultural theory.

CONCLUSION

In this article we have sought to map out one approach to the incorporation of critical theory into a lower-division college course. This approach strives to be attentive to students' resistance to complex theory by productively employing critical terminology in relation to texts they know well, thus establishing the usefulness and relevance of theory in the context of everyday viewing. Toward this end, we shift the focus of education from the reproduction to the production of knowledge.

We try to structure our course so that it provides an opportunity for students to come to grips with the myriad ways in which they are constructed through media, subscribing to a critical pedagogy that stresses the questioning of what students believe and why they believe it. Such a pedagogical style necessitates risk on the part of both instructor and student if students are to undertake the difficult task of examining and potentially revising their ideological stances. We subscribe to a pedagogy that situates itself largely in opposition to dominant institutions and in some cases this may mean the academy itself for, as John Higgins observes, "a critical pedagogy is critical of a system that too often merely provides disciplined automatons for the labor force, rather than working toward a critical consciousness that helps students examine their assumptions about life and society" (19).

The above description of our methods and results in teaching "Narrative Strategies" as a course connecting critical theory to the ideological analysis of audiovisual productions is not intended as a guidebook to instant success. Every class, every teacher, every school is different. We do not intend to intimate that we have some mystical power as teachers that cannot be replicated. To do so would be to reinstate what Stan Denski calls pedagogy as "voodoo" (4).

It is difficult to completely understand the position of a newcomer to film and television studies when looking out from inside the discipline. Our commitment to establishing the usefulness of critical theory must be tempered by an awareness of the difficulty of mastering the terms of analysis. As Peter Lehman has pointed out, "The new academic film discourse frequently was and still is a highly specialized one, with an abundance of obscure terminology often imported from related fields such as semiotics and psychoanalysis" (44). In our experience, moving students beyond their initial frustration with daunting terminology can be accomplished in large part by employing a pedagogical style that incorporates humor, excitement, and strong political conviction. We think that the success we have had with teaching our version of "Narrative Strategies" stems from our ability to teach critical theory in an accessible way. We try to showcase our excitement about critical inquiry, rather than suppressing it to conform with an outdated notion of professorial gravity.

Sympathy for the students' struggles with the theory is also required. This means spending extra time in office hours talking with large groups of students and working hard to be clear about theories that are not necessarily coherent. It means extra work in the library refreshing memories about semiotics, psychoanalysis, and ideological theory. It requires extra time responding to papers that attempt to forge sophisticated connections between theory and texts. Merely correcting grammar will not suffice for this class to work successfully. And, of course, facilitating students' application of theory requires watching many, many films and television shows. Most intriguing, it means letting the papers lead you to new film and television texts with which you are not already familiar. In short, teaching this class is a tremendous amount of work.

In fact, we suspect that such versions of undergraduate courses get taught so rarely not because of teachers' political leanings, but because the work such courses require is not supported or rewarded within the academy. Working hard on such a course does not help finish one's dissertation, get tenure, or complete one's latest book. What this course does accomplish when one teaches it successfully is a renewed belief in the joy of a political criticism that transforms one's vision of the cultural landscape. As teachers, we will never look at texts such as *The Wizard of Oz* or *Beavis and Butthead* again without watching through the insights offered by our students.

While the above preachings are awfully impressionistic, we do have confidence in our main theoretical suggestion. We advocate embracing the sophisticated analysis of popular culture as a means to empower students' already formidable understanding of these artifacts. We feel confident that the quality of papers described above would not have been written in such large numbers had we focused on traditional media studies content.

Naturally, the brightest of students could have produced skillful analyses of *Citizen Kane* and *All in the Family*. But, such canonical texts reproduce a field in which much of what can be said has already been said. Because the teachers know the history of criticism of this field, that again produces us as experts who can evaluate the quality of students' ideas. The students can sense the formulaic nature of a class taught in the same way for the past twenty years. Only by keeping the material fresh, by focusing on the texts that matter to the students, can the binary opposition between student and teacher be deconstructed.

We have taken the position that it is crucial for undergraduates to be challenged by the important concepts of critical theory, and that, in fact, such theories are the logical correlative to aesthetic understanding. When students come to understand the ideological positions inscribed within Hollywood films and other media, they can act more autonomously on these texts. We hope that as a result of our course students find their interactions with contemporary culture permanently politicized.

Of course, the long-term potential for activating social change can only be guessed, but perhaps a few anecdotes will suffice to demonstrate the nature and scope of the effects of this class. First and foremost, "Narrative Strategies" is a course for production students. Repeatedly, we are stopped in the halls by former students who provide status reports on their own and other students' progress in their production classes. One person, who engaged in many debates about feminism, reported that one of the students in his section went on to use the materials presented in "Narrative Strategies" to make feminist film projects for "Film I." While most students want to be the next Steven Spielberg, there are a few who take the theory and apply it to their filmmaking in interesting ways. This is exciting to us because it reveals the flip side of our profession: while we forge theory out of texts, politicized production students make texts out of theory.[21]

In another instance, one of our students became interested in the representation of women's bodies in the cinema, particularly in the representation of violence against women. In a brave act of critical confidence, she went to a lecture by Oliver Stone, who was on campus plugging his new film, *Natural Born Killers*. Standing in front of an audience of five hundred Oliver Stone fans, she interrogated the director about his choice of showing a knife assault on a woman's breast. She asked why he chose to use such invasive imagery against a woman's body but not against a man's, invoking the example of Nagisa Oshima's *In the Realm of the Senses* (1976) that we discussed at office hours. Stone's answer was patently uninteresting, and the audience typically did not consider the implications of her question, but nonetheless she engaged in a political intervention in a public forum.

None of these anecdotes is to suggest our responsibility for the transformation of these students. It is very likely that they were engaged with such issues before taking our class, and would have engaged in similar activities had they never heard of "Narrative Strategies." But, at least the course offers a space wherein such students can hone their critical skills. For one of our favorite teaching spaces—the review session for the final exam—we reserve a big conference room for an afternoon to chat with the students as they wander in and out with questions and comments.

One semester, a group of students initiated a provocative discussion about pedagogy, only tangentially related to their exam preparation. We had shown Frederick Wiseman's *High School* (1968) that semester. Part of the discussion we led in teaching the film was a critique of the teachers' reenforcement by memorization. Our students aggressively questioned us during the review session about our hypocrisy in criticizing the *High School* teachers' pedagogical methods and then making them take a final exam wherein they had to memorize all sorts of technical and critical theory terms and concepts. We talked for quite a while about the difference between pure memorizing and applying something that has been committed to memory. We defended our pedagogical approach as a compromise between memorization and empowerment of the students over their own education by learning to write critically about things that mattered to them. But, the significance of the conversation for us was that they were able to apply an analytical tool they learned in the classroom to their lived experience.

The most common sentiment that former students relate to us is invariably articulated in the following formulation: "I loved your class, but I hate you because I can't enjoy movies or TV anymore. My friends don't want to go to the movies with me because I ruin it for them." Here, we finally come to the crux of why we enjoy teaching "Narrative Strategies" so much: not because we are sadists, but because the course's political effect on students is quite formidable. By using popular film and television to introduce critical theory, we can politicize students' vocabulary and activate critical dissent to what the mainstream media produces for viewers. We hope that students emerge from the course with a variety of new implements in their "cultural tool kit" (to borrow a term from Jerome Bruner). We are delighted if, having taken this course, students find themselves increasingly unwilling to treat television viewing as doing nothing, and increasingly unable to file silently out of the theater. In an anti-intellectual and increasingly conservative culture full of Forrest Gumps (both inside and outside of Congress), this is one of the most valuable contributions to an informed citizenry that we can make.

NOTES

1. By theories of "radical politics," we refer to the teaching of what is commonly known as critical theory: Marxism, feminism, ideological criticism, Queer Theory, and the like. We acknowledge that our political activism here is located within the confines of the classroom. However, as we demonstrate, the effects of our work are not so neatly confined.

2. By "lower-division survey course," we mean a course primarily aimed at first-year students and sophomores. Typically, the lower-division coursework is taken during the first two years, in preparation for entry into upper-division work, which entails smaller, more specialized courses in the major, taught primarily by faculty members. The lower-division courses, on the other hand, tend to by taught at many institutions by graduate students or adjunct faculty.

3. We collaboratively taught this course at the University of Texas at Austin from 1994–96 while we were both Ph.D. candidates in the Department of Radio-Television-Film. The course was piloted there by Thomas Schatz in the 1970s. Diane Negra is now an assistant professor in the Department of Radio-Television-Film at the University of East Anglia, UK, while Walter Metz is now an assistant professor in the Department of Media and Theatre Arts at Montana State University in Bozeman.

4. In terms of "Narrative Strategies," content refers to the nuts and bolts of the production of audiovisual narratives. This is the material that the curriculum deems

important for production students to know about the history of the production of film and television narratives. The topics we are encouraged to cover include: narrative theory (plot-story relationships, three-act structure), film style (editing, *mise-en-scène,* sound, lighting), television production aesthetics (multiple-camera proscenium shooting), etc.

5. Our paper attempts to build a connection between the apolitical and anti-intellectual aspects of American culture. While it is clear that one could be an intellectual but not be interested in politics, our assumption is that given the pressing realities of human oppression within the culture, this is not a morally defensible position.

6. Examples of teaching strategies and student writing come from both the fall 1994 and spring 1995 versions of this course. We would like to thank the students for their verbal permission to quote from their essays.

7. Instructors' sensitivities to student tastes are of extreme importance to this method. After having taught media studies for over ten years now, it is remarkable to discover that students have a canon all their own. For example, after a number of references in class, a film or television show that we would have never seen left to our own devices becomes fodder for next semester's course. Examples of this include *The Shawshank Redemption, Fight Club,* and *South Park.*

8. One of the tendencies we are trying to resist here is the frequent use in pedagogical papers of "the class" as a euphemism for, or a projection of, what the teacher wanted to be said in discussion. In this paper, when we report a student insight, it is, to the best of our recollection, the student's own words and meanings.

9. *The Bell Curve: Intelligence and Class Structure in American Life,* by Richard J. Hernstein and Charles Murray, attempts a neoconservative assault on liberal social policy, explaining difference as the result of nature and not social inequities. The authors argue: "It is time for America once again to try living with inequality, as life is lived" (551). The book has been thoroughly critiqued by academics; Andrew Hacker likens it to a return to the discourses of the antebellum plantation. Three book-length critiques of the insidious racialist arguments presented in *The Bell Curve* are: Claude S. Fischer's *Inequality of Design: Cracking the Bell Curve Myth*; Bernie Devlin's *Intelligence, Genes, and Success: Scientists Respond to the Bell Curve*; and Joe L. Kincheloe's *Measured Lies: The Bell Curve Examined.*

10. One strategy we have used as instructors is to share our own arguments (orally or in print) with students. This has been pertinent in our teaching of the ABC soap opera *One Life to Live* and the hour-long show *Lois and Clark* as well as in the case of *True Lies.* In teaching the film, one of the instructors tells his students that in exchange for handing in their first papers, he would in turn give them a copy of his paper about *True Lies.* If they wanted it, the students were told, they could stop by the instructor's office to pick up a copy. A number of students did so, and came by later to discuss and argue with the interpretation. If students trust you to be interested in—and not defensive about—their critiques of your own work, this is an effective way to model a student's analytical eye toward media criticism.

11. We have deliberately refrained from making rigid distinctions here between what work the students are doing on their own and what ideas are being directly forwarded by us as "experts." As we stated earlier, the teaching of critical consciousness is a gradual process of exchanging ideas. At the beginning of the course, we perform much of the interpretive modeling. As the course progresses, students feel more empowered to take

risks and articulate their own hypotheses about their cultural landscape. When the course is working well, the distinctions between student and teacher become indistinguishable. Often, we will instill ideas that students will develop, and, most exciting for us, students will forward ideas which will lead us down interpretive paths we had never before considered. One colleague who has read this manuscript took grave issue with our rejection of the professor's status as expert. He argued that only in the humanities would such "nonsense" be given any serious consideration. Interestingly, he cited the ludicrous nature of a nuclear physicist coming into class and claiming to her students that they were just as much experts as she. Our paper of course argues for the important distinction between students of nuclear physics and media studies. Students have been saturated with media from the inception of their consciousnesses, so in this sense, they are just as much "experts" as we. Furthermore, our colleague's comments point directly to the pedagogical problem we are critiquing. That is, the nuclear physics students do have something valuable to contribute: they have suffered under the trauma that the nuclear age has created, and could contribute quite a lot to a critical discussion of the topic. Even nuclear physics pedagogy could learn a great deal from the critical thinking–based model of instruction articulated in this paper.

12. Of course, this impulse toward oversimplification is the major problem in teaching complicated material of any sort. We emphasize to our students that it will take more than one semester to completely understand any of the concepts that we teach them in this survey course. Our goal, as we envision it, is to get the students to at least begin to take seriously concepts not dealt with in their everyday experiences, in this case psychoanalysis's articulation of the unconscious. Once at this stage, the students can continue to learn about the intricacies of each particular critical method. Another one of our colleagues asked how we keep the students from thinking that any long item is a phallic symbol. In our experience, student resistance tends to take an opposite tack, one of resisting symbolic presence altogether. Our students argue, "sometimes a cigar is just a cigar," like a mantra, to which we typically reply, "but sometimes a cigar is much more than a cigar." One of our primary goals is to get students to notice and think critically about the symbolic structure behind the surface sheen of reality that they assume they know so well.

13. *The Wizard of Oz* is a perfect example of a popular film with which most students are intimately familiar from multiple family viewings at holidays, such as Thanksgiving, Christmas, and Easter (*It's a Wonderful Life* and *The Ten Commandments* are other potential candidates in this small category). When looked at from a critical perspective, these films can yield fabulous ideological insights. Pedagogically, this process is vital, for it demonstrates to the students that the films they would have sworn to be "safe" from our methodology are also deeply susceptible to it.

14. Earlier in the paper, the student argued that the tornado which sweeps Dorothy away to Oz represents the initiation of Dorothy's psychic trauma. The phallic tornado begins Dorothy's transition through the Oedipal trajectory.

15. Because of this paper's effectiveness, we included *The Wizard of Oz* on the next semester's syllabus and successfully used this film to teach psychoanalysis. Here again, the teachers and the students can work together to dialogically construct the course.

16. It certainly could be argued that our positioning of this student's paper is just as condescending as the traditional models of pedagogy that we are critiquing. Phrases such as "rough yet elegant" and "even lower-division undergraduates . . . have the tools" could

seem insulting. However, we offer this critical analysis to resist the temptation in pedagogical articles to present only the unusually stellar student work. Our central contention is that a large percentage of the work in our class engages concepts ordinarily deemed too advanced for introductory students in thoughtful and provocative ways.

17. These were the major reality shows at the time we taught the course. Since then, of course, the reality television genre has flourished. We believe our methods could be adapted to teach any of the current crop of reality shows, such as *Survivor, The Bachelor, Joe Millionaire,* or *Fear Factor,* to name just a few.

18. The term "equilibrium" was introduced by us, deriving from an Aristotelian theory of narrative in which the flow is from equilibrium to disequilibrium and back to a new equilibrium.

19. In his first paper, this student performed an intertextual analysis of Shakespeare's *Macbeth* and the gangster film *White Heat* (1949). Ordinarily we might have hesitated about making this connection for fear of intimidating the student. But, by this late in the semester, we had discussed enough literature for us to feel confident that he would find this suggestion very useful.

20. For example, we discuss the narrative structure of James Joyce's *Ulysses* in relationship to Richard Linklater's independent film *Slacker* (1991). We also explore the ways in which an episode of the cartoon *Animaniacs* simultaneously deconstructs Herman Melville's *Moby Dick* and Aaron Spelling's *The Love Boat.*

21. Of course, we do not mean to imply that we think ill of our students who want to become the next Spielberg. As educators working for large bureaucratic institutions, we know the necessities of the marketplace all too well. However, we do mean to expose our students to ways of thinking beyond the logic of commodification. Just as we have pursued careers that put the goals of others ahead of our own material gain, so too could filmmakers use their creative work for motives beyond profit maximization. If such a pedagogical project be associated with Paulo Freire's "consciousness raising" strategies, so be it.

WORKS CITED

Althusser, Louis. "Ideology and Ideological State Apparatuses." *Lenin and Philosophy and Other Essays.* London: New Left Books, 1971.

Bruner, Jerome. "The Narrative Construction of Reality." *Critical Inquiry* 18 (autumn 1991): 1–21.

Denski, Stan W. "Critical Pedagogy and Media Production: The Theory and Practice of the Video Documentary." *Journal of Film and Video* 43.3 (fall 1991): 3–17.

Freire, Paulo. *Pedagogy of the Oppressed.* New York: Continuum, 1990.

Grossberg, Lawrence. "Bringin' It All Back Home—Pedagogy and Cultural Studies." *Between Borders: Pedagogy and the Politics of Cultural Studies.* Ed. Henry A. Giroux and Peter McLaren. New York: Routledge, 1994. 1–25.

Hauerwas, Stanley M. "The Morality of Teaching." *The Academic's Handbook.* Ed. A. Deneef, C. Goodwin, and E. McCrate. Durham: Duke UP, 1988. 19–29.

Higgins, John W. "Video Pedagogy As Political Activity." *Journal of Film and Video* 43.3 (fall 1991): 18–28.

Lehman, Peter. "Politics, Film Theory, and the Academy." *Journal of Film and Video* 40.2 (spring 1988): 43–51.

McLaren, Peter. *Life in Schools: An Introduction to Critical Pedagogy in the Foundations of Education.* New York: Longman, 1989.

Mercer, Kobena. "1968: Periodizing Postmodern Politics and Identity." *Cultural Studies.* Ed. Lawrence Grossberg, Cary Nelson, and Paul Treichler. New York: Routledge, 1992. 424–38.

Scholes, Robert. "Narration and Narrativity in Film." *Film Theory and Criticism.* Ed. Gerald Mast and Marshall Cohen. 3rd ed. New York: Oxford UP, 1985. 390–403.

Willis, Paul. *Common Culture.* Boulder: Westview, 1990.

Worland, Rick. "Politics, Film Studies, and the Academy: A Commentary." *Journal of Film and Video* 46.4 (winter 1995): 42–56.

The World in a Frame
Introducing Culture through Film

GERALD DUCHOVNAY

BACKGROUND

Texas A&M University at Commerce, a regional university sixty-five miles northeast of Dallas, Texas, has a university core that includes "Capstone" courses. For the last two decades or so, all students have been required to take two of these courses in their junior or senior year. The courses seek to synthesize aspects of previous years of instruction via interdisciplinary, multi-cultural readings that require critical thinking and substantive writing "to help students develop more sophisticated reasoning skills" (*2003–2004 Undergraduate Catalog* 41). In many departments these courses offer faculty members the opportunity to teach special topics courses that might not normally be available, and provide an opportunity for team teaching.

These courses also encourage students to "look outward, [by] providing a . . . broader view than is the normal focus of upper division courses," and familiarize them with disciplines outside their own (41). Because of the desire to have students look beyond their major and minor fields and add breadth rather than depth to their studies, some departments require students to take capstones outside their major. Capstones have included: *Our Endangered Planet, Ethics in the Media, Psychology and Sociology of Diverse Populations, Voyages of Discovery, Making of the Atomic Bomb, Medieval Canterbury, Lord of the Rings as Literature and History, American and Japanese Cultures,* and *World in a Frame: Movies and Culture.* It is this latter course that I want to discuss, while suggesting how, through the use of film, instructors in different disciplines might adapt or modify the films and pedagogical heuristics I use to suit their own disciplines.

AN EARLY EXPERIMENT WITH FILM
AND TEAM-TEACHING DIGRESSION

Shortly after I joined Texas A&M University at Commerce (formerly East Texas State University) in 1990, I offered to coordinate and teach a capstone course on Vietnam and American culture.[1] Most students I encountered knew about Vietnam primarily from the films they had seen. Originally, I wanted to explore the myths about Vietnam and American culture via film. Because there were so many other important facets of the conflict and its impact on our culture, I decided to invite specialists in other disciplines (history, political science, French, humanities, music, literature, and Vietnamese culture) to team-teach the course. Seven instructors agreed to participate, as well as a former POW and a member of Special Forces. The success of this course demonstrated that students were hungry to learn about topics that were remote to them—even though family and friends had served in or were impacted by the Vietnam conflict. The faculty members were enthusiastic about the opportunity to team-teach a course, share in the grading, and engage in dialogue with colleagues and students; the students were extremely enthusiastic about the opportunity to hear professors debate topics, engage in the debate themselves, and learn something about facts and myths regarding the conflict in Vietnam and how it has been presented in various discourse communities. This course, which led to the development of several other courses in history, political science, and English, indicated how willing faculty members were to share their knowledge in courses outside their programs, how students warmed to the opportunity to hear visiting experts, and especially how important culture and media are in the lives of our students.

NEW WINE IN OLD BOTTLES:
WORLD IN A FRAME, MOVIES AND CULTURE

When another colleague expressed interest in taking over the course on Vietnam, I decided to incorporate some of the best aspects of that course into a new capstone whose focus would be on introducing students to aspects of other cultures through film. To anyone who studies the conflict in Vietnam or reads about Kosovo or our relations with China, India, Afghanistan, or Iraq, it seems apparent that what is often missing in our relations with other nations is an understanding of their cultures. This "lack" of understanding of key elements of Vietnamese culture explains in part our military failures and "pacification" programs. Today, many corporations require their employees who interact with international clients to undergo training in cultural differences to better prepare them to understand the culturally conditioned behavior and decision-making processes of their international clients, and books such as *Kiss, Bow, or Shake Hands: How to Do Business in Sixty Countries* are taking up more and more space on bookstore shelves and Internet listings.

While there are numerous excellent texts that deal with culture and media from ideological, political, and theoretical perspectives and others that focus on a particular country,[2] the primary textbook in this course, *Communication Between Cultures,* is useful in that its culture general approach (i.e., considering cultural traits and behaviors common to most or all cultures) stresses how "Our cultural perceptions and experiences help determine how the world looks and how we interact in that world" (xii); the text translates ideas and concepts into practices that assist in intercultural communication, as the authors make a concerted effort to "keep in check" their own ethnocentrism. In addition, the text shows how communication and culture interact, and how cultures shape and modify our view of reality; it also examines the differences between verbal and non-verbal messages (especially useful when discussing film), and provides overviews of how cultures approach business, health care, and education. The relevance of the latter to this course depends upon film selections and student interest. The textbook is very accessible to students who have had little interaction with intercultural communication, dovetails nicely with the films and other writing assignments, and provides useful activities that complement the course assignments.[3]

Even though there are useful introductory textbooks on film (such as Giannetti's *Understanding Movies,* Bordwell and Thompson's *Film Art,* and Phillips's *Film: An Introduction*), I do not require one for this course.[4] I spend the first few classes dealing with approaches to viewing films and connect those viewings with aspects of culture that we will be discussing during the semester. These include: attitudes toward women, family, language, food, economic systems, social stratification, political systems/organizations, age stratification, sex and culture, religion, magic and the supernatural, marriage and the family, the arts, space, and time. I also distribute reviews or articles about the particular films from different venues: the local press, *Newsweek* and *Time,* and scholarly articles, to model different kinds and levels of readings of the films.

The specific objectives of this course,[5] which could be accommodated to courses in a variety of disciplines, are:

1) to improve one's skills in reading "texts";

2) to consider how the elements of film are used by filmmakers to speak to an audience and how the films are cultural narratives;

3) to broaden one's understanding of ideas and values drawn from different cultures and thereby increase one's understanding of processes involved in cultural interactions;

4) to write focused and effectively developed short responses to the readings, viewings, and other cultural artifacts for the purpose of self-understanding and understanding of others;

5) to make connections (global) between the world of the texts and our world (regional and local) and to understand what it is like to be a member of another group in another place, possibly in another time;

6) to examine multi-cultural texts to help one better understand different cultures. Seeing different perspectives makes available options and choices not accessible from one perspective; and

7) to encourage and enhance one's critical thinking skills.[6]

In a recent class of forty students, it is no surprise that all them watched movies at home or went to the theater several times a month. Only seven, however, had traveled outside the United States (four others went to Mexico for the first time during spring break), and of these, three had lived or traveled abroad for more than three months, including one student who was raised and schooled in Korea. While it is a cliché that around the world people know about the United States through television, music, and movies, most of our students are ethnocentric, primarily because they have not been exposed to other cultures and have not had a need to know about "others" or "otherness." Yet many of these same students will be teachers in school districts in which ethnic diversity is commonplace, and others will wind up working in metropolitan areas such as Dallas or Chicago with their plethora of cultures. Knowledge of other peoples and other cultures through the use of movies, film clips, newspaper articles, focused research papers, and speakers provides an entry to topics and concepts that are, literally and figuratively, foreign to most of our students. This is not because they may not be interested, but many have never had the opportunity to be introduced to foreign films, ethnic restaurants, or an international student population.

While a sizeable percentage of our students commute from the Dallas Metroplex area, the majority of the undergraduates are from East Texas and are often the first in their families to have attended college. With a university enrollment of approximately 8,000 (5,000 undergraduate and 3,000 graduate), less than 100 undergraduates (2 percent) engage in summer study abroad each year. As I explain to the students when the class first meets, some of them may never have left Texas, while others may never have traveled outside the United States. Some may never want to interact with individuals from other cultures, while others may have already done so and may want to continue to do so. As Kurt Spellmeyer notes, "Although we might ordinarily conceive of learning as preparing for public life, we tacitly understand that every culture affords its members a variety of public lives—affords them many different and often dissonant modes of social existence, each having its own knowledge, or its own take on a shared knowledge" (229). Today, even listening to popular music requires knowledge of diverse cultures. The crossover star Ricky Martin, for example, says, "'I play with cultures.'" His "songs are less Latin workouts . . . than frothy cocktails of global pop styles" (Chambers and Leland 73). Understanding other cultures helps us to better understand ourselves and what we value as we learn to accept differences and appreciate similarities. As we discuss in class, knowledge of other cultures is a necessity in the workplace, is practical as well as financially and intellectually rewarding, and is becoming essential to social discourse. In our current global business and social environment, an understanding of how individuals are shaped by their cultures and how they communicate is useful, if not essential, in understanding and dealing with others.

World in a Frame: Movies and Culture uses foreign films as a key element in "introducing" students to foreign cultures by getting them to look closely not only at an entire foreign feature film, but at small segments (through frequent use of clips) that relate to other cultures. We begin with clips from films with which they might be familiar (*Pretty Woman, Thelma and Louise*) to establish a foundation on how to "read" film as text and to consider how "loaded" with culture even small segments of a film could be. For example, I play the first eight minutes of *Thelma and Louise* (1991) and then ask the students to list all the things they saw and what the film demonstrates about filmmaking. After some comments about how the focus of the film is on Thelma and Louise, who and how different their characters are, I play the opening again, stopping every few seconds to discuss how much information is supplied and how film is a collaborative art. I go over basic things, such as the various professionals who contribute to the film (screenwriter, director, cast), and introduce the much maligned concept of *auteur*; I then ask them to identify other films by the director (they can name other songs by rock groups or rap artists, so why not films by directors?), or other films that the actors have been in and what image those films convey of the actor. I then mention the distributor and the studio (important aspects to the business of film and film history). They pick up on the music, and then discuss why the opening shifts from black and white to color. We talk about the images and metaphors used (the road, the sky and mountains, the cars that Thelma and her husband drive). Once the two cars are compared, I ask how many can tell me what the license plate on the husband's car says and how it reflects his character. Our discussion continues, as we analyze the significance of the Thunderbird convertible, the way the characters dress, and their verbal and non-verbal communication. What, for example, does it do to audience expectation when Thelma drops a gun into her purse when she is packing? Why does Louise turn down the picture of her boyfriend when she calls him and gets his answering machine? We conclude this discussion with remarks on the importance of the film's title and its link to genre films and other "buddy" and "road" movies.

Because many of the students have seen this movie before, a careful viewing of the opening minutes introduces them to the many "elements of film" that one might discuss in a film course. Its primary function, though, is to demonstrate how one might read films. This heuristic is continued with the next two film clips, one from *Pretty Woman* (1990) and the other from *Fools Rush In* (1997). Everyone in the class has seen *Pretty Woman,* often several times. Looking at those first few minutes, we consider aspects of social class; why Julia Roberts and not Laura San Giacomo is the heroine; how clothing, music, dialogue, verbal and non-verbal communication, and set designs function. We also discuss how the studio changed the ending of the film to meet audience expectations, the use of the "Cinderella syndrome" and how it reinforces and reflects certain cultural values, as well as the tenor of the time in which the film was made. This heuristic is also a form of modeling what they will be asked to do for their third paper in the course.

Fools Rush In is an easy film for students to understand, as the harried New Yorker (Matthew Perry) has a one-night stand with a beautiful and self-reliant Mexican American (Salma Hayek) while he is on assignment in Las Vegas. Her pregnancy, their subsequent marriage, and the interaction of the protagonists and their families serve as a template for stereotypical patriarchal behavior, male-female interaction, differences in attitude between WASP and Hispanic cultures, tastes in decorating, and a score of other cliché-driven plot points and dialogue. Even with its simplistic presentation, *Fools Rush In* serves nicely as a primer for aspects of intercultural communication, and as a smooth transition from the representation of culture in Hollywood plots to international cinema.

At the beginning of the semester, I asked students to briefly define what they understand culture to be. Because most of the class had never really thought through what culture is, we adopted the textbook's working definition of it as "the deposit of knowledge, experience, beliefs, values, actions, attitudes, meanings, hierarchies, religion, notions of time, roles, spatial relations, concepts of the universe, and artifacts acquired by a group of people in the course of generations through individual and group striving" (Samovar et al. 36). To better assist them in getting a handle on particular aspects of culture, the students are asked early in the term to choose a particular country to research for the rest of the semester. Once we come to closure on those choices—often after some discussion of the importance of considering countries other than those in Europe—I demonstrate that their research and readings don't have to focus on large issues, that sometimes something small, something that we take for granted, might reflect important aspects of culture. Using the clips from films like *Fools Rush In,* we began to refine our working definition of culture. To get the students to think in terms of manageable topics and representations of culture, and to reinforce and refine what they mean by the term, I placed before them a glass Coca-Cola bottle and asked them how they used it and what the object represented to them.

While a few saw the connection that was coming, most were reminded at the next class meeting how a simple item such as the bottle could represent many things to us (a place to put flowers, capitalism, a drink, the need for recycling, and so on); it could also mean something very different to Bushmen in the Kalahari as presented in Jamie Uys's *The Gods Must Be Crazy* (1981). What followed was a discussion of geography (only one student had ever heard of Botswana), the artificiality of the juxtaposition of "civilized" vs. "savage" images for comic purposes, the "reel" vs. "real" nature of the Bushmen of the Kalahari, cultural perceptions, and myths created for comic purposes by filmmakers. A clip from a documentary *Culture Change* made a few years later showed how those same Bushmen were being displaced by elephants and were forced to organize as a political force in order to gain permission to dig a well for water for their families. The contrast of images led to a discussion of differences between documentary and narrative films, how audiences often take fictional images on the screen as "truth" rather than as often-distorted representations of a culture, and how cultural myths are established.

COURSE FOCUS

The focus of the course, then, is to engage one another in a voyage of discovery as we look at and talk about how diverse cultures are reflected on film and other sources. The idea behind this particular course is not to say whether a particular culture or country is better than another, but to consider how (and if) movies are ambassadors of culture and if they communicate aspects of particular cultures. This is not a film course *per se* with its attendant weekly feature film showing. The class meets twice a week for seventy-five minutes, with five scheduled classes (announced in the semester schedule) running an additional seventy-five minutes to permit viewings in full of five foreign films. Film clips from documentaries, news clips, and feature films are worked in throughout the semester as the topic and need arise. During the spring 1999 semester, for example, the films, film clips, and presentations included: *Pretty Woman, The Gods Must Be Crazy, Cinema Paradiso, The Nasty Girl, Women on the Verge of a Nervous Breakdown, My Fair Lady,*

American Tongues, Night and Fog, Like Water for Chocolate, Guantanamera, Not without My Daughter, Bandit Queen, and news clips on honor killings in Pakistan and Jordan. Guests or countries examined included: Botswana, Ukraine, Italy, France, Spain, Germany, Austria, Iran, Pakistan, Jordan, Cuba, Mexico, Peru, Bolivia, Uruguay, India, and Iceland. In addition, the students shared their findings about the countries through oral reports or abstracts, which added still more films and countries to the scope of the course.

While I could focus on one or two countries during a semester and be culture specific, I have chosen to use the culture-general method by focusing on traits and behaviors that are common to most cultures. As a result, to further personalize class responses, readings, and films, and to help the class separate fact from fantasy, I invite guest speakers to discuss foreign cultures and aspects of intercultural communication, and encourage students who have traveled abroad to share their experiences with their classmates.

The last time the course was taught, students spoke about life in Germany and South Korea, and outside guests shared information about Ukraine, Spain, Mexico, Cuba, Peru, Bolivia, Uruguay, and Iceland. The presentation on Ukraine was made by a visiting Fulbright lecturer who happened to be on campus; the year before, it was a visiting Fulbright lecturer from China. The presentation on Iceland was a matter of serendipity. While sitting in on a dissertation defense in the College of Education, I happened to meet a graduate student from Iceland who was completing hours for his doctorate at our university, and who agreed to talk to the class about his country. His presentation, which was added to the schedule, gave all of us insights into a country that we rarely think about. While there are few feature films indigenous to Iceland (*Children of Nature, Cold Fever, The Juniper Tree, Remote Control*), our speaker's comments were contextualized in relation to the other films and countries we discussed earlier in the semester. To better assist the students in understanding Iceland's culture, he created a course-specific Web site to provide information on such topics as movies, education, health, jobs, and music. The site included visual charts on divorce and education, still images of the country and its people, maps, historical textual information, and links to other sites about Iceland. The guests who spoke about the other countries were either students on campus or faculty members. Each person I approached was enthusiastic about visiting the class and sharing information about her culture. Some spoke on aspects of culture, supplemented with visual aids such as maps, food products and cooking implements, images of specific locations downloaded from Web sites, and indigenous costumes, while others used clips from films to demonstrate aspects of culture.

Over time guests in the course have taken a variety of approaches to introducing aspects of their culture. One of the invited guests spoke about cross-cultural communication, focusing on the unconscious process of how we communicate with one another and how that is reflected in everyday behavior. By focusing on cultural patterns, she was able to demonstrate with role-playing amongst the students and the use of a French film and a U.S. remake (*Three Men and a Cradle* and *Three Men and a Baby*), how seemingly "similar" actions are very different and reflect differences in humor, morality, and communication. By examining the visual text of the film, the interaction between characters, and the personalities of the characters in the scenes, she was able to demonstrate major cultural differences in verbal and non-verbal communication, proxemics—how we use space and distance to convey messages—and the differences between what E. T. Hall calls high and low context cultures—what some cultures pay attention to and what others ignore.

On another occasion, a guest introduced a variety of cultural aspects from Spain, presented facts about Spain in a handout, and then moved on to examine how the clothes of the female characters in *Women on the Verge of a Nervous Breakdown* (1988) reflect social and political mores over several decades: the movement away from the dark clothes worn during Franco's dictatorship, followed by the Jackie Kennedy look that infiltrated Spanish culture and is worn by one of the middle-aged women (Lucía, played by Julieta Serrano), to the total freedom of expression in choice of clothes, colors, and accessories worn by several of the female characters (Pepa, played by Carmen Maura; Candela, played by María Barranco; and Marisa, played by Rosy de Palma). Thus, we are told a great deal about Spain and its culture, beliefs, and attitudes at a particular moment in time by examining the clothes worn by these women. Other guests have spoken about the role of women in India and the caste system, and the factual and mythic qualities in the film *Bandit Queen*; the importance of food to Mexican culture in language and action, and how aspects of that are reflected in *Like Water for Chocolate*; and the impact of communism on Cuba as seen in *Guantanamera,* which clearly presents many of the country's current bureaucratic nightmares and how many citizens live by an underground economy that continues to valorize the dollar. Not all presenters used film clips. Some did presentations and invited discussion. On other occasions, if the logistics could be worked out, I established a roundtable. The last time the course was taught, for example, four graduate students participated in a roundtable discussion on the cultures of Bolivia, Uruguay, and Peru, complemented by a computer presentation that used visuals and the Internet to show aspects of their cultures.

SHORT WRITING ASSIGNMENTS

As an introduction to geographical and cultural units, I distribute maps of a continent and ask the students to work in groups to identify the various countries. As recent surveys heralded on the national news have indicated, as a nation we are geographically illiterate. My students have a difficult time locating states and naming capitals in their own country; they are often embarrassed when asked to name the countries, let alone the capitals, in, for example, Latin America. Presenting the task as a collaborative effort lessens the stigma of ignorance, helps to acquaint the students with their classmates, and attempts to familiarize the class with the world we inhabit. I also ask them to read daily newspapers for foreign news.

In previous classes, I have asked students to keep reading logs based on the assigned texts. This task was not as productive as I had hoped, and I now ask students to prepare for each class meeting a one-paragraph summary and a two- or three-paragraph commentary on a current newspaper or Internet news article about some aspect of a foreign culture. The article must be submitted with the written material. The newspaper summaries involve them in thinking about cultural issues, and the films serve as a visual way in to foreign lands and ideas rarely considered before. When students see *The Nasty Girl,* based on a true story, followed by a *60 Minutes* interview with the real-life protagonist, and then experience Alain Resnais's powerful Holocaust documentary *Night and Fog,* Bosnia, the Sudan, and Kosovo take on new meaning. When we travel by car across Cuba with a husband and wife who are trying to bury a friend's body in Alea's *Guantanamera,* not only do we see a sly attack on Fidel Castro's cultural, political, and social reforms, but we experience politics through art as we witness Cuba's informal economy and flourishing black market, and encounter social bureaucrats and lapsed idealists.

Once the students have chosen the country they plan to focus on for the semester, I encourage them to use articles about their country of choice in order to immerse themselves in that culture. While the class is culture general, the students are encouraged to make their work culture specific. A few who have traveled abroad, know another language, are working on projects in history or political science classes, or want to surf the Internet to find newspapers (in English) from another country may select this option, but almost all prefer to be culture general and learn a little about a number of countries. Another contributing factor may well be the paucity of international news in the local and regional newspapers. Occasional substitutions for this assignment include a comparison/contrast of the coverage (or lack of coverage) of a story on one of the national evening news programs (ABC, NBC, CBS, CNN, Fox) with a foreign language news program (e.g., Univision) or World News or ITN news on PBS stations; a restaurant review; or a review of a substantive television documentary about their country of choice.

Students liked the options, but opinions were divided on the newspaper assignment, with some indicating that it was an easy grade, while others said they were willing to do whatever it took to get a decent grade. At the start of the course, most students indicated they rarely read newspapers, and one even asked in what part of the paper he might find international news. A majority of the students said the summaries were worth doing because they provided useful and exploratory venues to foreign cultures, required thought, helped to better understand U.S. culture in light of other cultures and belief systems, and provided possible topics for papers. The students also appreciated the openness of choice of subjects. As one student noted, overall this assignment was "an opportunity, not a burden." Others felt they were "pesky but not difficult," or monotonous busy work that infringed upon time for other courses and jobs, or that its only benefit was the opportunity to clip coupons in the paper. One student was concerned for my well being and suggested I would have more time for other tasks if I didn't have to read their responses.

Required response papers were brief (5–10 minutes), in-class writings that were used to "prime the pump" about some aspect of the readings, films, or ideas being discussed. These responses occurred at the very beginning of class. For example, after looking at *American Tongues* and a clip from *My Fair Lady,* students were asked to respond to the question of whether or not the United States government should require all residents to speak a single language and whether there should be support for speakers of other languages. This idea linked to how those who live in other countries know more than one language, and ethnocentric attitudes toward language in the United States. At other times, students were asked to respond to the previous day's speaker. By asking them to synthesize what they took away from the presentation and any questions they had about what was said, I learned what they considered to be the key points and what was worth discussing; the students also practiced breaking down and organizing a presentation to its key components, which in turn helped enhance their exam-taking skills and prepared them for oral reports or abstracts later in the semester.

For each film shown students were given study questions.[7] The students responded to the questions in writing, in small groups, or in class discussion. These questions helped them to focus on particular cultural or cinematic aspects of what they were watching. When students were shown a documentary on a particular country, to encourage active viewing, I supplied a list of terms for them to become familiar with to better prepare for the speaker's comments.[8]

PAPER ASSIGNMENTS

The course required three short papers. Two papers focused on different aspects of foreign culture, and the third was on a film indigenous to their country of choice. The papers were 3–5 pages each.[9] The film paper had to focus on a foreign film made after 1965. The country focus remained the same for all papers. For the short papers on culture, the students were asked to use three different secondary sources, including the Internet or interviews. I also encouraged them to read or talk about their films and topics with others. Depending upon the size of the class, I offered two additional options at the end of the semester: brief oral presentations (6–8 minutes) detailing what they learned about their country, or an abstract covering their three papers and distributed to all members of the class. Thus, in one format or another, the students were able to share with their peers what they learned during the semester.

Most students at Texas A&M University at Commerce have to drive sixty miles or more to see a foreign film in a theater. While I would like to say that a majority of students did make that drive during the semester, that is not the case. A few did. However, initial resistance to the idea of seeing foreign films—"Do you mean I have to read subtitles?"—quickly disappeared after the first film. After seeing *Cinema Paradiso,* a film about movies, isolation, memory, childhood, frustrated love, and friendship that works much of its charm through silences and images rather than dialogue, students were heard to say: "it wasn't as bad as I thought it would be" and "after a while I forgot that I was reading the subtitles." Students have access to a variety of foreign films in our Media Center, and I lent out films from my personal collection when a particular film was not available. As we moved through the course, I tried to link the film selections to aspects of culture and themes or topics, while introducing the students to history, politics, geography, and other aspects of culture. Using film and the various readings and presentations, we covered topics such as characteristics of communication, how to understand the complexities of culture, alternative views of reality in cultural diversity, culture and family, religion as a worldview, the importance of language to culture, the problems of translation, verbal and non-verbal communication, and cultural influences on business, health, and education.

World in a Frame is a voyage of discovery to distant shores. Through film and other supplementary materials, we are able to navigate through the often murky waters of intercultural confusion. By understanding the various modes of intercultural communication, including film, keeping abreast of and thinking about what is happening in current affairs, and being receptive to what others tell us about their native lands, we will be better able to interact successfully with people from different cultures.

NOTES

1. The course on Vietnam was truly a team-taught course, whereas the culture and film course was collaborative. In the Vietnam course, while two of us could have "taken credit" for the course as part of our teaching load because of the anticipated size of the class, my colleagues declined, and yet most instructors attended each of the sessions. We engaged each other and the students in debate, we saw each other teach, and we each contributed to the evaluation process because each paper and each exam was graded by at least two of the instructors. For the last class meeting, we arranged a luncheon for the students, all the instructors, and our guests. (During the semester, in addition to the instructors, we invited a POW who was in the Hanoi Hilton and had written a book about his experience, and another member of our faculty who was part of an elite secret force in Vietnam.) Even the local press attended and wrote up the class. Because of the need to submit grades almost immediately, we all came together in the classroom to read and evaluate the final exams. We learned from each other, and we learned from our students. Faculty members and students saw a variety of teaching styles, engaged administrators (the instructors included two deans and two department heads), and shared political and theoretical differences as we engaged in debate and discussion.

Only one instructor was listed, but the way the course was going to be taught was publicized on campus. Capstone courses on our campus are limited to thirty-five students because of the amount of writing required, the need for interaction, and the emphasis on critical thinking and writing skills. Because of the shared responsibilities and the uniqueness of the course, we permitted fifty-six students to enroll. It was a thoroughly enjoyable, if not remarkable, experience for teachers and students alike.

With *A World in a Frame,* I collaborated with instructors and guests before the semester began as to what they would do in the class, which helped me to select the readings and films. While the students engaged the speakers and their instructor on the topics at hand, unlike the course on Vietnam, the guest instructors only participated in the classes in which they spoke. Students were able to interact with most of them—although not the Fulbright lecturer—outside of class, and many did. In addition, as a result of their presentations, some students decided to take classes from some of the guest instructors.

2. See, for example, Shohat and Stam's *Unthinking Eurocentrism* or Boyd-Barrett and Newbold's *Approaches to Media* for the ideological, political, and theoretical perspectives; and White and Barnet's *Comparing Cultures: Readings on Contemporary Japan for American Writers* for a cultural-specific text.

3. For those who are interested, there is an accompanying reader, *Intercultural Communication: A Reader* by Samovar and Porter, that deals with such matters as context and meaning, dominant cultural patterns in a particular country, verbal and non-verbal communication as reflections of reality, and the importance of setting to cultural understanding.

4. Ellen Summerfield's *Crossing Cultures through Film,* one of the very first texts to explore culture through film, notes that film can explore cultural aspects such as "gender, age, physical ability, class, sexual orientation, and religion" (x). While a somewhat useful primer on the topic, I found it unsuitable as a required textbook. Robin Buss's *The French through Their Films* is useful in its methodology but too culture-specific for the objectives of this particular course. Robert Singer's *Teaching from a Multicultural*

Perspective: Focus on International Film is a slim primer for teachers and is more note-like than sustained analysis. One text that came in too late for me to review thoroughly, but might work for a course like this is Robert Kolker's *Film, Form, and Culture*, which includes a CD-ROM of "key film elements and techniques." For historians who want to examine Latin American history through film, Donald F. Stevens's *Based on a True Story: Latin American History at the Movies* may offer a starting point. Journals such as *Film & History* and *Film History* offer detailed analyses of particular films or aspects of film history, and *Post Script: Essays in Film and the Humanities* includes an annual bibliography of film studies in approximately fifty English-language journals that is an accessible and inexpensive reference.

5. In addition to these objectives, a number of the students taking the course are in our Teacher Certification programs. Texas requires that students pass what were called ExCET tests (now TExTs) in their major and in professional development before they can be certified. Recent results indicate that our workshops are working very well. For a fuller discussion of the impact of assessment on the English program at Texas A&M University at Commerce and our strategies to meet this challenge, please see my brief article in the summer 2000 *MLA Newsletter*.

6. As detailed to the students, characteristics of critical thinking include: requiring imagination and creativity, as well as logic and reasoning; understanding the relationships of the parts of an argument; making valid inferences from information more than finding information to back up already-formed opinions, thereby stressing reading and listening sympathetically as well as skeptically; requiring identification of relevant criteria for judging an issue; solving a problem; requiring self-awareness, especially of one's self as a learner, a skill especially important in knowing one's capacity for risk taking; identifying one's assumptions and biases; seeing from multiple perspectives and understanding diversity; understanding that critical thinking occurs in different ways at different individual levels of cognitive development; and understanding that critical thinking always occurs in a context (a discipline, a discourse community, a social setting).

7. Representative of the type of study questions are these on *Bandit Queen* (India, 1994, dir. Shekhar Kapur): What did you learn from the film? What did you find different or strange? What would you like to know more about? What did you find disturbing and why? What do you know about the caste system in India and its meaning to the country's culture? How would you compare the treatment of women in *Bandit Queen* and how women are treated in other countries? Do you see any similarities or differences? What is the view of marriage in India? Is it similar to what you are familiar with in your own culture or co-culture? (I have adopted the term co-culture as used by Samovar, Porter, and Stefani, rather than *subculture*.) How important is it to you that people marry for love? Think about the treatment of Phoolan Devi at age eleven. Are there other cultures that treat young girls like that? What do you think of that treatment and why do you think that way? What is the difference between urban life and rural life in India? In China? In the United States? In Mexico? In Germany? In Italy? In Australia? Are there elements in *Bandit Queen* that echo any aspects of American culture either today or in our past? In other words, could the film in any way be used as a "gloss" of aspects of our culture or other cultures that you know about? Is *Bandit Queen* a documentary film? Why or why not? Is it an accurate portrayal of history? What U.S. films have you seen that are like *Bandit Queen* in their filmic presentations of historical events? What happens when history and film meet?

8. Supplemental terms for India include: Shiva, Siva, Akbar, caste system, importance of villages, Veda, RigVeda, Sanskrit, Benares, Aryans, Hinduism, Gandhi, Ganges, Indus, Brahmaputra, Bombay, Calcutta, Dharma, Bhagavad-Gita, Upanishads, and Brahamanas.

9. Sample subjects selected by the students and film titles they chose for papers included: Argentina: The Gaucho, soccer, *Tango: Our Dance*; Australia: education for the Aborigines, arranged marriages, *Muriel's Wedding*; Greece: Greek folk dancing, Greek wedding traditions, *Zorba the Greek*; Japan: Japanese bonsai, collectivism in Japan, *Fireworks*; Mexico: Totonic art, expatriate fathers and family life, *Erendira* and Days of the Dead (*los Dias de los Muertos*), corn in the Mexican diet, *Like Water for Chocolate*; Peru: evolution of native Peruvian populations, Peruvian Amazon life, *We're All Stars* (*Todos Somos Estrellas*); Venezuela: Miss Venezuela pageant, Carnaval, *The Day You Love Me* (*El Dia Que Me Quieras*).

WORKS CITED

2003–2004 Undergraduate Catalog: Texas A&M University–Commerce. Commerce: Texas A&M University–Commerce, 2003.

The Bandit Queen. Dir. Shekhar Kapur. Kaleidoscope Productions, 1994.

Bordwell, David, and Kristin Thompson. *Film Art: An Introduction.* 5th ed. New York: McGraw Hill, 1997.

Boyd-Barrett, Oliver, and Chris Newbold. *Approaches to Media: A Reader.* London: Arnold, 1995.

Buss, Robin. *The French through Their Films.* New York: Ungar, 1988.

Chambers, Veronica, and John Leland. "Lovin' La Vida Loca." *Newsweek* 31 May 1999: 72–74.

Children of Nature. Dir. Óskar Jónasson. Icelandic Film Corporation, 1991.

Cold Fever. Dir. Friorik Pór Frioriksson. Zentropa Entertainments, 1995.

Culture Change. Prod. John Bishop. Coast Telecourse series, *Faces of Culture,* Coast Community College District, 1983.

Fools Rush In. Dir. Andy Tennant. Columbia, 1997.

Giannetti, Louis. *Understanding Movies.* 8th ed. Upper Saddle River, NJ: Prentice Hall, 1999.

The Gods Must Be Crazy. Dir. Jamie Uys. Fox, 1981.

Guantanamera. Dir. Tómas Gutiérrez and Juan Carlos Tabío. Cine 360, 1995.

Hall, E. T. *Beyond Culture.* New York: Doubleday, 1976.

The Juniper Tree. Dir. Nietzchka Keene. Wea Corp, 1987.

Kolker, Robert. *Film, Form, and Culture.* Boston: McGraw Hill, 1999.

Legacy: India. Narrated by Michael Wood. Dir. Peter Spry-Leverton. Maryland Public Television and Central Independent Television, PLC, 1991.

Like Water for Chocolate. Dir. Alfonso Arau. Miramax, 1992.

Morrison, Terri, Wayne A. Conway, and George A. Borden. *Kiss, Bow, or Shake Hands: How to Do Business in Sixty Countries.* Holbrook, MA: Bob Adams, 1994.

The Nasty Girl. Dir. Michael Verhoeven. Miramax, 1990.

Night and Fog. Dir. Alain Resnais. Criterion Collection, 1955.

Phillips, William A. *Film: An Introduction.* Boston: Bedford/St. Martin's, 1999.

Pretty Woman. Dir. Garry Marshall. Buena Vista, 1990.

Remote Control. Dir. Óskar Jónasson. Skífan, 1993.

Samovar, Larry A., and Richard E. Porter. *Intercultural Communication: A Reader.* 8th ed. Belmont, CA: Wadsworth, 1997.

Samovar, Larry A., Richard E. Porter, and Lias A. Stefani. *Communication Between Cultures.* 3rd ed. Belmont, CA: Wadsworth, 1998.

Shohat, Ella, and Robert Stam. *Unthinking Eurocentrism: Multiculturalism and the Media.* London and New York: Routledge, 1994.

Singer, Robert. *Teaching from a Multicultural Perspective: Focus on International Film.* Northport, NY: Justin Books, 1992.

Spellmeyer, Kurt. *Common Ground: Dialogue, Understanding, and the Teaching of Composition.* Englewood Cliffs, NJ: Prentice Hall, 1993.

Stevens, Donald F., ed. *Based on a True Story: Latin American History at the Movies.* Wilmington, DE: Scholarly Resources, 1997.

Summerfield, Ellen. *Crossing Cultures through Film.* Yarmouth, ME: Intercultural Press, 1993.

Thelma and Louise. Dir. Ridley Scott. MGM, 1991.

Three Men and a Baby. Dir. Leonard Nimoy. Touchstone, 1987.

Three Men and a Cradle. Dir. Coline Serreau. Samuel Goldwyn Co., 1986.

White, Merry I., and Sylvan Barnet. *Comparing Cultures: Readings on Contemporary Japan for American Writers.* Boston: Bedford/St. Martin's, 1995.

Women on the Verge of a Nervous Breakdown. Dir. Pedro Almodóvar. Orion Classics, 1988.

To Show or Not to Show

The Use of Film in Teaching Cross-Cultural Courses

BAN WANG

Teaching literature and culture produced in countries outside North America and Europe has become a fact of life in American universities. Though still contested, the "non-Western" courses are now taught under a variety of institutional rubrics: comparative literature, world literature, ethnicity studies, race studies, area studies, globalization, and so on. They are often designated as multicultural or cross-cultural courses. Much has been written about issues and tensions arising from encounters between fundamentally different cultures. Though theoretical insights and findings are crucial to these courses, more inquiry should be made into the workaday mechanisms in teaching practice. As cross-cultural courses are mostly taught through translations and facilitated by media images, this essay attempts to address the use of film in the pedagogy of such courses.

Unlike the regular courses of a settled discipline whose validity is relatively self-evident, the implications of the cross-cultural course need to be assessed beyond the confines of a discipline or major. The increasing importance of the cross-cultural curriculum must be gauged through a broader perspective. In the last decade or so there has been a gathering momentum in universities in the United States to institute and develop the multicultural canon, which includes not only texts by minority writers within the United States but also those from non-Western cultures. Multiculturalism has joined hands with the academic discourse of post-colonialism to foster a new interest in or a sharpened curiosity about cultures beyond the West. In my institution, State University of New York at Stony Brook, knowledge of non-Western cultures has for some time been a requirement of undergraduate general education. The institutional components include the curriculum on non-Western literature and society, such as World Literature; the faculty positions established for teaching and research in non-Western cultures; and various research centers for Latin American, Asian, or African studies. Similar endeavors and programs are surely underway or already well established elsewhere across the country. "Diversity" is now a catch-word favorably uttered in many quarters of campus life, and a multicultural consciousness, a multi-ethnic sensibility, and cross-cultural orientation seem to be gaining ground.

The educational emphasis on cultural diversity reflects the need to keep up with the social and economic developments of the last two decades, especially the period after the Cold War. As demographic changes have brought diverse ethnic populations to the mainstream U.S. economy, the population of college students is becoming multi-ethnic, multicultural, and multi-lingual. The need has arisen to address minority students' cultural backgrounds and to provide them with alternative symbolic resources for working out their self-identity in college education. On the international scene, the end of the Cold War has led to a massive expansion of trans-national corporations around the world and the influx of global capital into less developed as well as wealthy countries in Europe and Asia. This glob-alizing trend is quickly breaking down regional, national, and local bound-aries. U.S.-based transnational corporations are increasingly aware of the cultural differences of foreign countries and are interested in domesticat-ing and repackaging ethnic and native flavors for marketing and sales (Palumbo-Liu 5). On the home front, corporate America needs to train an increasingly diverse workforce to function efficiently and harmoniously. A multicultural awareness is thus necessary for managing conflict arising from ethnic and cultural difference in the workplace and for ensuring pro-ductivity. All these issues put multicultural education and cross-cultural understanding on the agenda for higher and public education.

This essay addresses the teaching of cross-cultural courses through the medium of film. The above perceptions about multiculturalism raise some concerns of a hidden ideology that will affect the actual reception of "for-eign" texts. The inclusion of the heretofore marginalized cultures in the curriculum has certainly broadened the educational horizon and offered alternative resources for the cultivation of a democratic, tolerant, critical

mindset. But the mere inclusion of culturally diverse texts does not guar-
antee that they be read with due sensitivity to their differences or otherness. An apparently open-minded embrace of an unfamiliar culture may
conceal a narcissistic close-mindedness which subsumes the other in the
self. It is helpful to make a distinction between the celebration of multiculturalism as pluralism, and the training of the critical mind nourished
on a genuine cross-cultural knowledge.[1] Based on a refined aesthetic
assumption about the text, the celebration approach is inclined to read an
ethnic or foreign text as one more aesthetic artifact, a *fait accompli* from
the past, in no way different from the highly rarefied texts by Shakespeare
or Milton. If an instructor romanticizes or lifts the foreign text from its
specific context of production as a transcendent "essence," he or she reduces
the text's complex roots in history into a "common" standard tailored for
aesthetic appreciation. As a tributary to a common pool of the American
or universal "world" culture, foreign texts are stripped of their own history and of their own tradition of meaning making. Trained to read non-
Western texts from such a neutralized, universalistic stance, students will
lose sight of the particular circumstances in which these texts were produced, and of the tortuous process of struggle in which history and text
interact, intertwine, and negotiate to come to the present shape.[2]

Closely related to this pluralistic and universalistic approach is a deeply
engrained "orientalist" attitude towards non-Western, especially Asian, cultures. The word "orientalist" recalls Edward Said's influential book
Orientalism, which discusses a body of discourses, practices, attitudes, and
symbolic representations that maintains the imbalance of power between
the West and the East. While Said's book has generated a pervasive critique
of orientalism, we may still note a more implicit and "benign" orientalism
in educational discourse and in the students' attitude toward "oriental" cultures (the difficulty of using a less general and loaded term than "oriental"
is a sign of the tenacity of the attitude embedded in language). In my six
years of teaching comparative and cross-cultural courses on Asia, especially
China, I found that American students tend to perceive Chinese or Japanese
culture in the past tense—that is, as an already completed whole, like
exhibits on display in a museum. In literature classes, for example, they are
more likely to become interested in the ancient, religious aspects of Chinese
literature than in the contemporary literary developments fraught with

modernist anxieties and problems. China, for instance, is often perceived as a timeless, mystical entity with lots of precious wisdom to offer, as if contained in a fortune cookie ready for unraveling and perusal. Chinese Americans themselves are no exception. Though exposed to Chinese culture and language in the ethnic communities like Chinatown as they grew up, they are not exempt from the static view that flattens the native culture into mere spectacles and images. This kind of orientalist stereotyping could be attributed at least in part to the influence of the mass media. Even in the post–Cold War era, media representations of Asia still retain the residual ideology that sees the East-West relation in terms of a rigid standoff—Them vs. Us. When students read Chinese texts, they often fall back on a set of themes characteristic of the media's stance: a tyrannical government vs. a rebellious people; a backward country vs. the post-industrialized West; a timeless, soothing utopia vs. stressful modern life in the West; and so on. All these images color the perception of a vast and complex culture.

BALANCING CONCEPT AND IMAGE

The following pages will discuss how film can be used productively with written texts in teaching a course with multicultural materials. I call this kind of course "cross-cultural" in order to set it apart from courses focused on a "foreign" culture from "native" perspectives on the one hand, and courses on multi-ethnic, multi-racial experiences within the United States on the other. The cross-cultural course involves a much more fluid interaction between non-Western and Western materials and perspectives, and aims at cross-fertilization and mutual illumination. Drawing on a graduate seminar I taught with Professor Ann Kaplan at SUNY–Stony Brook in fall semester 1997, I will discuss lessons and experiences in addressing the give-and-take between text and film in a cross-cultural context. While our course proved to be very successful and produced several published papers in addition to an anthology in the making, I will deal mainly with the problems that arose in the course and whose adjustments and solutions yielded valuable lessons. The course is entitled "Trauma, Memory, and History: The Case of China and American Perspectives." Offered by the Program in Comparative Literature and the Humanities Institute at Stony Brook, we had fourteen graduate students enrolled from various departments and from a variety of cultural and ethnic backgrounds. In our symposiums and film screening, we also attracted a large number of undergraduate students.

This brief quotation from our course's statement of purpose may give a glimpse of what we planned to do:

> Traumatic memory cripples our feeble yet necessary attempt to understand our extreme century. It tears violently at our age-old schemes in picturing, in the face of all holocausts big or small, ourselves as worthy of humanity.
>
> This course offers an occasion for reflecting on how a culture remembers its past through art forms such as literature and film. We focus on how cultural memory flounders on the experience of catastrophe, genocide, annihilation, etc.—experiences that explode our inherited kits of meaning, representation, and symbolization, and how traumatic memory motivates as well as disfigures the fashioning of individual, gender, and communal identity. (Kaplan and Wang)

Trauma, as the note presupposes, is a trans-cultural experience in the twentieth century. Figuring traumatic memory is as relevant to Americans as to Chinese. People of different nationalities and ethnic backgrounds feel a strong need at the turn of the millennium to take stock of the bloody twentieth century. Film or visual material in this regard takes on enormous importance as a pedagogical tool. This is due to the imagistic and nondiscursive character of traumatic memory. The traumatic experience shatters the usual capacity of linguistic and literary expressions in representing and making sense. As an ineffable experience, it is particularly fitting for imagistic figuration, or more precisely, disfiguration. The trauma cripples the matrix of symbolic means and impacts directly on the body and emotion. The traumatized body is more prepared to reach out to another victimized body in another culture.[3] On the basis of this assumption about trauma's trans-cultural communicability and visual character, we assigned ten films representing traumatic events as primary course material.[4]

Any course should have a common theme. But in teaching a course with many films from widely divergent cultures, the demand to hold strenuously onto a frame of reference is much greater than in a course which is, say, based entirely on an aspect of American culture. Paradoxically, the frame should be the written text, or a body of written texts that defines clearly the line of exploration and analysis. The visual text, unlike the written one, is much less definable and much more ambivalent and open to interpretation. Although we did have trauma theory as a starting point, the specific, cross-cultural questions were not firmly set up. As a result, the discussion and analysis of the class became so randomly subjective and free-floating that the meaning was strictly in the eyes of the beholder. This soft, freewheeling tendency was aggravated with a weekly screening of films from America, China, and France. The films included, among others, Zhang Yimo's *To Live* (1994), Tian Zhaungzhuang's *The Blue Kite* (1993), Oliver Stone's *JFK* (1991), Alain Resnais's *Hiroshima, Mon Amour* (1959), and Carma Hinton's *The Gate of Heavenly Peace* (1995). As primary text, one film a week is not overload, but a steady stream of images, especially from unfamiliar and foreign films, caused confusion and frustration.

With cinematic images in excess of the conceptual command, the students experienced bewilderment akin to a mildly traumatic experience.[5] They had so much to watch yet so little time to digest. They had difficulty locating a mooring in the disorienting plethora of diverse images of suffering, mutilation, and brutality. There was much discussion but little grip on anything. Some students complained about the confusion. Since most of the films depict traumatic events, the frequent viewing of such scenes without a deeper understanding of their historical implications even rendered some students insensitive to their traumatic effect.

About three to four weeks into the semester, it seemed necessary to restate the theoretical framework of the course. Although we already had a clearly pronounced focus buttressed by a group of theoretical essays on trauma and history, it was still useful to reflect on what we were doing and to find the "signposts" for orientation. We spent a whole three-hour session exclusively on this concern. The book *The Ironist's Cage* by Michael Roth, a cultural historian who has written widely on trauma and history, proved to be extremely helpful. The book contains a number of essays dealing with a range of issues: the shift in historiography from monumental history to memory, historians' skepticism and self-questioning about the literary and rhetorical nature of their trade, the danger of beautifying a traumatic event through narrative conventions, the persistence of the past in unresolved traumas, and the need for a pious attitude toward the burdens of history. All these themes are included within an overarching, coherent concern. They boil down, in Roth's own words, to "What does it mean to claim to have a reasonable, legitimate, or worthwhile connection between the present and the past?" (1). How do we make meaning and find direction from change over time, and for what purposes? To ask the question more specifically, how do the films embody and reflect this general urge to picture a usable past in the shadow of trauma, a past with which we can live?

Elaborating the central questions established a rough sense of direction and clear lines of inquiry. The themes enabled the students to perceive and employ a number of key terms that served as handles in a media-suffused, multicultural viewing experience. Conceptual clarification, moreover, was able to bring out the potential of a comparative analysis embedded in the cross-cultural material. It placed the students behind the screen and significant scenes to imagine what the filmmakers were trying to do in order to come to terms with the unresolved traumas in history. Seeing the varied versions of the Kennedy assassination or the Vietnam War, for instance, the students who knew something of these traumas were more prepared to search for similar experiences and to hypothesize the expressive attempts behind a Chinese film. This way the Chinese films, some of which at first glance seemed to be awash in misery and suffering without a "perceivable" reason, lost their "strangeness," and came to resonate with the traumatic experience depicted in American films.

Using a set of concepts as a common ground for understanding multicultural visual material begs the questions of cultural imperialism. No common denominator is innocently "common" enough to be fair to different cultural trajectories and territories. The trauma theories we studied derived mostly from Holocaust studies, psychoanalysis, and poststructuralism, whose relevance to non-Western materials cannot be taken for granted. For pedagogical and analytical purposes, however, a thematic structure needs to be set up as an expedient device, as a starting point. Once again, there is the aforementioned danger of mistaking the other for the self, of bringing the unfamiliar to the familiar, thus narcissistically or arbitrarily subsuming or ignoring cultural complexity and differences. But what can prevent this universal approach from colonizing the other is the insistence that the matrix of concepts functions no more than a formal device for organizing culturally diverse film images. Whether this matrix is productive or counterproductive depends on how dialectically one uses it. There is something to be gained by placing different cultures under a common denominator. If in analysis the "common" denominator does not dissolve the differences into the same, but rather dialectically foregrounds them, historicizing in turn the conceptual denominator itself and revealing its limits, a truly critical cross-cultural understanding can be achieved. In the dialectic process the divergent histories become intertwined and different territories overlapped. It is as unproductive, we should note, to exaggerate cultural differences as it is wrong to homogenize them. Without a "procedural" common ground, cultural differences are absolutized, fetishized, or obscured, as exemplified by the most combative forms of identity politics among some militant minority groups. In such a scenario students will be caught in a Babel of languages and opinions and swamped in endless superficial differences.

FRAGMENTS VS. HISTORY

One central question in a cross-cultural course, therefore, is how to give due to the uniqueness of a different culture. Even a finely tuned, comprehensive, thematic grab bag cannot adequately address cultural differences embedded in Asian materials. The reason is simple: the formal and procedural matrix of concepts is precisely that, and needs to be substantiated with history. However, foreign material—Asian films in this case—can be broken down into three levels: content, production, and reception. In his well-written, useful book *Teaching History with Film and Television,* the historian John O'Connor outlines these three levels of analysis of what he calls the "moving-image document." The content level addresses what occurs on the screen, and asks the question, "How is this information determined by the visual and aural texture of the film? What is the connection between the medium and the message?" The thematic frame is capable of dealing with this level. The next two levels, production and reception, seem more directly relevant to the difficulty of foreign texts. The question of production asks, "What influences were at work in shaping the moving image document and, perhaps, served to limit or bias the information it conveys?" (9). Reception concerns interpretation, controversies, social significance, and even public impact surrounding a film work immediately or long after its release. These issues involve the specific history of a foreign cultural production. Thus an Asian film proves difficult for the viewer to comprehend when its production and reception history remains obscure. This does not mean Asian filmmakers have developed a cinematic language unfamiliar to the American audience. Since the 1930s, Chinese filmmakers, for example, have indeed evolved a particular film style on their own, a unique pattern of camera movement, framing, lighting, editing, narrating, and so forth. But since the film, with all its technical resources and expressive syntax, is fundamentally a medium introduced from the West to Asian countries, a crash lecture about film styles and their modifications in Asian cinemas may fill the gap.

In our course, which centered on the style-defying trauma, the appreciation of formalistic and stylistic features is intimately implicated in the changing patterns of historical consciousness concerning pains in the past; hence, the need to delve into the analysis of production and reception. To talk about the history of production and reception of a particular film is to venture into the muddy waters of history and culture. Now, the difficulty in this exercise does not lie in the lack of information, for the instructor can always assign a reasonable amount of background reading. Rather, it arises from an unconscious and tenacious tendency to treat foreign images merely as images. The soft "orientalism" mentioned above found a good variation in our class. The students were in the habit of watching images of foreign culture as fragments or snapshots. They tended to remain content with fragments as fragments. The fragmentary coverage of the "World News" by the national media is partially responsible for this viewing habit. Just consider the countless accounts of earthquakes, famine, and civic unrest around the world that are extremely brief yet deliberately dramatic. In foreign countries, no news is not good news. The news must be either very bad, or out of this world.

The format of television and its setting also contribute to this viewing habit. The TV program is constantly punctuated by commercial interruptions, and while watching, the viewer may carry on casual conversations, do lots of channel surfing, or eat dinner. How this pattern of TV viewing shapes the viewer's faculty for understanding films or other visual media is a question for a valuable sociological study of the media, and there is no lack of work on this subject.[6] In our course, this fragmentary viewing involved a ready satisfaction with visual bits and pieces, a thirst for movement and action, and a shallow fascination with technical innovation or "special effects." Transferred to reading foreign texts, this viewing habit tended to de-historicize, stripping a text or an image of its complex history, its historically circumscribed chain of significance or lack thereof.

The documentary filmmaker Carma Hinton's work *The Gate of Heavenly Peace* is a good occasion for analyzing the importance of history in relation to the inability, exemplified by this fragmentary viewing habit, to be curious about the history behind the fragment. As an important item in our viewing list, this documentary offers a day-to-day documentation of the student protest in Tiananmen Square in Beijing, China, during the spring of 1989. It differs from other accounts of the event by weaving a far-reaching cultural history into its narration. The film was directed by Carma Hinton and Richard Gordon, who know the Chinese language and are well informed about Chinese culture and politics. A distinguished team of Chinese scholars was also consulted concerning the historical and narrative implications of the film. The film reconfigures the themes of trauma, narrative, and history in ways that radically challenge media versions of this event, which frequently exaggerate the shock and drama of the student protests, zeroing in on exciting fragments at the expense of an intelligible history. Despite the fact that the American media coverage of the bloody Tiananmen event took up more time than all the coverage of China in the previous ten years, the student demonstration was presented largely as an American drama. The protesting students were seen as bringing the news—refreshing and self-flattering to many Americans—of China's struggle for America's dear old democracy. The audience suddenly "discovered" that Chinese students were just "like us," as much into democracy and even more daring in their pursuit. Assuming the students were following the "American teacher" and pursuing the American dream, the media consciously or unconsciously assumed an authoritative position of supervising the students. The "real" protagonist of the TV coverage was thus often the anchorman and anchorwoman. Standing on Tiananmen Square, the TV personalities were center-stage, interviewing student protesters. Not knowing the Chinese language and often not bothering to interpret what the students were saying, they would often arbitrarily switch the camera to the more dramatic, theatrical, action-packed scenes. Rarely was an interviewed speaker on the square allowed to finish his or her statements. The swiftness and action, as well as the discrete and fragmentary quality of the coverage, were meant to create a dramatic spectacle and to serve up the thrill of news that might draw the jaded American viewers during their dinner time.[7]

Trauma theories in our reading are derived from poststructuralist and deconstructionist epistemology. At the risk of simplification, it is pertinent to point out that poststructuralism and deconstruction are basically anti-epistemic and anti-narrative in their conceptualization of representation. With the emphasis on the gap between signifier and signified, on the breakdown of structures and paradigms, there is a hasty or uncritical rejoicing in the free play or infinite deferral of meaning. One logical outcome is the celebration of fragments, which mirrors the television format. A variation in trauma theory is the insistence on the impossibility of apprehending trauma and on the necessary fragmentary nature of trauma-ridden representation.[8] Through our reading we became quite accustomed to the close link between traumatic experience and its fragmented, "ineffable" representation.

This conviction of the unrepresentability of trauma was challenged by a comparison between *The Gate of Heavenly Peace* and the fragmented media coverage. The disjointed, superficial coverage of the student demonstration does more to glide over its traumatic implications and tensions than to suggest any genuine understanding of the significance of what was going on at Tiananmen Square, an understanding due to the trauma. For the American students, fragments of TV coverage were simply a matter of style and surface, blithely unencumbered with a frame of meaning, devoid of the cherished stories in Chinese culture. The fragments are not made conscious of what they are fragments of; freely floating above and beyond history, there is no hint of the tragic breakdown of meaning, of the shattering of the fondest utopian hopes of Chinese history, no scars, no wounds. They fly in the face of the audience as perpetual present without depth.

Keeping in mind this viewing habit and its de-historicizing danger, we encouraged the students to pay special attention to the portrayal of historical continuity in *The Gate of Heavenly Peace*. We even brought the director in to speak about her original plan for the film. The director agreed with us that the film foregrounds the historical narrative as a means of making sense of this apparently irruptive student movement.

The film has the power to shock deeply, not because of its visual impact, but because it incorporates historical storytelling and "forgotten" data of Chinese history into its narration. The film juxtaposes the images of the

ongoing activities with footage taken from the image bank of modern
Chinese history spanning an entire period from 1919 to the spring of 1989.[9]
Most uncannily striking are the journalistic photos of the student demonstration in the May Fourth movement in 1919, the clips from the progressive films of the left-wing filmmakers in urban centers in the thirties and
forties, the scenes from documentaries made in the era of Mao, the episodes
from the classic films made in the fifties and sixties glorifying the Chinese
revolution, and the melodies deeply ingrained in the popular imagination.
These images are not presented just for the sheer pleasure of viewing but to
render modern Chinese history alive in all its pathos, hopes, setbacks, traumas; in all its living intensity and complexity. By being inserted into this
chain—a broken yet continuous chain of narrative and meaning—*The Gate
of Heavenly Peace* is able to project compelling tragic, epic, comic, and far-
cical dimensions unheard of in the numerous documentaries and books
addressing the student protest in June of 1989, let alone all the media coverage of the incident. If the real event of June Fourth is not traumatic to
everybody concerned, the film seems able to intensify its shock value and
offer compelling opportunities for understanding trauma. The film is able
to bring out the traumatic implications of the June Fourth incident, precisely
because it is able to give historical depth and significance to a demonstration
that was seen largely as another media event to audiences around the world.
The film gives trauma its due because it uses narrative to hark back to the
fondest dreams and aspirations of Chinese history; it links up the May
Fourth movement with June Fourth, tracing the continuity and frequent
shattering of those deep dreams and aspirations that got uncannily re-
enacted in the student protest and bloody massacre on June 4, 1989.

HISTORICIZING FILM STYLE AND PRODUCTION

Just as the students zeroed in on a few images about China, they tended also
to privilege a select list of films as quintessentially "Chinese." For the themes
of our course, trauma and history, there were already quite a few appropriate Chinese films, well known through repeated international awards and
Oscar nominations. They are also available in the university or public library,
even in video rentals: Zhang Yimo's *To Live* and *Raise the Red Lantern,* Chen
Kaige's *Farewell My Concubine,* and Tian Zhaungzhuang's *The Blue Kite.*

To varying degrees, these films depict the trauma of the Cultural Revolution and decades of political victimization or repression.

The potential danger in teaching these films is the accumulated glamour and fetishism through the mass media. The films' award-winning prestige, their critical acclaim in the West, and their popularity and availability in the market already elevated them to a prematurely fossilized canonical status. Once canonized, they became THE Chinese films, THE Chinese directors, and some actors and actresses, especially Gong Li, became THE Chinese superstars. The European and American audiences suddenly "discovered" that Chinese directors made great films, and these films were dramatically exciting and politically subversive.

The assumption is that these films signify a sudden outburst of the filmmakers' creativity, as if they had fallen out of the blue. In our course we showed these celebrated films because of their proven appeal with the American audience. The problem with privileging these films was, once again, the danger of depriving the students of a much-needed consciousness of historical complexity or contingency, which is the precondition for critical analysis. To unravel historical complexity and foster critical thinking, the class looked at two aspects of production. We tried to learn something about the actual production history and the cinematic tradition these films inherit and depart from.

The production history of these "canonical" films reveals that they were not produced purely as "Chinese" films. The directors are known as the "fifth generation" filmmakers. They made films during the mid to late 1980s that consistently explore and engage pressing problems in Chinese society and culture.[10] In fact, this generation of filmmakers, though all good storytellers and entertainers, already evolved a historically reflective and politically critical pattern of filmmaking in the 1980s, with the film *Yellow Earth* as their classic achievement. The earlier films pondered deeply the traumatic breakdown of meaning and value after the historical catastrophe, the Cultural Revolution; critiqued communist ideology and discourse; and revealed the bankruptcy of received expressive means, including film language. They had powerful appeal to the traumatized Chinese audience. They were well known in China but little known in the West. As China was becoming more commercially open and vibrant, the filmmakers were compelled to make commercial films. The late 1980s and early 1990s thus saw an influx of foreign capital into China, and filmmakers started to have joint adventures with the transnational entertainment corporations.

This means that the Chinese filmmakers now worked under the constraint of economic rules. They had to make films that catered to worldwide audiences/consumers. The quickest way to enter the international market was winning awards at European film festivals in Cannes, Berlin, and Venice, or winning Oscar nominations for best foreign films. The filmmakers now had their eyes on the preference of the award committee. They packaged "innovative," Western elements into their works: depiction of sexual repression, rebellion, voyeurism, and perversity; hints of homosexuality; oriental exoticism and mysticism; oriental beauty and harmony; inflated melodramatic narrative; political oppression; and so forth.[11] On the other hand, they still tried to keep their artistic autonomy and endowed their work with the reflective strain and historical consciousness that marked their earlier, noncommercial phase. Thus, the celebrated Chinese films of the 1990s could be placed midway between a residual desire to explore Chinese problems and the imperative to pursue commercial interests. Learning about the peculiar history of this group of films made students reluctant to generalize them as "Chinese" films whose meaning should be kept open for analysis and contestation. They were able to see several often incompatible influences at work in the process of film production, and to separate the implicit attempt to ponder cultural and historical problems from commercial pursuits or the vying for awards.

The other level of historical understanding is knowledge of the native cinematic tradition. To avoid a truncated impression made by those celebrated, well-marketed films, we included some earlier, less-known films in our viewing list, supplemented with background reading. The viewing of these earlier films enabled the students to see the recent Chinese films not as something isolated and static, but as both continuous and discontinuous within an established Chinese cinematic tradition dating back to the 1930s. By focusing on certain narrative segments and themes, one or two episodes from a different period, the students were able in a short time to identify the similarities and differences between the new works and the old. This method is crucial to apprehending the changing modes of cinematic representation of traumatic memory.

The viewing of the films *To Live* and *The Blue Kite*—the most traumatic of the fifth generation films—in conjunction with the films by the "fourth generation" can be cited as a lesson in the development of cinematic style in the portrayal of trauma. These two films depict the Cultural Revolution as the climatic stage following several decades of political victimization. Both focus on the way a family is steadily ravaged and destroyed by political rage. One symptom of traumatic memory, we learned from trauma theory, is that the patient repeatedly returns to the primal scene of injury, death, or disaster. The two films dramatize this sickness and are structured as a cyclical visitation of catastrophes on innocent people huddled together as a family. There is no obvious attempt to explain and redeem the "blindness" and irrationality of history. At the first viewing, the students found the films depressing, dragging, enigmatic, and repetitive. Their impressions were quite right, but for the wrong reasons. They expected to see drama or melodrama in the films with historical and epic dimensions. To provide a different angle, we showed *Hibiscus Town* and *Legend of Tianyun Mountain* directed by Xie Jin, the best-known director of the fourth generation. These two films focus just as much on the traumatic suffering of average people, but they strive to redeem the unspeakable trauma and catastrophe through a highly melodramatic narrative and extremely cathartic effects. In plain words, Xie Jin's films are powerful tearjerkers that tend to wash out historical trauma. The typical narrative has its own explanation of historical trauma: the historical catastrophe is depicted as a drama between evil and good. Its basic message is that beauty, kindness, love, and human sympathy may suffer in times of adversity but eventually these values will triumph. One telling scenario in the film *Hibiscus Town* is an instance of redeeming historical suffering through love. A young man and a young woman, branded as counter-revolutionary, are condemned to the hard labor of sweeping the town's streets. Immersed in hazy, bluish light, the couple's degrading labor is magically transformed into a ritual of romance and courtship. The man starts teaching the woman how to waltz with broom in hand while sweeping the streets. Accompanied by melodious music, this "Shall we dance?" act celebrates the triumph of beauty and love against darkness.[12]

In comparison with the cyclic catastrophes of *The Blue Kite,* this dance in adversity looks like a sugar-coating of history's bitter pills. The contrast enabled the students to see the depressing and uncathartic qualities of *The Blue Kite* with a new understanding and interest. The film's depressing qualities are precisely the effect of a refusal to explain away trauma in comforting terms and to emotionalize painful historical events through melodramatic narrative.

Reviewing changing patterns in the cinematic tradition, the students had an opportunity to apprehend both the historically circumscribed film style and the corresponding mode of historical consciousness, and to appreciate both the cinematic mode and the culture's way of representing trauma. Our initial intention was to historicize film style so that the students might have a longer and less truncated view of the evolution of Chinese cinema, but this exercise eventually and fruitfully led to a broader context of exploring the changing modes of historical consciousness in grappling with traumatic memory.

NOTES

1. David Palumbo-Liu makes a distinction between multiculturalism as pluralism and a critical multiculturalism. Pluralism regards racial and cultural differences as merely part of one all-encompassing culture, and thus different histories or symbolic systems are subjected to judgment or assimilation by the mainstream standards. Critical multiculturalism, on the other hand, "explores the fissures, tensions, and sometimes contradictory demands of multiple cultures, rather than (only) celebrating the plurality of cultures by passing through them appreciatively" (5).

2. The tendency to regard peoples of pre-industrial or traditional communities merely as static aesthetic objects is well reflected in the visual structure and viewing habit of what Fatimah Rony calls the "ethnographic film," films made by anthropologists as documents of native people. The people filmed in this kind of film are meant to be seen as exotic, as savages and primitives, "without history, without writing, without civilization, without technology, without archives" (7). Implied in this approach is that these people are stuck in the spectrum of historical change as a fixed object for anthropological and aesthetic contemplation.

3. In her brilliant book *The Body in Pain,* Elaine Scarry argues that physical, traumatic pain, unlike other states of consciousness, "has no referential content" (5). It is unspeakable, anterior to language. While Scarry does not rule out the function of language in expressing pain, she stresses the human body as the crucial referential point for apprehending the pain of another person. "If the felt-attributes of pain are . . . lifted into the visible world, and if the referent for these now objectified attributes is understood to be the human body, then the sentient fact of the person's suffering will become knowable to a second person" (13).

4. For a further elaboration of image outweighing word in traumatic experience, see Cathy Caruth (3–12).

5. This happens even more to undergraduate classes. Without a clearly defined theme, without a planned agenda for discussion, preferably equipped with a set of questions, discussion of visual images can spawn endless airings of personal, subjective opin-

ions. Heated as a discussion may be, it is more detrimental than conducive to the rigorous and painstaking analysis, formulation, and articulation based on solid evidence. Reasoned discourse and clear articulation, not just soft, ineffable intuition, should be the goal of humanities courses. Research on teaching history with film confirms this. For a fuller exposition of the necessity of a discursive frame in the face of visual texts, Arthur Marwick observes that without an analytical frame, "Talk, in a university teaching situation, of the 'imaginative penetration' of films can too readily degenerate into the soft option of smart cocktail chat . . . unrelated to any hard analysis" (151). See Marwick for a fuller exposition of the need for "hard analysis" in the use of films.

6. David Harvey has commented on how TV viewing shapes contemporary perceptual structures and fosters an ahistorical sense of reality. He notes that in the TV culture one's relation to history has shifted, and "there emerged an attachment to surfaces rather than roots, to collage rather than in-depth work . . . to a collapsed sense of time and space rather than solidly achieved cultural artifact" (61).

7. In her talk at SUNY–Stony Brook, which was a part of our course, Carma Hinton said what motivated her to make a film about Tiananmen was the frustration and anger she felt while watching the major TV networks' coverage of the event. This accounts for her effort, palpable in the texture of her documentary, to bring historical depth and complex cultural and nationalistic meanings into her own narrative and representation.

8. Cathy Caruth, for example, rightly insists that the trauma remains unrepresentable through conventional narratives. There is a danger, she warns, of integration of traumatic experiences into a coherent representation, which may destroy the sting of the negative force of historical traumas. But a misreading of this view easily leads to a premature emphasis on fragmentary representation deemed appropriate to trauma. See Cathy Caruth, pages 151–57.

9. Hinton and Gordon spent six years doing research for this film and analyzed more than 250 hours of historical and contemporary archival footage. Obviously, they did not treat the Tiananmen event as an isolated incident, but conceived it as part of a continuous endeavor of Chinese modernity in the twentieth century.

10. The fifth generation filmmakers were the first group of graduates from the Beijing Film Academy after the Cultural Revolution. They launched their diverse careers in the early 80s and established their reputation in a few years. Prominent members of this group include Chen Kaige, Zhang Yimo, Tian Zhuangzhuang, Hu Mei, Wu Ziniu, and Huang Jianxin. It is often noted that the first significant achievement was *Yellow Earth,* directed by Chen Kaige. The film that marks the end of their searching, historically reflective style is *Red Sorghum.* The "celebrated" films here belong to the post–fifth generation phase. Though lacking the strong historical reflection of the previous works, these films still retain a concern with historical narrative and traumatic memory. For a discussion of their unflinching depiction of historical traumas, see Wang.

11. Dai Jinhua describes the trajectory of the fifth generation filmmakers from a historically reflective mode to a half-hearted catering to the international market in their desperate attempt to keep the artistic integrity of their works.

12. The fourth generation filmmakers were trained during Mao's era (1949–76) and exhibited more ideological allegiance to the Party ideology than the younger generation of the fifth. After the Cultural Revolution (1966–76) they began criticizing the socialist

system and the Party, but the criticism was basically directed at re-adjustment and even apology. Their films dramatize the historical trauma of the Cultural Revolution as the wrongs of evildoers or momentary lapses in the fundamental health of the system. Following a pattern of disaster and redemption, they prove uncritical of the traumatic Chinese history by resorting to an overly melodramatic account of the painful past. The fifth generation, on the other hand, by eschewing the melodramatic mode, concentrated on the traumatic experience as unredeemable, and developed a critical historical consciousness that refuses to embrace an easy resolution of the trauma. See Wang.

WORKS CITED

Brown, Nick, et al. *New Chinese Cinemas: Forms, Identities, Politics.* New York: Cambridge UP, 1994.

Caruth, Cathy, ed. *Trauma: Explorations in Memory.* Baltimore and London: Johns Hopkins UP, 1995.

Dai, Jinhua. "Huangdu di shang de wenhua kulu (Hard journey on yellow earth)." *Wenhua piping yu huayu dianying (Cultural Criticism and Chinese Films).* Ed. Zheng Shushen. Taipei: Rye Field Press, 1995. 69–94.

Harvey, David. *The Condition of Postmodernity.* Cambridge, MA: Blackwell, 1990.

Hinton, Carma. "Introduction to *The Gate of Heavenly Peace,*" and "Making Sense of Remnants of the Past." *The Gate of Heavenly Peace* Symposium. 13–14 November 1997. SUNY, Stony Brook.

Kaplan, E. Ann, and Ban Wang. "Syllabus of the Graduate Seminar 'Trauma, Memory, and History: The Case of China and American Perspectives.'" Fall 1997. SUNY, Stony Brook.

Marwick, Arthur. "Film in University Teaching." *The Historian and Film.* Ed. Paul Smith. London and New York: Cambridge UP, 1976. 142–56.

O'Connor, John E. *Teaching History with Film and Television.* Washington: American Historical Association, 1987.

Palumbo-Liu, David, ed. *The Ethnic Canon: Histories, Institutions, and Interventions.* Minneapolis: U of Minnesota P, 1995.

Rony, Fatimah Tobing. *The Third Eye: Race, Cinema, and Ethnographic Spectacle.* Durham and London: Duke UP, 1966.

Roth, Michael. *The Ironist's Cage: Memory, Trauma, and the Construction of History.* New York: Columbia UP, 1995.

Said, Edward W. *Orientalism.* New York: Vintage Books, 1979.

Scarry, Elaine. *The Body in Pain: The Making and Unmaking of the World.* New York: Oxford UP, 1985.

Thompson, John B. *The Media and Modernity: A Social Theory of the Media.* Stanford: Stanford UP, 1995.

Wang, Ban. "Trauma and History in Chinese Film: Reading *The Blue Kite* against Melodrama." *Modern Chinese Literature and Culture* 11.1 (1999): 125–55.

Through the Looking Glass

Pedagogical Uses of Literary Film Adaptations

KAMILLA ELLIOTT

While any use of film or television adaptations can vivify a litera-ture class, in my experience, the richest uses of them occur when they are integral rather than merely illustrative parts of the course. Rather than using literary film and television adaptations simply to lure students from the rising tide of popular culture to the higher, dryer shores of literary analysis, I teach them as recent developments in a long history of narrative fiction and as modes of literary criticism and interpretation.

English survey courses typically trace the journey from oral to writ-ten poetry, hail the rise of drama in the Renaissance, attend at the birth of the novel, watch its growth to a majestic Victorian bulk, and detail its breakdown and reconstruction in the twentieth and twenty-first centuries. Narrative film and television grow out of this narrative history. They derive techniques, stories, and ideologies from literature, adapt it, and thereby engage in a lively cultural and economic exchange with it.

Narrative film and television derive not only from visual arts and tech-nological innovations, but also from theatrical and literary traditions. As Sergei Eisenstein attested, there was no virgin birth of cinema: it grew out of a rich cultural heritage and was a child of Charles Dickens as well as of Thomas Edison.[1] From Dickens, claims Eisenstein, early Western film-makers like D. W. Griffith borrowed the narrative structures and an empirical mode of representation. The influence is not limited to Dickens: Leon Edel and others have claimed, "Wherever we turn in the nineteenth century we can see the novelist cultivating the camera-eye and the camera movement."[2] Although Eisenstein sets this heritage in opposition to the theater, these were qualities of theater as well, from which the Victorian

novel drew many of its techniques. And the narrative influence has not
been a one-way affair. As Keith Cohen, Claude-Edmonde Magny, and
others have shown, the narrative structures of modern novels have been
shaped in part by cinematic techniques, such as ellipsis, temporal discon-
tinuity, fragmented vision, cross-cutting, and multiple viewpoints, and
have in turn shaped cinema.[3]

Christian Metz has further argued that there is a continuity between
the social role of the nineteenth-century novel and twentieth-century film:

> Inasmuch as it proposes behavioral schemes and libidinal proto-
> types, corporeal postures, types of dress, modes of free behavior or
> seduction, and is the initiating authority for a perpetual adolescence,
> the classical film has taken, relay fashion, the historical place of the
> grand-epoch, nineteenth-century novel (itself descended from the
> ancient epic); it fills the same social function, a function which the
> twentieth-century novel, less and less diegetic and representational,
> tends partly to abandon.[4]

Film theorists and historians have noted not only the techniques and cultural roles inherited from and exchanged with literature, but also more
generally certain linguistic properties of cinema. Metz has adduced that
"To go from one image to two images, is to go from image to language"—
that is to say, the spaces between images create syntactic relationships
between them that can be read as narrative.[5] The preponderance of college textbooks and publications on film whose titles include the words
"read," "language," "rhetoric," or "grammar" has reinforced the semiotic
connections between literature and cinema.[6]

The lively exchange between literature, film, and television in literary
film adaptation, as well as in the reverse process of novelization, indicates a
shared audience. George Bluestone finds evidence that more copies of
Wuthering Heights were sold in a single year after MGM's 1939 film was
released than in the ninety-two years between its publication and the film.
There were similar dramatic increases in the readership of *David Copperfield*
in 1935 and of *Pride and Prejudice* in 1940 following the release of films
of these books.[7] More recently, Robert Giddings, Keith Selby, and Chris
Wensley cite a 1985 survey on the effects of television dramatization of novels upon reading habits. The study found that 46 percent of viewers had

bought or borrowed a book directly as a result of seeing a television adaptation.[8] And almost any glance at a bestseller book list reveals the ongoing influence of films on popular literary consumption.

Since my area of literary specialization is the British Victorian period, I take a particular interest in films of Victorian fiction. Apart from films of Shakespeare, no other literature has been so frequently adapted to film. I have found over 1,500 films of Victorian prose fiction. Studying a Victorian text adapted to several films enables varied pedagogical emphases. Students can study the transition from Victorian novel to film through early theatrical adaptations recorded by early silent films. Films of *Vanity Fair, A Tale of Two Cities,* and *David Copperfield* made between 1911 and 1913 are readily available on videocassette. Often I shift from this focus on the origins of filmic adaptations of novels in theater to later films of the same text to explore developing filmic techniques as well as changing social and cultural contexts of adaptation. *A Tale of Two Cities* is particularly apt for this study because of its connection of social identity to disguise and theatricality, particularly the courtroom scenes which establish identity and social value. The 1935 MGM film, a 1958 British film, a 1984 cartoon version, and the 1989 Anglo-French PBS miniseries all provide excellent material to examine the development of film and television adaptation, as well as changing cultural factors that influence literary film interpretation and the construction of character and identity. Studying representations of identity links semiotic and cultural issues in adaptation as we ask: What is a literary character? What is a filmic character? How have film and literature influenced ideas of social identity in the nineteenth and twentieth centuries?

A more general advantage of studying several films of a single text is that students can engage a variety of critical concerns without simultaneously having to grapple with new authors, characters, and plots. I have found that the level of analysis students can attain is much higher and that the variety of films keeps students from getting bored with the material.

I do not stress adaptations as translations; to limit discussion to fidelity or changes from the original is akin to limiting a literary class to the discussion of foreign language translations of the text. I therefore consider adaptations as critical interpretations. While semiotic shifts do form some part of the analysis, equally interesting and influential are the social and cultural factors that come to bear on adaptation. Several film and television adaptations of *Wuthering Heights,* for example, provide a lucid sense of how film and television have used and interpreted literature at various historical junctures in various genres for various audiences. Clearly, William Wyler's 1939 MGM film set in late-Depression pre-war Hollywood, Luis Buñuel's 1953 film shot in Mexico, a 1950s Westinghouse live television theater production targeting housewives, a McGraw-Hill text film for children, an international production in the new censorship climate of 1970, a Japanese adaptation in 1988, and a British television adaptation from the late 1990s are products of widely varying contexts. We also address semiotic and narrative issues, some of which intersect with context and some of which are endemic to shifts in media. We note how post-Freudian narratives of repression as the root of pathology have caused inversions of villain and hero in some adaptations, like the Fantasy Island episode filmed in 1979 and Jane Campion's *The Piano* (which she has designated her "tribute" to *Wuthering Heights*). In these productions, Edgar is the more violent and rapacious character while Heathcliff emerges as a Harlequin romance figure. We ask how film and television can approximate the "I am Heathcliff" declaration with the didacticism of the grammatical syntax when the actors who play Heathcliff and Cathy look so physically different. More generally, we ponder whether any effective dramatic representation of these characters is possible, since many dramatizations of this novel degenerate into scenes of domestic bickering and violence, a far cry from the Gothic, quasi-heroic creatures evoked by Brontë's language.

I have taught film and television adaptations of Victorian fiction in classes that are exclusively about the relations between literature and film and in classes that are predominantly about Victorian literature. The two endings of *Great Expectations* form the focus of a major debate in the novel's criticism. The six film adaptations available on videocassette offer six additional endings—all different from the two prose endings. David Lean's film, shot at the end of World War II, symbolically dramatizes the fantasy of returning soldiers rescuing women imprisoned inside blacked-out homes as Pip arrives to rescue Estella from the similarly curtained house in which she seems doomed to follow Miss Havisham's solitary fate. He tears down the curtains and pulls her out into the sunlight. Joseph Hardy's 1974 film, heavily influenced by British method acting, ends with a chastened Estella (Sarah Miles) suddenly revealing to Pip (Michael York) that she has loved him all along and was only cruel to hide her feelings for him. Jean Tych's 1983 animated version portrays Pip jovially announcing to Biddy that he is going to London to "find himself" and Biddy responding with a cheery cartoon guffaw. These variant endings are all culturally and contextually conditioned and form the basis for lively discussion.

I also teach a more general literature and film course that includes American literature adapted to film. I have found that reading books along-side film adaptations raises questions that do not arise when the literature is studied separately. Positioning excerpts from Thomas Dixon's novels *The Leopard's Spots* (1902) and *The Clansman* (1905) beside D. W. Griffith's *The Birth of a Nation,* which adapted them in 1915, was one of my most forma-tive experiences as a teacher of American narrative. I had planned a fairly traditional lecture, comparing the narrative techniques that promote racism in the books with those that foster it in the film, when I received a note from a student taking the class. She asked, "I want to know why, when watch-ing the film, I found myself cheering for the Ku Klux Klan and hating the African American characters, when I myself am an African American." I immediately threw away my lecture notes and began to research spectator identification. I found that the novels had no such impact on students—indeed, they aroused primarily aversion and scorn—but that many stu-dents, even though they found the film dated and somewhat tedious to watch, were powerfully drawn to identify with the Ku Klux Klan. They too wanted to know why they had identified with a movement they ideo-logically abhorred. We found that, while both the novels and the film eroti-cize politics by attaching them to love stories and representing opposing views as a threat of defiling rape to these romances, and that, while both media employ a melodramatic structure of hero, villain, and heroine to fos-ter narrative suspense and identification with white southern interests, other narrative techniques differed sharply between novels and film. The novels typically employ debate, metaphor, excessive rhetoric, slurs, and outmoded scientific theories to press their racism. The film more viscerally harnesses survival instincts to its melodramatic plot structure, most intensively in its chase and ride-to-the-rescue scenes. Victims are pursued by villains to be res-cued by heroes at the last minute. The fast pace of the editing and the dire narrative straits of the characters allow no time for critical distance. This class provided a basis for discussions throughout the semester concerning how films lead audiences to identify with viewpoints with which they rationally disagree.

Interdisciplinary analyses of *The Strange Case of Dr. Jekyll and Mr. Hyde* and its film adaptations also raise questions that do not arise when the novella and films are studied separately. Stevenson is elusive in describing Hyde, because he wants to keep the notion of "evil" abstract and open to individual interpretation. But films specify evil, attaching it to various visual representations, persons, ideas, and actions that vary considerably over the twentieth century into the twenty-first. Over many films and decades we thus trace various social constructions of "evil." For example, a 1920 silent film starring John Barrymore in the title roles suggests that evil enters via sexual temptation, whereas Mamoulian's 1932 film states an exactly opposite view: that evil is unleashed through sexual repression. These two films reflect essential differences between certain nineteenth- and twentieth-century theories of personality according to moral and psychological codes. Class and gender issues emerge in these filmic castings of "evil." Many films imply that women and the lower classes are catalysts for evil; most tinge the lower classes with various racial representations. However, just as many films make middle- or upper-class father figures the catalyzers which change the "good" Jekyll into the "evil" Hyde. (In the novella, Jekyll is not purely good: he is a mixture of good and evil.) In the 1920 film, the father of Jekyll's fiancée is a tempter spouting Wildean cynicisms, luring Jekyll from his philanthropic interests in the lower classes to erotic ones. In the 1932 film, Jekyll's intended father-in-law is a rigid, repressive military general, whose refusal to allow Jekyll's early marriage to his daughter drives Jekyll to become Hyde and find sexual satisfaction elsewhere. However, evil is not always a purely sexual affair. *Jekyll and Hyde . . . Together Again* (1980) playfully equates evil with drugs and popular music, while Eddie Murphy's remake of *The Nutty Professor* (1996) aligns it with the cult of thinness.

Building on this discussion, Stevenson's novella and its films allow for further study of gender issues. The variety of films keeps the class from grinding to a bored halt, while the continuity of the basic plot and characters pushes students to move from these safer considerations towards deeper and more nuanced analysis and theoretical explorations. Typically, we begin with a study of male-male relations in the text, then consider the marginalization of females (including female imagery and its use in describing inanimate objects or Hyde himself). We ponder homoerotic readings of the novella, peruse biographical information about Stevenson and his father, and read Henry James's opinion as to why Stevenson minimized women characters in his writing. When we turn to the films, we see that they all add female characters—and many such characters—most commonly an upper-class virginal fiancée for Jekyll and a lower-class performer or hooker for Hyde. (Of course, Jekyll is always somewhat intrigued by this lower-class woman and is torn between philanthropic and erotic interest in her.) We discuss whether this addition of female characters (a tradition that began with the earliest stage adaptation in 1886) is simply a dramatic convention or whether it points to sexual subtexts in the novella itself. We note how women displace and mediate relations between men, particularly those between Jekyll and Hyde. Two later films, *Dr. Jekyll and Sister Hyde* (1972) and *Dr. Jekyll and Ms. Hyde* (1995), cast Hyde as a woman. We consider the social context of these films (the rise of feminism in the 70s and issues surrounding women in the corporate world that films of the 80s and 90s commonly address), and relate these adaptations to wider social anxieties about gender roles. We explore these films through psychoanalytic theories (and test the theories with the films), including those that address male fears of the female body and its reproductive powers. The Jekyll of the 1972 film believes that female hormones are the elixir of life, but paradoxically engages in the murder of women to "harvest" their ovaries for his research. Sister Hyde seeks the hormones for a different reason: so that she can take over Jekyll and render him permanently female. To do this she must also kill women and harvest their reproductive organs. Ms. Hyde's (Sean Young) threat in the 1995 film lies more in women taking over the corporate world and the threat to male bodies emerges principally in the form of cross-dressing. Dr. Richard Jacks (the Jekyll character, played by Tim Daly) lacks ambition and drive, as well as social skills. His career and love life are floundering, and no one respects him. Helen Hyde is powerful, beautiful, an excellent housekeeper, with superior social skills, and further uses her sexuality to gain promotions in Jacks's company. Rescued by his fiancée, a chastened Jacks emerges from Helen Hyde at the end of the film still wearing her dress and lipstick, preaching about "the woman in all of us," before planting a firm heterosexual kiss on his fiancée's lips. But the presence of

302 Through the Looking Glass

homosexual characters and homoerotic moments in both of these films leads to a more complex discussion of sexual identity, one that eventually leads us back to homoerotic tensions in the novella itself.

Not every literature-film connection offers multiple adaptations, nor are multiple adaptations necessary for a richly varied pedagogical experience. I have taught the book and film of *Gone with the Wind* several times, with great success. The novel and film are unparalleled in terms of popular consumption and represent a rare instance of a book and film that have been equally successful. Moreover, this pair provides a forum for many issues that can be discussed over several weeks (which allows students time to read the novel and to see the film in two parts if necessary), from racist fictionalizations of history posing as truth to how a vast readership influenced the film's casting. We spend one class addressing how the book and the film responded differently to the stresses of the Great Depression, considering what Margaret Mitchell called "gumption" against motion picture palace escapism. We look at the special effects used to produce the illusion of glamour in the film (the documentary *The Making of Gone with the Wind* offers an excellent resource). We address why the book has a lower cultural status than the film, addressing prejudices against female authors and the romance genre and examining the awards won by each text. I extend this discussion to consider more generally what kinds of books win Pulitzer Prizes (Mitchell's book beat out Faulkner's *Absalom, Absalom!* that year) and which authors and genres win Nobel prizes. We analyze the phrases used to award Nobel prizes to gauge what are the underlying values of the award. In the same way, we study films that have won Academy Awards and Cannes Film Festival prizes, contrasting the values represented by each through the films they congratulate. And for students tired of one-sided gender studies—feminist approaches—Mitchell's novel offers a look at female sexism and stereotypes about males.

I have also frequently taught Cornell Woolrich's short story "Rear Window" (1942) with the 1954 Hitchcock film, in order to provide an undergraduate introit to contemporary film theory, particularly psychoanalytic accounts of voyeurism. Setting this material in the context of the McCarthy era, where surveillance becomes a political issue, offers a cultural way in which to regard voyeurism as well. We begin with the short story and ask how one identifies a crime, how one interprets visual experience and makes a narrative from it. We discover that seeing and meaning are unstable: the narrator continually revises the meaning of what he sees. We move towards psychoanalysis when we discover that a key to identifying the criminal in the short story is identifying *with* the criminal, asking what he would have done in the criminal's place. Hitchcock plays further on these connections of identification and crime to taunt and embarrass his audience. He makes the audience culpable voyeurs of his implicated voyeur-detective, who is associated not only with the surveyed criminal, but also with the pathology and criminality of McCarthyist surveillance. The film is humorous and light—an apt counterbalance for the heavier politics and pathological theory we probe.

I also teach Shakespeare and film. In the interest of filmic range and analytic depth, I limit the class to four plays over a sixteen-week semester. I selected *The Taming of the Shrew, Othello, Macbeth,* and *Romeo and Juliet,* because they provide a wide range of films and issues. In addition to weekly screenings (we see about fourteen films together), each student researches and reports on an additional film not screened in class, so that by the end of the semester, we have seen at least part of thirty to forty films. Some films are simply recordings of theatrical productions; others are cinematic affairs; some are televizations; yet others are cartoons. (There are pornographic films available as well.) This range of films provides a solid base for considering genre and medium.

We begin by reading and discussing criticism on performance in general, from Charles Lamb's assertion that Shakespeare should not be performed to Harold Bloom's more recent critique of certain contemporary dramatic interpretations. We then study each play thoroughly before turning to its adaptations. I require each student to research criticism on the play at hand and I give a brief overview of the central critical issues in literary studies. I pay particular attention to the criticism current at the time the adaptation was made. We then discuss what some of the issues might be for adapters. Only then do we see the films.

I might not select *The Taming of the Shrew* for a straightforward literary survey of Shakespeare's work, but it offers a terrific array of films: a silent D. W. Griffith production in 1908, an early talkie with Douglas Fairbanks and Mary Pickford, a 1950 live television dramatization with Charlton Heston as Petruchio, a musical (*Kiss Me Kate,* 1953), a lavish Zeffirelli feature starring Elizabeth Taylor and Richard Burton (1967), and a recent modernization set in an American high school, *10 Things I Hate about You* (1999). The films allow for a skeletal historical overview of film styles and genres and open up discussions ranging from the oxymoron of silent Shakespeare to modernizing his language. We look at how much of the verbal conflict in the play has been translated to slapstick in the Griffith film and discuss how the addition of sound in the 1929 Fairbanks/Pickford production punctuates the dialogue and visual editing (whips cracking and laughter both feature prominently). We look at how Zeffirelli substitutes a visual punctuation for the dialogue, using shots instead of sounds as pacers. The musical *Kiss Me Kate* provides an especially good forum for discussions of soliloquy's relationship to modern musical numbers and of the influence of dance choreography and theater on film technique. Turning to the 1950 televization, we spend more time analyzing how the commercials that interrupt the dramatization pick up themes, lines, and characters from the play to sell Westinghouse products: his and her radios for the college graduates and fans to cool fractious households. The latter commercial even ends with a rhyming couplet: "There's nothing like mobile air anywhere." We also read between films, particularly considering Kate's famous closing speech and how it is performed, from Mary Pickford's ironic wink to Elizabeth Taylor's insistence on doing her speech straight, most likely in an effort to restore her sullied moral profile. We consider how the 50s televization ridicules male domesticity in a Three Stooges style presentation of Petruchio's household (the message is clearly that a woman's touch is required) and the taming of Kate in this production from a woman who wears trousers to one who wears dresses. The position of this adaptation following the end of World War II certainly influenced its gender representations, as women left the work force when men returned home. In *10 Things I Hate about You*, we discuss modernizations of language and romance and raise the inevitable question, is this still "Shakespeare"?

Turning to *Othello,* a comparison of films with Orson Welles, Laurence Olivier, and Laurence Fishburne in the title roles highlights contrasts between cinematic and theatrical adaptations. The Olivier production is pure filmed theater; the Welles film is far closer to pure cinema (indeed, its most effective scenes are wordless); the Fishburne adaptation is a blend of the two. In the 1995 production, Kenneth Branagh in the role of Iago gives a brilliant theatrical and aural delivery of his lines, while Fishburne relies heavily on a powerful facial and physical presence as Othello. These generic differences within the film heighten not only contrasts between the two characters, but also the uneasy relationship between theater and film in adaptations of Shakespeare. Starting with speeches from the play, we examine their performance in these various films, moving from vocal performance to the visual and aural accompaniments to these speeches, like cinematography, editing, sets, costumes, casting, lighting, and music. We ask whether the language has been adapted to any of these things or whether they are simply accompaniments, like music for lyrics. We ask whether there is a clear line demarcating foreign language translations of Shakespeare and adaptation of his words to other sign systems.

Macbeth allows us to study the work of two great cinematic Shakespearean directors who are not Anglo-America: Akira Kurosawa and Roman Polanski. It also offers another terrific adaptation: Trevor Nunn's theatrical piece, made especially for television in 1977. Kurosawa's *Throne of Blood* (1957) introduces the subject of intercultural adaptation, particularly marked in this post-war critique of Japanese feudalism and in his blend of Eastern and Western philosophies and artistic techniques. Characters and movements from Noh theater, perspectives from Japanese painting, and Buddhist philosophy blend intriguingly with Darwinian survivalism and a ruthless competitive individualism that undermines feudal relations, tinged with a trace of despairing Western nihilism. Alternations between Western close-ups privileging individuals and extreme long shots emphasizing groups and the human figure in relation to the landscape intensify these effects.

Polanski's film was made immediately following the murder of his pregnant wife, Sharon Tate, by the Charles Manson gang, a connection that is evident in the representation of the murder of Lady Macduff and her son. Yet the film contains other disturbing biographical resonances (in spite of his ardent denials of any biographical connections). Polanski's sympathetic representation of a young and beautiful Lady Macbeth stands in striking contrast to the disfigured and loathsome elderly witches, whom he figures grotesquely naked. The language of the play and much literary criticism casts Lady Macbeth as a fourth witch; Polanski's refusal to make this association is more in accord with virulent statements he has made about the hideousness of female bodies after twenty-five and his preference at the time for young girls. While I rarely indulge in biographical criticism, such discussions are important for understanding filmic theories of auteurism during this period, in which the film manifests a personal statement of the director. From here we ponder how auteurism intersects with the cult of Shakespeare as author.

Finally, we turn to *Romeo and Juliet,* with a particular emphasis on its centrality in modern American youth culture and its frequent appearance as a mandatory high school text in curricula. Films viewed include *West Side Story* (1951), Zeffirelli's enormously popular 1968 film (the first to cast teenagers in the title roles), Baz Luhrmann's 1996 postmodern futuristic MTV-style production, a cult film produced in the same year, *Romeo and Juliet*, and more recently, the martial arts hip-hop combo, *Romeo Must Die* (2000). We spend considerable time pondering America's obsession with this play and high school academia's insistence on its presence in their curricula. I have students research teaching manuals on this pedagogy as well as draw on their own memories of studying the play in high school.

These are just skeletal indications of far wider ranging and also deeper investigations made in the course of various classes over numerous semesters. I turn now to more general pedagogical concerns about teaching film together with literature. Colleagues frequently ask questions about the process. For example, how does one prepare students to study film when they have little or no background in the discipline? First, most students are thoroughly familiar with film and television and need only slight promptings to begin deeper investigations of it. Film shares with literature many plot and character structures and many narrative and rhetorical strategies, like point of view. However, because film operates on so many channels and goes by so quickly, and because the Hollywood classical style that dominates film and television stresses invisible editing and seamless transitions, students must often be prompted to watch films differently. I have developed a handout on film analysis (Appendix A) which students can glean quickly by way of prelude to in-class analytical exercises. In seminars, one pedagogical strategy that I have developed involves showing a brief clip and assigning each student to observe one element of the film. One attends to the music; another to sound effects; a third considers editing rhythms; a fourth studies lighting; a fifth interprets costume, hair, and makeup; a sixth focuses on acting; a seventh on set design; and so on. Afterwards, each student reports back to the class and a composite analysis emerges in discussion.

Another common question is, what kind of assignments are best for these classes? I find that regular brief and simple quizzes on the books and films work far better than midterms and finals to keep students reading and viewing and the class discussion rich and fully participatory. Most students are happy to have these irksome quizzes in place of bulky exams, and the class runs far better this way. Students of course write essays and the final exam includes questions on class lectures and discussions to encourage regular and awake participation in that element of the course. I also ask students to undertake a creative project. My original intention in making this assignment was to counter what I perceived to be a rather pervasive student scorn for failed adaptations. In requiring them to design, make, or perform one aspect of an adaptation, I thought they would learn something about how difficult it is to adapt a narrative from one medium to another. One student who made a film of her own poem affirmed in her report how hard it was to get her actors to cooperate, and to procure appropriate sets and lighting; much of what she had imagined simply could not be filmed with the materials available to her, so that her adaptation of her own work ended up entirely changing the meaning of her poem. But the outcome of this assignment far exceeded my original intention. I was completely unprepared for the amazing creations that students produced, and learned a great deal from them about the interaction between various art forms (each student was required to append a verbal account of his/her creative process). The instructions for the creative project are included in Appendix B. Students were given two choices: either they could engage in an aspect of adaptation (costume or set design, screenwriting, novelization, musical composition, etc.) or they could create a more general exploration between two media (words, images, music, artifacts, etc.).

The day the projects were due, my desk was piled high with films, musical compositions, collages, posters, photographic projects, book illustrations, costume and set designs, sculptures and tactile projects, and an ingenious array of contraptions using projectors, turntables, and chemical reactions. One student (a part-time bartender) designed drinks for a panoply of characters. Another, inspired by the narrator's assertion that no two people described Hyde in the same way, painted three oil paintings of Hyde: one after late-nineteenth-century realism, one impressionistic, and one Cubist. Even the brick wall behind Hyde differed in each painting.

Her written analysis of how each style of art changed Hyde was incisive and scholarly. Another student created an Alice in Wonderland layer cake, with a layer for each of three chapters, containing ingredients in strange combinations. The Caterpillar chapter layer blended poppy seeds, gummy worms, and caramelized mushrooms; the Queen of Hearts layer combined strawberries and licorice and rose petals. Her essay on the cake made insightful connections between Carroll's strange linguistic combinations and the unappetizing effect of combining ingredients that would not normally be consumed together, though each was quite palatable alone. Another student designed a game based on *Gone with the Wind,* in which characters moved forward when fortuitous circumstances befell them or when they performed praiseworthy deeds, and moved backwards when calamity occurred or when they engaged in morally dubious actions. She made game cards for each character based on the actions and events surrounding them. Scarlett's protagonist pile was of course the largest, but she could never progress because of her calamities and immoral actions. The African American characters did not have enough cards to move more than a few spaces. No one could finish the game. The project led me to ponder the difference between the rules of romance narrative and the rules of competitive games and how incompatible they are in Western culture.

Students in the Shakespeare and film seminar also produced creative projects: theatrical, cinematic, balletic, and musical. Again, I learned new lessons about the plays from these projects. One student intercut the deathbed scenes of *Othello* and *Romeo and Juliet.* Keeping the language intact, but rearranging it, she revealed compelling connections and contrasts between the two tragic conclusions. Most poignant was Juliet's awakening just as Desdemona expired. Another student choreographed a ballet with only the four women of Juliet's household in it, including the Nurse's dead daughter. As I watched the ballet, I saw much more clearly the female complicity and agency in the tragedy so heavily obscured by male rivalries and heterosexual bartering in the play. A student musician composed vocal motifs for Othello, Iago, Desdemona, and Emilia. Each began separately, then intertwined in various harmonic and atonal combinations that powerfully represented relationships between characters. What was particularly brilliant about this composition is that the lyrics as well as the music created different verbal statements. Another student made a film of *Macbeth* that explored intercultural resonances of the play in a Korean setting. The film, filled with distorted angles, metamorphosing images, and narrative circlings, superbly evoked the confusion and ghostly dimensions of the play.

The creative project is vivifying to the learning enterprise and inspiring to most students (of course there is always one who, the night before, slaps magazine pictures and headlines on a piece of cardboard and entitles it, "Words and Images"). I make time during class to present projects that can be performed, and set up displays of the art and artifacts.

No other classes I teach so fully engage the students and lead to such animated discussion and creative work. These classes are as intellectually rewarding as they are aesthetically vivid and culturally elucidating. However, no other classes I teach involve so much preparation. It obviously requires twice the time to study a book and its criticism together with a film and its criticism than to prepare a book by itself, and even more time must be spent locating points of connection and conflict between the arts and preparing film clips to show in class (I use videocassettes and DVDs, not actual film). But the rewards of these labors have been inestimable, as I see students responding not only on intellectual levels, but also on aesthetic, emotional, and ideological levels to the material. Furthermore, no other classes draw such a range of students from other disciplines to literature and film narrative. These students greatly enrich the class experience and create an interdisciplinary class population that augments the interdisciplinary material.

APPENDIX A
A QUICK INTRODUCTION TO INTERPRETING AND ANALYZING FILMS

Besides the analysis of a fiction film's

story line

characters (includes casting, acting, star system, etc.)

genre (is it silent? animated? a miniseries? Hollywood? foreign? independent? etc.)

social, political, historical context (includes marketing, financing, film censorship, etc., as well as broader social contexts)

ideology and modes of representation,

there are a number of formal features crucial to understanding each film, which can be used to enhance interpretations of how various issues, characters, events are represented. The following list is suggestive rather than exhaustive:

Framing: What's in the shot? What is excluded? (What's off-screen can at times be more compelling than what's on-screen.) What is centered/foregrounded/peripheral? How do the elements in the shot relate to each other? Are hierarchies of representation created?

Depth of Focus: Related to framing, what is in focus, what is softened and obscured? Why?

Shot Size determines how large or small an object appears in the frame, what parts are shown, etc. Most commonly used to describe how characters are shown, a *close-up* is usually of the face alone; a *mid-shot* shows the character from the waist up; a *long-shot* shows the full figure. There are lots of variations on these sizes: *extreme close-ups* may show only an eye or a mouth; *mid-close-ups* show head and shoulders; *extreme long-shots* render the whole figure very small in the shot, etc.

Camera Angle: A character can be rendered imposing when shot from below (*low-angle shot*); vulnerable when shot from above (*high-angle shot*). Central to camera angle is point of view: is it omniscient, first-person, etc.? How does it shift and change and what effect does this have? Is the angle reassuring or disorienting?

Camera Movement can interact with point of view, add lyricism, turmoil, unfold elements of a scene in a certain—sometimes even suspenseful—order, etc.

Lighting adds emotive and aesthetic effects to a scene; is sometimes symbolic. Shadows can become quasi-literal, psychological elements, e.g. a man being chased by his own shadow.

Color can be symbolic; is strongly emotive. Even in black-and-white films, shades of black, white, and gray can have powerful aesthetic and representational effects.

Music: Another element that adds psychological and emotive effect. Most scores attach motifs to characters and often to settings (e.g. the Tara theme in *Gone with the Wind*). Distinguish between music that is a literal part of the story and music that lies outside of it.

Scene design, costumes, makeup, props: The landscape and weather often take part in a filmic pathetic fallacy; indoor spaces reflect the characters who live in them and have decorated them; clothing and makeup reflect class, culture, personality, gender, etc.; props (as in theater) are often central to characterization or important wordless clues to the story, etc.

Editing: It's reading between shots that makes the visual story unfold. Consider not only the sequence but also the duration of shots, the rhythm of editing, the spaces between the shots, and how one shot moves to the next (cut? dissolve? etc.) and with what effect.

Other: A partial list includes slow or fast motion, grain of film stock, movement within a frame, sound and sound effects, dialogue, voice-over, special effects, allusions to other films, and credits.

Finally, be sure to consider how these elements interact with each other: e.g. is the music in harmony with the lighting or does it play in counterpoint? Does camera movement interact with editing to create multiple layers of narrative transition?

For a fuller discussion of these and other issues, in addition to our text, I recommend David Bordwell and Kristin Thompson's *Film Art: An Introduction* (3rd edition): a quick read yet full of further references for in-depth research.

APPENDIX B
THE CREATIVE ASSIGNMENT

The creative project differs from the analytical work in this course in that you are asked to do an *artistic* exploration of the relationship between any two media: text and image, image and music, music and text, etc. (You don't have to be an artist in a given field to do an artistic exploration. If you can't create or perform music, you can select it. If you can't draw, you can photograph or make a collage or shoot a short film, etc.)

Some possibilities:

Doing Adaptation

Some examples: Write a treatment (an overall description of your film) or a few pages of a screenplay; design costumes or sets; compose music; construct miniature sets; draw characters for an animated version or cast characters for a live-action film (ideally with photos and commentary about why you chose them); make a video excerpt from your film adaptation, design a poster or book cover for your adaptation, do an intercultural adaptation (of a text to a film in another culture).

NOTE: *If you choose the screenwriting option,* avoid simple reproduction of dialogue in the text in a screenplay format: even though that's part of adaptation, it's not the most creative or elucidating aspect. Feel free to consult screenwriting handbooks for correct format but *be sure to include visual descriptions of what your film will look like, not just dialogue.*

You can also adapt a movie back into a text (e.g. write interior monologues or thoughts of an underrepresented screen character), or write a description of a music video to accompany a song (give me a cassette tape recording of the song if you do this), or adapt a movie to another movie.

Exploring Modes of Representation

Another possibility (if you're more philosophical or avant-garde) is to do a piece of art or music or writing that explores more generally the relationship between literature and film: a collage, a song, a poem, a video. Draw illustrations to accompany a poem, make a collage of words and images that comment on each other or clash with each other, etc.

You are not limited to the films/texts we have studied in class, but if you choose another text, you MUST provide me with a summary of the text. If your project is written (a screenplay excerpt) you MUST provide me with a photocopy of the passages you are adapting so I can compare language and style. (Help me on this: I cannot assign a grade without this information!)

Each creative project must be accompanied by a *brief* description of your creative process: what was going on in your mind, how you made the decisions you made, where problem spots were, anything you learned about the two media by trying to adapt or connect them, etc.

Checklist

- Creative project
  (Be sure to give me as much as you can; e.g. if you are choosing songs to go with certain characters for a movie, make a tape of those songs; if you are writing interior monologues for minor characters in a film, loan me a copy of the film, etc.)
- Brief description of your creative process
- Summary and/or photocopy of any text outside our 173 syllabus

You will be graded on the creativity of your project and on what I learn about the relationship between the two media from your project. I look forward to seeing these projects!

NOTES

1. Sergei Eisenstein, "Dickens, Griffith, and the Film Today," *Film Form: Essays in Film Theory,* ed. and trans. Jay Leyda (New York: Harcourt, Brace and World, 1949), 195–255.

2. Cited by David Lodge in "Thomas Hardy As a Cinematic Novelist," *Thomas Hardy after Fifty Years,* ed. Lance St. John Butler (New York: Macmillan, 1977), 78–89.

3. Keith Cohen, *Film and Fiction: The Dynamics of Exchange* (New Haven: Yale UP, 1979); Claude-Edmonde Magny, *The Age of the American Novel: The Film Aesthetic of Fiction between the Two Wars* (New York: Frederick Ungar, 1972).

4. Christian Metz, *The Imaginary Signifier: Psychoanalysis and the Cinema,* trans. Celia Britton, Annwyl Williams, Ben Brewster, and Alfred Guzzetti (Bloomington: Indiana UP, 1977), 110.

5. Christian Metz, *Film Language: A Semiotics of the Cinema,* trans. Michael Taylor (1974; Chicago: Chicago UP, 1991), 46.

6. Most famously, James Monaco's *How to Read a Film* is in its third edition (New York: Oxford UP, 2000). A few of the many others are Metz's *Film Language,* cited above; John Harrington, *The Rhetoric of Film* (New York: Holt, Rinehart and Winston, 1973); Daniel Arijon, *Grammar of the Film Language* (Los Angeles: Silmon and James P, 1991).

7. George Bluestone, *Novels into Film* (Berkeley: U of California P, 1957), 4. Bluestone cites other instances of increased circulation of *The Good Earth, Moby Dick, War and Peace,* and *Lost Horizon.*

8. Robert Giddings, Keith Selby, and Chris Wensley, *Screening the Novel: The Theory and Practice of Literary Dramatization* (London: Macmillan, 1990), 22–23.

WORKS CITED

Andrew, Dudley. *Concepts in Film Theory.* New York: Oxford UP, 1981.

Beja, Morris. *Film and Literature.* New York: Longman, 1976.

Bluestone, George. *Novels into Film.* Berkeley: U of California P, 1957.

Bordwell, David. *Narration in the Fiction Film.* Madison: U of Wisconsin P, 1985.

Bordwell, David, and Kristin Thompson. *Film Art: An Introduction.* 3rd ed. New York: McGraw-Hill, 1990.

Boyum, Joy Gould. *Double Exposure: Fiction into Film.* New York: Plume, 1985.

Brady, Ben. *Principles of Adaptation for Film and Television.* Austin: U of Texas P, 1994.

Branigan, Edward. *Narrative Comprehension and Film.* New York: Routledge, 1992.

Braudy, Leo, and Marshall Cohen, eds. *Film Theory and Criticism: Introductory Readings.* 5th ed. New York: Oxford UP, 1999.

Cartmell, Deborah, and Imelda Whelehan, eds. *Adaptation: From Text to Screen, Screen to Text.* New York: Routledge, 1999.

Chatman, Seymour. *Story and Discourse: Narrative Structure in Fiction and Film.* Ithaca: Cornell UP, 1978.

Cohen, Keith. *Film and Fiction: The Dynamics of Exchange.* New Haven: Yale UP, 1979.

Cook, David A. *A History of Narrative Film.* 3rd ed. New York: Norton, 1996.

Corrigan, Timothy. *Film and Literature: An Introduction and a Reader.* New York: Prentice Hall, 1999.

Enser, A. G. S., ed. *Filmed Books and Plays: A List of Books and Plays from Which Films Have Been Made, 1928–1991.* Metuchen, NJ: Scarecrow Press, 1995.

Fell, John L. *Film and the Narrative Tradition.* Norman: U of Oklahoma P, 1974.

Giddings, Robert, and Erica Sheen. *The Classic Novel: From Page to Screen.* Manchester: Manchester UP, 2000.

Larson, Randall D. *Films into Books: An Analytical Bibliography of Film Novelizations, Movie, and TV Tie-Ins.* Metuchen, NJ: Scarecrow Press, 1995.

Magny, Claude-Edmonde. *The Age of the American Novel: The Film Aesthetic of Fiction between the Two Wars.* Trans. Eleanor Hochman. New York: Frederick Ungar, 1972.

McFarlane, Brian. *Novel to Film: An Introduction to the Theory of Adaptation.* Oxford: Clarendon, 1996.

Metz, Christian. *Film Language: Semiotics of the Cinema.* Trans. Michael Taylor. New York: Oxford UP, 1991.

———. *The Imaginary Signifier: Psychoanalysis and the Cinema.* Trans. Celia Britton, Annwyl Williams, Ben Brewster, and Alfred Guzzetti. Bloomington: Indiana UP, 1977.

Monaco, James. *How to Read a Film: Movies, Media, Multimedia.* 3rd ed. Oxford: Oxford UP, 2000.

Naremore, James. *Film Adaptation.* New Brunswick, NJ: Rutgers UP, 2000.

Orr, Christopher. "The Discourse on Adaptation." *Wide Angle* 6.2 (1984): 72–76.

Reynolds, Peter, ed. *Novel Images: Literature in Performance.* New York: Routledge, 1993.

Ross, Harris, ed. *Film As Literature, Literature As Film: An Introduction to and Bibliography of Film's Relationship to Literature.* New York: Greenwood, 1987.

Seger, Linda. *The Art of Adaptation: Turning Fact and Fiction into Film.* New York: Henry Holt, 1992.

Spiegel, Alan. *Fiction and the Camera Eye.* Charlottesville: U of Virginia P, 1976.

Wagner, Geoffrey. *The Novel and the Cinema.* Rutherford, NJ: Fairleigh Dickinson UP, 1975.

Merchant-Ivory Tames the Shrew in *Howards End*

ELYSE BLANKLEY

The 1992 release of the film *Howards End* heralded another triumphant Ismail Merchant–James Ivory adaptation in the "heritage" tradition, featuring lush views of novelist E. M. Forster's Edwardian England, sepia-tinted and authentic down to the last shoe button. Audiences applauded the film's capacity to evoke an historical period. At the same time, critics praised the faithfulness of Ruth Prawer Jhabvala's screenplay, which transported great swaths of dialogue intact from novel to film. What is generally overlooked, however, is the film's considerable liberties with one very minor character, namely Jacky Bast, the trashy wife of the hapless clerk Leonard Bast. Tinkering with Jacky seems innocent enough, as at first glance she functions simply to provoke narrative coincidence and move the plot forward. Yet Forster's original Jacky was a complex and essential component of the novel's moral and political universe.

I propose that Jacky Bast represents a crucial juncture in both film and text where past and present collide. By cross-reading Forster's Jacky against the Jhabvala version, we see how Jacky originally mingled race, class, gender, and empire in such a volatile mix that she nearly catapulted the novel into chaos. Conversely, Forster's contemporary adapters fail to translate these unsettling possibilities and concoct instead a gentle Jacky tinged with contemporary politics. What did Forster see in Jacky that her contemporary adapters are unwilling to acknowledge, and why? Walter Benjamin cautioned that "every image of the past that is not recognized by the present as one of its own concerns threatens to disappear irretrievably" (255). Those "disappearances" in the Jhabvala screenplay provide instructions for recovering a significantly more complex character in the novel; at the same time, they suggest avenues for sketching the limitations of contemporary postcolonial and post-feminist thinking. They help us see, moreover, just how nonhistorical the film is, despite its celebrated attention to historical detail. The film's own unidentified political agendas complicate not just the film's evocation of a selected historical past that constitutes identity in the present, as Benjamin suggests, but also the present it hopes to bury within its retrieval of the past.

Of course, representing and reproducing history have been vexing issues for all the recent cinematic "heritage" literary adaptations, including the current surge of Jane Austen and Henry James translations.[1] For this reason, history and adaptive fidelity are preliminary issues I wish to address before beginning my rereading of *Howards End*. The Forster reworkings for screen (of which there have been five) present an interesting case because their popular and critical success is largely rooted in their perceived fidelity to Forster's cultural moment. Indeed, *Howards End* struck many viewers as a crowning achievement in the heritage adaptation genre, which is a thriving subcategory of film marked by its revered literary sources, its attentiveness to period recreation, and its dedication to a stylized view of the English past.[2] Nonetheless, this capacity to reanimate the past with such meticulous detail and style—what Gabriele Annan of the *Times Literary Supplement* knowingly calls the "toffee-colored light of 1910" (18)—proved for some viewers of *Howards End* a liability.[3] The sumptuous costumes and sets, for instance, have been criticized for diminishing the viewers' interest in the ironies and social criticism that all Forster's novels foreground (N. Annan 4; Higson, "Representing" 120). Moreover, unlike old photos that evoke nostalgia for time past, the films that serve up the past (as heritage adaptations do) have been accused of succeeding precisely because they create an illusion of history that is coextensive with the present. In consequence, time and space are collapsed, giving us a view of the past that is not really past at all (Wood 30–31, qtd. in Wollen 186). Thus the risk of historical misrecognition or occlusion is neutralized; viewers may enjoy the sensation of a complete and accessible universe, untroubled by gaps in their knowledge of this past. This is why Peter J. Hutchings laments the reassuringly "static" nature of all the Forster films, which, he claims, offer audiences a placid "historical husk" in what amounts to an "Edwardian theme park" that papers over the conflicts of a hundred years ago with tepid romantic machinations (218).

Hutchings's complaint about the inauthenticity of a film like *Howards End* implicitly also reveals his fear that by catering to a modern mass audience's assumed lack of historical awareness and unwillingness to mix unpleasant truths with entertainment, the film may dupe or mislead viewers unfamiliar with the novel. Scholar-teachers whose emphases are primarily textual and not filmic may be further concerned that today's hypervisual student will substitute viewing for reading and, in a case such as *Howards End,* will mistake what David Lyons describes as Ivory's "visual candies" and production value "cholesterol" for the more substantial meal: the novel itself (18). This fear that film will replace and deface its literary sources is as old as the film medium; in the 1920s Virginia Woolf likened a silent film adaptation of *Anna Karenina* to a "parasite" that feeds upon its source with "immense rapacity" for an audience of "the savages of the twentieth century" (Geduld 86–91, qtd. in Boyum 6). To be sure, Woolf reveals a clear class bias, in favor of high cultural productions such as the innovative fiction she and her modernist peers were creating and against low or mass culture, whose new technology of moving pictures she feared might completely displace her art. Yet Woolf (and to some extent Hutchings) implies that film adaptations must always fall short, and in doing so they jeopardize the very texts on which they are based. The calculated compressions, flattening, simplifications, and distortions that are essential for any literary translation from page to screen must, it would seem, inevitably dilute *Howards End,* whose nuanced political/historical moment cannot be reproduced for contemporary viewers.

I would like to address these complaints directly, as they appear to offer a compelling argument for discouraging literature students from viewing adaptations, even—or especially—if these films are as reverently executed as director James Ivory's *Howards End* is. To be sure, most recent film adaptation criticism avoids judging translations strictly on issues of fidelity, preferring instead to analyze the ways in which literary conventions such as narrative voice or symbolism are reinvented in another medium.[4] Yet although critics of film adaptations focus naturally enough on film, they unwittingly tend to privilege the literary source by making its meaning a stable, fixed point against which the adaptation negotiates its shifting shape. Looked at this way, the heritage film will triumph if its evocation and recovery of the past closely parallels our understanding of the novel's particular temporal moment, which is implicitly more available to us through the experience of reading. That is, *Howards End* the novel will presumably yield its braided meanings, historical moment, and cultural codes unproblematically to a reader a century later, and it is this allegedly more genuine vision by which an adaptation must be judged. But as Donald R. Larsson cautions, the so-called "spirit" of a literary work in fact transforms "in the historical matrix within which we read the novel" (75); adds Joy Gould Boyum, film adaptations are always "interpretations of interpretations" (61). Even if the past is always a "forgery" on-screen (Giddings 31), there isn't a static *Howards End* against which we confidently judge a film. Instead, we have one art object from the past and another art object imitating an idea of the past. We can only ever recover the past in fits and starts, and the book's cultural moment is not necessarily more accessible or more visible than the interpretation of history that the film promotes. Books and films are flexible sites of meaning because both are susceptible to complex critical practices; each has specific genre conventions, a distinct cultural moment in which it was produced, and a set of conventions that we as readers and viewers bring to our historical engagement with these works of art.

I prefer to rethink the assumptions governing the reading of novels and their film adaptations. Specifically, I wish to view *Howards End* the novel as a contested location of meaning that *Howards End* the film can potentially reshape. This is the spirit in which Peter Hutchings, noting that Edwardian novels and contemporary films possess different aesthetic and cultural meanings, urges us to review issues in the Forster novels that become legible as a result of their being translated into a contemporary film (214). My method is even more specific: to look at a minor film deviation from a textual detail and subsequently to cross-read its multiple meanings against the novel. By putting *Howards End* the film and the novel into a particular kind of "dialectical debate" (Reynolds 11), we can locate culturally constructed meanings in each that become visible when these texts interrogate each other. Specifically, a film adaptation may in fact provide avenues for recovering meaning in a source novel by virtue of the interpolations that are essential to the adaptive process. Issues that we may not easily recognize in a 1910 novel may, paradoxically, become vividly accessible when we view a contemporary cinematic interpretation, which finds itself incapable of reproducing meanings that are occluded, invisible, or unavailable to the contemporary reader of the text.

Consider, for instance, Merchant-Ivory's addition of Risley's trial in their adaptation of *Maurice*; or Adela Quested's overtly eroticized con-

sciousness in David Lean's *A Passage to India*; or Merchant-Ivory's truncated vision of Miss Lavish, the "lady novelist," in *A Room with a View*: I
am intrigued by the possibility that these films take their greatest screen
liberties with minor details or nuances in the source text that are presumably so transparent and inconsequential as to be infinitely malleable.[5] Such
is the case with the portrayal of Jacky Bast in *Howards End,* a minor thread
easily pulled from the entire carpet of the novel's design. Only when we
identify the clever changes wrought by screenwriter Jhabvala to Jacky's
character do we recognize that Jacky is in fact the novel's turbulent synec-
doche. Jacky on-screen functions as the critical rabbit hole through which
we tumble past a spectacle of history and into our present moment, via
Merchant-Ivory, in order to see more clearly Forster's fictional vision of his
present moment, which is a glimpse of our history.

In both novel and film, Jacky Bast's entries and exits are minimal but
staged nonetheless for maximum dramatic effect. The story depends on
Jacky's unlikely appearances to set in motion its most contrived narrative
events, including the unveiling of Henry Wilcox in public as an adulterer.
Throughout all this, Jhabvala's Jacky is cozy, blowzy, and likable. The
appealing contours of this character send us back to the novel, where we
discover a portrait that surprisingly seethes with undiluted venom from
start to finish. Examine, for example, the economy with which Forster's
narrator first makes Jacky visible, in a photo held by her soon-to-be husband, Leonard Bast:

> [The photograph] represented a young lady called Jacky, and had
> been taken at the time when young ladies called Jacky were often
> photographed with their mouths open. Teeth of dazzling whiteness
> extended along either side of Jacky's jaws, and positively weighed her
> head sideways, so large were they and so numerous. Take my word
> for it, that smile was simply stunning, and it is only you and I who
> will be fastidious, and complain that true joy begins in the eyes, and
> that the eyes of Jacky did not accord with her smile, but were anx-
> ious and hungry. (50)

Although the narrator admits that Jacky's eyes betray pain and privation,
this passage's smugly dismissive tone invites us to contemplate, at a bemused
and safe distance, a vision of female vulgarity. The narrator mocks Jacky's
name and her pose; the cartoonishly exaggerated mouth, with its carnality

and suggestive eroticism, announce that we are in the presence of something debased, something that may not even be fully human. Indeed, the weighty and visible teeth invite comparisons with horses or apes, thereby hinting that this is a photo of an atavistic throwback to an earlier evolutionary stage, exemplifying what Anne McClintock calls the "primitive archaic" (41). Significantly, Jacky is the only woman in the novel whose physical particulars are lavishly detailed, and at least one reader has found this objectionable and unfair (Duckworth 122). But Forster quite deliberately wants Jacky to serve as a clear counterpoint to other characters like Leonard, whose elevated spiritual and cultural longings make him a worthy pet project for the bohemian bourgeois Schlegel sisters, Margaret and Helen. In this scene, we occupy the place of anthropologists, studying, over Leonard's shoulder, the empirical evidence of another tribe: the lower-class female.[6] Forster asks that our superior gaze participate in a convention of social hierarchy and surveillance, a subtlety muddied by the film's rich surfaces and generally approving air.

Thus the novel's first image of Jacky telegraphs to Forster's audience powerful messages regarding class and the erotic female body. The fact that Jacky is initially "framed" in the book is noteworthy, as well. Leonard subsequently drops this photo, shattering the glass. If the frame suggests a need to contain Jacky's corporeal energy, the dangerous consequences of that energy unleashed are symbolically suggested by Leonard's bleeding hand, pierced by a glass shard. Quite literally, Jacky draws Leonard back into the body, just as her beckoning voice later calls to him "from the darkness beyond the kitchen" (i.e., their bedroom; 57). In the flesh, Jacky is no less formidable. Forster writes,

> Her appearance was awesome. She seemed all strings and bell-pulls—ribbons, chains, bead necklaces that clinked and caught—and a boa of azure feathers hung round her neck, with the ends uneven. Her throat was bare, wound with a double row of pearls, her arms were bare to the elbows, and might again be detected at the shoulder, through cheap lace ... The face—the face does not signify. It was the face of the photograph, but older, and the teeth were not so numerous as the photographer had suggested, and certainly not so white. Yes, Jacky was past her prime, whatever that prime may have been. (52–53)

Here Jacky's accessories turn her into a Victorian parlor, evoking beaded lampshades and lacy, antimacassared sofas. Her exposed flesh mingles an available body amidst all that furniture, like Manet's Olympia. Without a signifying face, Jacky is not human, trapped in an essentialist web of nineteenth-century signifying practices that equate overt female sexuality with animality. As the text progresses, the dehumanizing references multiply: she is "worse than dull" (135), an "old bore" (153), "an extravagant imbecile" (199), and "bestially stupid" (236). The film purges this prickly revulsion, however, and makes Jacky the clichéd sweet "tart with the heart of gold." True, the clothing that Jacky (actress Nicola Duffett) wears provides a colorful counterpoint to the Schlegel girls' relatively sober suffragette mufti—I think of the occasional tie, cardigan, and shirtwaist blouses worn by Emma Thompson as Margaret. Nonetheless, Jacky's screen image as a zaftig, marabou-ed Janis Joplin with Madonna's cutaway fishnet gloves is a surprisingly contemporary image devoid of any real transgressive impact because those garments no longer signify exclusive class issues but have circulated more recently as a kind of shabby chic.[7]

Forster's Jacky stands for a kind of "female" insofar as she deviates from norms anchored in tropes of family and home. In the novel's first glimpse of Jacky, we see Leonard weakly attempting to rebuff the painful weight of Jacky's "massive" form on his knee, fondling him. Ironically, his only escape is into the kitchen, to prepare dinner—further proof of the misrule in the Bast household, where the female has abdicated conventional domesticity and moves about the public urban space decorated like a house turned inside out.[8] As the critic Anita Levy has brilliantly argued, middle-class female ideals served throughout the nineteenth century to erase "other women" by making all women accountable to a bourgeois standard that would come to be regarded as ahistorical and universal by sociologists at home and anthropologists abroad. Both would use converging languages to diagnose or describe what in *Howards End* is the role of Jacky: the woman who shows exactly what respectable women are *not* (Levy 21–33).

Jhabvala's Jacky, however, is a predictable showgirl type, her blowzy exterior harboring a kind heart and dull head—in other words, a perfect victim.[9] The film's first glimpse of Jacky resonates with an altogether different tone—loving, solicitous—that can be achieved only by ignoring

Forster's narrative condescension and finicky revulsion at this apparition in the flesh.[10] Forster's Jacky is witless ("Is that a book you're reading?") and pathetic ("But you do love me, Len, don't you?" (54). In contrast, Merchant and Ivory's first view of Jacky presents a faithful girlfriend waiting worriedly at home for her man, delayed (she fears) by an accident or illness. Her fleshiness, moreover, is clearly part of her charm. Through the filmmakers' lens, the dragging of Leonard's book from his hands is not a violation but a clever bit of foreplay, as Jacky teasingly paws her resistant but chuckling lover, who yields to her seductive entreaties. Without Forster's acerbity, the film's Jacky provides broad comedy, a tidy counterpoint to the film's other pairings, which Marie-Anne Guérin describes as tragic—Leonard/Helen— and bourgeois dramatic—Margaret/Henry (25).

This simpler Jacky is arguably more easily represented, but by suppressing Forster's discomfort and distaste, Merchant-Ivory unwittingly (and perhaps unknowingly) flattens the turbulent fin-de-siècle political and social terrain of which Jacky is acutely emblematic. James Ivory admits he deliberately tinkered with both Jacky and Leonard because he felt Forster's portraits of these characters were deficient:

> There is something patronizing, even intolerant, in [Forster's] portrayal of the poor bank clerk, Leonard Bast, and his poor and poor-spirited wife, Jackie [*sic*]. It is almost as if somehow they were lesser beings, for whom Forster could not feel the same empathy or sympathy he felt for those nearer to his own social background. In adapting the novel into a film, we felt we had to build up the relationship between Leonard and Jackie to show more of her clinging love and gratitude to him and his pity, leading to tenderness, for her. (xviii)

One can hardly fault Ivory's motivations, which are both socially responsible and cinematically shrewd. In rescuing Jacky from Forster's venom, however, Ivory elides not just Forster's class bias but also his complicated sexual politics as well. The Merchant-Ivory Leonard is arguably a more multidimensional Leonard, but the improved Jacky becomes another character altogether. In this way, an entire sociopolitical universe slips from the film's grasp.

Because Jacky is tamed in the film, Merchant-Ivory has no need for the framing or containment metaphor, and so that striking detail has been comfortably dropped, as has its curious second appearance in the novel when Margaret breaks a framed photo of Dolly, Charles Wilcox's wife, on a visit to Ruth Wilcox in London. In her own way, Dolly is also a transgressive female, although in appropriately diminutive terms as suggested by her name.[11] Dolly, described as "a rubbishy little creature" (95), must be policed and governed by the Wilcox males because she fails to behave properly. She says things out of turn; she offers deliciously uninformed opinions on everything; she eavesdrops; and as a result she continually has to be "put in her place," or anchored back into her role as the dumb dutiful wife. But her indiscretions are valuable, nonetheless; only through Dolly, for example, does Margaret inadvertently learn the story of Ruth's will and the foiled legacy of Howards End. Dolly, like Jacky, holds the Wilcoxes to a standard of honesty that they would sooner repress, although she does so unintentionally and so lacks any moral force in the novel.

If Jacky were merely an unchanging, immutable figure of transgressive femininity, she would be little more than a polarity or point of contrast for defining the Schlegel sisters. But Jacky's most intriguing dimension is her fluidity, her unfixed quality. What becomes increasingly peculiar as the novel develops is the way in which, with each appearance, Jacky refuses to cooperate as the recognizable nineteenth-century portrait of female "otherness." More interesting still is the way in which the novel's heroines, Margaret and Helen Schlegel, develop unlikely resemblances to Jacky just as Jacky begins to mimic *them*. As if in anticipation of this dramatic turn of events, the Schlegel sisters instinctively begin to build protective walls when Jacky turns up on their doorstep, looking for her lost husband. Forster pointedly avoids direct presentation of this scene and chooses, instead, to let Helen narrate the incident, thereby transmuting the experience through a specific lens of class and sensibility:

> "Annie opens the door like a fool, and shows a female straight in on me, with my mouth open. Then we began—very civilly. 'I want my husband, what I have reason to believe is here.' No—how unjust one is. She said 'whom,' not 'what.' She got it perfectly. So I said: 'Name, please?' and she said: 'Lan, Miss,' and there we were."
> "Lan?"
> "Lan or Len. We were not nice about our vowels." (117–18)

First, Jacky's accent is mocked; then her worrisome visual spectacle is remarked: she is described as "magnificently dressed and tinkling like a chandelier" (117), with "a face like a silkworm" (118). Curiously, Annie, the servant, admits a "female" to the household, which suggests that at least the Schlegel servants are distinguishable by name but Jacky is not even identified by species: the dismissive "female" (female *what?*) differs subtly but crucially from the more specific "woman," which Jacky by implication is not.[12] Helen instinctively polices the class boundaries here and exercises her privilege through mockery. Jacky, however, has already begun to work her ideological deviltry in this scene when Helen, caught unaware with *her* "mouth open," reprises Jacky's photo and suggests the first sly blurring of boundaries that will be amplified when Helen herself becomes a loose sexual signifier and unwed mother.

Merchant-Ivory films this scene omnisciently and thus rob Helen's viewpoint of some of its authority. Indeed, Jacky in the film hurls a wounded, stinging riposte at the condescension of Margaret and Helen. In Jhabvala's screenplay Jacky accuses the Schlegel sisters of "having a laugh" at her expense, thereby endowing Jacky with a self-awareness and subjectivity lacking in Forster's portrait. She is, in the film, a woman with pride and a voice—even if she has lost her figure, her looks, and her reputation. Yet Jacky's bite in this scene becomes merely a tease, a prelude to her sentimentalized decline into a conventional woman more sinned against than sinning. In contrast, Forster's original revelations here are rather darker, exposing Margaret's delicate fear of future "contact with such episodes as these," a fear clearly shared by the novel's narrator as well (119).

For Forster, the scene concludes with the swirling of Jacky's scent: "the dining room reeks of orris-root," comments Helen dryly (118). Henceforth Jacky recurs throughout the novel as an odor: "Mrs. Lanoline had risen out of the abyss, like a faint smell, a goblin footfall, telling of a life where love and hatred had both decayed" (119). The subtlety of these signifiers— odor, appearance—would not have been lost on an Edwardian middle-class audience, which would clearly have read this as code for prostitution. As the critics Peter Stallybrass and Allon White have astutely observed, the link between public sanitation and social pollution (the lower class in general, prostitutes in particular) was particularly acute for nineteenth-century urban architects and moral reformers, who spoke of sewers and streetwalkers with the same vocabulary (138).

Jacky is in fact descended from a long pedigree of fallen women populating English fiction since the late eighteenth century. In the nineteenth century "fallen" woman was an elastic term suggesting a range of so-called deviant female figures in urban England (Anderson 2), from prostitutes to adulteresses, victims of seduction, and even "delinquent lower class women" whose simple presence in the streets made them suspect. These images of lost womanhood crystallized cultural anxiety about sex, female purity, social misrule, and urban pollution. As the nineteenth century progressed, fallenness was increasingly focused on a specific issue—prostitution—owing to the Contagious Diseases Acts. The C. D. Acts, which legally mandated compulsory medical examinations of women in the sex trade, precipitated long and acrimonious public discussion. By the time these acts were repealed, in 1886, nearly twenty-two years after their first enactment, they had helped make prostitution a public issue even for middle-class women, who for the first time could speak openly of sexual passion and danger in parliamentary debates, in print, and in highly visible urban demonstrations (Walkowitz, *City* 9).

By 1910, when *Howards End* was published, "prostitution" in England had begun to shift its meanings once again. Fin-de-siècle England's literary men and their peers uneasily watched as socialist demonstrations country-wide threatened bourgeois stability with the spectre of the mob; and the prostitute could still convey that unruliness with stunning metaphoric ease. Indeed, Victorian complacency was being swept aside by "religious self-doubt . . . radical challenges to liberalism and science, anxiety over imperial and national decline," and even mounting anxiety over consumer culture, whose fluctuating values further helped to defamiliarize social life (Walkowitz, *City* 17). The fallen woman, with her associations of disease and decadence, could still be the focus of public furor and thereby deflect the middle class's panicky perception that as a class, it was losing control.

Merchant-Ivory's Jacky has lost all these disturbing associations, even if she still aids with the progress of the plot. But this transmutation may have more to do with reading "fallenness" through a 1990s lens than with any compelling aesthetic or narrative issues. The middle-class film audience can be compassionate toward Jacky because she no longer represents a measurable cultural threat. Forster perhaps saw her as the first Europeans on the North American continent saw the indigenous peoples: as savage, dangerous, and nonhuman. Eighteenth-century enlightenment commentators like Rousseau could transform these same peoples into images of benevolent nature—childish, simple creatures—only when their aggressive resistance to European imperialist designs had been successfully neutralized. Perhaps in similar fashion the century has recovered Jacky in benevolent and romanticized terms. Amidst the Edwardian set pieces, Jacky is the film's looking glass, through which we may walk and see our own age.

The novel's subtext of prostitution becomes context in the climactic wedding scene, where Jacky the unwilling interloper reveals Henry Wilcox as a former lover. In his earliest sketch of the novel, Forster had already envisioned this event: "Idea for another novel shaping . . . Mrs. Wilcox dies, and some years later Margaret gets engaged to the widower, a man impeccable publicly. They are accosted by a prostitute" (qtd. in Furbank 165). Merchant-Ivory recognizes the pivotal plot value of this scene, because here Henry's moral duplicity will be fully revealed by the woman from the past who collides with his carefully arranged present. Nonetheless, the film scene unfolds with differing nuances of meaning. First we view Jacky's recognition and fond (albeit tipsy) salute of Henry Wilcox:

Jacky: Why if it isn't 'enry! [laughter]. 'Ello 'enry! Fancy seeing you here. Don't you remember Jacky? 'enry! Aren't you going to say 'ello?

Met with a polite inquiry from Margaret (*Do you know this woman?*) and a rebuff from Henry Wilcox, Jacky reacts further:

Jacky: Know 'enry? Who doesn't know 'enry! We've had some gay old times, haven't we, 'en?

Her tone of voice is increasingly desperate, as Wilcox strides away.[13] Here the consistently unproblematic vision of Jacky that Jhabvala has crafted works efficiently to coalesce as the pitiable, kind-hearted girl with a past, a figure capable of generating audience sympathy (for herself, a project worth saving by the noble Leonard) because she radiates a sweet innocence through all of this. For Merchant-Ivory, Jacky's fateful recognition of Henry quickly dissolves in tearful, intoxicated confusion. Compare this, however, to Jacky's confident, "professional" appraisal of Henry in the novel, where the scene unfurls quite differently:

Mrs. Bast was still in the garden; . . . Margaret found this woman repellent. She had felt, when shaking her hand, an overpowering shame. She remembered the motive of her call at Wickham Place, and smelt again odours from the abyss—odours the more disturbing because they were involuntary. . . .

> "Henry!" [Jacky] repeated, quite distinctly. . . . Jacky pointed with
> her cake. "You're a nice boy, you are." She yawned. "There now, I
> love you. . . ."
>   "Why does she call you 'Hen'?" said Margaret innocently. "Has
> she ever seen you before?"
>   "Seen Hen before!" said Jacky. "Who hasn't seen Hen? He's serv-
> ing you like me, my dear. These boys! You wait—Still we love 'em."
> (241–43)

No tears here: this Jacky is bold and brassy. If the novel seeks social harmony by revalorizing the Ruth Wilcox model of "the feminine," then Jacky
is the vicious reminder that middle-class "woman," however carefully constructed and maintained as a cultural ideal, may quickly be contaminated
as Margaret is by Jacky's inclusive innuendo, that tell-tale "we" who "serve"
Henry. In the figure of "woman," class and gender merge in *Howards End*
to form a cultural signifier that floats from the nouveau riche (Henry) to
gentility's nether edge (Leonard), eddying ever closer to the Schlegel sisters.
At the same time, Jacky is trying to swim upward toward the Schlegels. In
the opening sequence, for instance, she returns from having "tea at a lady
friend's" (53). Moreover, despite the squalor of the Camelia Road flat, Jacky
nonetheless enjoys marginally middle-class status there as a non-working
woman whose husband can keep her (albeit with increasing difficulty, as
his financial woes mount).[14] But these "airs" of gentility cannot mask the
odors of her previous status and profession, and when Margaret excoriates
Henry for having "yielded to a woman *of that sort*" (251, emphasis mine),
his sin is not simply adultery but adultery with the wrong class—the class,
one might add, that doesn't even have the "class" to stay in its place.
Although such a liaison uncovers Henry's moral vacuity, it poses a greater
threat to Margaret Schlegel by potentially collapsing all women into one
potent—and essentialist—erotic symbol.
    One might indeed argue that Margaret herself only dimly recognizes
the extent to which she is complicitous in this dangerous conflation. She
eventually gets Henry to agree to find employment for hapless Leonard,
but she achieves this goal only through a series of subterfuges: "Margaret
had winced, but she was influencing Henry now, and though pleased at
her little victory, she knew that she had won it by the methods of the
harem" (240, emphasis mine). "Harem" clearly suggests Forster's sense of
the thin membrane separating trashy Jacky from superior Margaret, in

terms of sexual politics. The filmmakers, however, have neutralized Jacky's edges, and as a result Margaret can be a much more appealing character because she doesn't have to police these class/gender boundaries as brutally as does her fictional counterpart. Moreover, the film's changes underscore the extent to which we have lost sight of the danger in cross-pollinating the New Woman and the prostitute. From our historical perspective, we must work to recover that moment in the history of social hierarchy when, as was the case circa 1910, a middle-class modern woman wasn't also automatically a self-consciously sexual, autonomous being.

Jacky's professionally-tinged appraisal of Henry, absent from the Merchant-Ivory production, reminds Forster's audience of the ambiguous relationship between prostitution, morals, and economics, another potent combination of ideologies that threatens Margaret and Henry alike and makes them natural allies in the scene. The prostitute, as Lynda Nead reminds us, occupies an ambiguous space in economic terms because she "stands as worker, commodity and capitalist and blurs the categories of bourgeois economics in the same way that she tests the boundaries of bourgeois morality" (99). Thus Jacky violates codes of both public and private order, as the would-be domestic queen who has also been an enterprising capitalist, the "unnatural supplement to bourgeois femininity [that] does not even conform to the laws of the market-place" (Nead 99).

The most important deviation of film from novel occurs when we learn of the unlikely circumstances that united Jacky and Henry long ago. The location was British-controlled Cyprus, where Henry, we are told in both novel and film, spent time for "sport and business" at a Cypriot garrison town (159). Here Ruth Prawer Jhabvala feels compelled to construct an elaborate past for Jacky that absolves her of personal responsibility and denies her any real agency.

> *Leonard*: Mr. Wilcox met Jacky before, out in Cyprus, when she was sixteen. I told you you didn't want to hear about it.
> *Helen*: Go on. Why was she in Cyprus?
> *Leonard*: Her father was a clerk in an export business, so after her mother died she'd gone out to be with him. Then he died, accidentally drowned because he couldn't swim. Jacky was left having to fend for herself 'til she managed to get back home.[15]

Given that screenplays generally compress and conflate their sources, such deliberate additions are noteworthy. To say as the film does that Jacky was a vulnerable sixteen-year-old abandoned in a foreign country after the death of her parents is to confirm Jacky as victim and to invoke late-nineteenth-century England's anxieties about topics like the so-called white slave trade or the traffic in "five pound virgins." As historian Judith R. Walkowitz reminds us, there is little hard evidence for white slave trade or trafficking, although the popular press whipped public sentiment into a frenzy over these issues (*Prostitution* 246–47). But simple calculations in the novel tell us that Jacky, a "massive woman of thirty-three" (54), was in her mid-twenties during the Cyprus episode—a bit too old to be seduced and abandoned, and more in line with the outer age limit of girls who were working prostitutes and who, in their twenties, tended to leave the streets "to resume respectable employment or to settle down with a man" (Walkowitz, *Prostitution* 18).

To complicate this picture further is the matter of whether "Jackies" were likely to be figures on the colonial scene at all. At least one social historian claims that "British empire- builders never took their own prostitutes with them. Their presence was thought to be bad for prestige. Indeed, any British prostitute found in India or elsewhere was sent home" (Hyam 142).[16] Jhabvala's inventions obviate this point, but Forster provides no such explanation.[17] Whatever the factual improbability, Forster nonetheless instinctively imbricates Jacky with his critique of imperialism, as if imperialism's full moral horror can best (or perhaps *only*) be represented by the unruly female. In her accent, dress, demeanor, and pollution, as well as her realignment of bourgeois capitalism's rules, Jacky disrupts the norms of class. Through all this is interwoven her dangerous gender status, because her "fall" and subsequent "rise" mark her as a mobile woman with a history in a culture where a "female" in middle-class terms is expected to be natural, stable, outside history, or even prehistorical (McClintock 30). Finally, she emblematizes the empire's corrosive moral influence. While Henry Wilcox's exploits receive mixed reviews from a censorious Forster (if only because the pursuit of empire also make possible leisure, wealth, and the pursuit of Art and Literature), her position in Cyprus is morally unambiguous, particularly when we recall that Cyprus was reputed to be the birthplace of Aphrodite and, by 1829, the word "cyprian" connoted "prostitute."

Merchant-Ivory makes Jacky imperialism's victim by suggesting that her fall was the result of personal bad luck, not systematic exclusionary class politics and sexism. Perhaps this is more in line with a contemporary unwillingness to see class and gender as intransigent mechanisms of social control. Forster, however, does not provide heart-warming details of Jacky's pathetic past because his version of Jacky functions generically in both class and caste terms: Jacky's fall is so natural as to make commentary irrelevant. And here Forster may reveal the principle weakness of his imperialist critique, which would otherwise unveil the ruthless opportunism of Henry Wilcox: if Jacky's fall is naturalized by Forster then so, too, is its imperial context, whose excesses may likewise by extension unwittingly be seen as "natural," or unavoidable. In this way, Jacky functions as a sort of substitution for imperialism: viz., *her* evil can be easily identified and delineated, whereas Wilcox's ruthless opportunism is a pervasive but essential feature of a market economy in which even the bohemian Schlegel sisters must partake.

The critic Fredric Jameson has argued that despite *Howards End*'s critique of imperialism, the colonized are completely unthinkable in the novel which, like other works of high early modernism, imagines imperialism in terms of competing First World powers and not in terms of Third World "others" (a way of thinking more characteristic of our "postcolonial" moment). He identifies the novel's imperial presence as chiefly a spatial metaphor for the faraway places where imperialism happens. Jameson also distinguishes between the novel's treatment of the urban poor and the colonial subject: "This internal subsumption [of poor people] is sharply to be distinguished from the exclusion of an external or colonized people (whose absence is not even designated): the distinction would correspond roughly to that which obtains in Freud between repression (neurosis) and foreclosure (psychosis)" (59). To be sure, Jacky Bast is literally not a colonized subject, but she nonetheless tantalizingly partakes of both the world of the indigenous poor and the dangerous polluting "other" in a distant colony. In *Howards End*, Jacky carries the full weight of insurgent otherness on both national and international levels.

Merchant-Ivory's adaptation of the wedding scene at Oniton elides these troubling issues of gender, class, and imperialism by interposing Jacky as the watchful eye framing the fateful departure of Helen and Leonard in a boat.[18] The scene is calculated to evoke feelings of protective pity for poor, harmless Jacky by asking the audience to share, even briefly, the space of Jacky's subjectivity. If the erasure of colonial subjectivity is a hallmark of imperial thinking,[19] Merchant-Ivory avoids this issue by showing us that Jacky is clearly capable of interiority (this may be why all the beast-like descriptions of her have been dropped in the film). One might speculate, too, whether twenty-five years spent imagining Indian "alterity" in her novels and short stories have made Ruth Prawer Jhabvala especially sensitive to representing cultural "otherness" in general. Thus it is not surprising that she and James Ivory give us a clear chance to see the world from Jacky's viewpoint, thereby suggesting that Jacky's perspective matters. But Forster's Jacky is differently presented. He denies Jacky an interior life, and by demonizing her as an erotic, liminally human Other, Forster exposes sentiments common to his class at the turn of the century. Drunk and gorged on sweets, she is the snake in Henry's Oniton garden who must be expelled.

The novel's tensions regarding Jacky's tainted status are strained to the breaking point when Helen "falls" into Jacky's category and experiences illicit sexuality. Forster has prepared us for this and indeed suggests that the boundaries have already begun to bleed when Margaret earlier admits using the "methods of the harem" to gain Henry's favor. As argued previously, Margaret is complicitous with the dangerous conflation threatening to pull both Schlegel women down to Jacky's level. Her refuge in the power of a woman's sexuality underscores her enormous lack of authority and privilege as a woman that her class status cannot offset. Just as Margaret, Forster's more sober heroine, slowly transforms into the odalisque, the impetuous Helen now plunges headlong into the dark waters where Jacky treads. The plunge, moreover, is especially toxic because it is so unnatural: Helen cannot even pretend to have fallen for economic reasons, as could arguably have been lower-class Jacky's motivation.

Thus one important consequence of the collision between Wilcox's adultery and Helen's illegitimate pregnancy is that the natural role of woman is being interrogated. If polluted Jackies can enter the cohesive social order as "respectable" married women (Jacky is anxious that Leonard "make it all right" in legal terms [54]), then Wilcox must struggle to reassign her the prostitute role that absolves him of moral responsibility founded on *class* expectations. Moreover, if unlawful pregnancies are freely chosen by middle-class

New Women, then Wilcox must again work to reassign the woman's role in terms instantly recognizable to the nineteenth-century middle-class ideal. Thus Henry demands to know the name of Helen's "seducer," to know who has "done" this to her, thereby reassuring himself that Helen is merely the recipient and not the agent, a passive victim easily identified within prescriptive norms of class and gender. But sexual self determination leading to cultural anarchy was a perceived if not an actual threat of the emerging New Woman of the period, and Henry's inquisition seeks to avoid any potential parallel with Jacky and her circumstances. Also, and perhaps most important, it attempts to stop Helen's dangerous free-fall into the New Woman category, where boundaries between respectable and non-respectable womanhood might dissolve, prefiguring chaos.

The pregnancy of Helen likewise provokes reactions from Leonard. He accepts full responsibility: "it never occurred to him that Helen was to blame" (331), because that would impute motivations and meanings to Helen that are in Leonard's mind likewise inconsistent with her class. "It was as if some work of art had been broken by him, some picture in the National Gallery slashed out of its frame. When he recalled her talents and her social position, he felt that the first passer-by had a right to shoot him down" (332).[20] He also feels that the event has brought him down to Jacky's level, with one important difference: while he broods on the moral force of these events, Jacky's "hungry eyes" reveal "nothing that she could express," thereby reinforcing the novel's contention that Jacky must remain the beast. The fall of Helen, trembling with such apocalyptic possibilities, serves only to instruct Leonard that women like Helen and Jacky must not, indeed cannot, be equated.

Not surprisingly it was Helen's (unnatural) downfall and not Jacky's (natural) past history that deeply troubled so many of the novel's first readers, who otherwise lauded the novel. *The Morning Leader* unhesitatingly stated that Helen "had been seduced" (qtd. in Gardener 127); Helen's coupling with Leonard is an "extraordinary act of self-sacrifice," claimed the *Spectator*'s reviewer (qtd. in Gardener 133); the *Observer* opined, "The story of Helen's fall is disagreeable; perhaps it was necessary for the purpose, but it introduces a jarring note" (qtd. in Gardener 135); the "seduction," claimed *Athenaeum*'s critic, is "unconvincing" (qtd. in Gardener 151). The only scathing assessment of the book, from Edmund Gosse, fixated on those elements that struck him as "sensational and dirty and affected":

> I should like to know what you think of the new craze for intro-
> ducing into fiction the high-bred maiden who has a baby? It is the
> craze of the moment; it is beginning to attract the wonder of the
> Continent. I have read three new English novels this autumn of
> which it is the motif . . . I think it is a mark of feminisation . . . I do
> not know how an Englishman can calmly write of such a disgusting
> thing, with such sang-froid. . . . (qtd. in Furbank 189)

Interestingly, writer and New Woman Katherine Mansfield assessed
Helen's fall in droll counterpoint: "And I can never be perfectly certain
whether Helen was got with child by Leonard Bast or by his fatal forgotten
umbrella. All things considered, I think it must have been the umbrella"
(120). Whether Forster meant to suggest otherwise, many readers were only
too willing to assume the seduction/betrayal motif to explain the inexplicable. And if Forster can be shown to believe Helen capable of agency here,
then the gap between Jacky and the Schlegel sisters closes, despite their
attempts to patrol those pungent odors from the abyss.

In contrast, the compassion Merchant-Ivory extends to Jacky throughout the film again characterizes her final appearance on-screen, the night
before Leonard's fateful trip to Howards End. Jacky tenderly asks after
Leonard's health, reconfirming her sympathetic portrait from the film's
opening scenes. By contrast, her silent, somnolent form in the novel highlights Leonard's character, at the expense of hers: their marriage has been
a test of his moral resolve, through which he has learned to pity his wife
"with nobility" and through which we, in turn, are asked to pity Leonard.
Forster wants us to view Leonard as generous enough to recognize that
Jacky lacks malice but shrewd enough to understand she occupies an order
considerably lower than his.

In a novel that interrogates the role of history and place in the present,
Jacky Bast tellingly has no "home," no surname, no "people" to recover, no
past to honor. Infertile and uncontainable, Jacky carries odors that do more
than just contaminate the Schlegels' refined airs: they threaten the very survival of national stability, whose linchpin is the reproductive bourgeois
female. Forster struggles to limit Jacky's role to that of the conventional fallen
woman narrative, the unredeemable version. But the historical contingency
of the New Woman demanded that Jacky be erased before she could successfully "reproduce" herself in Helen and Margaret. Moreover, she provided a convenient figure on which Forster might displace his own anxieties

about Empire, which made possible the leisure necessary for good bourgeois sons like himself to write novels like this one.

Conversely, the New Woman has lost her transgressive edge in the contemporary film. Audiences instantly recognize screen images of embryonic New Womanhood because those images have been familiarized by popular culture, such as Virginia Slims ad campaigns. There's a quaintness to these radical women of the teens, whose infractions have become commonplace. Therefore Jacky need no longer serve as the visible boundary of acceptable femininity. For Forster, however, Helen's removal from metropolis to countryside was a strategic necessity, designed to separate her from London's loose "old" women (like Jacky) and loose New Women, alike. This spatial logic resonates only dimly for a modern audience, for whom the contagious carnival of postmodern urban life is a fact, not a threat.[21] Jacky's urban turf has presumably long since been mapped, surveyed, and surveilled; and the sexualizing of the middle-class woman has in the later twentieth century become such a commonplace that "Jackys" are no longer potent figures of metropolitan chaos. Jacky's rich role in evoking empire has been likewise modified. Coded by Forster as a fractious "other," Jacky is considerably softened by Jhabvala's postcolonial sensibilities. Henry Wilcox is, however, a different story altogether. In the lens of Merchant-Ivory, he is a recognizable prototype of the modern downsizing, stock-raiding, multinational CEO, for whom a contemporary audience can have undiluted scorn.

Howards End the film is more than just a "complacent Tory tract on the pleasures of property," as one critic complains (Monk 34). By reducing Jacky to farce, Merchant and Ivory have made her class distinction more rigid, and more apparently natural. The final irony may be that Jhabvala has unwittingly restored a stable discourse of class, gender, and empire that even Forster, in his historical moment, could not conjure innocently.

NOTES

1. In a lively collection of essays about recent Austen adaptations for the screen, contributors repeatedly identify the films' historical inaccuracies, presumably incurred to satisfy contemporary audience expectations for feminist heroines, emotionally expressive heroes, visually seductive surroundings, or vast country houses. See Troost and Greenfield, eds.

2. The four previous Forster adaptations constitute an influential part of this "heritage" genre. See David Lean, *A Passage to India* (1984); James Ivory, *A Room with a View* (1986) and *Maurice* (1987); and Charles Sturridge, *Where Angels Fear to Tread* (1992). Significantly, Sturridge also directed *Brideshead Revisited,* arguably the founding ancestor of all recent heritage cinematic adaptations (at least in terms of popularity and influence). For works dealing with the question of English "heritage" and cinematic representation, see Higson ("Heritage"), Wollen, and Cairns. Regarding critical responses to *Howards End,* most reviews that appeared in large-circulation newspapers and magazines were positive and often effusive, calling it "sublime" (Travers in *Rolling Stone* 41), "elegant" (Blake in *America* 299), "handsome and intelligent" (Rafferty in *The New Yorker* 4), even "perfect" (Anderson in *Films in Review* 117). Stuart Klawans's comment in *The Nation* is representative: the film "is so good I wouldn't have believed it if I hadn't seen it with my own eyes" (570).

3. Of the more than thirty reviews I surveyed, only half a dozen were strongly negative, for reasons varying from film content (Leonard and Jacky are lower-class "caricatures" according to Billson [33]) to visual excessiveness, as with Donald Lyons's complaint about Ivory's "Hallmark vulgarity" (18).

4. See, for instance, Griffith (1997), McFarlane (1996), Reynolds (1993), Orr and Nicholson (1992), Chatman (1990), and Sinyard (1986).

5. My current project is a detailed analysis of these novels and films. Recent readings from this work in progress include my 2001 MLA conference presentation, "Homosexual Difference and the Importance of being Risley," in which I cross-read Forster's *Maurice* against the Merchant-Ivory adaptation.

6. Anita Levy has analyzed the way nineteenth-century anthropology helped universalize an idea of "woman" rooted in English middle-class behavioral and cultural prescriptions, against which all other women, both nationally and globally, would be judged. Any woman falling short of this image would be seen as "improperly gendered" (12), and this photo of Jacky Bast certainly suggests an improperly gendered woman who falls far short of the middle-class ideals of propriety, domesticity, and reproductivity.

7. Director James Ivory does not, moreover, have the luxury of disembodying every woman on-screen except Jacky. Costumes must work for him to reflect character transformation, and thus Margaret's "New Woman" look yields to increasingly opulent garments as her engagement with Henry Wilcox develops, thereby reinforcing Margaret's personal recalibrations as she moves into the Wilcox arena. These tasteful velvets and laces vibrate with a sensuality absent from Forster's portrayal of Margaret in the novel.

8. The haphazardly "domestic" female would later find comic expression in Rebecca West's "Indissoluble Matrimony" (1912), and she resurfaces in T. S. Eliot's *The Waste Land* (1922) as an emblem of cultural chaos in the figure of the young typist, clearing the breakfast things at teatime and preparing her dinner out of "tins."

9. Only a very few film critics acknowledged the disjunction between Jacky on-screen and on the page. Noel Annan commented that her film version is "far more appealing to us than she was to Forster" (4), a sentiment shared by Gabriele Annan (18).

10. To be sure, many if not most of Forster's women are misogynistic portraits in generalized ways—women frequently precipitate textual crises of all sorts (see Adela Quested in *A Passage to India,* for instance), or they are more insidiously effaced by

narrative tone (as with Maurice's sisters). Jacky Bast, however, is somewhat *sui generis,* because of her class affiliation and its capacity for complete female "embodiment," a possibility only hinted at in other Forsterian female portraits.

11. She is never called "Mrs. Wilcox," only Mrs. Charles or Dolly. This hints that she will never partake of the adaptive strategies that marked Ruth's incorporation into Henry's worldview.

12. What passes virtually unnoticed here is the naturalness with which Annie, the servant, is dismissed as a "fool"—presumably for opening the door to a "female" who will not be so neatly corralled by Helen's social advantage. Indeed if, as Jane Marcus has commented, bourgeois English women "traded their own freedom for power over servants (or natives in the colonies) which replicated the master/slave relationship of husbands and wives" (149), then Jacky represents a simmering insurrection, a much more dangerous species of "fool" over which Helen may have limited control or none whatsoever. Robert H. MacDonald likewise identifies the connection between class rhetoric and colonial politics, both partaking of similar discourses in national and imperial contexts (38).

13. Film transcription is mine.

14. Historian Angela V. John describes this as "a lady*like* manner" (3).

15. Film transcription is mine.

16. That emigration might *build* moral character was, as Lynda Nead reports, the hope of mid-nineteenth-century social commentators like William Acton, who argued in 1857 that "for the sufferings of labour, for the immorality of the community, my nostrum is, marry and colonize—colonize—colonize" (qtd. in Nead 209).

17. It is unlikely Forster possessed any credible information about prostitution at this time, since by his own admission he did not in 1910 even fully understand the mechanics of heterosexual coupling. See Furbank 37.

18. James Ivory has justified the interpolated boat scene as a function of dramatic necessity. Nowhere in the novel does Forster create a sexual context for Helen and Leonard, and Ivory surmises that perhaps "Forster just could not, or would not, conceive of a semiliterate bank clerk having a physical relationship with an educated upper-middle class young lady, though he could—and did—portray such a relationship when the middle-class protagonist was not a young lady but a man" (xviii). Hence the Merchant-Ivory creation of the boat scene as the site where the crucial sexual encounter takes place. More relevant to my purposes here, Forster could not imagine viewing this scene sympathetically through Jacky's eyes, which is exactly what happens in the film as the rowboat with Leonard and Helen slips from the shore.

19. One might argue that the novel's unidentified narrator sustains a colonial relationship to Jacky throughout the novel, as Jacky's consciousness is as impenetrably dark and presumably meaningless as is Conrad's Africa. Her muteness reinforces the narrator's contrasting intelligence and insightfulness, just as Edward Said argues that, in *Heart of Darkness,* "Marlow's narrative takes the African experience as further acknowledgement of Europe's world significance; Africa recedes in integral meaning, as if with Kurtz's passing it had once again become the blankness his imperial will had sought to overcome" (165).

20. Here, Helen, like Jacky and Dolly before her, is figured as a woman unframed. The difference is that Leonard sees himself as initiating the act.

21. Forster's fear of the encroaching "red rust" of London suggests a literal terror of the machine, even though Leonard Bast's job as a clerk already reveals a major twentieth-century shift away from production-oriented economies toward service-oriented, post-industrial economies that now characterize major developed nations.

WORKS CITED

Anderson, Amanda. *Tainted Souls and Painted Faces: The Rhetoric of Fallenness in Victorian Culture.* Ithaca: Cornell UP, 1993.

Anderson, Pat. Rev. of *Howards End,* dir. James Ivory. *Films in Review* 43.3–4 (March–April 1992): 117–18.

Annan, Gabriele. "Faithful to Forster." Rev. of *Howards End,* dir. James Ivory. *Times Literary Supplement,* 1 May 1992, 18.

Annan, Noel. "Oh, What a Lovely War." Rev. of *Howards End,* dir. James Ivory. *The New York Review of Books,* 14 May 1992, 3–4.

Benjamin, Walter. "Theses on the Philosophy of History." *Illuminations.* Ed. Hannah Arendt. Trans. Harry Zohn. New York: Schocken, 1968. 253–64.

Billson, Anne. "Our Kind of People." Rev. of *Howards End,* dir. James Ivory. *New Statesman and Society,* 29 May 1992, 32–33.

Blake, Richard A. "A Tired Season." Rev. of *Howards End,* dir. James Ivory. *America,* 11 April 1992, 299–300.

Boyum, Joy Gould. *Double Exposure: Fiction into Film.* New York: Universe, 1985.

Cairns, Craig. "Rooms without a View." *Sight and Sound* 1.2 (June 1991): 10–13.

Chatman, Seymour. *Coming to Terms: The Rhetoric of Narrative in Fiction and Film.* Ithaca: Cornell UP, 1990.

Duckworth, Alistair. *Howards End: E. M. Forster's House of Fiction.* New York: Twayne, 1992.

Forster, E. M. *Howards End.* 1910. New York: Vintage, 1989.

Furbank, P. N. *E. M. Forster: A Life.* Vol. 1, *The Growth of the Novelist 1879–1914.* New York: Harcourt Brace Jovanovich, 1978.

Gardner, Philip, ed. *E. M. Forster: The Critical Heritage.* London: Routledge and Kegan Paul, 1973.

Geduld, Harry M., ed. *Authors on Film.* Bloomington: Indiana UP, 1972.

Giddings, Robert, Keith Selby, and Chris Wensley. *Screening the Novel: The Theory and Practice of Literary Dramatization.* London: Macmillan, 1990.

Griffith, James. *Adaptations As Imitations: Films from Novels.* Newark: U of Delaware P, 1997.

Higson, Andrew. "The Heritage Film and British Cinema." *Dissolving Views: Key Writings of British Cinema.* Ed. Andrew Higson. London: Cassell, 1996. 232–48.

———. "Representing the National Past: Nostalgia and Pastiche in the Heritage Film." *Fires Were Started: British Cinema and Thatcherism.* Ed. Lester Friedman. Minneapolis: U of Minnesota P, 1993. 109–29.

Howards End. Prod. Ismail Merchant. Dir. James Ivory. Screenplay by Ruth Prawer Jhabvala. Perf. Anthony Hopkins, Emma Thompson, Vanessa Redgrave, and Helena Bonham Carter. Sony Classics, 1991.

Hutchings, Peter J. "A Disconnected View: Foster [*sic*], Modernity, and Film." *E. M. Forster.* Ed. Jeremy Tambling. New Casebooks Series. New York: St Martin's Press, 1995. 213–28.

Hyam, Ronald. *Empire and Sexuality: The British Experience.* Manchester: Manchester UP, 1990.

Ivory, James. Introduction. *Howards End.* By E. M. Forster. New York: Modern Library, 1999.

Jameson, Fredric. "Modernism and Imperialism." *Nationalism, Colonialism, and Literature.* Ed. Terry Eagleton, Fredric Jameson, and Edward Said. Minneapolis: U of Minnesota P, 1990. 43–66.

John, Angela V. Introduction. *Unequal Opportunities: Women's Employment in England 1800–1918.* Ed. Angela V. John. Oxford: Basil Blackwell, 1986. 1–41.

Klawans, Stuart. Rev. of *Howards End,* dir. James Ivory. *Nation* 27 (April 1992): 568–72.

Larrson, Donald R. "Novel into Film: Some Preliminary Reconsiderations." *Transformations in Literature and Film.* Selected Papers from the Sixth Annual Florida State University Conference on Literature and Film. Ed. Leon Golden. Tallahassee: UP of Florida, 1982. 69–83.

Levy, Anita. *Other Women: The Writing of Class, Race, and Gender, 1832–1898.* Princeton: Princeton UP, 1991.

Lyons, Donald. "Traditions of Quality." Rev. of *Howards End,* dir. James Ivory. *Film Comment* 28.3 (May–June 1992): 14–16, 18.

MacDonald, Robert H. *The Language of the Empire: Myths and Metaphors of Popular Imperialism, 1880–1918.* Manchester: Manchester UP, 1994.

Mansfield, Katherine. *The Journal of Katherine Mansfield.* Ed. J. Middleton Murry. London: Constable, 1927.

Marcus, Jane. "Britannia Rules *The Waves.*" *Decolonizing Tradition: New Views of Twentieth Century British Literary Canons.* Ed. Karen R. Lawrence. Urbana: U of Illinois P, 1992. 136–62.

McClintock, Anne. *Imperial Leather: Race, Gender, and Sexuality in the Colonial Context.* New York: Routledge, 1995.

McFarlane, Brian. *Novel to Film: An Introduction to the Theory of Adaptation.* Oxford: Clarendon, 1996.

Monk, Claire. "Sexuality and the Heritage." *Sight and Sound* 5 (October 1995): 32–34.

Nead, Lydia. *Myths of Sexuality: Representations of Women in Victorian Britain.* Oxford: Basil Blackwell, 1988.

Orr, John, and Colin Nicholson, eds. Introduction. *Cinema and Fiction: New Modes of Adapting, 1950–1990.* Edinburgh: Edinburgh UP, 1992.

Rafferty, Terrence. "Yes, But." Rev. of *Howards End,* dir. James Ivory. *New Yorker,* 4 May 1992, 74–76.

Reynolds, Peter, ed. *Novel Images: Literature in Performance.* London: Routledge, 1993.

Said, Edward. *Culture and Imperialism.* New York: Vintage, 1994.

Sinyard, Neil. *Filming Literature: The Art of Screen Adaptation.* New York: St Martin's, 1986.

Stallybrass, Peter, and Allon White. *The Politics and Poetics of Transgression.* Ithaca: Cornell UP, 1986.

Travers, Peter. Rev. of *Howards End,* dir. James Ivory. *Rolling Stone,* 2 April 1992, 41.

Troost, Linda, and Sayre Greenfield, eds. *Jane Austen in Hollywood.* Lexington: UP of Kentucky, 1998.

Walkowitz, Judith R. *City of Dreadful Delight: Narratives of Sexual Danger in Late-Victorian London.* Chicago: U of Chicago P, 1992.

———. *Prostitution and Victorian Society: Women, Class, and the State.* Cambridge: Cambridge UP, 1980.

Wollen, Tana. "Over Our Shoulders: Nostalgic Screen Fictions for the 1980s." *Enterprise and Heritage: Crosscurrents of National Culture.* Ed. John Corner and Sylvia Harvey. London: Routledge, 1991. 178–93.

Wood, Michael. "You Can't Go Home Again." *Arts in Society.* Ed. Paul Barker. Glasgow: Fontana, 1977. 21–30.

I Don't Want to Talk about It

Using Spanish Feature Films to Teach Literature

CARMEN CHÁVEZ

We may not want to talk about it, but it is a reality. As Russell A. Berman addresses in *Profession* (1997), our undergraduate literature courses are undersubscribed (71). We are confronted with products of the video generation, students who want a quick fix and who do not have memorization skills or long attention spans. Literature may have stopped being "cultural" when literary texts were replaced with television and the Internet. We in foreign language departments are designing culture classes in which students are not required to read anything longer than two pages in Spanish. Professors find themselves trying to accommodate different learning styles and at the same time teaching them what they need to know to be educated, bilingual people.

This essay describes how the technology that replaced literature can be used to bring literature, writing, and grammar back into the language classroom. Students improve listening, reading, and writing proficiency and learn grammatical nuances when feature films are used to relay the information to the student. Through a variety of traditional and nontraditional ways of generating the language—such as listservs, chat rooms, bulletin boards, class discussion, Web portfolios, essays, and reading—students learn how to express complicated ideas in written and spoken Spanish as they discover the thrills of learning another language.

According to Berman, foreign language and literature teachers have dedicated themselves, in order of importance, to three distinct goals: the scholarly study of works of literature, the learning of language, and a general knowledge of the cultural history of other countries.[1] Berman also champions the need for more interdisciplinary involvement in our language classrooms, stating, "it is fair to suggest that interdisciplinarity may

soon have to be regarded as a transitional phase, a mediation or a redefinition of the field, and not an end in itself" (67). He suggests the possible
alliance between cultural studies and the language-instruction function
within departments, calling for a rethinking and redefinition of goals in
the training of graduate students, which would lead to a change in how
we teach undergraduates. In essence, language instruction and cultural
studies should be presented as an intertwined unit and not treated as separate entities.

In "When Did Literature Stop Being Cultural?" Sandy Petrey identifies the phenomenon of choosing between cultural studies and literary
studies as the seesaw model: one can only triumph if the other fails.[2] He
argues that faculty trained in literature should not retreat to the other side
of the seesaw simply because the perception is that cultural studies is on
top. On the contrary, he sees literature as having enough material to please
all students interested in learning language and culture. Petrey asks what
the incentive is of learning a second language in an interdisciplinary cultural studies program, if one does not have to actually know how to read
or speak the target language.

Several years after Berman's and Petrey's essays were written, one sees
a shift in interest. Now a general knowledge of other cultures is first
emphasized, followed by a desire to learn the technical aspects of the language, and, finally, the study of literature. Students are not interested in
"literature." They want to learn about the culture. So, as second language
teachers, how can we convince our students that one of the most penetrating ways to learn another culture is to know its literature? One answer
lies in the mesmerizing quality of the visual media, which captivate the
student's attention and therefore prove to be an ideal method of transmitting cultural information.

There are many ways of incorporating film/video clips into the beginning and intermediate language classroom. In this essay I describe how to
use films to reintroduce literature to students, how to teach them presentation skills in Spanish, and how grammatical structures and current language
usage can be learned by using feature films in the upper-level second language classroom. Teaching literature through film alleviates the stress that
students feel when they approach the literary text. Professors can highlight
the cultural aspects of literature by explaining how the visual metaphors in

a film are reflections of the metaphors that writers use in their texts. One principal motivation for offering a class on Hispanic film is to incorporate the literary text in some fashion, either by reading the entire text or by selecting crucial passages that are reflected on-screen. Many students do not enjoy literature because they do not have the skills to read at the level that is required of them. As demonstrated in the debate mentioned at the beginning of this essay, students prefer taking courses that focus on language, conversation, and culture "bytes." With this in mind it is not surprising that when an instructor integrates video technologies into the study of language and the cultural aspects of literature, the student is much more motivated to learn to communicate in Spanish. Some of the topics that may be discussed in class include: the different registers of language in Latin American and Spanish texts; the various ways of expressing historical events depending on the epoch in which the text was written or the film was shot; and the cultural manifestations of Hispanic identity through film and literature.

Teachers must of course consider the availability of Hispanic films in the United States. I have purchased several videos in Spain that are not subtitled, but fortunately there are many subtitled films based on literature besides the ones distributed in Spain. There is an ample selection of videos that are technically and thematically interesting for the student, and, with the advent of Digital Video Disc (DVD) in the United States, one can now take advantage of the DVD titles available in Spain and Latin America.[3] Many literary Spanish classics have been adapted into film and are available in the United States (see Appendix A). Among the questions that a professor must ask herself is which literary texts are linguistically accessible to the undergraduate level? Are the films based on these texts subtitled or not? Are the films too scandalous or violent? Will the themes interest the student or alienate him? How much technical film vocabulary will the instructor have to teach the student? How many literary texts and films should he or she cover in one semester?

Among the topic-generated themes that I have taught are "The Visual Metaphor: Film Adaptations of Hispanic Fiction," "The Concept of Gender in Hispanic Film", and "Spanish Identity and Culture through Films." All the topics are broad enough to cover both Spanish and Latin American film titles as well as a variety of themes. My main intention for the film adaptation class is to encourage students to read literature written in Spanish.

The texts that I selected for this course were: *El burlador de Sevilla* (written by Tirso de Molina), *Don Juan Tenorio* (written by José Zorrilla), *Los santos inocentes* (written by Miguel Delibes), *Extramuros* (written by Jesús Fernández Santos), *Como agua para chocolate* (written by Laura Esquivel) and "De eso no se habla" (written by Julio Llinas). The videos that accompanied each text respectively were: *Don Juan, My Love* (directed by Antonio Mercero), *Don Juan en los infiernos* (directed by Gonzalo Suárez), *Los santos inocentes* (directed by Mario Camus), *Extramuros* (directed by Miguel Picazo), *Como agua para chocolate* (directed by Alfonso Arau), and *De eso no se habla* (directed by María Luisa Bemberg).

While difficult for a typical undergraduate to read, I selected the Don Juan texts because I wanted the students to be familiar with the importance of the Don Juan myth in Spanish society, and the films as modern adaptations of this classical theme. I highlighted the difference between Tirso's and Zorrilla's versions and compared the difference to the film versions of Mercero where Don Juan, after spending centuries in purgatory, tries to find redemption when he is given a second chance; and Suárez, who portrays Don Juan as a victim of destiny whose punishment is to live with the consequences of his sins with no chance for redemption. The films directed by Mercero and Suárez capture how Don Juan was portrayed in the theatrical representation of Tirso and Zorrilla. Tirso de Molina, concerned with the theological importance of predestination in the seventeenth century, portrays Don Juan as a trickster and philanderer who shows no remorse for the damage he has done. Zorrilla, on the other hand, shows a repentant nineteenth-century Don Juan redeemed by his love for doña Inés. The most challenging text for the students to read in this class was Fernández Santos's *Extramuros*. Students found the historical references and the religious theme extremely difficult to decipher, but the film version provided enormous help with the text. In contrast, *Los santos inocentes, Como agua para chocolate,* and "De eso no se habla" are reader-friendly texts that the students thoroughly enjoyed because of the simpler language.

The three-hour class, with a one-hour additional lab for screening films, met twice a week in an audio/video language lab with multi-standard VCR, computer equipment, and a video projector with a 100-inch diagonal screen.[4] Students may listen to the film using the headphones or they may listen to the audio feed from the room speakers. As I organized the syllabus, my initial impulse was for the students to read the literary works first and then show them the films to reinforce their reading. However, when I considered the difficulty of the literary texts, the amount of reading that I was asking them to do, and the language ability of an average undergraduate student, I decided to show the films first. This was a wise pedagogical decision. Most of the time the students were able to complete the reading because they knew what to expect. They commented that if they had not seen the film they would have not understood the reading. They also stated that being able to visualize a person as they read the text was extremely beneficial and helped them manage the material.

Every two weeks I showed a film based on the novel, play, or short story that the students had started to read for that day. I reinforced their readings by requiring students to use chat rooms to discuss abstract topics, such as themes, and to provide an opportunity for students to critique the texts and films. I used bulletin boards, email, and a listserv to cover specific material on characterization, plot, and other concrete issues. Given the nature of learning in a computer classroom, students typically come prepared to discuss the readings and if they are not prepared, they immediately confess it. If I had taught this course in a regular classroom environment, more of the eighteen students could easily have remained passive, listening silently as the more vocal students, even if they were in a minority, carried on the discussion. In a computer classroom, even the weakest student will tend to have something to write in a chat room about the theme, and they are more willing to ask questions about plot or other confusing elements of the text or film. The computer classroom demands student-centered learning, with participation documented in writing. The timid or less proficient language student typically will not volunteer orally in a traditional classroom, but in a computer classroom environment this same student, who often times is more skilled in written discourse, feels comfortable and will participate in writing because his or her oral competency are not in question. The lack of written participation in a computer classroom, heard as "silence" in a conventional classroom dominated by oral discourse, attracts more attention in a computer classroom. The less proficient language student may take longer to express an idea, but he or she feels compelled to make the attempt when participating in a chat room. In a computer classroom students tend to articulate an idea that might go unexpressed in a traditional environment where the more language proficient student will excel.

An obvious benefit of using instructional technology in an upper-level class is that it allows both strong and weak students to participate actively and equally in the written discussions. Typically this environment provides an even playing ground for everyone. With technology-assisted instruction, students are more responsible for their learning and participate more actively. Gender, racial, and ethnic disparities are not as prominent in this environment as they are in a traditional classroom, perhaps because the students feel shielded from scrutiny and are judged exclusively on their comments. For instance, women and men usually contribute more equally and there is an increase in racial and ethnic cultural sharing. Students seem to view this community as safe and typically tend to be more open in their opinions regarding the assignment.

The listserv provides an additional resource for the student who has problems with basic plot comprehension in Spanish. Students can ask each other questions and discuss the book or film before face-to-face class discussions. Using feature films helps improve the five content standards, known as the 5 Cs: communication, cultures, connections, comparisons, and communities, as outlined by the collaborative project of the eleven-member team, the *National Standards for Foreign Language Learning.*[5] While the chat room is ideal for brainstorming and starting discussion online after viewing a film and before meeting in class, I noticed that the students preferred face-to-face discussions in class after everyone had a chance to read the text. Why? Immediacy. Once the student is engaged in the story, he or she wants details quickly, and face-to-face discussions are ideal for transmitting information without having to formulate a question in written Spanish. Students with better oral skills were the power brokers in charge of verifying or discovering crucial facts regarding plot, which highlights another lesson that second language teachers want their students to learn: language is power.

If I were to use the listserv again, I would prepare directed short answer questions and essay questions and have students respond to them as homework exercises. This would be extremely beneficial for the students who have not learned how to decipher the important details of a text, and it would prepare them for the type of essays that I ask them to write in Spanish in class and on tests. In addition to reading in this film class, students are required to write constantly in the target language. It is not uncommon to see a student writing between an intermediate mid-level and an advanced mid-level in this type of class.[6] The focus in this class is on reading, but the student's comprehension is measured by their ability to express their ideas in written Spanish. However, students also improve their listening comprehension skills by viewing feature films in the target language with no English subtitles. The learning process is reinforced first by the visual message received from the film, then from a detailed reading of the literary text, ending with the class discussing how the visual image is a metaphor for concepts presented in the literary text. Throughout the semester the students and I discuss the importance of the visual narrative in relaying a message within a shorter period of time than is possible in a written narrative. Of utmost importance is the ability to contrast and compare the visual image with the written word in Spanish. In many cases the visual images represented similar, if not almost identical, ideas as had been presented with the written word. When there were differences, the student's challenge was to express how the director used the visual image to capture the author's intent.

For the course on gender I require two texts: Richard M. Gollin, *A Viewer's Guide to Film: Arts, Artifices and Issues* (New York: McGraw-Hill, 1992) and Ramón Carmona, *Cómo se comenta un texto fílmico* (Madrid: Cátedra, 1991). In this class, the main course objective is to promote learning the technical aspects of studying film. Students learn how to analyze and critique Hispanic films, incorporating specialized vocabulary to describe cinematographic techniques that the director uses to structure his or her film. They discover that film viewing is not passive, but interactive. Students learn that the filmmaker, like the literary author, constructs meaning through images, supporting the thematic conventions visually. Additionally, students are required to read additional materials and share their findings with the class through weekly analyses.

In this class, I have more freedom to select a variety of texts because I am not bound by the availability of literary adaptations. In the past, students have viewed *La historia oficial, Camila, La boca del lobo, Verónico Cruz, El nido, La mitad del cielo, El pájaro de la felicidad,* and several Almodóvar films. While showing Almodóvar films is a little problematic for our conservative student body, he is a wonderful director to analyze from a cinematographic point of view. Almodóvar's affinity for portraying the darker side of societal institutions makes it challenging for the instructor, but his cinematographic technique enables her to study how the visual image serves to capture within a matter of a few seconds what would take pages to convey in a written narrative. Almodóvar's films are colorful, both visually and thematically. He uses bright colors, especially red, in his films to show passion and desire. The beginning of each of his movies usually startles the viewer because he introduces a character in a compromising and sexually-explicit situation, using vivid colors to reinforce the shocking image the audience witnesses. His characters are rich portrayals of nontraditional members of society. For instance, in his movie *Entre tinieblas* (1983), the Spanish director offers his audience a religious satire showing a convent full of nuns addicted to drugs, with the Mother Superior falling in love with the young singer, Yolanda. Almodóvar's films exemplify post-Franco Spain during the years of transition and *la movida* (the cultural movement). In what is considered Almodóvar's most accomplished film, *La ley del deseo* (1987), he tells the story of a mentally unstable man, Antonio, obsessed with a cocaine-addicted film director, Pablo. Almodóvar introduces the audience to an array of characters from the underground nightlife of Madrid as erotic homosexual sex dominates the screen. Both *Entre tinieblas* and *La ley del deseo* are films that are visually appealing, thematically rich, and representative of the flamboyant style that has made Almodóvar an international success.

This class met twice a week for one hour and fifteen minutes, and students were required to view the movies on their own in the library or at home. Unlike the Film Adaptation class, the students came prepared to present a scene analysis. They selected a sequence, explained how the scenes are representative of the major theme, and then, using the technical vocabulary that I provide, explained shot by shot how the director visually reinforces some aspect of the theme. In addition to the reading assignments in Appendix B, students were required to bring an outside reference in Spanish or English to support their observations. Articles were placed on reserve in the library before class so that everyone had a chance to read them. Many students found current information on the Internet and shared these resources with the class. Others brought selections of the literary text and explained how the director adapted the original source. Given the technical aspect of this class, we used the computer language lab so that students could freeze frames to discuss camera angles and study details that might have gone unnoticed upon first viewing.

The strong oral component in this class worked on several levels. First, during presentations the students were allowed to use note cards, but were asked not to read their analysis. Students found that the visual media supported their oral comments, which is particularly beneficial to the public speaking aspect of the class. The level of oral proficiency in this course oscillated between intermediate and advanced levels. However, the amount of language produced in Spanish increased as the students learned how to use the technical vocabulary in Spanish to describe the cinematic nuances of Hispanic film. As in the previous class, students learned idiomatic expressions of the period and increased their Spanish vocabulary because of the exposure to the language. As language faculty familiar with the *National Standards for Foreign Language Learning* know, communicative competence requires more than mere rote memorization. While memorizing vocabulary and grammatical structures serves as a building block to language acquisition, the true challenge is learning how to apply these structures to strategies that will promote oral competence. In my film classes, grammatical structures and syntactical complexity are noted, but students are not penalized for specific errors made in Spanish. I have found that bean-counting errors will not produce the outcomes that I desire in written or oral communication, fluidity that can only come if a student is not afraid to share his or her ideas in writing or orally. As Melinda Reichelt states, it is difficult, if not impossible, to know whether grammatical structure usage improves when it is targeted because of grammar instruction or simply because the student has practiced writing more.[7] When learning how to express complicated ideas in their second language, however, students should be allowed to make errors and concentrate on grammatical accuracy only after they feel comfortable expressing their ideas in Spanish.

This third class, "Spanish Identity and Culture through Films," taught in the audio/video language lab twice a week for seventy-five minutes each meeting, included an additional hour when the student was to view the film. I focused on defining the meaning of culture as it relates to the identity of post-Franco and contemporary Spain. I have used various film texts for this course, which is ideal if one does not have easy access to international films or if the instructor prefers to limit his or her repertoire to a personal collection or the university lab collection. In addition to the regular oral presentations that the students do in Spanish, I asked them to design a Web portfolio about the films and directors studied. The intent of this assignment is to encourage the students to synthesize and articulate their definition of culture as it relates to Spanish film. The students were asked to include written analyses of various films and to visually reinforce and organize the themes discussed in class. Each Web site is as unique as the person who designs it. As is typical in upper-level language classes, there was a wide range of oral proficiency. Again, as the guiding principle for learning a second language, I required that students develop all content standard areas by asking them to analyze scenes orally, write essays about the films, and express their opinions and listen to other students accurately using film vocabulary to discuss movies in Spanish. They were asked to expand on personal observations by reading secondary sources and making connections between their findings and what they observed about Hispanic culture on-screen.

As one might imagine, these presentations dramatically improved the students' oral and written proficiency. Each student was required to study a sequence and surpass the concrete exercise of retelling plot. They learned how to analyze and speculate in Spanish and bring very creative ideas into the classroom. We spent a considerable amount of time using chat rooms and listservs to discuss similarities and differences between the United States and Hispanic cultures.

In addition to developing writing skills, using computer technology also provides the student with an immersion-type experience. Students begin to think in Spanish and realize that expressing their ideas through writing is powerful; they also show more motivation in their writing as they learn how to express their ideas about the films and/or literary texts. In addition to writing more, they speak more Spanish and develop critical thinking skills in the language. When stimulated by a visual image, students are willing to leave their comfort zone, use more difficult grammatical structures, and attempt to articulate difficult ideas in Spanish.

In these courses, students must spontaneously apply the critical theory that they have learned to specific scenes selected by the instructor. Most of the films are not subtitled, which requires careful attention to idiomatic expressions, popular slang, and nuances of the language delivered on-screen. On occasion selections from the films were recorded and students translated or synthesized the main idea of the passage. Using visual media to represent cultural meaning and identify is another way that instructors can use Spanish feature films to teach language and critical thinking skills in a second language. Students must communicate the director's message via images, learning to watch a film for more than just entertainment as they grasp the importance of film structure.

Using Spanish feature films is inherently more challenging for the English-speaking student because not only must the student comprehend the language, but he or she must also understand the culture. The student must be able to "read" the cultural images in order to correctly analyze and comment on the importance of the film. As Dudley Andrew writes:

> Cinema is not only a good index of culture, but better, perhaps, than painting, music, or poetry, because it visibly partakes of the stuff of cultural life. . . . How does a film exist in culture and culture in film? As satisfying as is the metaphor of movie screen as cultural mirror, the power of the camera to set the scene of culture is a power much stronger than that of mere reflection. The cinema literally contributes to a culture's self-image, inflecting, not just capturing, daily experience.[8]

Integrating film technology in the upper-level Spanish class has allowed me to teach literature and language to students who think that they will not enjoy it. Students not only learn how to critically view a Spanish film, but they are also engaged in the learning process through writing and oral expression. Watching a film in Spanish without subtitles improves the students' listening comprehension skills and requires them to be attentive to the culture cues displayed on-screen. Teaching film in the language classroom allows the instructor to concentrate on the three goals that Berman and Petrey cite as the reason for our existence—teaching language, culture, and literature.

In the end, however, perhaps another paradigm will work better for us, one in which the professor is not limited to one goal, but can enjoy a fusion of all three. In *Literary into Cultural Studies,* Antony Easthope suggests that cultural studies creates a new paradigm that includes both high culture and popular culture instead of the traditional opposition that has existed between the canon and popular culture.[9] Feature films are an effective method of delivery for the student learning another language because they provide visual cues as to the importance of culture and increase the chances that the student will understand the spoken language. If we can engage our students in the subject material, then we have succeeded in teaching them the importance of visual and written narratives while teaching them what we love about the humanities.

APPENDIX A
VIDEO AND LITERARY TEXTS
Film Adaptation Class

Don Juan, My Love (directed by Antonio Mercero) based on the Don Juan myth in *El burlador de Sevilla*, written by Tirso de Molina.

Don Juan en los infiernos (directed by Gonzalo Suárez) based on the Don Juan myth in *Juan Tenorio*, written by José Zorrilla.

Los santos inocentes (directed by Mario Camus) based on *Los santos inocentes*, written by Miguel Delibes.

Extramuros (directed by Miguel Picazo) based on *Extramuros*, written by Jesús Fernández Santos.

Como agua para chocolate (directed by Alfonso Arau) based on *Como agua para chocolate*, written by Laura Esquivel.

De eso no se habla (directed by María Luisa Bemberg) based on "De eso no se habla," written by Julio Llinas.

El abuelo (directed by José Luis Garci) based on *El abuelo*, written by Pérez Galdós.

El perro del hortelano (directed by Pilar Miró) based on *El perro del hortelano*, written by Lope de Vega.

La tía Tula (directed by Miguel Picazo) based on *La tía Tula*, written by Miguel de Unamuno.

La colmena (directed by Mario Camus) based on *La colmena*, written by Camilo José Cela.

Bodas de sangre (directed by Carlos Saura) based on *Bodas de sangre*, written by Federico García Lorca.

Las bicicletas son para el verano (directed by Jaime Chávarri) based on Fernando Fernán-Gómez's play with the same title.

Bajarse al moro (directed by Fernando Colomo) based on José Luis Alonso de Santos's play with the same title.

¡Ay, Carmela! (directed by Carlos Saura) based on José Sanchís Sinisterra's play with the same title.

Historias del Kronen (directed by Montxo Armendáriz) based on the novel by J. A. Mañas with the same title.

Tiempo de silencio (directed by Vicente Aranda) based on the novel by Luis Martín Santos with the same title.

Historia de una escalera (directed by Ignacio Iquino) based on Antonio Buero Vallejo's play with the same title.

Esquilache (directed by Josefina Molina) based on Antonio Buero Vallejo's play *Un soñador para un pueblo.*

Cinco horas con Mario (directed by Josefina Molina) based on Miguel Delibes's novel with the same title.

Vicente Aranda's adaptations of Juan Marsé's novels: *La muchacha de las bragas de oro, El amante bilingüe,* and *Si te dicen que caí.*

Requiem por un campesino español (directed by Francesc Betriu) based on Ramón Sender's novel with the same title.

Como ser mujer y no morir en el intento (directed by Juanjo Puigcorbé) based on the novel by Carmen Rico Godoy with the same title.

Boquitas pintadas (directed by Leopoldo Torre Nilsson) based on Miguel Puig's novel with the same title.

Winter Barracks (directed by Lautaro Murua) based on Osvaldo Soriano's story with the same title.

El hombre muerto (directed by Hector Olivera) based on Jorge Luis Borges's short story with the same title.

Yo, la peor de todas (directed by Maria Luisa Bemberg) inspired by Octavio Paz's "The Tramp of Faith."

Fresa y chocolate (directed by Tomás Gutierrez Alea) based on Senel Paz's story "El lobo, el bosque y el hombre nuevo."

La ciudad y los perros (directed by Francisco Lombardi) based on Mario Vargas Llosa's novel with the same title.

No se lo digas a nadie (directed by Francisco Lombardi) based on Jaime Bayly's novel with the same title.

Golpes a mi puerta (directed by Alejandro Saderman) based on Juan Carlos Gené's play with the same title.

APPENDIX B
FILMS AND READINGS FOR THE
CONCEPT OF GENDER COURSE

Ver: *La historia oficial,* Luis Puenzo, Argentina, 1985.
Tarea: Gollin 5–25. *Screen Credits, Film Viewing and Audience Participation.*

Terminología y ejemplos de tomadas en *La historia oficial.*
Ver: *Camila,* María Luisa Bemberg, Argentina, 1984.
Tarea: Gollin 26–64. *Camera Conventions: Dramatic Space.*

Análisis

Ver: *Los santos inocentes,* Mario Camus, España, 1984.

Tarea: Gollin 65–89. *Editing Language: Composing Space and Time.*

Análisis

Ver: *La boca del lobo.* Francisco J. Lombardi, Perú, 1988.

Tarea: Gollin 90–117. *Dramatic Conventions and Screen Acting.*

Análisis

Ver: *Verónico Cruz,* Argentina, Miguel Pereira, 1989.

Tarea: Gollin 118–30; 155–56. *Genre Conventions.*

Análisis

Ver: *El nido,* Jaime de Armiñan, España, 1980.

Tarea: Gollin 160–200. *Historical Contexts and Why People Go to the Movies.*

Análisis

Ver: *La mitad del cielo,* Manuel Gutiérrez Aragon, España, 1986.

Tarea: Carmona 9–12; 13–17; 30–41.

Análisis

Ver: *Como agua para chocolate,* Alfonso Arau, México, 1990.

Tarea: Carmona 43–45; 47–53; 72–79.

Análisis

Ver: *Don Juan mi amor,* Antonio Mercero, España, 1991.

Tarea: Carmona 94–115.

Test

Carmona 117–31; 183–98; 254–70.

Ver: Pedro Almodóvar (documental), España, 1983.

Introducción al cine español.

Ver: *La ley del deseo,* Pedro Almodóvar, España, 1987.

Análisis

Alternate video: *Matador,* Pedro Almodóvar, España, 1986.

Ver: *Entre tinieblas,* Pedro Almodóvar, España, 1983.

Análisis

Ver: *La flor de mi secreto,* Pedro Almodóvar, España, 1995.

Análisis

Ver: *El pájaro de la felicidad,* Pilar Miró, España, 1993.

APPENDIX C
ONLINE RESOURCES
Websites

http://www.tulane.edu/~latinlib/internet.html

http://lanic.utexas.edu/la/region/cinema/

http://www.facets.org/

http://www.homefilmfestival.com/

http://www.filmforum.com/distributor.html

http://www.cinespain.com/

http://www.lavavideo.org/lava/

http://www.cubacine.cu/

http://chavales.iespana.es/chavales/INFOCINE.htm

http://www.cinenacional.com/

Course Syllabi

http://people.clemson.edu/~cchavez/02s407sy.htm

http://communication.ucsd.edu/courses/syllabi/110.W98.html

http://www.msu.edu/user/colmeiro/spanish891.html

http://www4.ncsu.edu:8030/~jmari/FLS318-Spr01-Readings.htm

http://www.msu.edu/user/colmeiro/spanish830.html

http://ll.truman.edu/filmvideo.html

http://lilt.ilstu.edu/smexpos/cinergia/cinergia.htm

http://www4.ncsu.edu/~jmari/film%20links.htm

http://lamar.colostate.edu/~fvalerio/hispaniccinelit.html

NOTES

1. Russell A. Berman, "Graduate Education Toward a Foreign Cultural Literacy," *Profession* (1997): 61–74.

2. Sandy Petrey, "When Did Literature Stop Being Cultural?," *Diacritics: A Review of Contemporary Criticism* 28.3 (1998): 12–22.

3. If one is purchasing a DVD player for the first time, he or she should consider a code-free player (also referred to as a region-free or non-region player). This region-free player converts the feed so that any DVD purchased anywhere in the world will play on the machine. The six regions are: Region 1, United States; Region 2, Europe and Japan; Region 3, Asian Pacific; Region 4, Australia, New Zealand, Latin America; Region 5, Africa, Russian, Eastern Europe; and Region 6, China and Hong Kong.

4. See <<http://people.clemson.edu/~cchavez/AudioVideoComputerLabs.html>>.

5. For a copy of *The Standards for Second Language Learning,* see

<<http://www.actfl.org/public/articles/execsumm.pdf>>.

6. These ACTFL (American Council on the Teaching of Foreign Languages) descriptors are delineated and explained by Karen E. Breiner-Sanders, Elvira Swender, and Robert M. Terry in the revised document published in *Foreign Language Annals* 35.1 (2002): 9–15.

7. Melinda Reichelt, "A Critical Review of Foreign Language Writing Research on Pedagogical Approaches," *Modern Language Journal* 85. 4 (2001): 578–98.

8. See Andrew, "Cinema and Culture."

9. See Easthope, *Literary into Cultural Studies.*

WORKS CITED

Andrew, Dudley. "Cinema and Culture." *Humanities* 6.4 (August 1985): 24–25. Also online: <<http://www.csulb.edu/~jvancamp/361_r3.html>>.

Berman, Russell A. "Reform and Continuity: Graduate Education Toward a Foreign Cultural Literacy." *Profession* (1997): 61–74.

Breiner-Sanders, Karen E., Elvira Swender, and Robert M. Terry. *Foreign Language Annals* 35.1 (2002): 9–15.

Cárdenas, Karen. "Technology in Today's Classroom: It Slices and It Dices, but Does It Serve Us Well?" *Academe* 84.3 (May–June 1998): 27–29.

Easthope, Antony. *Literary into Cultural Studies.* London: Routledge, 1991.

Ehrmann, Stephen C. "Technology's Grand Challenges." *Academe* 85.5 (September–October 1999): 42–46.

Miller, Pat. "My Life as an Infomercial: On Time, Teaching, and Technology." *Profession* (2001): 137–41.

Monegal, Antonio. "La pantalla de papel: Proyecciones intertextuales, o la economía del préstamo." *Letras Peninsulares* 7.1 (spring 1994): 185–92.

Montes-Huidobro, Matías. "Análisis fílmico-literario de *Los santos inocentes.*" *Letras Peninsulares* (spring 1994): 293–311.

Newson, Janice. "Techno-Pedagogy and Disappearing Context." *Academe* 85.5 (September–October 1999): 52–55.

Petrey, Sandy. "When Did Literature Stop Being Cultural?" *Diacritics: A Review of Contemporary Criticism* 28.3 (1998): 12–22.

Phillips, June K., project dir. *Standards for Foreign Language Learning in the 21st Century: Including Chinese, Classical Languages, French, German, Italian, Japanese, Portuguese, Russian, & Spanish.* Lawrence, KS: Allen, 1999.

Reichelt, Melinda. "A Critical Review of Foreign Language Writing Research on Pedagogical Approaches." *Modern Language Journal* 85.4 (winter 2001): 578–98.

Tomasulo, Frank P. "Resources for Teaching Film and Video Courses." 18 October 1999 <http://www.cinemastudies.org/temp.htm>. First published in *Cinema Journal* 34.4 (summer 1995): 71–88.

Zatlin, Phyllis. "From Stage to Screen: Transformations of Twentieth-Century Spanish Theater." *Letras Peninsulares* 7.1 (spring 1994): 119–42.

Veiling Practices, Invisibility, and Knowledge Production in the Documentary Films of Trinh T. Minh-ha, Barbara Hammer, and Lourdes Portillo

ADRIENNE McCORMICK

> What is one to do with films that set out
> to determine the truth from falsity while
> the visibility of this truth lies precisely
> in the fact that it is false?
>
> TRINH T. MINH-HA,
> *When the Moon Waxes Red* (1991)

Film is not just an accessory but a central component of several of the courses I teach: Drama and Film, and Women and Film, for example. But as each year passes, film takes a more and more central place in my Introduction to Women's Studies, Feminist Theory, Multiethnic American Literature, Black Women Writers, and Major Women Novelists courses as well. In a culture thoroughly saturated in the visual, students enter college classrooms with an arsenal of reading experiences rooted in the visual that thoroughly overpowers their engagement with written texts. Finding ways to enhance their reading skills when they encounter visual texts, and to translate those visual reading skills into broader critical literacies, are two of the key goals I set for myself in utilizing film in the classroom.

Of course, the encounter with visual texts is much more complex than this, and the larger challenges include how to successfully teach critical thinking and reading skills, and raise awareness about the extent to which visual modes of representation are steeped in social, cultural, and political ideologies. This is where I find the documentary film most useful, regardless of the particular classroom setting into which it is incorporated. In the 200-level Drama and Film, for example, pairing Trinh Minh-ha's documentary filmmaking practices with the plays of Bertolt Brecht leads to invaluable learning experiences. While many of my colleagues despair of teaching Brecht to undergraduates at the 200-level, especially when they are not English majors (as many in this general education course are not), I have had success largely due to the interesting pairing of Brecht's plays with Trinh's films. Teaching Brecht's *Mother Courage and Her Children*, for example, beside either Trinh's *Shoot for the Contents* (1991) or *Surname Viet Given Name Nam* (1989) foregrounds how both Brecht and Trinh utilize a variety of techniques to distract viewers from becoming emotionally sutured onto the particular form of visual representation (play or film) they view. The tactics that characterize Brecht's epic theater resonate in many ways with the veiling practices Trinh utilizes in her documentaries (which I discuss at length later in this chapter); each set of techniques interrupts the passive viewers' desire to sponge information from the visual image before them, and requires instead that spectators position themselves as critical readers intellectually engaging with and questioning what they view.[1] Yes, undergraduates find this one of the most challenging units of the course, but they get it. And more importantly, they take away from this unit a different awareness of themselves as spectators, as readers of visual texts. My pedagogy in this class continually returns to the question of how knowledge is produced through visual representations, in the theater and on film. Does a film or a play package information for its audience to passively absorb, or does it present itself in such a way as to engage and position audience members as active agents in the production of knowledge?

Experimental documentary filmmaking practices such as Trinh's are also incredibly useful in Introduction to Women's Studies, Feminist Theory, and Women and Film classrooms. While Trinh questions the use of any labels in fixing her work as either "experimental," "feminist," or "third world," her films exemplify feminist theorizing in numerous ways. In keeping with contemporary feminist theorizing both globally and in the United States, Trinh challenges overly simplistic categories rooted in false binaries such as first and third world feminist, and produces more complex approaches to differences that are situated at the intersections of race, class, gender, national, and sexual power relations. She refuses simplicity, singularity, and any too-easy politics of identification; she advocates complex understandings of difference, of context, and of how meanings (gendered, racial, national) are shifting and embedded in relations of power.

The image of the veil is but one example of a culturally fraught symbol with which Trinh and the other filmmakers mentioned in this chapter engage. She neither embraces the veil as a total symbol of women's repression, nor espouses an apolitical relativism in her readings and visual positionings of veil-images. Thus, her use of veil-images and veiling practices are immensely beneficial in classrooms where multiple, supple approaches to feminist thought and documentary filmmaking practices are taught, and where issues of political agency and cultural relativism are at issue.

The analyses of veil-images and veiling practices in this chapter arose organically from my teaching experiences in the classes mentioned above. Seeing these images over and over again led me to start asking myself and my students whether or not there are similarities between their separate realizations. I also ask why women directors are using veil-images, and what these images allow these directors to explore. To list a few examples of what I mean by veil-images and veiling practices, I could begin with Anne Marie Fleming's *You Take Care Now* (1989)—an experimental documentary that "documents" a woman's experiences being raped in Brindisi and run over by a car in Vancouver.[2] Several scenes feature a woman's body tightly wrapped in a shroud-like veil as the body bends and sways near a body of water. A man, whose back is to the camera, looks on. In one scene, the veiled body is prone on the ground and Fleming has hand-painted lines onto the celluloid surface of the film, lines that further surround and veil the woman, circumscribing her motions. The veil-images and veiling practices here suggest the resulting invisibility and immobility the woman experiences after these two separate violent episodes. Another example can be found in Ngozi Onwurah's *The Body Beautiful* (1991), in which Onwurah uses veils and sheers as set dressings the camera must peer through in order to see one of the most controversial scenes: the fantasy sex sequence in which the filmmaker's actual mother, Madge Onwurah, has a sexual encounter with a young black man. Madge is white, in her sixties, overweight, has had a mastectomy, and suffers from rheumatoid arthritis. Hers is far from the "body

beautiful." The veiling practice here alludes to the complexities of spectatorship, voyeurism, fantasy, and the layers of mediation and positioning—
along the lines of gender, race, ability, age, sexuality—to which all cinematic
gazes are subject.[3] A third example can be found in Mona Hatoum's
Measures of Distance, an experimental pseudo-documentary composed of still
photographs of the filmmaker's nude mother. The images are always slightly
out of focus, and also always veiled by Arabic script that covers the visual
images on-screen. While functioning as a kind of veil over the woman's
body, the script evokes images of barbed wire while the text recounts the
family's experiences with Palestinian exile, male ownership of female sexuality, and barriers between mother/daughter intimacy.[4]

Two more documentaries I could include in this chapter, but which
would require an entire chapter of their own, are Tania Kamal-Eldin's
Covered: The Hejab in Cairo, Egypt (1995) and Claire Hunt and Kim
Longinotto's *Hidden Faces* (1990). Both documentaries overtly address the
practice of veiling in Egypt, and utilize numerous techniques to question the
political ramifications of veiling for Muslim women. What is most interesting about these two films is the degree to which they remain unaware of the
filmmaking apparatus itself as having the power to veil and unveil the mind
of the viewer. While directly addressing the politics of veiling in Egyptian
culture, Kamal-Eldin and Hunt and Longinotto fail to push the boundaries
of the documentary form to a position where they might examine how their
own filmmaking practices reveal veiling effects. Kamal-Eldin's film includes
interviews with a variety of Muslim women, both veiled and unveiled, as
well as with Muslim religious authorities who defend the practice. But the
film fails to include in interview form any outright challenges to the practice of veiling, opting instead for a more culturally relativist positioning as
the counterpoint to those who defend the practice.[5] Similarly, Hunt and
Longinotto include numerous, sensational images of veiled women, obviously designed to portray the practice as oppressive. But the voice-overs and
interviews in the film again do little to examine the politics of veiling in all
of its complexity. And, as is the case with Kamal-Eldin's film, Hunt and
Longinotto's documentary remains completely unaware of itself as such,
going even so far as to film another documentary crew in Egypt talking to
Dr. Nawal el Saadawi, whom the directors of this film also interview, but
never reflecting on their own filmmaking practice. This is unfortunate, or

perhaps understandable, due to the hostility with which the film subjectively positions Dr. el Saadawi.[6] The politics of veiling in these two films could fill an entire chapter, but they are worth mentioning to illustrate the richness and complexity that characterize contemporary feminist documentaries on the topic of veiling alone. All of these examples taken together reveal that veil-images and veiling practices are not limited to singular manifestations. They are evident in, but not limited to, literal fabrics that function as veils and produce veil-images; metaphoric symbols that represent the layers of mediation through which the camera always looks; and abstract representations that reveal how social, political, and cultural relationships veil, obscure, and mediate the production of knowledge about nationalities, histories, sexualities, ethnicities, and genders.

Examples of veil-images and veiling practices are especially noticeable in films directed by Trinh Minh-ha, who theorizes quite extensively about her uses of the veil-image in relation to voyeurism, filmmaking genres, identities, and gender. The remainder of this chapter examines Trinh's theories of the veil-image, and how they intersect with her work on identity and authenticity, the filmmaking apparatus, and the in/visibility of knowledge production in documentary film. A close reading of Trinh's *Shoot for the Contents* (1991), followed by a shorter reading of her most recent film, *A Tale of Love* (1995), reveals the extent to which Trinh's theories of identity/authenticity, and of the filmmaking apparatus, intersect with veil-images and veiling practices. Trinh's theories provide a useful means of reading Barbara Hammer's documentary *Nitrate Kisses* (1992)—which examines how gay and lesbian histories and sexualities are erased from historical memory—as well as Lourdes Portillo's "melodocumystery" *The Devil Never Sleeps* (1996)—which prods the edges of documentary, narrative, and autobiography as the filmmaker investigates her own uncle's death in Mexico.[7]

Trinh Minh-ha's work is crucial to any discussion of veiling practices in feminist documentary filmmaking. Indeed, she functions as her own film critic and theorist in that she writes numerous essays and grants many interviews addressing her filmmaking practices. Furthermore, her filmscripts are easy to access, making her work a key body of visual and textual information upon which to theorize more generally about women's documentary filmmaking and the veiling practices and veil-images found therein.

One of Trinh's key tasks in her films and in her theorizing is to render *more visible* how the filmic apparatus works to produce meaning, and by extension, to render *less visible* the contents of documentary films that are usually positioned as fixed, factual, and authoritative. Veil-images and veiling practices are key tools utilized by Trinh in approaching these tasks, and can be found working in complementary manners in the films of Hammer and Portillo. Each filmmaker is concerned with how knowledges are made more or less in/visible through documentary filmmaking practices, and how those same knowledges get constructed around shifting national, gendered, sexual, ethnic, and historical narratives. Reading Trinh together with Hammer and Portillo is fruitful for a number of reasons. Hammer and Portillo take very different approaches to veil-images and veiling techniques, so provide for a range of discussion. Furthermore, their films reveal a more sustained use of veil-images and veiling practices and connect them more directly to the production of documentary filmmaking itself than the other films mentioned at the beginning of this chapter do. Thus, the links between Hammer and Portillo and Trinh's theorizing are most generative to explore. The importance of these three filmmakers combined in the classroom stems from their consistent moves to interfere with the tendency of spectators to fix the meaning of the Other as portrayed in documentary film or any filmic representation. Trinh, Hammer, and Portillo—each in her own way and using her own techniques—require critical thinking of their audiences, instilling in them a healthy skepticism for filmic representations which portray themselves as objective, as *merely documenting* or *transmitting* meanings rather than *actively constructing* meanings and knowledge about their subjects.

One final note before I discuss Trinh's theorizing more directly. Trinh's veiling practices and her theories on filmmaking in general constitute an important contribution to contemporary feminist theorizing about the female spectator. A central concept in feminist film theory, the female spectator has been the subject of many feminist film critics' attentions. Inquiries regarding the female spectator began in response to Laura Mulvey's 1975 article "Visual Pleasure and Narrative Cinema" published in the British journal *Screen*—an article which was largely silent on the female spectator in comparison to its trenchant feminist psychoanalytic analysis of the male spectator in relation to concepts of voyeurism and scopophilia. Mulvey sparked many responses, especially in the form of attempts to theorize the/a female spectator on whom Mulvey was silent (since that was not her primary concern). Linda Williams asked what happens "When the Woman Looks," the title of an important essay that asks basic questions about female spectatorship. In *Women and Film: Both Sides of the Camera* (1983), E. Ann Kaplan asked "is the gaze male?" Kaplan also responded with concern to Mulvey's call for the elimination of visual pleasure in cinematic representation (Mulvey 15–16; Kaplan 33). In her most recent book, *Looking for the Other: Feminism, Film, and the Imperial Gaze* (1997), Kaplan extends her consideration of the female spectator by differentiating between an oppressive, male gaze that is not reciprocal, and a more fluid "look" that can be attributed to male and female spectators, and which is complicated in its movements along the lines of class, national, gender, ethnic, racial, and sexual affiliations (xvi–xix). Larger debates that stemmed from Mulvey's discussion tended to shift between psychoanalytic readings of the female spectator—which were frequently ahistorical and limited to theorizings of the white spectator—and more ethnographic, sociologically based readings—which frequently failed to complicate their approaches to women's "real" experiences.[8] Trinh's contribution to the discussion of the female spectator is important for the manner in which she bridges these divisions (though I am not claiming that she is necessarily the first to do so). She cannot be categorized into any particular theoretical camp; she posits neither a strict psychoanalytic model for the female spectator, nor relies solely on ethnography. Rather, she combines contemporary theoretical frameworks with situated attention to "actual" representations of her subjects. In doing so, she produces filmic representations that open up new possibilities for conceptualizing how the female spectator looks, when she looks, and why—in her own films as well as in the films of other women directors such as Hammer and Portillo.

TRINH MINH-HA ON IDENTITY, AUTHENTICITY, AND DOCUMENTARY IN THE FILMMAKING APPARATUS

The title sequence of Trinh T. Minh-ha's film *Shoot for the Contents* (1991) begins with the word "*SHOOT*" accompanied by a gunshot and the sound of breaking glass. The words "*FOR THE*" flash on the screen barely long enough to be seen, followed by "*CONTENT*," which remains on the screen a few seconds before scrolling off to the left. It then scrolls back on from the left, and an "S" comes on from the right so that the word reads "*CONTENTS.*"

In this first image, Trinh exposes the viewer to a set of practices that will continue throughout the film: first, the sequence emphasizes the word-play on "shoot," which resonates in terms of shooting to kill, "shooting" a film, and shooting as in guessing or divining (shoot for, guess, or divine the answers/contents, an actual Chinese game the film addresses); second, the sequence introduces an emphasis on and interrogation of the nature of content(s). The speed with which the words, "*FOR THE,*" enter and leave the visual space emphasizes the multiple relationships between the key words "shoot" and "content(s)": the title can be read as either *Shoot for the Contents,* or more directly, *Shoot Contents.* Trinh's title places under fire the notion that filmmakers have unmediated access to a "real" as a known and knowable set of contents which can be reproduced without distortion for a viewing audience. The game and the title of the film provide the first veiling practice. What Trinh emphasizes is how the camera as the film-making apparatus necessarily veils the content of the film, mediating it and obscuring it before it is ever presented to an audience. The title sequence insists that filmmaking is as indeterminate a process, as constituted and constituting, as the game of divination from which the title is taken, a game in which the contents of the boxes are always veiled by the external materials surrounding the thing itself inside.

Trinh's *Shoot* examines notions of documentary and scientific objectivity, as well as modes of narrative representation and how they intersect with documentary knowledge production. In targeting traditional documentary practices, Trinh theorizes and enacts filmmaking techniques that undermine the manner in which visual representation has been used in anthropological and ethnographic filmmaking practices to fix ethnic and cultural others into positions of "identity-authenticity" (*Woman* 89).[9] In writing this, Trinh challenges notions of the "expert anthropologist," such as Bronislaw Malinowski, who positions himself as the objective observer who can capture and make knowable the (usually) savage other.[10] In contradiction to this notion, Trinh points out that "[w]hat a man looks for . . . [in anthropology/ethnography/documentary] is fortunately what he always/never finds: a perfect reflection of himself" (*Woman* 59). The fantasy this relationship reveals is that if the other's representation corresponds without mediation to a "real" (identity-authenticity), then the self looking at the other corresponds to a "real" as well. This is the key notion Trinh seeks to destabilize. Trinh's critique is in concert with Peggy Phelan's discussion of the many manifestations of "the real," in which she argues that "the very proliferation of discourses [of the real] can only disable the possibility of a 'Real-real'" (3). What both seek to do is locate more supple positions relative to representation than contemporary film and psychoanalytic theories allow.

While I do not intend to develop a psychoanalytic focus on Trinh's work, these comments on the real and how they relate to the filmic gaze and spectatorship bear mentioning to contextualize the projects Trinh engages in. In taking issue with the "self-see(k)ing" cinematic look of the Western anthropologist/ethnographer, Trinh's work engages with Jacques Lacan's theories of the Real and the gaze. Feminist film theorist Jacqueline Rose provides a useful summary of Lacan's theory of the Real as rooted in a sense of loss; this loss stems from the subject's transition from the realm of the Imaginary to the realm of the Symbolic (54). The Imaginary is characterized by "the ego and its identifications" (54), as well as by the "myth" of the mirror stage and its misrecognition of the "smoothness and totality" of the self (53). The Symbolic refers to the realm of language, and the lost sense of plenitude the subject experiences after the transition from one stage to the other. In reference to Lacan, Rose writes that "the real was then his term for the moment of impossibility onto which both [the Imaginary and the Symbolic] are grafted" (54), or, in other words, the Real is "the point of the subject's confrontation with an endlessly retreating reality" (183). Slavoj Zizek further elucidates the "impossibility" of the real in relation to its paradoxical status: "the paradox of the Lacanian Real, then, is that it is an entity which, although it does not exist (in the sense of 'really existing,' taking place in reality), has a series of properties—it exercises a certain structural causality, it can produce a series of effects in the symbolic reality of subjects" (163). Thus Lacan's theories of the "Real" relate to processes of identification in complex ways. The subject seeks the plenitude of the Imaginary and the mirror stage, the loss of which produces the subject's desire for the Real, which is "forever impossible to realize (to make real) within the frame of the Symbolic" (Phelan, *Unmarked* 3). But the subject keeps trying anyway, and this is where Trinh's concern with the spectator of ethnographic documentaries relates to Lacan's theories of the Real and how they intersect with his theories of the gaze.[11] Lacan describes the gaze in *The Four Fundamental Concepts of Psycho-analysis* (1978): "In our relation to things, in so far as this relationship is constituted by the way of vision, and ordered in the figures of representation, something slips, passes, is transmitted, from stage to stage, and is always eluded in it . . ." (73). This slippage refers to the inability of the subject to satisfy the desire to get back to the pre-Symbolic self, the realm of the "Imaginary," which in turn "explains" the dynamics of the Western subject fixing its gaze on the ethnic/cultural other in an attempt to see "himself." Thus, as Phelan writes, the "gaze guarantees the *failure* of self-seeing" (15), or as Lacan writes, "I am unable to see myself from the place where the Other is looking at me" (*Scilicet* 120; quoted in Phelan 15). This (albeit oversimplified) explanation of the Lacanian gaze does nothing to affect change in the existing structures between self and other, and in effect, preserves the look of the (Western) self at an (ethnic/cultural) other: "the (failed) desire for a reciprocal gaze keeps the looker looking" (Phelan 21). Here is where Phelan and Trinh's concerns overlap the most. Phelan wants to challenge any notion of visibility as power, for as she astutely points out, "if representational visibility equals power, then almost-naked young white women should be running Western culture" (10). This is obviously not the case. Trinh also problematizes easy assumptions about the visibility and representation of identity as providing access to empowerment for marginalized groups of people.[12] Thus, Phelan's theories of the visible and Trinh's cinematic praxis complicate any theory of a "Real-real," and particularly, of a cinematic/representational real that purports to have access to the other's identity and mimics the function of the gaze in fixing ethnic and cultural others.

In *When the Moon Waxes Red* (1991), Trinh states that "there is no such thing as documentary—whether the term designates a category of material, a genre, an approach, or a set of techniques. This assertion—as old and as fundamental as the antagonism between names and reality—needs incessantly to be restated despite the very visible existence of a documentary tradition" (29). In Trinh's theorizing, there is no such thing as documentary that communicates a real, or actual, set of events or facts in an unmediated presentation. This is a crucial point to emphasize in the classroom, since young people are trained by today's visual culture to absorb rather than to question the material that is presented to them, especially through visual images. Television channels based in documentary modes of representation permeate contemporary cable TV, ranging from the Travel Channel and Animal Planet to the Discovery, Learning, and History Channels. Students need to gain basic skills in interpreting how many layers of mediation exist between the actual subjects filmed for representation on these channels, and their later re-presentation under the guise of objective documentary, whether in relation to religious practices in India, voting procedures in the United States, or the mating habits of crocodiles in Australia.

Trinh critiques the notion that documentary communicates a "Real-real": "The real? Or, the repeated artificial resurrection of the real, an operation whose overpowering success in substituting the visual and verbal signs of the real for the real itself ultimately helps to challenge the real, thereby intensifying the uncertainties engendered by any clear-cut division between the two" (*Moon* 33). By asking these questions, Trinh coaxes her spectators to extend them to her own work as well: she, too, works within the (Western) filmic apparatus so inextricably rooted in looking. Trinh demands that the spectator—especially the Western spectator—consider how meaning is constructed in Trinh's own films, and in all documentaries by extension. Quoting Barthes, she writes:

> *The West moistens everything with meaning, like an authoritarian religion which imposes baptism on entire peoples* (Roland Barthes).[13] Yet such illusion is real; it has its own reality, one in which the subject of Knowledge, the subject of Vision, or the subject of Meaning continues to deploy established power relations, assuming Himself to be the basic reserve of reference in the totalistic quest for the referent, the true referent that lies out there in nature, in the dark, waiting patiently to be unveiled and deciphered correctly. (*Moon* 50)

Trinh's documentaries work against this project of finding the "true referent," of totalizing quests, and especially of unveiling and deciphering the object, or the Other. She uses many formal techniques to achieve this project, but the elements I am most concerned with are her use of veiling practices and veil-images, and her attention to modes of looking and spectatorship on-screen, as well as between the screen and the audience.

The relationship between the looking subject and the looked-at other, particularly when the two stand in different cultural or ethnic spaces, is a primary concern of Trinh's in each of her films.[14] Whereas mainstream documentaries frequently establish themselves as unmediated records of objective truth (the represented is the real), with the interviewed/documented other fixed in terms of a single, unified, and knowable identity,

Trinh's films focus on how the mediation of film provides a milieu for using the falsity of representation as a tool for exploration.[15] That which is open for exploration is a multiplicity of identities, truths, meanings: "Difference in such an insituable context is *that which undermines the very idea of identity,* deferring to infinity the layers whose totality forms 'I'" (Trinh, *Woman* 96).

Trinh's interrogation of how film represents the "real" through her use of veil-images and veiling practices results in a questioning of any monolithic concept of truth, a concept that has significant currency in today's cultural debates on historical revisionism. When I first became familiar with Trinh's work in 1995, questions such as whose version of historical or cultural events is "true" or "accurate" appeared daily in the *Washington Post* and on local news stations in Washington, D.C., in references to the "commemorations" of the fiftieth anniversary of the bombing of Hiroshima and the twentieth anniversary of the fall of Saigon. Who has the right to represent such cultural signifiers as the Enola Gay or the role the American government played in the Vietnam War? If revision is happening, what "truth" is being revised? This mode of inquiry provides rich material for classroom debate. Such questions take center stage in our attempts to determine which version of history should be "documented," and thus made official. A more contemporary example of a "current event" that is subject to multiple interpretations is the election of George W. Bush as president in 2000. *The Nation* recently featured a cover story focusing on this very topic, the subjective interpretation of events following election day 2000 and leading up to Bush's inauguration. This particular history can be documented in any number of ways. The debates surrounding these events themselves acknowledge the possibility for multiple readings and representations of history; the dynamics behind these questions compose a key concern of Trinh's theoretical and filmmaking aesthetic(s).[16] For example, her film *Surname Viet Given Name Nam* (1989) looks specifically at how Vietnam is represented through visual images. She stays away from stock war footage, and focuses instead on juxtaposing images of human suffering from the Vietnam War with contemporary footage from the country in the 1980s. The same technique is evident through *Shoot for the Contents*, especially in her refusal to include stock media images of the Tiananmen Square uprising while her narrators discuss it. The absence of

these images requires the spectators to engage with the narratives surrounding Vietnam and the democracy uprising in China in different contexts than those produced by mainstream media. She wants to present
complexities and contradictions, not the denuded "content" (such as the
Enola Gay without any accompanying written text) or the stock image
(such as the lone student facing down a row of tanks). One final comment
on this issue: it is noteworthy that the text that was to accompany the
exhibit of the Enola Gay in 1995 was considered so controversial in its treatment of the plane's history that the director of the Smithsonian Air and
Space Museum was eventually dismissed. However, a short documentary
film was produced that was considered safe enough in its modes of representation to include in the exhibit. The film included interviews with the
crew of the plane, and their reflections on their role in ending the war.[17]
The assumptions about the film as objective, and the written text as subjective, are unmistakable.

However, Trinh makes it clear that her practices are not simply "anti-
documentarian," as they are often characterized (Wallis 61).[18] In an interview, Trinh states, "Breaking rules is not my main concern since this still
refers to rules" (qtd. in Penley and Ross 95). Trinh argues that the "claim for
an ethnic and/or female identity is necessary at a certain stage of the feminist fight, [for] it helps us to beat the Master at his game. But it is not an end
in itself" (qtd. in Penley and Ross 103). Making identity an "end" creates an
ideal situation for Western voices to say, "We no longer wish to erase your
difference, [sic] We demand, on the contrary, that you remember and assert
it" (Woman 89). Thus the ethnic/woman finds herself restricted again within
a discourse defined and controlled by a Western cultural viewpoint. The
question of Trinh's positioning with "the feminist fight" itself is closely
linked to her work on the problem of "identity-authenticity." The ramifications of her bid to redesign the economies of exchange between the
Western self-see(k)ing viewer and the (usually ethnic) other extend beyond
a critique of Western anthropological and ethnographic filmmaking practices to feminist documentary practices as well. Trinh writes that if "feminism is set forth as a demystifying force, then it will have to question
thoroughly the belief in its own identity" (Woman 96). The theme of
"consciousness-raising" that characterizes many feminist documentary films
in the 1970s and 1980s remains rooted in questionable notions of "giving

voice to," "accessibility," and the possibility of *cinéma vérité,* or representing "women's real environments" (Lesage 229, 234–35).[19] From the mid-1980s on, Trinh has been asking of such a feminist aesthetic: Who gives voice to whom? To (for) whom are these films made accessible, and how?[20] The use of "realistic" techniques in the feminist documentaries of the late 1960s and early 1970s is understandable as a claim for an identity in the early stage of that "feminist fight," just as it was in the early stage of the fight for an ethnic and/or female identity. One good example of a feminist documentary shot in a realistic format in the 1980s is Johanna Demetrakas's *Right Out of History: The Making of Judy Chicago's Dinner Party* (1980). Demetrakas's documentary is a wonderful tool for teaching about early feminist collective activism and techniques related to consciousness raising, but the self-reflexivity found within the art collective is not reflected at all in the film-making techniques. Such traditional documentary forms certainly have their place and time, but to promulgate *cinéma vérité* as a viable aesthetic for ongoing feminist documentaries—without any self-reflexivity on the role of the apparatus in shaping the realities portrayed—is to attempt to "dismantle the master's house" while using "the master's tools" (*Woman* 80).[21] Both embrace a notion of filmic objectivity that produces gaps in their documentaries, especially in moments where subjectivity most obviously shapes the selection of shots, the voice-over, or the interviewees chosen for the films.

According to the "Great Masters" of anthropological discourse, such as Malinowski, the tools of anthropological and ethnographic practice posit, and indeed demand, objectivity as a means of looking at the other. Trinh argues and reveals through her film that such looking is impossible. In *Moon,* Trinh writes:

> The real world: so real that the Real becomes the one basic referent— pure, concrete, fixed, visible, all-too-visible. The result is the elaboration of a whole aesthetic of objectivity and the development of comprehensive technologies of truth capable of promoting what is right and what is wrong in the world, and by extension, what is "honest" and what is "manipulative" in documentary. (33)

In order to counter this "aesthetic of objectivity," Trinh cannot simply posit an "aesthetic of subjectivity." To do so would be to remain within a binary that, if it values objectivity as truth, must value subjectivity as lies, or untruth.

In order to avoid such a limitation, Trinh locates her work in the field of representation, takes the apparatus and makes it highly visible, and thus exposes the lack of reciprocity between the visual image and any fixed identity or "real." To illustrate this disjuncture, Trinh utilizes numerous veil-images and veiling practices. These are not reducible to singular readings, readings which tend to read veils as oppressive for women: "the veil is oppressive, but it can also become a form of resistance . . . the way we all partake in the politics and aesthetics of veiling is complex and often paradoxical" (Trinh, *Cinema Interval* 239). The paradoxical veil provides Trinh with a supple tool for examining how the act of looking is always mediated on film and in the process of filmmaking. The veil obscures what is seen, while also drawing attention to, making more visible, filmic modes of looking. The following sections of this essay examine several of Trinh's veiling practices in both *Shoot for the Contents* (1991) and *A Tale of Love* (1995), and explore Trinh's theories of veiling in relation to Barbara Hammer's *Nitrate Kisses* (1992) and Lourdes Portillo's *The Devil Never Sleeps* (1995). After reading these four films, what emerges is a set of veiling practices that force the audience to consider the complex interrelationships between gendered spectatorship and voyeurism, un/covered sexualities and histories, and especially how knowledge about each is recorded and reconstructed.

UN/VEILING AUTHENTIC IDENTITIES AND HISTORIES IN *SHOOT FOR THE CONTENTS* (1991)

Veiling practices are central to Trinh's theorizing of narrative and documentary modes of representation. Each of her films utilizes veiling practices in different modes and degrees. These veils are not all literal, nor are they all symbols of oppression. Trinh theorizes a relationship between visible likeness and a concept of the invisible life force of things in one particular scene in *Shoot for the Contents* (1991). Three women wearing traditional Chinese dresses with long, extended sleeves dance behind a blue, backlit screen.[22] The screen functions as a veil between the camera and the "contents" it shoots, as well as between the spectator and the subjects of the documentary. The scene begins with the following commentary by "performer" Ying Lee-Kelly, or Voice 1: "What is manifestly real to some eyes looks strangely stiff and conventional to others. You do not catch the vital spirit of things in formal likeness, said Chang Yen-Yuan of the T'ang period. What seems unrealistic may transmit the life force of things in ways no mastery of their visible likeness can" (*CI* 160). Voice 1 is not "present" at the dance, thus the commentary works both with and against the visual image of the women dancing. Using the screen as a veil-image emphasizes the many mediating factors between what is purportedly seen as "real" and what the camera represents. The women appear more complex than when they were filmed earlier in the sequence without the mediating screen/veil. Their sleeves—accentuated by slow motion—hover over and around their bodies, evoking images not only of dancing women, but of Chinese textual brushstrokes and of the dragon bodies that are drawn in several other instances in the film. Trinh's shooting here reveals the complex layers of representation at work in any particular shot. In an interview titled "The Veil-Image," Trinh comments that "what we have in the film-viewing process is the layering of one kind of veil over another, or the encounter of an indefinite number of screens: mind screen reacting to film screen, and to other mind and body screens" (*CI* 77). Every image seen is viewed through a screen, Trinh asserts. In this image, she makes the screen literal, and reveals that the screens we look through always mediate what we see. The women are transformed into abstractions; the mind-screens we look through also transform what we see (women, for example) according to the social forces that have shaped the screen. If we think of the cinematic apparatus as a screen through which all filmed subjects are viewed, then we must acknowledge that the subjects have likewise been transformed through that viewing practice.

Just as the screen reveals the mediation of the camera, the juxtaposition of the voice-over with the image on the screen reveals the mediation of the spoken as well as the seen:

... There is a tendency to apprehend language exclusively as Meaning. IT HAS TO MAKE SENSE. WE WANT TO KNOW WHAT THEY THINK AND HOW THEY FEEL. (*Moon* 59–60)

Images, not only images, but images and words that defy words and commentary.[23]

This passage reveals Trinh's dedication to juxtaposing multiple discourses. Just as these two columns speak to and against each other on the page, the image of the women dancing in *Shoot* speaks to and against the spoken words, defying their "meaning" and the "Meaning" of commentary in general. The presence of the screen as a veil-image, and the analogous mediating subjectivities of Voice 1 and the filmmaker, force the viewer to ask, "what *is* manifestly real?"[24] What is *the,* or *a,* vital spirit, and according to whose definition?

Trinh establishes a defiance and questioning of objectivity when she offers the following as the first exchange between the two voices/narrators of the film:

> VOICE 1: Any look at China is bound to be loaded with questions.
> VOICE 2: Her visible faces are minuscule compared to her unseen ones. [A few seconds of silence elapse before the voice continues] Or . . . is this true? (*CI* 152)

The question accompanies the camera's slow pan over a group of Chinese men and women in a public space playing table games, socializing, and with some (significantly) looking into the camera.[25] The use of some of China's "visible faces" looking directly into the camera does more than add self-reflexivity to Trinh's project. Such self-reflexivity can be found in many ethnographic studies that do not seek to realign the act of looking in the way Trinh does. In fact, James Clifford uses just such an example in the opening paragraph of his chapter "On Ethnographic Authority" in *The Predicament of Culture* (1988). He describes a picture from Malinowski's *Argonauts of the Western Pacific* (1922), in which a "native" stares into the camera. Clifford identifies this stare as evidence that the "predominant mode of modern fieldwork authority is signaled: 'You are there . . . because I was there' " (22). Though he questions Malinowski's authority in this example, Clifford's argument is not one that ultimately challenges authority, but one that relocates it. Clifford elevates self-reflexivity as exemplary of "scientific rigor" and the ethnographer's methodological authority; what his version precludes is a concept of self-reflexivity in filmmaking which "prevent[s] meaning from ending with what is said and what is shown— as inquiries into production relations—thereby challeng[ing] representation itself while emphasizing the reality of the experience of film" (Trinh, *Moon* 46, 47). Trinh does not pursue a mode of reflexivity that simply validates information-gathering techniques, but one which seeks to expose the constitutedness of subjectivities and filmic techniques as determining meaning at all points along the "ethnographic" spectrum. Trinh discusses these differences in *Woman, Native, Other* as significant for what they reveal about authoritative discourses, especially in the sciences. Malinowski uses ethnography to solidify his own position of power, more than to promote communication between culturally different groups of people (57). Her critique is informed by much more than a difference of discipline, but reveals how power and language are at play in all disciplines (57).

Immediately after the sequence on China's visible faces, the viewer is introduced to the two Chinese women who function throughout the film as narrators, Voices 1 and 2. Positioned near the beginning of the film, the two women are filmed discussing and then playing a Chinese game called "shoot for the contents," in which the players are given an unlimited number of attempts to ascertain the contents of a closed box. By beginning with these two women and using their voices as "narrators" throughout, Trinh frames the film as a conversation. This framing has two effects: it portrays the entire film as a set of observations, images, and commentaries filtered through the two women's consciousnesses, and it also aligns the making and the viewing of the film with a game of divination. Each subject will divine her own reading of the materials represented. Thus, Trinh represents a cultural "look" that is divorced from structures of authenticity which revolve around the invisibility of filmic techniques (*Moon* 39).

Significantly, their introduction and explanation of the game "shoot for the contents" portrays the two women surrounded by veil-images in the form of white squares constructed of paper.[26] The women are actively cutting the paper to construct even more boxes. The paper and the boxes function as veil-images in that they obscure the contents within the boxes, which the two women "shoot for." In one shot, Ying (Voice 1) actually holds a sheet of paper up over her face, veiling herself from the camera's look. The game, however, is scripted, a common technique of Trinh's. The viewer must always remember in a Trinh film that anything the film appears to be uncovering on one level (such as the dragon that Voice 1 guesses at, or shoots for, in this sequence) is also always being covered, or veiled on another level.[27] At the end of the film, the two women discuss their respective roles as "an activist" (Voice 1) and "an actress" (Voice 2), which further de-emphasizes the narration as objective, or even transparently subjective, and brings in the possibility that the voices "perform" their roles throughout the film. The performativity is evident in how their voices coalesce, agree and disagree, observe and embellish on images seen by the viewer, and tell stories and challenge narratives about China, whether stemming from China or the United States. The voices are not always discernable one from the other, so the listener must struggle to identify the speakers as much as the images seen. In the same conversation at the film's conclusion, the viewer discovers that Voice 1 describes herself as Chinese, but Voice 2 defines herself as "a fourth-generation, American-born Chinese." Their different "identities" do not come through in a pronounced manner in their voices, nor in their dress or physical appearance. In casting them as the "narrator/performers" for the film, Trinh undermines the notion that film can capture an authentic identity through the visible. In fact, after Voice 2 describes herself to Voice 1 and asserts that her parents were "steeped in Chinese culture," Voice 1 asks, "How did they maintain that through three generations? and what does it mean being Chinese?" (*CI* 176). The question can be reformulated as how is meaning constructed, especially in relation to the visible field on screen.

The questioning that Voices 1 and 2 inaugurate continues throughout the film as their conversation and commentaries work together and against each other, thus revealing how the women themselves function as veils that obscure and reveal notions of documentary representation as rooted in visible truths. They refer to various elements in Chinese history and usually disagree in their perceptions of those histories. Voice 1 comments at one point that "there is [*sic*] a thousand trillion Chinas, as a Chinese storyteller would say: the China of people's imagining" (*CI* 153). The two voices, then, put forth only two of many possible versions of Chinese cultural and historical events. There is no unified China represented or representable, nor are these women "unified" representers of China or Chinese culture. The viewer of *Shoot* "sees" China as nothing so much as dynamic: China is a dragon. Voice 1 goes on to elaborate, through the example of the dragon, the difficulties of the type of interrogation Trinh's film enacts:

> Interpreting orientation and form is not without risk, because in the Ancient books, the beast exists in a thousand forms; has ten thousand aspects; stands or crouches; is huge or tiny, unruly or obedient, reserved or extravagant. Infinitely in metamorphosis, it dives deep, rises high, meanders, coils, leaps, and takes its flight. (*CI* 153)

The beast is the imperial dragon, or the dragon representing the "body" of China's histories. The commentary coincides with the visual representation of two artists (two separate scenes) painting dragons; the paintings associate the commentary with artistic, thus artificial, representation. The dragon continues to operate throughout the film in its many manifestations: artistic, mythic, historic.

Another cultural construction the two voices investigate is the figure of Mao Zedong. Voice 1 refers to him as "a son of the earth" who "cultivated many flowers." Voice 2 responds shortly after with her own rendition of the man: "Mao was no peasant. When he immersed himself in manual labor, it wasn't forced labor. He was cultivating his own garden" (*CI* 157). These comments do not correspond to any visual images of Mao. In fact, the film never represents Mao visually at all. Rather, the various instances in which the voice-over/commentary refers to him accompany shots of the Chinese countryside, village life, and often representations of artists and calligraphers depicting dragons and/or Chinese characters. At one point, Voice 2 says, "Dead at last! Without your death China would have gone to pieces." Voice 1 immediately follows, saying, "How dare you!" (*CI* 157). This first interchange reveals that the two voices often do not even speak to each other, since the two statements are intoned without any dialogue or commentary between the two on their disagreement. The second exchange, on the contrary, reveals a response from Voice 2 to Voice 1 (How dare you?).

The references that the voices make to Mao as a cultivator of flowers and as a peasant allude to some of the major rhetorical and political premises of the periods preceding and during the Cultural Revolution. The film refers repeatedly to the speech Mao made in 1956 after the Communist victory and before the Cultural Revolution began: "Let a hundred flowers blossom. Let a hundred schools of thought contend" (*CI* 157). The idealism of the statement is parodied later in the film in an "interview" in which the "interviewee" tries to remember Mao's words and fails: "Mao's let a hundred blossoms, let a hundred flowers blossom, let a hundred something contend" (*CI* 163). The film investigates the multiple representations of both Mao and the Cultural Revolution as cultural signifiers produced by various voices and sources. Shortly after this exchange, Voice 1 comments: "The truth about 'China' is more often than not full of surprises, because ruptures and continuities occur side by side" (*CI* 164). The coming to power of the Communist party and the ensuing Cultural Revolution can be seen both as a break from the past, and by others as a progression; the teller of the tale determines the tale told, translating and transforming meaning(s) with each telling.

Trinh's film communicates this necessary condition of language by placing no more value on a supposedly factual telling of a historical event such as the Cultural Revolution than on the telling of a fable. One example is her inclusion of a Chinese fable in the form of a conversation between an alligator and a frog:

"The Dragon King issued a decree yesterday to the effect that all aquatic animals that have tails are to be beheaded. 'I am an alligator. I weep because I am afraid of death. But thou art a frog and have no tail. Now, why weepest thou, then?' Thereafter he heard the plaintive reply, 'I am indeed fortunate to have no tail at present. But the fact that I did once bear a tail as a tadpole might be recalled!'" (*CI* 165). The inclusion of this tale in the dialogue/polylogue on the Cultural Revolution exemplifies Trinh's inclusion of that which would be termed "non-factual" by objective, anthropological accounts of "the" history of the Cultural Revolution in China. The tale itself functions as an allegory for the experiences of Chinese people whose ideas (tails/tales) did not correspond to those of the party during the Cultural Revolution. This story is accompanied by footage of rice fields and other rural countryside scenes, so again there is no overt representation of the more emotionally inflammatory public parades of the Cultural Revolution.

In several other instances, the two women's voices focus on the 1989 student uprising at Tiananmen Square. Again, the verbal sequence is not accompanied by any of the famous media images from Tiananmen Square, but rather by rural images of China. Voice 2 characterizes the event:

> A thousand-year sleep. A ten day wake. It was a short spring, but a memorable one. For the world wept at the sight of the massacre. Fear was the name of the wild shooting at a crowd. They couldn't distinguish all the different forms, so they were aiming blindly at the contents. That night, China's hundred flowers were again trampled ruthlessly. (*CI* 164)

By linking the student uprising in Tiananmen Square to the "trampling" of the one hundred flowers associated with the Cultural Revolution, Voice 2 identifies a historical continuity between events in the 1960s and those of 1989. But again, the visual image defies the commentary by representing village scenes and rural activities of a Chinese experience at odds with the experience of university students in Beijing. There can be no single, or authentic, "reading" of either the Cultural Revolution or the Tiananmen Square "uprising"/"massacre"/"revolution"; all who record, write, film, or tell of any event, whether the Cultural Revolution or the shootings at Tiananmen Square, will necessarily shape the "meaning" of the event told in ways informed by their own particular political biases and ideological leanings. Thus, the disconnect between the voice-overs and the visual images on-screen at any point in the film functions as a veiling practice. The image seen is linked to the topic of discussion, but is mediated by the camera's and the filmmaker's subjective point of view.

Another important aspect of the commentary on Tiananmen Square is its return to the issues of form and content: not being able to discern the (individual) forms (of students), "they" could only aim blindly at the contents, signifying both the students' words and the students' bodies. The passage implies that if "they" could have discerned the forms, the "shooting" would not have been blind, an argument which resonates in several ways with Trinh's opening sequence and raises the question: what is the alternative to "shooting blindly"? In the context of Tiananmen Square, would discerning the forms have meant that "they" could have shot in a more accurate manner? And if the shooting guns parallel shooting a film, this infers that by recognizing form, a film can be shot in a more "accurate" manner. These resonances seem to be at odds with Trinh's methods of releasing and expanding, not fixing, meaning(s). Yet these questions are not at odds with Trinh's project in the sense that the inclusion of this sequence *extends her critique of unified meanings to her own film*. Not only is there no such thing as a single "authoritative" reading of history, but also, there is no such thing as an "accurate" representation of it. Filmic representation, including hers, is always veiled and veiling regardless of the approach the particular film takes to discerning or eliding the nature of its form.

Trinh develops the analogy between the danger (and power) of shooting guns and shooting films even further in a reference to Mao's words on guns: "Mao said it loud and clear. Political power grows out of the barrel of a gun. Only with guns can the whole world be transformed" (*CI* 165). Considering this reference in terms of the parallel between guns and film, Trinh alludes both to the negative and positive transformational aspects of filmic representation: film can both convince the world of the fixity of the other by keeping invisible the means by which the camera fixes meaning, or it can represent, in an unfixed manner, the other in all of her multiplicity by making visible the apparatus as a location for producing multiple meanings and representations.

A final example of a veiling practice from this film I want to discuss relates to Trinh's use of interviews. Interviews constitute another element of Trinh's filmmaking praxis that is essential to her refusal of "authoritative" and "authentic" representations of culture and history. Trinh works against common ethnographic uses of the interview by not identifying the names or titles of anyone "interviewed" in her films, nor does she use any intertitles to mark the interview or subtitles for the purposes of translation.[28] Interviews are also the only place where Chinese is spoken in the film. The voice-over is all English, and Trinh vacillates between translating and leaving untranslated many of the Chinese interviewees' commentaries. The very first interview features a man singing a Chinese song, which remains untranslated. Later in the film, an interviewer asks a Chinese artist, "Why did you immigrate to the United States?" (*CI* 173). His response is untranslated, an obvious attempt by the film to frustrate the viewer by withholding information that would "inform" the viewer about this particular man's immigration story. Leaving this particular response out highlights, through omission, the many narratives circulating in the United States today about why people immigrate to the United States. The omission is especially poignant given the numbers of Chinese immigrants who are now being smuggled into the United States (and Great Britain) at great risk to their lives.

By manipulating the filmic techniques of framing, focus, light, and language, Trinh distracts from the "interview's" authenticity. These techniques work to call into question the viewer's culpability in attributing authority and identity-authenticity to the proverbial "talking head." The veiling practices evident in her interviews stem from technical manipulations that again make the viewer more aware of the filmic apparatus, and thus less sure of her knowledge of the subject/content being interviewed/shot.

One example of the de-authenticized interview is the scholar trying to remember Mao's one hundred flowers speech discussed above. Though he is not identified in the film as Caribbean, his words draw similarities between "studies" of China and the Caribbean.[29] Thus, Trinh's casting of him expands her frame of reference to include representations of others within what is geographically the "West" but who are still outside; that is to say that they are also on the receiving end of the normative "Western" anthropological and ethnographic looks. The reference to the Caribbean is in a segment of the interview in which the man gives his "reading" of anthropological and ethnographic techniques:

> I also find it very amazing that people can . . . attempt to become experts on another country, whether it's China or the Caribbean. For me it's virtually impossible. I think the most interesting anecdote is that people don't even know themselves. These very experts have to go to a psychiatrist to tell them what's happened to them, what's the matter with them. (*CI* 163)

Although it seems Trinh would agree with the interviewee, his words and comments on psychoanalysis are also subject to veiling practices; as the man talks, another recording of his voice comes on and overlaps with what he is saying on-screen. His synchronized voice becomes less audible as the voice-over continues, thus forcing the viewer/listener to think about which voice she should listen to. The second voice veils the first, aurally signifying the multiple narratives at play in any documentary knowledge production. A decision has to be made, a decision mirroring the decisions made by Trinh the filmmaker and scriptwriter in what to include and what to cut. Trinh reveals the multiple levels at which interpretations and meanings are determined by individual choices.

The framing of this interview sequence also undercuts the on-screen speaker's authority. The entire time the man speaks, Trinh moves the camera over his face, from one portion to the next; down to his hand and a burning cigarette; up with the smoke to his bookshelves; from shelf to shelf focusing on particular titles; then back to his face. This movement of the camera results in a heightened awareness of the subjectivity of the camera and the filmmaker and the role that each plays in determining the meaning of the "interview." The "unnatural" motion of the camera thus results in its own "unveiling." The apparatus is rendered more visible through its non-traditional movement, contributing to a veiling effect for the subject, in that the viewer's attention is drawn not to the content of his words, but to the random motion of the camera.

Another "interview" sequence in the film employs even more of the technical tools of filmmaking that are available for determining meaning, and is perhaps more overt as a veiling practice. This time the subject is a male Chinese filmmaker who speaks only in Chinese. Each time he is "interviewed," the screen portrays three figures, none of whom are identified with subtitles. Trinh chooses not to use any subtitles for translation either.

The first sequence places the man and an unidentified woman in chairs with their backs to the camera.[30] They face a green screen with some outlines of vegetation on it. For several moments, the viewer hears the man speaking uninterrupted Chinese, but he does not turn to face the woman beside him. As the voice of a woman begins translating the man's speech ("There is no independent cinema in China"), the camera begins to pan slowly to the right, and a third woman appears, the translator. The positioning of the camera situates the interviewee's head as a veil, covering the face of the translator who faces him and the camera. She sits in a chair facing the man, and as she translates she speaks to the other woman, who appears to be Trinh. Thus, the scene makes visible through a veiling practice three of the levels of mediation through which any interview passes before it reaches the viewer's eye: the speaking subject, the filmmaker, and the translator, who translates, imbues, and alters meaning. In this scene, the translator's face is the only one that is ever seen on-screen.[31] Trinh films that which is usually left invisible: the impact "translation" has on "meaning." When the translator and other mediating factors in filmic representation remain invisible, monolithic concepts of meaning and language remain intact.

Thus, the film returns again to the question of visibility. As Peggy Phelan formulates it, the visual field is a trap, and visibility does not equal access to power. Trinh's film reveals that invisibility has its ties to Western structures of power. Where Phelan exposes representational visibility as a trap, Trinh exposes the invisibility of (the processes of) representation as a trap. But Phelan and Trinh are not "saying" the same thing. Phelan's argument for returning to an "unmarked" position which revalues the unseen and unspoken remains firmly within a binary construction that derives its value in a polar manner: the marked valued, the unmarked not. For Phelan, the unvalued, unmarked position is a position of power. For Trinh, power derives from breaking away from binary formulations of thought: they are as inappropriate to her critical and filmic work as is the Western psychoanalytic paradigm of the self-see(k)ing other. Trinh argues for a multi-polar frame of reasoning, where two poles cannot cancel each other out, and where multiple "meanings" are derived out of a theory of subjectivity which infiltrates all that we do and see. This theory of subjectivity is reflected in her sometimes contradictory use of veiling practices and veil-images. Veiling traditionally signifies something being covered, made less visible, and while Trinh uses her veil-images in this manner in some instances, in others she uses veiling to make more visible the function of the filmic apparatus in constructing meaning. These complexities are even more evident in her next film, *A Tale of Love* (1995).

THE VEIL, VOYEURISM, AND IN/VISIBILITY IN *A TALE OF LOVE* (1995)

For those unfamiliar with the film, *A Tale of Love* tells the story of Kieu, a contemporary Vietnamese American woman living in San Francisco. She works as a writer researching the Vietnamese nationalist poem "The Tale of Kieu," and as a model for a photographer. Veiling practices are numerous in this film; they range from Kieu's literal veiling in her photography sessions with Alikan, where actual veils are used to illustrate his refusal to feature her head in any of his shots, to window curtains, mosquito netting, blindfolds, and the visual matting of camera shots as veils.[32] Trinh's uses of the veil in this film are as complex and sometimes contradictory as these different "fabrications" would suggest, though she retains many of the same approaches to how film produces knowledge about its subjects as seen in *Shoot*.

By having Kieu model for Alikan, Trinh forces the spectator of *A Tale* to consider her own role as a voyeur. Most audience members do not like Alikan; Trinh includes anecdotal evidence of this in her book *Cinema Interval* (1999), where she transcribes a "dialogue between voyeur and voyeur after a screening" (267). One dislikes Alikan because his veiling practices seem too evident; Alikan makes no efforts to hide his dislike for models that look back at him, who do not uphold the traditional relationship of man as voyeur/bearer of the look and woman as object/to-be-looked-at-ness.[33] The second speaker points out to the first that while Alikan is indeed a man on-screen, the photographer he plays and his voyeurism are much less attached to his gender than the first speaker suggests:

—Are you so sure the photographer is a man? It may appear so ultimately. But who's he? The photographer in the film, Alikan, who is a man, or the photographers of the film—the director who is a woman, the co-director who is a man and the director of photography who is a woman, not to mention all the women camera assistants. And what about you? I'm Alikan. We are Alikan.
—Oooh! Isn't that fascinating. . . . I hated Alikan. (*CI* 267)

Alikan does indeed represent the oppressive qualities of the veil and the detestable qualities of the voyeur, but the audience member's disapproval of Alikan implicates herself. The audience member's demand that the film not be self-evident, or transparent, or aware of its fabricatedness, is the same as Alikan's demand that his models not look back. Since the expectation of most spectators is that the film not look back, Alikan is a surrogate for the spectator in the audience. In this film, Trinh seeks to "enhance the inevitably fabricated effect [of the characters' interactions] rather than hiding it . . . I used actors," Trinh states, "but was interested in the intensity of a veiled theatricality, not in naturalistic acting" (*CI* 5). Thus, the spectator's disgruntled response to Alikan is the same as Alikan's disgruntled response to his models when they want to break the naturalism of their poses.[34]

Trinh highlights Alikan's role as a surrogate for the audience member in two scenes where we see Alikan with a blindfold over his eyes engaged in a sexual act with a woman who is also blindfolded. Neither of them can see the other, which emphasizes that it is the audience doing the looking. The audience as voyeur is not a new concept in film theory.[35] However, Trinh's particular take on it is significant for how she utilizes the veil as a tool to illustrate the audience's complicity in voyeurism. To accentuate this complicity, Trinh mattes the scenes with Alikan blindfolded, so that the audience sees this image only in a narrow bar on the screen. The matte serves as a kind of veil, situating the audience member as the voyeur that she is, peeping through an opening in order to watch the sexual act on-screen. Here, the gendered roles are loosened; we see blindfolds as veils over the eyes of the man and the woman on-screen, and we also know that the director and the cinematographer of the film are women.

These scenes complicate the gendering of the spectator and the voyeur as male, as do several others in the film. We also see women watching women

through veils elsewhere in the film. In one scene, a woman approaches a curtained window, and sees the girl next door climbing out of a window to meet
her lover. The actress draws the curtains closed, so that she can continue to
watch through the veil/curtain as the girl meets her lover and drives away.
In another scene, a woman (her aunt) watches Kieu as she bathes herself out-
doors in the moonlight, lifting cups of water from a basin and pouring them
over her skin. There is a voice-over in Vietnamese from "The Tale of Kieu."
The subtitles read:

> A lover's mind is full of the loved one.
>
> Beneath the moon, summer cuckoos cried.
>
> Above the wall, pomegranates kindled fire.
>
> Now, in her chamber, at a leisured hour,
>
> She let the curtain fall for an orchard bath.
>
> Her body stood as Heaven's masterwork. (*CI* 127)

The lines of the poem and the image on-screen evoke the woman's body
as a site of pleasure for women themselves; Kieu revels in the feel of the
water on her skin, and her aunt silently enjoys watching her. Men are
absent from this scene, and the veil is present in the lines of the poem: the
water as the curtain that Kieu lets fall in order to enjoy her own body.

In each of the scenes described above, veils function both to obscure and
reveal women and their sexualities. They are oppressive to the women who
model for Alikan, yet Kieu talks back to Alikan despite the veil, resisting
his attempts to silence her and reduce her to a headless pose. For the audience, the veil functions as a sign of how all images are mediated by the screen,
a key point that Trinh insists upon in each of her films. She is not after a "visible likeness," or a "real," but rather seeks to capture the veil itself as a tool
for emphasizing mediation, illusion, indirection, and unlikeness. The reality of the filmic space is disturbed when characters look directly into the camera, as Kieu does, thus seeing through the veil of the screen. The film seeks
to break the illusion of reality that the screen as veil produces—while also
retaining the aesthetic pleasures that result from producing visual images
through the cinematic apparatus. The presence of the numerous veils in the
film—Kieu's modeling costumes, the netting she sleeps and writes under,
the matted scenes, sheets of water that veil images of Kieu—all of these are

sensual deployments of veiling practices. Appealing to multiple senses through her veiling practices—the touch of water, the smell of perfume, dissonant sounds—complicates singular definitions of the veil as visually oppressive, opening up spaces for filmic resistance. These appeals to the senses also provide for the possibility of multiple pleasures in addition to the visual to occur.

The final comment I'd like to make about Trinh's use of the veil-image before moving on to readings of Hammer and Portillo pertains to her exploration of history. To reiterate points made in relation to *Shoot for the Contents,* Trinh is always examining how the film produces knowledge about groups of people and historical events that constitute a nation's or a people's past. In questioning how these knowledges are produced, she must also question and explore the edges of genre and categorization. She resists discreet units such as "experimental documentary" and "narrative," since, as she argues:

> "experimental" is not a genre and "documentary" does not really exist since everything goes through fictional devices in film. Rather than reverting endlessly to these established categories, I would prefer to speak about different degrees of staged and unstaged material, or about different spaces of resistance—such as that of enriching meaning while divesting it of its power to order images and sound. (*CI* 227–28)

Trinh's films flow from narrative to documentary and back again. There is no central plot driving *A Tale of Love,* nor can it be called a documentary. Yet it juxtaposes narrative moments and historical moments, tearing away the veil that ostensibly exists between the two. *Shoot* demonstrates this tactic especially well, in that the title and the entire film emphasize the degree to which "content" is always "shot for," as in "guessed at" as well as determined by that which the camera "shoots," as illustrated in my earlier comments on Mao, the Cultural Revolution, and the uprising in Tiananmen Square. Trinh destabilizes the narratives that have made up what we call history, and thus emphasizes the impossibility of "speaking about" history through documentary with a singular authority and authenticity. What Trinh does, rather, is "speak nearby," or through a veil, always seeking to "make visible the invisible" (*CI* 218).

UN/VEILED HISTORIES AND SEXUALITIES:
BARBARA HAMMER'S *NITRATE KISSES* (1992)

Hammer's veiling practices differ significantly from Trinh's; whereas Trinh seeks to add obscurity to knowledges that have been perceived in terms that are reductively transparent, Hammer seeks to add clarity to knowledges that have been obscured from popular visual culture. But there are several key similarities between the two as well: 1) Hammer also uses veiling practices to illustrate the veil's oppressive and resistant effects; and 2) she uses the veil to explore how histories and sexualities are mutually silenced, constructed, reconstructed.

Nitrate Kisses opens with a short piece on Willa Cather, which juxtaposes images of a young cross-dressing Cather with two voice-overs that contradict each other: one is the voice of a tour guide who leads visitors around Cather's home in Red Cloud, Nebraska, which erases Cather's history as a lesbian author; the other voice is Sandy Boucher, a feminist author who reinscribes that history.[36] The images on-screen are torn photographs being reassembled, as a history that has been erased is also being reassembled. Hammer relies heavily upon Walter Benjamin's "Theses on the Philosophy of History" in the film, using intertitles with several quotations, including the oft-quoted "Nothing that has ever happened should be regarded as lost for history" (254). The early sequence on Cather presages the focus of the entire film upon the loss of lesbian and gay histories in a visual culture firmly rooted in heterosexist representations. The final image we see in the Cather sequence, after numerous photographs of Cather have been reassembled, are strips of lace being reassembled into a veil-image over the camera. Veiling the screen with lace represents the covering and uncovering of lesbian and gay histories which the film exposes.

Another veiling sequence that is crucial in the development of this film involves the use of text as a veil over the image on the screen.[37] The entire film is composed of four separate sequences that intertwine depictions of lesbian and gay lovers having sex with voice-over interviews and commentary from a wide variety of interviewees, scholars, and commentators. The second sequence portrays a gay male couple, one white and one black. The key scene I am concerned with includes a close-up of the two men's genitalia. Over this screen image, Hammer scrolls the Motion Picture Code of 1930, veiling the multiple "obscenities" present on-screen: sex itself, gay sex at that, and miscegenation to top it all off. The veil practice here represents how such an image would have been impossible to screen in the 1930s, and is indeed impossible to screen in many theatres today. Gay sex is often not only veiled, but erased, hidden, or at best, toned down to chaste hugs and kisses in mainstream Hollywood's much ballyhooed forays into representations of gay love and lifestyles in films such as *Philadelphia* (1993), *The Birdcage* (1996), and *In and Out* (1997). So the Motion Picture Code as a veil both covers the image and uncovers the politics of veiling, thus resisting censorship as an oppressive form of veiling in itself.

The final veil practice I would like to mention in Hammer's film involves the filmmaker herself. In the fourth sequence of the film, the lovers are two women of color, whose bodies feature multiple tattoos and piercings. (All four of Hammer's couples come from gay and lesbian communities that are as likely to be censored or rendered invisible *within* the broader gay and lesbian community, as they are to be censored by mainstream heterosexual society: women in their seventies; interracial couples; S&M, butch/femme, and body art practitioners.) Interspersed with images of these two women are several shots of Hammer herself holding her camera. At first, she seems to be peeping through a curtained door at the couple as they have sex. Then she raises her hand to wave at herself, and her hand can be seen in the field of the camera as well as on the door. We discover that this shot incorporates two pertinent images of Hammer: as voyeur, who watches and records the love-making of each of the four couples in the film, and as a spectator who also looks at herself through her own camera, catching her reflection on, or through, the veil of the door, which she is both outside of and within. It is a complex image that reveals the filmmaker's implicatedness in the acts of looking, shooting, and un/covering. This particular use of the veil also redefines the voyeur not as one who only lasciviously watches, but one who also watches in order to remember, record, and ensure the survival of that which is seen. It is an unveiling that functions as not only resistance, but counterdiscourse. Various unattributed intertitles are mixed in with these shots of Hammer filming herself; she does not always reveal her sources when using quotations, just as Trinh does not reveal the identities of her interviewees through subtitles. Hammer uses intertitles that admonish the viewer to

Unravel the knot of history, narrative, and desire.

Find traces of a counterdiscourse.

Produce a genealogy of survival.

Perhaps the most important and poignant of these intertitles is the final one in this sequence, which reads: "Effective history does not retrieve events/ actors lost by official history, but shows the processes that produced those losses, those constructed silences."[38] Thus, Hammer positions herself as producing "effective history" through her emphasis on how silence has been constructed around gay and lesbian sexuality. By choosing not to reveal any sources for several of her intertitles, Hammer veils the authority of the speaker, setting these words into play in a more widely resonant sense as imperative statements directly addressing the spectator in the audience as well as the interested subjects featured in the film. Hammer's uses of the veil-image and veiling practices are thus different from Trinh's in some crucial ways, though they share similar concerns with how knowledge is produced and recorded, and how the filmmaking apparatus can be used to affect the relative in/visibilities of different histories and experiences.

Just as Trinh emphasized how histories and understandings of Vietnam and China are contextual and relational, Hammer emphasizes how the histories and understandings of all sexual activities are likewise "contextual and relational." And pulling again from theories of sexuality that are influenced by the work of Foucault, Hammer's intertitle asserts that "no specific identity and sexual desire can be historically denied." The questions of who sees and how need continually to be unraveled and explored, and veiling practices in films such as Hammer's provide excellent opportunities for exploration.

THE FILMMAKER UN/VEILED: LOURDES PORTILLO'S *THE DEVIL NEVER SLEEPS* (1996)

Portillo categorizes *The Devil Never Sleeps* as a "melodocumystery" (qtd. in Fregoso 307); Portillo coined the term in order to capture how her film combines melodrama, documentary, and whodunit qualities. Giving it this hybrid moniker, Portillo shows how the genres of experimental film, documentary, and narrative are inadequate to the task she sets herself in her work. In short, Portillo returns to Mexico to make a film about her Tio Oscar's death, which was ruled suicide by the police, but many family members believed otherwise. Portillo does not set out to uncover any truths, but rather is interested in juxtaposing the many interviews she holds on film, which enable her to explore the same contested terrain of history that both Trinh and Hammer find so compelling. Each family member and colleague gives a different story about Tio Oscar, ranging across his family commitments, infidelities, questionable business activities, and hypothetical homosexual activities. These juxtapositions raise questions about the im/possibility of reconstructing the past, either through film or narrative devices. This does not mean that Portillo's project stands in opposition to Hammer's, for example, who seeks to reconstruct various tellings of the past. Rather, there is a continuity between the two (as well as with Trinh) since each focuses on the "relational and contextual" condition of all identities, knowledges, histories.

Portillo plays with the blurred edge between documentary and fictional narrative when she includes Oscar's widow, Ofelia, in the film. In a phone conversation, Ofelia refused to be interviewed. Portillo decided to include the phone conversation since she could not get Ofelia on film. The viewer thinks throughout the film that what is heard is actually Ofelia's voice recorded on tape, but the credits reveal that Ofelia was "read" by another woman, thus reenactment passes for reality and Portillo pulls a "veil" over the audience's eyes (and ears).

Veils also figure in two other sequences in the film: through the cultural narrative of the embalmed virgin and through Portillo's reflective sunglasses. First, the bride. In this sequence, Portillo explores a traditional fantastic story typical in Mexican cultures. One Chihuahua legend tells of the owner of a bridal shop whose daughter was killed in an accident on the day of her wedding; legend has it that the distraught mother had her embalmed and put on display as a mannequin in her bridal gown and veil. One shot in the film shows a crowd in front of the store window, and the workers are lifting the gown as if to "prove the truth of the legend" (Fregoso 313). This moment crystallizes Portillo's concern throughout the film with the difference between reality and "tele-reality," the latter term playing on the melodramatic realities depicted within Mexican *telenovellas*. In her reading, Rosa Linda Fregoso writes that "the legend's location in this scene has less to do with the process of gathering empirical evidence or 'knowledge' for documentary truth and more to do with underscoring the veracity of popular forms of knowledge for making sense of one's reality" (314). Thus, the bride's veil and the fabric of her gown signify resistant veiling practices. They resist forms of knowledge that rule out the fantastic, the fabricated. Including this legend in the film links Portillo's work to Trinh's through the veil-image as well as through the prioritizing of multiple subjectivities in constructing and documenting the "realities" depicted within the film.

· The final veil-image, which is also a veiling practice, used in Portillo's film is her polarized sunglasses. In a few scenes, Portillo turns the camera on herself during an interview while she is wearing polarized sunglasses. Thus, what the audience member sees on-screen is from the point of view of the interviewee, as well as the interviewer. Fregoso writes that it is "the on-screen absence of the filmmaker's visual range ... that gives film its veneer of transparency" (311). It is precisely this transparency that Portillo's veiling practices challenge. She places herself in front of the camera, wearing reflective sunglasses that "veil" her own eyes and reflect back yet another image. Thus, Portillo emphasizes both "how the filmmaker (camera) sees, as well as how she (it) is seen by an external witness" (Fregoso 311). As a result, no single vision, or viewing practice, is prioritized. Portillo advocates instead a plurality of modes of looking within the filmic apparatus, as do Trinh and Hammer. Each places the practice of looking into play in order to examine how histories are constructed and erased, to posit new ways of producing "effective histories," and to resist oppressive modes of veiling and voyeurism, thus releasing both of these practices into more divergent possibilities.

CONCLUSION
(WHICH IS REALLY MORE OF A
BEGINNING THAN AN ENDING)

As I write this conclusion, the prospect of revising several syllabi lies before me. Next semester, I teach Introduction to Women's Studies, Black Women Writers, and Women and Film. My institution is also instituting a freshman seminar program, and I will be teaching a mini-course on Women and Visual Culture, which is designed to get freshman interested in analyzing contemporary visual images such as those found in television, in film, and in the proliferating advertisements we (and especially young people) are bombarded with daily. All is possibility as I consider my options for these four courses and ponder how film will shape the experiences of each. The

Introduction to Women's Studies course will include documentaries such as Demetrakas's *Right Out of History: The Making of Judy Chicago's Dinner Party* in our unit on women artists, as well as Ngozi Onwurah's *The Body Beautiful* and Mona Hatoum's *Measures of Distance* in our unit on body politics. When I last taught Black Women Writers, I began the class with Pratibha Parmar's film *A Place of Rage* (1991), a documentary featuring Alice Walker, June Jordan, Angela Davis, and Trinh Minh-ha (who comments on how influential black women's writing and activism have been on her work). In one scene, Jordan discusses some of the failings of the black power movement, such as consciousness raising sessions that revolved around tests for blackness. In a room full of black people, she states, no one could pass the test for being "black enough" as it was being defined at the time. Thus, issues of authenticity and identity are put in question from day one. The documentary provides a great tool for discussing the expectations that students in a majority white institution (something around 94%) bring into a class titled "Black Women Writers." This is important in my particular situation in order to raise awareness in the students about the veils and screens through which they view black women in general, and black women's writing in particular.

In Women and Film, an entire unit of the course is dedicated to feminist documentary filmmaking, and how filmmakers such as Trinh, Hammer, Portillo, Onwurah, Hatoum, Fleming, and Parmar represent an abundance of women's concerns and issues while also producing challenging new understandings about how knowledge is produced in relation to these concerns and issues at one and the same time. If I can instill in my freshmen a set of tools for understanding how visual images produce knowledge about gendered relationships, and how so many of the visual images in today's popular culture intersect with racist, heterosexist, and ethnocentric ways of seeing, I will have accomplished no small task. Given their broad exposure to visual images, if not their literacy in decoding them, starting with film makes sense. Film provides a key location for examining how meanings about differences—based in gender, race, sexuality, class, nationality—are understood in the contemporary United States. The resonance of veil-images and veiling practices in particular provide but one small element in the vast resources offered by contemporary film with which to begin implementing more critical reading skills in today's (and tomorrow's) spectators.

NOTES

1. For a brief and accessible introduction to epic theater and its tactics, see Brecht's "Theatre for Pleasure or Theatre for Instruction"; in it, Brecht writes that in epic theatre, the spectator is "no longer in any way allowed to submit to an experience uncritically (and without practical consequences) by means of simple empathy with the characters in a play" (qtd. in Worthen 890).

2. On using the term "experimental" here, I refer to the fact that this documentary is only eleven minutes long and utilizes non-traditional modes of filmmaking, such as hand-painted celluloid, symbolic intertitles, and frequent disjunction between the narrative voice-over and the visual image on screen. These elements are characteristic of Fleming's work in general. She is usually referred to as an experimental filmmaker. A Canadian national, she has several award-winning shorts in her filmography. Some of these films are available on the compilation of her work, *Pictures Don't Tell You Anything,* available from the artist.

3. Stemming from her experiences as a Nigerian-British woman of color, Onwurah's work is particularly useful in the classroom. Each of her films addresses issues of race intersecting with gender to position the woman of color as exoticized Other, mostly in British contexts. An earlier film, *Coffee Coloured Children* (1988) addresses the effects of having a mixed racial heritage on children, and the more recent documentary *And Still I Rise* (1993) interviews numerous black women artists, dancers, writers, and cultural critics on the representation of black women in the media.

4. Mona Hatoum is a Palestinian multi-media artist located in London. Video is only one of many emphases in her work, including sculpture, installation and performance art. Central to each of these artistic endeavors are questions regarding representation of the body. See Archer.

5. Tania Kamal-Eldin's documentary films have been featured in many festivals. Her most recent work—*Hollywood Harems* (1999)—examines representations of Egyptian and other Middle Eastern peoples in Hollywood films ranging from the 1920s to the contemporary period. In a discussion following a viewing of Kamal-Eldin's film *Covered* at SUNY Fredonia, Dr. Nawal el Saadawi referred to the film as a fine example of the "veiling of the mind" revealed in many contemporary feminist readings of the practice of veiling. Dr. el Saadawi points out that all three of the monotheistic religions practice veiling: Islamic women take the veil; many orthodox Jewish women "veil" with wigs; and Christian women, nuns in particular, also cover their heads. But the feminist community remains fascinated only with Islamic veiling. The question "why?" is a complex one, not unrelated to the continuation of Orientalist thinking in the West.

6. *Hidden Faces* is a complex film. Originally intended to be a documentary on el Saadawi, the filmmakers shifted their focus and made a film tracing the homecoming of a young Egyptian woman who has been living in exile in Paris. The young woman reads el Saadawi's work throughout the film, but is ultimately disappointed in her, and feels personally judged by some of el Saadawi's observations on her own dissatisfaction with living in exile. The subjective disappointment this narrator experiences is adopted uncritically by the documentary, which never examines its own culpability in portraying el Saadawi in negative terms (such as opening the film with an image of her in a disagreement, rather than with attention to her accomplishments working with women in rural Egyptian villages.)

7. Barbara Hammer has directed some forty-seven films, mostly focusing on lesbian sexuality in the United States as well as globally. *Nitrate Kisses,* perhaps one of her most recognized films, explores the perimeters of documentary filmmaking as a mode of representation that peers through veils to capture previously unseen images of marginalized peoples. *Out in South Africa* (1995) is another well-known documentary by Hammer, which explores the edges of racial and sexual oppression in post-apartheid South Africa. Lourdes Portillo has directed six films, and is perhaps best for her documentary, *Las Madres: The Mothers of Plaza de Mayo* (1985), which features the Argentinean mothers who protested the disappearance of their children for political reasons, and demanded information from the government. Portillo received an Academy Award Nomination for best documentary for this film. Her later work includes a documentary of Tejana musician Selena, titled *Corpus* (1999), which examines Selena's fame, her murder, and her role as cultural icon.

8. One excellent source to consult for an overview of discussions about the female spectator is the special issue of *Camera Obscura* 20–21 (1989) titled "The Female Spectatrix," edited by Janet Bergstrom and Mary Ann Doane. Other key sources on the issue of the gaze and the look include Doane's article "Film and the Masquerade: Theorizing the Female Spectator," an analysis of spectatorship in melodrama; Jane Gaines's reading of race in relation to the female spectator in "White Privilege and Looking Relations: Race and Gender in Feminist Film Theory"; and Judith Mayne's *Cinema and Spectatorship* (1993) and "Lesbian Looks: Dorothy Arzner and Female Authorship," which was originally published in another anthology of interest, Bad Object Choices' *How Do I Look? Queer Film and Video* (1991). Many of these articles are anthologized in Kaplan's *Feminism & Film* (2000).

9. In *Woman, Native, Other* (1989), Trinh points out that new ethnographers such as James Clifford and Georges Marcus, co-editors of *Writing Culture* (1986), critique previous anthropological methods as she does. But Trinh also notes that the new ethnography is not quite new enough in that it continues to legitimize "the production of knowledge" and to identify "unmediated meaning in the event observed" (*Woman* 157, n. 64).

10. Trinh quotes Malinowski from *Argonauts of the Western Pacific* (1922) to illustrate her point. Malinowski writes of the anthropologist that he "has introduced law and order into what seemed chaotic and freakish. [He] has transformed for us the sensational, wild and unaccountable world of 'savages,' into a number of well-ordered communities governed by law, behaving and thinking according to consistent principles" (qtd. in *Woman* 56).

11. I follow Peggy Phelan's model in distinguishing the Lacanian Real from other versions of the real by referring to the former with a capital "R." (*Unmarked* 181n5). Rose does not make this distinction, and I use her lower-case "r" for Lacan's real when using direct quotations from her. I also want to note here that Trinh herself never references Lacan in her work. It is a strategy of hers to decenter authoritative names such as Lacan's. Nor do Phelan or Rose address Trinh's work overtly (or vice versa, though Phelan references Rose quite a bit). I bring Phelan, Rose, and Lacan into this discussion because their interests in representational economies illuminate certain of Trinh's theories.

12. Joan Copjec would disagree and asserts that "Lacan's concept [of the gaze] disallows the notorious notion of the male gaze" (124). Copjec writes that "film theory's concept of the gaze is an unjustified amalgam of Lacanian and Foucauldian concepts,"

which lead away from Lacan's central emphasis on the failure of the gaze to see what it wants to see. It is this failure in which Copjec locates possibility. Phelan, however, complicates the idea of the failed gaze in order to move beyond its generative (looks and representations keep being generated due to this failure) but also negative (what are the social ramifications of those looks?) limitations.

13. Barthes is quoted from *Empire of Signs* (1982).

14. *Surname Viet Given Name Nam* (1989) focuses on Vietnam, and *Naked Spaces— Living Is Round* (1985) and *Reassemblage* (1982) focus on African nations. *Woman, Native, Other* (1989) mentions a fifth movie that was in progress at the time of its publication, *India-China*. But stills from the work-in-progress reproduced in *Woman, Native, Other* appear in *Shoot for the Contents* (1991), which suggests that Trinh split *India-China* into two projects. I have chosen *Shoot for the Contents* and *A Tale of Love* (1995) as my primary focus because they are Trinh's two most recent films.

15. I do not mean to imply that all documentaries other than Trinh's assume representational objectivity, but most do when compared to Trinh's documentaries. The interviewees in most documentaries, for example, are identified as experts through the use of subtitles giving their names and relative areas of expertise. This alone qualifies the interviewees as a trustworthy source, with little attention being given to the subjective process of choosing interviewees and constructing questions to ask them.

16. Many theorists have written on the question of history and historiography in relation to postmodern and poststructuralist modes of thinking. There are too many for me to engage with in this article, but a good place for others to start reading is Linda Hutcheon's *The Politics of Postmodernism,* especially chapter 3, "Re-presenting the Past" (62–92); and Trinh's "Grandma's Story," in *Woman, Native, Other* (119–51). For the *Nation* article, see McCormack.

17. See www.exploratorium.edu/nagasaki/Library/Enola.html for a discussion of the details of the events surrounding the exhibit, and a few articles from the museum's archive. See also Harwit.

18. Brian Wallis describes Trinh's work as "fundamentally anti-documentarian" in so far as it "employ[s] new methodologies to unceasingly question and fracture the rules of documentary. For today the real need is not to redefine documentary, nor to establish a new canon of 'politically correct' documentarians, but to shift the questions that are being asked to different grounds altogether and to question the structures of power while participating within them" (61). Trinh would not use this adjective herself, since it situates her as merely reacting to accepted notions of documentary filmmaking, hence remaining within a binary relationship.

19. Julia Lesage's article "The Political Aesthetics of the Feminist Documentary Film" (1984), is interesting to compare to Laura Mulvey's "Film, Feminism, and the Avant-Garde" (1978), which, though published six years earlier, correlates to Trinh's readings of feminist filmmaking practices more so than Lesage's. Mulvey summarily identifies the "heady," but "weak," use of the *cinéma vérité* tradition in early feminist films and goes on to emphasize the importance for later films of "probing [the] dislocation between cinematic form and represented material" (119). This is a progression Lesage never addresses, thus remaining within a discourse of identity-authenticity.

20. For a discussion of Trinh's oft-quoted method of "speaking nearby" instead of speaking for, see Kaplan's *Looking for the Other* (95–217). See also *Women, Native, Other*:

"speaking nearby or together with certainty differs from speaking for or about" (101).

21. Trinh quotes Audre Lorde's "The Master's Tools Will Never Dismantle the Master's House."

22. See *Cinema Interval* (189) and Kaplan's *Looking* (209–10) for stills from this scene.

23. This quotation is taken from *Moon,* but the article originally appeared under the title "Mechanical Eye, Electronic Ear, and the Lure of Authenticity" in *Wide Angle* 6 (1984): 58–63, where the words in the right-hand column read: "*The eternal commentary that escorts images*" (62). The quotation as it appears above was added to the version of the article in *Moon* (53–62).

24. I refer throughout this section to the performers Ying and Dewi as Voices 1 and 2 respectively, since they are not identified by their names anywhere in the film, and reveal little of themselves directly until the end of the film.

25. One still from this scene is reproduced in *Woman, Native, Other* in the top frame (115).

26. Stills of these images can be found in *Cinema Interval* (150, 154).

27. This practice is especially evident in *Surname Viet Given Name Nam* (1989) where the seemingly authentic or authoritative "interviewed" subjects constitute a large segment of the film, but are discovered to be "acting" roles at the film's end.

28. Trinh only refers to the "interviewees" in the credits, where their names are listed under the title "interviews/performers." The filmmaker, translator, and scholar are identified as Wu Tian Ming, Mayfair Yang, and Clairmonte Moore. Voices 1 and 2, Ying Lee-Kelly and Dewi Yee, are also identified in the credits as performers.

29. The filmscript reveals him to be Clairmonte Moore. He is also listed in the credits for the film, but is not linked to a particular interview.

30. See the cover of *Cinema Interval* and other stills in the unnumbered insert between pages 130–31.

31. This very image serves as the cover of Trinh's most recent book of interviews and filmscripts, *Cinema Interval* (1999).

32. *Cinema Interval* reproduces numerous stills of the veil-images in *A Tale.*

33. This is one of Mulvey's key assertions in "Visual Pleasure and Narrative Cinema" (19–26).

34. By "naturalistic," Trinh means unaware of itself as acting. This goes back to her connections to Brecht. Just as he sought to highlight the artificiality of what his actors were doing on stage, Trinh seeks to highlight the artificiality of what her actors are doing on screen. They are acting, not attempting to hide the fact that they are acting. So "natural" here is positioned as the opposite of "artificial," or enacted.

35. Again, the special issue of *Camera Obscura* is a good source to consult about the history of critical discussions of spectatorship and psychoanalytic theories of voyeurism. Doane points the reader to work by Christian Metz, especially his article "The Imaginary Signifier" and the book of the same title; Stephen Heath's "Film and System: Terms of Analysis"; Julia Lesage's "The Human Subject: You, He, or Me? Or, the Case of the Missing Penis"; and Laura Mulvey's work (Doane 5–7).

36. See Foster for an interview with Barbara Hammer where she discusses the interplay of these various voices in the film. Hammer states, "I believe we need multiple voices to present multiple viewpoints" (125).

37. Trinh also utilizes text as a veiling practice to a great extent in *Surname Viet Given*

Name Nam, where she scrolls the text of the original interviews over the faces of the actresses enacting the absent interviewees. The effect on the viewer is to split their levels of perception, as they have to decide whether to listen to the words the women speak, or to read the text on the screen, which most of the time does not overlap directly with the women's performances.

38. This quotation, and the three which preceded it, are not attributed to any one theorist, but are obviously influenced by Foucault. The phrase "effective history" is Nietzsche's, but is not attributed either. See Foucault's "Nietzsche, Genealogy, History" for a discussion of "effective history" (76–100).

FILMOGRAPHY

Demetrakas, Johanna. *Right Out of History: The Making of Judy Chicago's Dinner Party.* Phoenix Films & Video. St. Louis, MO, 1980.

Fleming, Ann Marie. *You Take Care Now.* 1989. 11 min. 16 mm film. Available from Moving Images Distributors, 402 West Pender Street, Suite 606, Vancouver BC V6B 1TC, Canada.

———. *Pictures Don't Tell You Anything.* 106 min. VHS compilation (includes *You Take Care Now*). Available from Moving Images Distributors.

Hammer, Barbara. *Nitrate Kisses.* 1992. 63 min. VHS. Available from www.reel.com.

———. *Out in South Africa.* 1995. 51 min. VHS. Available from Women Make Movies (WMM) (www.wmm.com).

Hatoum, Mona. *Measures of Distance.* 1988. 15 min. VHS. WMM.

Hunt, Claire, and Kim Longinotto. *Hidden Faces.* 1990. 52 min. VHS, 16 mm film. WMM.

Kamal-Eldin, Tania. *Covered: The Hejab in Cairo, Egypt.* 1995. 25 min. VHS. WMM.

———. *Hollywood Harems.* 1999. 30 min. VHS. WMM.

Onwurah, Ngozi. *And Still I Rise.* 1993. 30 minutes. VHS, 16 mm film. WMM.

———. *The Body Beautiful.* 1991. 23 min. VHS, 16 mm film. WMM.

———. *Coffee Coloured Children.* 1988. 15 min. VHS, 16 mm film. WMM.

Portillo, Lourdes. *The Devil Never Sleeps.* 1996. 82 min. VHS, 16 mm film.

Trinh Minh-ha. *Shoot for the Contents.* 1991. 101 min. VHS, 16 mm film. WMM.

———. *Surname Viet Given Name Nam.* 1989. 108 min. VHS, 16 mm film. WMM.

———. *A Tale of Love.* 1995. 108 min. VHS, 35 mm film. WMM.

WORKS CITED

Archer, Michael, Guy Brett, and Catherine de Zegher, eds. *Mona Hatoum.* London: Phaidon, 1997.

Bad Object Choices, eds. *How Do I Look? Queer Film and Video.* Seattle: Bay Press, 1991.

Benjamin, Walter. "Theses on the Philosophy of History." *Illuminations.* Ed. Hannah Arendt. New York: Schocken, 1969. 253–64.

Bergstrom, Janet, and Mary Ann Doane. "The Female Spectator: Contexts and
    Directions." *Camera Obscura* 20–21 (1989): 5–27.

Bergstrom, Janet, and Mary Ann Doane, eds. *The Spectatrix.* Spec. issue of *Camera
    Obscura* 20–21 (1989): 1–378.

Brecht, Bertolt. "Theatre for Pleasure or Theatre for Instruction." *Brecht on Theatre:
    The Development of an Aesthetic.* Ed. and trans. John Willett. New York: Farrar,
    Strauss & Giroux, 1992.

Clifford, James. *The Predicament of Culture: Twentieth Century Ethnography, Literature,
    and Art.* Cambridge: Harvard UP, 1988.

Clifford, James, and Georges Marcus, eds. *Writing Culture: The Poetics and Politics of
    Ethnography.* Berkeley: U of California P, 1986.

Copjec, Joan. "Individual Responses: Joan Copjec." *Camera Obscura* 20–21 (1989): 121–27.

Covered: The Hejab in Cairo, Egypt. Dir. Tania Kamal-Eldin. Women Make Movies, 1995.

The Devil Never Sleeps. Dir. Lourdes Portillo. Women Make Movies, 1996.

Doane, Mary Ann. "Film and the Masquerade: Theorizing the Female Spectator."
    Screen 23 (1982): 74–88.

El Saadawi, Nawal. Public discussion at SUNY Fredonia. March 30, 2001. See also *The
    Nawal El Saadawi Reader.* London: Zed Books, 1997.

Fleming, Ann Marie. "Transcript: *You Take Care Now.*" *Screen Writings: Scripts
    and Texts by Independent Filmmakers.* Ed. Scott MacDonald. Berkeley, CA:
    U of California P, 1995. 264–69.

Foster, Gwendolyn Audrey. *Captive Bodies: Postcolonial Subjectivity in Cinema.* Albany:
    SUNY Press, 1999.

Foucault, Michel. "Nietzsche, Genealogy, History." *The Foucault Reader.* Ed. Paul
    Rabinow. New York: Pantheon Books, 1984. 76–100.

Fregoso, Rosa Linda. "Sacando los trapos al sol (airing dirty laundry) in Lourdes
    Portillo's Melodocumystery, *The Devil Never Sleeps.*" *Redirecting the Gaze: Gender,
    Theory, and Cinema in the Third World.* Ed. Diana Robin and Ira Jaffe. Albany:
    SUNY Press, 1999. 307–30.

Gaines, Jane. "White Privilege and Looking Relations: Race and Gender in Feminist
    Film Theory." *Screen* 29.4 (1988): 12–27.

Harwit, Martin. *An exhibit denied: lobbying the history of Enola Gay.* New York:
    Copernicus, 1996.

Heath, Stephen. "Film and System: Terms of Analysis, Part I." *Screen* 16.1 (1975): 7-17.

———. "Film and System: Terms of Analysis, Part II." *Screen* 16.2 (1975): 91–113.

Hidden Faces. Dir. Claire Hunt and Kim Longinotto. Women Make Movies, 1990.

Hutcheon, Linda. *The Politics of Postmodernism.* New York: Routledge, 1989.

Kaplan, E. Ann. *Feminism and Film.* Oxford: Oxford UP, 2000.

———. *Looking for the Other: Feminism, Film, and the Imperial Gaze.* New York:
    Routledge, 1997.

———. *Women and Film: Both Sides of the Camera.* New York: Methuen, 1983.

Lacan, Jacques. *The Four Fundamental Concepts of Psycho-analysis*. Trans. Alan Sheridan. New York: Norton, 1978.

Lacan, Jacques. *Scilicet* 2–3 (1970): 120.

Lesage, Julia. "The Human Subject: You, He, or Me? Or, the Case of the Missing Penis." *Jump Cut* 4 (1974). Reprinted in *Screen* 16.2 (1975): 77–82.

———. "The Political Aesthetics of the Feminist Documentary Film." 1984. *Issues in Feminist Film Criticism*. Ed. Patricia Erens. Bloomington: Indiana UP, 1990. 222–37.

Lorde, Audre. "The Master's Tools Will Never Dismantle the Master's House." *Sister Outsider*. Freedom, CA: Crossing Press, 1984. 110–13.

Mayne, Judith. *Cinema and Spectatorship*. New York: Routledge, 1993.

———. "Lesbian Looks: Dorothy Arzner and Female Authorship." *How Do I Look? Queer Film and Video*. Ed. Bad Object Choices. Seattle: Bay Press, 1991. 103–44.

McCormack, Win. "Deconstructing the Election: Foucault, Derrida, and GOP Strategy." *The Nation* 272.12 (March 26, 2001): 25–34.

Measures of Distance. Dir. Mona Hatoum. Women Make Movies, 1988.

Metz, Christian. "The Imaginary Signifier." *Screen* 16.2 (1975): 14–76.

———. *The Imaginary Signifier: Psychoanalysis and Cinema*. Trans. Cecilia Britton et al. London: Macmillan, 1982.

Mulvey, Laura. "Film, Feminism, and the Avant-Garde." 1978. *Visual and Other Pleasures*. Bloomington: Indiana UP, 1989. 111–26.

———. "Visual Pleasure and Narrative Cinema." *Screen* 16.3 (1975): 6–18. Reprinted in *Visual and Other Pleasures*. Bloomington: Indiana UP, 1989. 14–26.

Nitrate Kisses. Dir. Barbara Hammer. Frameline, 1992.

Penley, Constance, and Andrew Ross. "Interview with Trinh T. Minh-ha." *Camera Obscura* 13–14 (1985): 85–111.

Phelan, Peggy. *Unmarked: the Politics of Performance*. New York: Routledge, 1993.

Right Out of History: The Making of Judy Chicago's Dinner Party. Dir. Johanna Demetrakas. St. Louis, MO. Phoenix Films & Video, 1980.

Rose, Jacqueline. *Sexuality in the Field of Vision*. London: Verso, 1986.

Shoot for the Contents. Dir. Trinh T. Minh-ha and Jean Paul Bourdier. Women Make Movies, 1991.

A Tale of Love. Dir. Trinh T. Minh-ha and Jean Paul Bourdier. Women Make Movies, 1995.

Trinh Minh-ha. *Cinema Interval*. New York: Routledge, 1999.

———. *Framer Framed*. New York: Routledge, 1992.

———. "Mechanical Eye, Electronic Ear, and the Lure of Authenticity." *Wide Angle* 6 (1984): 58–63.

———. *When the Moon Waxes Red: Representation, Gender and Cultural Politics*. New York: Routledge, 1991.

———. *Woman, Native, Other. Writing Postcoloniality and Feminism*. Bloomington: Indiana UP, 1989.

Wallis, Brian. "Questioning Documentary." *Aperture* 112 (1988): 60–63.

Williams, Linda. "When the Woman Looks." *Re-Vision: Essays in Feminist Film Criticism*. Ed. Mary Ann Doane, Linda Williams, and Patricia Mellencamp. Frederick, MD: University Publications of America, 1984. 83–99.

Worthen, W. B., ed. *Harcourt Brace Anthology of Drama*. 3d ed. Fort Worth: Harcourt, 2000.

You Take Care Now. Dir. Anne Marie Fleming. Moving Images Distributors, 1989.

Zizek, Slavoj. *The Sublime Object of Ideology*. London: Verso, 1989.

There's No Light without Heat, and No Heat without Friction

Avant-Garde Film in the College Classroom

SCOTT MacDONALD

In my more than thirty years experience as a teacher at small liberal arts colleges, I have found no dimension of film history more useful than what is generally known as "avant-garde" and/or "experimental" film.[1] And yet, despite the remarkable potential of this immense body of work to invigorate the college classroom and instigate productive discussion—not simply about film, or even media in general, but about a broad range of aesthetic and philosophical issues—relatively few academics have been willing to take advantage of this remarkable resource. Indeed, a good many, if not most, of those who *could* use avant-garde films are not even aware that these films exist; or, if they are vaguely aware of this other cinema, they are not clear what its particular benefits might be or how to make use of them.

Given the stresses and distractions of contemporary academic life, who can blame anyone for avoiding a dimension of film history that even many cineastes know little about—especially since most avant-garde films pose challenges for anyone whose experience of film has been limited to commercial features and documentaries. However, while the under-utilization of avant-garde film may be understandable, it represents an astonishing waste of an incomparable pedagogical resource. I suspect that, if those committed to effective college teaching could find a way into this field, many would quickly become as excited about working with this alternative history as I have been all these years.

The function of the discussion that follows is to provide access to avant-garde film as a teaching tool, in three ways. First, I offer some background about how I came to use avant-garde film: my "conversion," while it was not an easy one, seems reasonably typical and will, I hope, provide a useful context for what follows. Second, I provide a set of suggestions about which particular films I have found most valuable in my teaching and some explanation of how I have used them. While another avant-garde enthusiast might choose a different list of particular films, my guess is that few would deny that the films I've selected are exemplary for teaching purposes. Finally, I provide a variety of practical tips about where to rent these films and what is essential for presenting them well; and I recommend some sources for general and specific information about avant-garde films and filmmakers.

BACKGROUND

By the time I finished my Ph.D. at the University of Florida in 1970, I knew that I wanted to find a job at a small, liberal arts college, where I could teach both modern American literature, which had been my major as a graduate student (my dissertation examined narrative perspective in Hemingway's short stories), and film history, which had become a passion. Like so many of us who came out of graduate school in the late 1960s and early 1970s, I had discovered the obvious—that cinema was worthy of the same kind of attention as literature—at what in retrospect seems relatively late in life (my mid-twenties). Indeed, I can remember standing with other students and my modern novel professor at DePauw University in 1963, when someone said, "You know, it'd be interesting to study movies in a course," and all of us, I think, laughed at the frivolity of such an idea. Not surprisingly, when I did land a job at Utica College of Syracuse University and began teaching a survey of modern American literature, introduction to film, and first-year writing, I was forced to play catch-up, especially in film: there was so much "foreign film" I hadn't seen and/or hadn't yet understood, and so many American auteurs I hadn't explored. My Introduction to Film course was the inevitable one-feature-a-week plus discussion, focusing on masterworks from the silent era up until the present.

During my second year at Utica College, I had an experience that was to transform my teaching, not only of film, but in many ways, of literature as well; and would lead me to some of the most exciting and, I believe, most effective classroom experiences of my life. The transformative experience was an afternoon screening of "avant-garde film," part of a weekend symposium hosted by the State University of New York at Binghamton. I had heard derogatory comments about avant-garde film during my graduate school years in Florida, but I decided to attend the Binghamton symposium because, as a very young, virtually untrained film professor in the wilds of central New York, I didn't feel I had the luxury of ignoring an opportunity to expand my horizons.

Now, more than a quarter-century later, I remember virtually nothing of that symposium except that afternoon screening, but I do remember that four films were screened, and the intensity of my reaction. We saw Larry Gottheim's *Barn Rushes* (1971), Ken Jacobs's *Soft Rain* (1968), Ernie Gehr's *Serene Velocity* (1970), and Stan Brakhage's *The Act of Seeing with One's Own Eyes* (1971). My guess is that these films remain relatively obscure, even to most film historians, so a bit of description might be useful, along with some detailing of my reactions. What was ultimately transformative for me was not simply seeing the films, but the evolution of my response to them during the months that followed.

Barn Rushes presented eight silent approximately three-minute shots made from a car slowly passing an upstate New York barn in different lights, at different times, and on different days. "Rushes" is a triple pun, referring to the unedited shots, each of which begins and ends with end-of-roll flares and perforations; to the tall weeds that are visible between the camera and the more distant barn; and, ironically, to the (actually quite slow) movements of the car carrying the camera past the rushes and around the barn, along the same route, over and over, at "silent speed."[2]

Soft Rain revealed a minimal cityscape—pedestrians and vehicles are seen across a vacant lot, moving through a soft rain, over and over: the film presents the same, approximately three-minute shot, in silence at eighteen frames per second, three times. In the upper left corner of the image a black space that at first seems a surreal interruption within the composition is moved slightly, half-way through, so that we recognize that the darkness isn't in the distance, which our assumptions about perspective have led us to conclude, but right next to the camera—no mystery at all, really, just a piece of cardboard.

If I had some vague understanding of the Gottheim film, which seemed reminiscent of Monet, I found the Gehr and Brakhage films not only inexplicable, but utterly infuriating. In *Serene Velocity* Ernie Gehr films an empty institutional hallway for twenty-three minutes from a camera mounted on a tripod. Having divided the focal length of his lens into equal increments, Gehr exposed four frames at a time, first from a focal point on one side of the mid-point; then from a focal point the same distance on the other side of the mid-point; then again from the next focal point on the one side, then from the next focal point on the other, and so on. The hallway is transformed into an eye- and mind-battering experience: as the focal lengths of the four-frame clusters grow further apart, the motion of the film seems increasingly aggressive—and yet nothing of a conventional sort happens: no one even walks down the hall.

Brakhage's film is now the best known of the four and has begun to be recognized as a landmark not only of avant-garde film, but of documentary.[3] At the time, however, it seemed even more outrageous than *Serene Velocity*: Brakhage's exploration of autopsies conducted at the Pittsburgh morgue grows increasingly visceral as the film proceeds, until his camera is swooping in for extreme close-ups of the results of the coroners' grisly work. Not only are the autopsies themselves shocking (many of the bodies are in terrible shape, even before they are opened up), but Brakhage's willingness to present us with this horrific visual information in close-up, with absolutely no explanation or justification of any kind (*The Act of Seeing with One's Own Eyes* is silent) seemed indefensible, shocking.

When the lights came on at the end of this nearly two-hour screening, I was furious. I felt as if I had been visually assaulted and insulted, and could see no reason for the experience. Doubly frustrating and infuriating was the fact that at least some portion of the audience, as well as the filmmakers who were present (Gottheim, Jacobs, and perhaps Gehr), took these films seriously, and seemed to expect something more than anger and rejection. "Horrible filmmakers and pretentious, to boot," I thought. I sometimes tell my students that I raised a vocal ruckus during the post-film discussion, but in reality I believe I sat there, silent and fuming, wishing for the courage and the language to express my outrage. I did vocalize my anger to the colleagues I had made the trip with, all the way from Binghamton back to Utica, and found comfort in the fact that they seemed to agree with my assessment of the films and filmmakers.

But try as I might, I couldn't put these films, and the experience they had created, behind me. For the first few weeks, I found myself telling the filmmakers off as I drove around town doing errands, and then, slowly but surely—to my amazement—I began to find that I was also *defending* the films *to* myself, answering my own attacks. Soon I realized that I actually admired the Gottheim film, especially the filmmaker's commitment to slowing the film experience down and offering a variety of subtle visual rewards to the patient viewer. Many of my students seemed addicted to a frenetic cinematic pace—and soon I was using *Barn Rushes* and other Gottheim films to model a more serene viewing experience. By the end of the next year or so, I also realized that the other films had also recontextualized my "normal" film experiences in ways that were beginning to affect my teaching.

Like (I assume) many academics teaching film appreciation and history during that era, I had generally assumed that the most effective way to broaden my students' cinematic horizons was to show them films they would immediately recognize as great. I chose films I was sure would impress them (with limited success: they didn't admire Renoir as I did, didn't enjoy the Marx Brothers as much as I expected they might), and spent class time talking about how the directors had created their effects and meanings. But while this method seemed reasonably effective, it seemed a little too easy (partly, no doubt, because of my very limited awareness of film language and my naiveté about auteurism!). More importantly, it felt far less fulfilling, less intellectually exciting, than teaching American Literature. The students' horizons might be broadened, but they were not forced to question their relationship to the film experience itself, the way reading Gertrude Stein, T. S. Eliot, William Faulkner, e. e. cummings, Wallace Stevens, or Richard Wright forced my literature students to question the experience of reading.

By the end of that first year after the Binghamton experience, I was searching for more film experiences that could create the level of engagement the Binghamton experience had created for me, and I had begun to use not only *Barn Rushes,* but *Serene Velocity* and films by Brakhage in order to interrupt the smooth continuities of my film course and the comfortable complacency that was created by the parade of narrative masterwork after narrative masterwork. Indeed, the Gehr film had become my metaphor for the way in which a new approach to cinema can re-invigorate an academic environment. That my intrusion of these new, confrontory films did indeed energize my classes was less surprising to me than the discovery that, by the end of the semester, many students recognized the initially frustrating experiences created by these films as among the most valuable experiences in the course.

In the end, I came to three general conclusions about the kind of viewing experience the Binghamton symposium had modeled. First, this experience—and those like it I had begun to instigate in my film courses—necessitated more thought about the nature and implications of the film experience, and of media experiences in general, than any of the conventional films I was likely to show. Second, the types of challenges created by avant-garde films were analogous to the challenges posed by the literature I expected my American literature students to come to grips with; and these challenges allowed me to be far more useful to my film students: certainly they didn't need my help to enjoy, even understand, *The Gold Rush* or *Psycho* or *The Grand Illusion* or *Rashomon*. The best I could do was to add something to their awareness. But they *did* need me to assist them in coming to grips with *Serene Velocity* and *The Act of Seeing,* the way my literature students needed my help with "Melanctha" and *The Sound and the Fury.* That I soon came to recognize more particular parallels between avant-garde film and "serious" literature opened up additional pedagogical avenues. Third, it quickly became obvious to me that the evolution of my reaction to the films I had seen at Binghamton—from fury to interest to fascination to professional commitment—was a prototype of my students' reactions to any effective interruption in the assumption, polemicized so effectively by Hollywood (and echoed more frequently than we'd like to admit by academics using film in the classroom), that easy pleasure is the only legitimate response to an experience of media. In the years that followed, I saw hundreds of students (at Utica College and Hamilton College) begin with anger and end with a deeper awareness, not only about particular films, but of many aspects of their cultural surround.

Since the mid-1970s, my research efforts—as well as much of my teaching energy—have been devoted to exploring all forms of alternative cinema and to helping other teachers become more fully aware of how to use these films in the classroom.[4] While there is no point in trying to survey this immense cinematic world in a single chapter, a brief discussion of a few of those films I have found to be the most useful pedagogically may be of value to readers. What follows is a listing of ten films (or sometimes pairs of films) that I believe offer a teacher remarkable opportunities. I describe the films and suggest how they can be used, not only within film courses, but in a variety of other academic contexts. And I offer suggestions designed to help potential users of these films avoid those practical hassles that can foil the most enlightened plans.

One other issue needs attention, however, before I discuss particular films: in-theater screening conditions. It has become standard in academic environments to rely on video, DVD, and laser disk projection of film and to accept mediocre screening conditions for 16mm films. Indeed, I often hear academics confirm that 16mm "is on its way out." While this situation may seem a matter of technological progress, in fact it represents a remarkable dereliction of responsibility. While it may be true that video/DVD/laser projection of commercial feature films is sometimes equal in quality and, once the investment in equipment has been made, less expensive than renting or maintaining 16mm prints of films made in 35mm, the situation is absolutely the reverse for most forms of independent cinema, and this is most especially the case for avant-garde film.

The films I discuss in the remainder of this essay were made in 16mm, specifically for exhibition in a theater space where excellent 16mm projection is available. I mean a room with two excellent 16mm projectors (Eikis are easy to work with and provide good light), a clear, unmarked screen, and an excellent sound system. To compromise on this is virtually to negate the considerable value of working with these films, for at least three reasons.

First, few of the crucial avant-garde films are available in any format other than 16mm, and the few videos available are inferior in quality not only to 16mm, but to videos of commercial film. Second, many avant-garde films rely on very subtle dimensions of the visual image; and anything less than very good screening conditions renders crucial aspects of a film invisible. For example, Peter Hutton's films are exquisite depictions of landscape and cityscape, usually filmed in black and white, often in relatively low-light conditions. Shown well, these films are among the most engaging avant-garde films, but when the projector bulb isn't strong enough, or the screening space isn't dark enough, or the "throw" from the projector to the screen is too long, the particulars of Hutton's subtly evolving images tend to disappear. Finally, since many avant-garde films provide particularly incisive critiques of mass-market, commercial cinema, they are best seen in a theatrical environment analogous to the normal movie theater.

Given the pervasive, often relentless demand to cut costs in academe, the struggle for the necessary screening situation for the films I describe may be the most frustrating dimension of working with these films. But few jobs are more pedagogically responsible as fighting for the most effective presentation of the films we choose to show. If we want our students to take film seriously, not simply in the sense that we need to seriously question many of the assumptions and tendencies of commercial media, but also in the sense that film history also offers exemplary practices and texts, works that provide progressive alternatives for thinking people, then we must do as our colleagues in music, the fine arts, and literature do. We must insist on a quality experience of quality work. Our battles for the necessary rental monies for 16mm prints and good screening conditions models a seriousness of purpose that can only have salutary impact on our colleagues and on our students. And, of course, the rental monies we liberate from academic coffers will literally help to keep a remarkable cultural achievement alive.

To put all this succinctly, quality films deserve quality screening conditions; avant-garde films demand them.

TEN RECOMMENDATIONS
1. *Fog Line* by Larry Gottheim

I have found *no* film more useful in the college classroom than Larry Gottheim's single-shot record of morning fog clearing over a lovely green landscape in central New York State. Because *Fog Line* is nearly eleven minutes long and because virtually nothing, certainly nothing of a conventional sort, seems to be happening during the continuous shot—other than the fog clearing fully enough for the landscape to be recognized *as* a landscape—Gottheim's film creates a remarkably powerful intervention into the velocity and density of the lives of our students and provides a powerful confrontation of their assumptions about how media art is supposed to function. Shot and presented in real time, *Fog Line* demands that we slow down.

But it does more than this, as well. It provides an opportunity for a new form of filmic perception and for in-depth discussion about a wide range of issues relevant to many sectors of academic life. The moment one asks students what, in fact, they *did* see during the seemingly endless eleven minutes of the film, a new, far more particular investigation of the filmic image can emerge, followed by a recognition that this "simple" film is both visually subtle and conceptually complex. Most viewers will remember that the image is roughly trisected by two sets of (telephone and/or power) wires, and will begin to question why—if Gottheim wanted to focus on a purely natural scene—he wouldn't avoid including the wires. Few will have noticed that in the bottom part of the image, just about halfway through the film, two horses are just barely visible as they graze across a pasture and across the film image from right to left. Indeed, the discovery that these horses actually passed through the image (it may be necessary to reshow the film to prove it) creates consternation in many viewers—how could we *miss* something when there was so little to distract us!—and an opportunity for discussing such issues as our shortening attention spans and the way in which most cinematic imagery focuses our attention exclusively on the center of the image and on visual information that requires little perceptivity on our part.

I have used *Fog Line* in a wide range of courses, often as a means of bridging gaps between conventional disciplines. In a film studies context the film is useful in demonstrating not only the distinction between real time and film time, but the ways in which film history is simultaneously an evolution and an ongoing resource. Gottheim's decision to use a single shot recalls the one-shot-equals-one-film approach of the Lumière brothers (and the ways in which the Lumière films were limited by their fifty-second duration); and his decision to arrange his shot so that the movement of the horses is the film's only real "action" recalls Eadweard Muybridge's early motion studies of horses that led the way toward the cinematic representation of movement. Of course, there is wry humor in Gottheim's allusion to Muybridge's motion studies in a film in which almost nothing seems to move!

Gottheim's subtle combination of natural process (the fog lifting, horses grazing) and technological development (as represented by the wires and by the lines of the film frame, even by the way in which the telephoto lens distorts the space, causing the horses to seem smaller than they should and the distant trees larger) makes *Fog Line* useful within an American Studies context. In a sense Gottheim reverses Leo Marx's famous paradigm of "the machine in the garden": here, we see a lovely, Edenic moment captured by and within the machine of cinema.[5] The film also seems a modern version of certain tendencies of nineteenth-century painting: it has much in common, for example, with Thomas Cole's *The Oxbow* (1836) and with those schools of painting that have come to be known as "luminism" and "tonalism."[6] Indeed, in an art history context it could demonstrate how the evolution of art doesn't simply leave earlier tendencies behind, but often redirects them into other cultural arenas. The film's combination of a "simple," "natural" image and an extended duration is also useful in a literary context: *Fog Line* is both analogous to a haiku *and,* paradoxically, takes up a space—or really a time, a duration—far greater than its content at first seems to justify. I even used *Fog Line* for a number of years as a subject for expository writing in my written communication courses: it offers a challenge to the student's observation and embodies the idea that there is often a good bit more in what we see, in both media and in the world, than first meets the eye and mind.

Indeed, for Gottheim the film has an epistemological dimension. Whenever we are faced with a new experience (a type of film we've never seen, an academic subject we've never studied, a change in environment such as going to college), we may at first feel ourselves to be "in a fog," but with patience and perception we not only realize where we are, but discover those dimensions of this new environment that can be valuable and pleasurable to us.[7]

While *Fog Line* is a remarkably suggestive film, I have used a variety of other films in much the same way. Robert Huot's single-shot, three-minute shot of snow falling—*Snow* (1972)—is both lovely and mysterious (since the particulars of his composition are difficult to decipher); and while it creates, on one hand, a meditative experience of a natural phenomenon, it also teases the eye into a perceptual rhythm that is quite different from the way we normally see snow: in *Snow* our attention moves from foreground to background to foreground to background in a manner that has as much to do with the mechanical apparatus of cinema as it does with snow falling. And Peter Hutton's films—especially *Landscape (for Manon)* (1985)—use an unusual editing strategy to interrupt conventional perceptual/conceptual rhythms and provide opportunities for cinematic meditation. *Landscape (for Manon)* presents a set of images recorded in the Hudson Valley—in part as an homage to nineteenth-century American landscape painter Thomas Cole. At first, these images are extended (twenty to twenty-five seconds) and relatively minimal (they're black and white, presented in silence), and *then* become even longer and quieter. The result is a fifteen-minute experience that seems to take us back in time, to a moment when the simple recording and projection of the world felt stunning and memorable.

2. *Window Water Baby Moving* (1959) by Stan Brakhage

While our students frequently assume, primarily on the basis of mass-media polemic, that American society and American cinema grow ever more open and accepting, in fact, a surprising number of films that seemed outrageous when they were first presented to audiences seem even *more* outrageous now. No film is a better instance of this than Stan Brakhage's document/interpretation of the birth of his first daughter: *Window Water Baby Moving*. If most students now see a human birth at some point during their formative years, in school or on television, Stan Brakhage's film of Jane Conger Brakhage giving birth continues to cause shock and consternation for most students because of the directness and complexity of Brakhage's approach. And the film provides a remarkable opportunity for considering a wide range of issues, including those that originally informed the film. For *Window Water Baby Moving* to function most effectively, however, it needs to be contextualized carefully.

For the Brakhage who made *Window Water Baby Moving* (he has evolved through various stages in a remarkably prolific career), one of the great tragedies of the modern acculturation of children is that, in order to train them to *conceptualize*—by creating educational institutions that focus on, even fetishize, the word—we *perceptually* impoverish them. Brakhage's famous line, "How many colors are there in a field of grass to the crawling baby unaware of 'Green'?" implied a new approach to filmmaking and film viewing.[8] Brakhage's films became an ongoing attempt to use a mechanical/chemical apparatus to create metaphors for the perceptual experience "under childhood": that is, before our ability to perceive, and especially to see, is corrupted by the domination of language. That this approach would result in films that would widely seem shocking is hardly surprising: from Brakhage's point of view, the training that privileges language and conception slowly but surely renders much visual experience increasingly taboo. In fact, by the time we learn to be members of society, we have internalized a deep resistance to a considerable range of visual experiences.

My experience suggests that for *Window Water Baby Moving* to have its most profound pedagogical impact, it needs to be seen once the instructor has discussed contemporary visual taboos with the class. I usually ask students to imagine those dimensions of experience that a six-month-old baby would have no trouble perceiving, might even be perceptually attracted to, that *we* have difficulty perceiving. This question generally instigates a very energetic discussion, since even enunciating our perceptual taboos feels risky, especially in a classroom. The list of taboo subjects, of course, is virtually inevitable: shitting and pissing, vomiting, menstruating, sex (not *representations* of particular kinds of people having particular forms of sex, but real people having real sex), physical aging, death and decay, physical handicaps . . . that is, virtually everything to do with the physical body *as a process*. Of course, *this* discussion can lead to a further discussion of who this set of taboos benefits and the ways in which contemporary mass media are complicit in maintaining them.

And then it is time for *Window Water Baby Moving*, introduced perhaps by the proposition: "Given the fact that this film was made nearly a half-century ago, and we feel much less visually constricted than people of the 1950s, see if *any*thing in the film causes you to feel uncomfortable or even to look away." It is also useful for students to know that Brakhage forgoes a soundtrack because he wants to focus on sight, assuming that any soundtrack would distract viewers from his visuals.

There is something amusing in the usual response to *Window Water Baby Moving*. A substantial percentage of students are always shocked (this was consistently true at Utica College and at Hamilton College during the many years I taught introduction to film history/theory courses at those institutions). When the lights come on, a good many women will tell me they know now that they'll *never* have children, and a good many men sit stunned, wide-eyed, as if women were an alien species. During discussion it becomes clear that the most troubling images are the fluids being expelled from Jane Brakhage's vagina and the expulsion of the placenta and the physician's subsequent examination of it. Of course, the reason for students' consternation involves Brakhage's way of presenting the birth: in order to combat his own resistance to visual taboo—he is, after all, a product of the same culture as his viewers—Brakhage moves his camera relentlessly *toward* what our visual training has taught us to suppress. Unlike most of the films about birth our students are likely to see on TV or in school, Brakhage eliminates clinical distance and "objectivity." His astonishment at the birth (exacerbated by the fact that in 1959 virtually no one other than physicians and nurses ever saw birth) and his anxiety about being at the event and filming it are evident in his gestural camera work, in his generally fast editing (the rhythms of Brakhage's cutting between imagery of the months leading up to the birth and the birth itself evoke the contractions that move the baby out of the womb and into the world), and in the mythification of birth, of women, of mother created by his close-ups projected within the public sphere of the movie theater.

While the candidness of Brakhage's first birth film resulted in its being seen "underground" in the late 1950s and early 1960s—that is, at membership film societies and in small theaters where censors would be unlikely to go—*Window Water Baby Moving* quickly became a classic of the film avant-garde. Indeed, this film (along with other Brakhage films in which birth is depicted: *Thigh Line Lyre Triangular* [1961], for example) may have had some influence in breaking down the societal tendency to hide real human birth not only from the general public, but from mothers and fathers.

Window Water Baby Moving offers a variety of avenues for discussion. Most obviously, Brakhage's representation of birth can be examined for the beauty of its visuals, for the intricacy and suggestiveness of its editing, and as one of a series of depictions of birth to come out of the avant-garde. For example, Gunvor Nelson's birth film, *Kirsa Nicholina* (1969), offers another unconventional vision of birth, shocking in its own way but less involved with a male's astonishment at a woman's ability to give birth, and, like Brakhage's film, implicitly critiques those versions of birth marketed by mass media. There are also powerful critiques of *Window Water Baby Moving,* including Carolee Schneemann's *Fuses,* which was conceived, in part, as a response to Brakhage's reduction of Jane to Mother: *Fuses* documents/interprets Schneemann's sexual relations with lover James Tenney as a way of reasserting the primacy of sexuality and the usual repression and control of the erotic in the interest of promoting the ideal of the nuclear family.

Further, since Brakhage's film simultaneously demonstrates the societally-taught restrictions on our vision and functions as a metaphor for the birth of a new way of seeing, students can be invited to do follow-up projects that demonstrate their exploration of other visual arenas they have learned to avoid and to fear, *and* of aspects of their visual environment that they routinely ignore. After all, *Window Water Baby Moving* doesn't simply record a birth; it lovingly examines subtleties of color, of texture, of light and shadow, of movement that are clearly around us everyday, if only we took time to see them.

For those teachers with a hunger to confront the visual complacency so endemic to modern American culture, Brakhage's *The Act of Seeing with One's Own Eyes* (1971) can function effectively as a companion piece to *Window Water Baby Moving* and a powerful extension of the ideas generated by the birth film. As I suggested earlier, *The Act of Seeing* documents Brakhage's visual exploration of the process of autopsy (the title is a literal translation of "autopsy"). One of the most visually taboo of modern societal rituals, the process of determining the cause of death is for viewers, as it was for Brakhage, an extreme test. Gradually, during the thirty-two minutes of the film Brakhage moves from a frightened distance to an in-close immersion in the horrific and visually stunning process of opening the corpses of men and women who have died and decayed. In the end, *The Act* argues the function of art, including cinema art, to transcend the death of vision and death itself.

3. *Zorns Lemma* (1970) by Hollis Frampton

Whether teaching film appreciation/history/theory is our academic focus or whether our using film is an attempt to broaden and deepen an exploration of other academic disciplines and interests, we are frequently confronted by the tendency of a good many students to see film as an escape from the intellectual rigors of other, older disciplines. The most obvious response to this tendency, at least during recent years, has been to demonstrate the complexity of cinema by turning to literature—to the considerable theoretical literature *about* cinema that has engaged academe during the past quarter-century. While this response is effective in demonstrating how film can instigate serious intellectual engagement, there is another approach, one that can transform one's understanding of what is possible in a movie theater. Some avant-garde films offer not just the opportunity for deeper thought *about* film, but an opportunity for thinking *in* film, *with* film. A particularly useful instance is the late Hollis Frampton's exploration of the ways we learn, *Zorns Lemma*.

For film historians in 1970, even those who considered themselves savvy about alternative forms of film, *Zorns Lemma* seemed unprecedented, both in terms of the experience it created and in terms of what it asked of an audience. Even the title could hardly have been more puzzling: mathematician Max Zorn's lemma is the eleventh axiom of set theory, the "existential axiom," which, stated crudely, argues that in any set of sets, there is a further set made up of a comparable instance from each set. *Zorns Lemma* uses the alphabet as its fundamental set: specifically, an early version of the Roman alphabet in which i/j and u/v are single letters (this twenty-four letter alphabet is an allusion to the twenty-four frames that, each second, pass through a movie projector running at sound speed). During the short first section of *Zorns Lemma,* there is no image other than the projected frame where imagery *should* be, but there is sound: a schoolmarmy voice reads twenty-four verses, originally published in English-speaking America's first grammar book, *The New England Primer.* Each verse reviews a biblical story, while highlighting an alphabetized word: "In *Adam's* fall, we sinned all"; "Thy life to mend, God's *Book* attend."

The long second part of *Zorns Lemma* (it accounts for forty-seven of the film's sixty minutes) is what made the film and Frampton famous and influential in alternative film circles. After a single review of the twenty-four-letter alphabet, Frampton presents set after set of alphabetized words filmed in the environment of Lower Manhattan and Brooklyn, where Frampton lived during the sixties. Each alphabetized word is on-screen for one second, and the sets of words follow each other relentlessly (and in silence). No sooner has one become accustomed to this phantasmagoria of words than Frampton begins to substitute other forms of imagery for the alphabetized words, one letter at a time. These "replacement images" include ongoing natural processes (tiny waves on a beach, a fire burning, an elm tree) and practical tasks (reading a book, frying an egg, changing a tire); the substitutions occur in no predictable order, though several of them are timed so that the particular practical task depicted concludes with the middle section of the film, when the final substitution of ongoing image for letter is made.

The final section of *Zorns Lemma* releases the viewer from the relentless visual rhythm of the second section, though the sound (six women read an eleventh-century treatise on the structure of the universe, one word at a time, one word per second) maintains the earlier rhythm. In the imagery, a man, a woman, and a dog walk across a snowy, upstate New York field into a distant woods, in four continuous nearly three-minute shots.

Once students have vented their frustration and/or fascination with their experience of the film, discussion can move into the reasons for the particular nature of this experience, the logic behind the film's unusual but undeniably ingenious structure. And since there are a good many ways of coming to understand the film, this discussion allows for considerable creativity. One particular dimension worth drawing students' attention to is the way in which *Zorns Lemma* uses the changing nature of the audience's experience as a basic set of metaphors for Frampton's assumption about the ways we learn. While for Brakhage, childhood (or really the period "under childhood") is a perceptual Eden destroyed by the cultural incorporation of the child into language, for Frampton childhood is a time of "darkness" during which whatever practical learning occurs is wrapped in moralism. But once we've learned the alphabet and know how to read, we are released from the intellectual darkness of early childhood. At first, we are faced with the exciting phantasmagoria of a language-dominated society, but we are quickly immersed within society's relentless schedules and demands. Our submission to societal demands is so thorough that when we try to escape them— by taking a vacation or by retiring to the country—we feel their rhythms even as we attempt to turn our back on them.

College students are a particularly appropriate audience for *Zorns Lemma,* since they are creatures of institutional scheduling. Indeed, I often show the film about two-thirds of the way through the semester so that I can help them recognize that their frustration with the seemingly endless demands of the second section of the film is analogous to the rising frustration and panic that develops in students once the early-semester euphoria has worn off and the various end-of-semester deadlines are approaching.

And even once the semester is over and they are "free," they know the limitations on their freedom and can hardly fail to hear the echo of earlier demands and the hint of new ones.

The film is also particularly relevant within an academic context, since it critiques the institutional structure of most institutions of higher education. We've come to think of the sciences as distinct from the arts and humanities, a separation Frampton never understood, since the *art* of cinema is a function of mechanics and chemistry. *Zorns Lemma* is simultaneously mathematical (in its general use of set theory, in the attempt of the eleventh-century philosophical treatise to explain the structure of the universe numerologically, using numbers from one to ten), *and* verbal (in its devotion to the alphabet, to words, to reading). It demands some awareness of both a mathematical proposition and of the history of the alphabet; it forces us to read and to count.

There are a good many other ways of making sense of the structure of *Zorns Lemma,* but the bottom line, at least for this brief discussion, is that Frampton has created a film which we cannot understand without questioning our conventional relationships to film, and to media in general. It's very much a part of the serious intellectual exploration we want college to be, rather than (still another) cinematic escape from it.[9]

4. *Riddles of the Sphinx* (1976)
by Laura Mulvey and Peter Wollen

For those who have taught women's studies or have explored feminist critiques of culture, Laura Mulvey will be a familiar name, most obviously for her "Visual Pleasure and Narrative Cinema," and possibly for her demonstration of the principles explored in that groundbreaking essay, in *Riddles of the Sphinx.*[10] While I have certainly used *Riddles* within a gender studies context, I most frequently use it in introductory film courses, where its considerable demands on viewers seem more pronounced. Indeed, the combination of the film's complex, demanding structure and its focus on the subject of childcare and domestic labor has caused me to develop a ritual that I conduct with students after they've seen the film, but before I attempt to talk about it with them. In order to understand the need for this ritual, some specifics about the film are useful.

Like *Zorns Lemma* (and to some degree, probably as a result of the influence of the Frampton film), *Riddles of the Sphinx* is structured to reflect its intellectual concerns, rather than to conform to conventional media expectations. Basically, the several sections of the film are organized into a mirror structure: the film's relatively brief first three sections are echoed by the final three sections (section 1 is echoed by section 7; section 2, by 6; section 3, by 5) and the long central section, "Louise's Story Told in Thirteen Shots," is implicitly organized around shot 7 so that each shot before 7 is echoed by the shot in a comparable position after 7 (shot 1 by shot 13, shot 6 by 8). Louise's story provides the film's central melodrama, though it focuses on an aspect of conventional life that melodrama routinely suppresses: the day-to-day struggles of young mothers to care for their children. While Louise and her husband separate during "Louise's Story," the focus is neither on the battles leading up to the separation, nor on the sexual alliances the new arrangement makes possible; but on Louise caring for her daughter: feeding her breakfast, tidying up her room, putting her in daycare so she can take a job to support the new arrangement, and so on.

Each of the thirteen shots of Louise's story is presented as a 360-degree pan, first to the right and, after shot 10, to the left, so that Louise's domestic labor is revealed from the right and left edges of the screen, an approach familiar from suspenseful moments in conventional movies—here used to reveal the opposite of what is usually considered suspenseful. Shot 7 is the pivot on which *Riddles of the Sphinx* turns; during the shot Louise and her colleagues at her new workplace discuss whether their union might make childcare *at* the workplace a priority.

Riddles critiques both *what* the movies depict and the conventional nature of these depictions. Not only do the 360-degree pans in "Louise's story" offer a new way of experiencing cinematic action, but the six sections that frame Louise's story provide a survey of important avant-garde approaches to film. Each section refers to a filmic procedure typical of a good many avant-garde films. The first section, "Opening pages," for example, is a single shot, more than a minute long, of hands turning the pages of a book (a book about the representation of women in the arts) and refers to the use of extended shots by a wide variety of avant-garde filmmakers. The third section, "Stones," is a close-in examination of the texture of found-footage imagery of the Egyptian sphinx, re-filmed through a number of generations;

it refers to the history of the "process film" in which filmmakers use the camera to explore the possibilities of rephotography (the most famous instance is Ken Jacobs's *Tom, Tom, the Piper's Son* [1969]).

At the conclusion of any screening of *Riddles* involving a student audience not well-versed in feminist issues, I ask students to write the name of the film on a piece of paper and then to crumple the paper into a small ball. Recognizing that for nearly every contemporary American college student, the slow pace of *Riddles of the Sphinx* is frustrating; *and* that the issues of childcare and domestic labor are the very *essence* of boredom, I tell them to direct their frustration with the film, and with me for showing it to them, into that little ball of paper and crumple it as tightly as they can. Then I ask them to stand. I close my eyes and tell them to stone me with the paper balls. They are always delighted to do so. *Then,* after a break, we begin to explore the film.

Once students have vented their frustration and can stop to examine what Mulvey and Wollen *have* accomplished in *Riddles,* the remarkable complexity and ingenuity of the film become obvious. The intricacies of any of the shots of "Louise's Story," the implications of any of the echoes of the sections/shots that mirror each other, can sustain a considerable discussion; and a film that may have seemed empty of pleasure during the screening becomes as engaging as any work of film, or literature or painting, where close reading discovers a surprising density of implication. And, of course, the overall structure of *Riddles*—its conscious evocation of Jacques Lacan's "mirror stage" of child development, its simultaneous rejection and reconfirmation of the climactic narrative structure endemic to commercial movies; its varied ways of engaging/challenging viewers— becomes a cinematic sphinx that will continue to resonate with students when they return to the commercial movie house, causing them to critique commercial conventions even as they experience them.

Because *Riddles of the Sphinx* was designed as an instigator of discussion, as a theoretical essay about cinematic pleasure, Mulvey and Wollen have always made sure that the text of the film, and the details of its structure, are available in printed form, first in *Screen* (18.2 [1977]), and more recently in my *Screen Writings* (see note 9).

5. *Un Chien Andalou ("An Andalusian Dog")* (1929) by Luis Buñuel and Salvador Dali; *Take Off* (1972) by Gunvor Nelson

Since many avant-garde films challenge the conventions of popular media and the audience expectations most of us have internalized, classroom screenings of these films often cause frustration, a level of frustration greater, or at least less repressed, than that caused by literature, painting, and music of a comparable level of experimentation. In several ways this frustration is an advantage for a teacher. First, it allows for discussion of the *reasons* why the student is *so* angry at this film: what in his/her/our training has caused *this* experience to be as annoying as it is? Second, as I suggested earlier, these more difficult films create a level of confusion that makes *us* necessary. When I taught literature, I always found Gertrude Stein and William Faulkner as much fun to teach as Willa Cather and Ernest Hemingway: while many students could come to an adequate understanding of a Cather novel or a Hemingway story without any assistance from me (I hoped I could *expand* their awareness, of course), I knew that without my assistance *The Sound and the Fury* and *Three Lives* would be nearly opaque, and *with* my assistance, they might become student favorites.

On the other hand, the discovery of pleasure and insight in a cultural form where one does not expect to find them can also be exciting, and avant-garde film provides a good many opportunities for this kind of surprise. Luis Buñuel and Salvador Dali's first collaboration, *Un Chien Andalou* ("An Andalusian Dog," 1929) may be the best-known instance of cinematic surrealism, and as a good many readers may know, remains as provocative in the modern classroom as it was for audiences in 1929—though *this* provocation is one many students are happy to experience. The film's shocking opening where a man, played by Buñuel himself, sharpens a razor and uses it to slice a woman's eye (the filmmakers cut away to a close-up of a dead donkey's eye being sliced by a razor, but the moment is remarkably visceral) creates a memorable metaphor for what Buñuel/Dali are doing to our conventional way of seeing, our complacency as viewers. This opening attack leads to a series of bizarre events, often as humorous as they are disconcerting. *Un Chien Andalou* continually breaks the rules of cinema, and a discussion of the particular acts of defiance in the film is always useful and productive. The film provides a valuable introduction for any course where students will be asked to reconsider their conventional ways of experiencing film, media, art—an introduction that simultaneously shocks contemporary students and pleases them; many of them will ask that the film be reshown to colleagues not in their class.

Un Chien Andalou is one instance of the considerable body of dadaist and surrealist film produced in Europe in the 1920s, and it is also a premonition of the considerable body of surrealist films produced in the United States from the 1940s until the present. Several of these films are very effective in the classroom, including Maya Deren's *Meshes of the Afternoon* (1943), in which Deren and her then-partner, Alexander Hammid, psychodramatize Deren's discomfort with domestic life. But of all the short surrealist films produced in the long wake of *Un Chien Andalou,* the one I've had the most luck with is Gunvor Nelson's *Take Off.*

To describe *Take Off* is to destroy the impact of the film for anyone who's not seen it. A stripper (her professional name was Ellion Ness) performs a striptease for the camera, accompanied by a jazz soundtrack. She dances seductively, removing her clothing, item by item, until she is entirely naked, at which point she proceeds to remove what we've assumed is her hair, then her limbs, her breasts, her head. At the end her torso "takes off" and is seen flying among meteors in outer space. Here is a film that is actually more interesting to work with now than it was when it was first available. Certainly audiences, and especially student audiences, are at least as surprised as the original viewers that Ellion Ness goes further than simple nudity—that she does indeed take it *all* off—but most contemporary students are surprised that a striptease is being shown in a classroom: some struggle with the question of whether to endure this exploitation or leave. I am careful to indicate before showing *Take Off* that Gunvor Nelson is a woman, in the hope that all will remain through the film, perhaps puzzling over the filmmaker's, and their professor's, motivation for presenting it. Of course, once Ness deconstructs her body, we realize that the film is deconstructing the ritual of striptease, revealing implicitly what the fetishization of women's bodies means to women. Indeed, the fact that Ness is older and heavier than most women polemicized as erotic by the mass media (both in the early 1970s and currently) causes even most progressive students to judge Ness as "fat," or at least as less attractive than she "should be."

On the other hand, the moment Ness removes her hair, beginning the film's critique of striptease, we realize that her smile is not, and *was* not during the earlier part of *Take Off,* an attempt to submit to the audience's male gaze. Rather it is/was a smile of complicity with the director, a smile at our naiveté and our presumptions about who Ness is. As her body disappears during the final minutes of the film, her intelligence and spirit—and the intelligence/spirit of Gunvor Nelson—become self-evident. Then it is obvious that the collaboration of Nelson and Ness (and a woman named Magda who had the original idea for the film) has allowed these women to appropriate a conventional, essentially misogynistic societal ritual (one virtually inevitable in at least a camouflaged form in mass market movies) and destroy viewers' complacency about it, hopefully forever.[11]

Nelson's film is very effective in an introduction to film context (I've often used it in conjunction with early Méliès films and Lucy Fischer's "The Lady Vanishes" (in John L. Fell, ed., *Film Before Griffith* [Berkeley: U of California P, 1983] 339–54]) but is as good a film as any (and, at ten minutes, shorter than most) for any course designed, at least in part, to confront the modern control and exploitation of women's bodies.

6. *Fireworks* (1947) and *Eaux D'Artifice* (1953) by Kenneth Anger

While *Un Chien Andalou* and *Take Off* can be used to exemplify two very different attitudes toward gender (the Buñuel/Dali collaboration rebels against a good many social and cinematic expectations, but is rather conventional in its depiction of women), Kenneth Anger's *Fireworks* and *Eaux D'Artifice* offer two very different, though complementary, depictions of gay desire. *Fireworks* may be the first openly gay American film; and that it was made in 1947 by a seventeen-year-old filmmaker suggests that the history of gay representation is older than most contemporary students may assume. What makes these Anger films particularly useful, however, is that they offer an opportunity for discussing what has become one of our most volatile political issues with a good humor and sensuality that films devoted to progressive polemic rarely reveal.

Fireworks is usually categorized as a "psychodrama," which in avant-garde film history has come to mean a filmmaker's dramatization of his/her disturbed state of mind.[12] Generally, psychodramas take the form of dreams or fantasies. In the case of *Fireworks,* Anger himself plays the protagonist whose dream life reveals his struggle to conceal his powerful gay desire from a society in which the expression of that desire often means danger. During the climax of *Fireworks,* if the reader can forgive the pun, the protagonist goes to the men's room in a bar frequented by sailors, where he is brutalized (it is clearly a pleasurable brutalization, a sado-masochistic fantasy) and then just before he wakes is seen lighting a firecracker protruding from the fly of his pants. This and the other phallic jokes that punctuate *Fireworks* are a form of whistling-in-the-dark humor that dramatize the poignant reality that no matter how hard this young man works at repressing his desire, his dreams reveal to him and to us his fundamental hunger. That Anger connects the desire for gay sex with fireworks is a way not only of alluding to the "explosions" that an honest expression of gay desire can create in society, but a way of suggesting that this independent filmmaker's willingness to be honest about who he is and what he wants represents just the independence of spirit and the personal courage we celebrate with fireworks on the Fourth of July.

Eaux D'Artifice (the title means "Waterworks") can be seen as a companion piece to *Fireworks,* even though it provides a very different kind of experience. Anger's careful choreography of the fountains in the gardens of the Villa D'Est, just outside Rome, to passages of music from Vivaldi, is one of the great sensual pleasures in the annals of independent cinema. I have never shown the film to an audience that found the film anything less than a sheer sensual delight. And it is this very accessibility that provides an opportunity for considering the sources of such enjoyment.

Anger had, between the making of the two films, moved to Europe, where he found a much more accepting climate for his art and his sexual preference. The gay desire that had to be so carefully controlled in America that it grew incandescent in dreams was finally freed, released, allowed to flow. The elaborate fountains at Villa D'Est are an emblem of this release. If *Fireworks* is a portrait of a man and a society at war with its own desire, *Eaux D'Artifice* reveals a maker now at harmony with himself, a cinematic conductor of music and image who uses film not to confess, but to share the pleasure of culture and nature, spirit and body in synchronization. That Anger needed to leave the United States and settle in Europe in order to be free makes the pair of films a useful critique of more traditional depictions of Europeans immigrating to America in the name of freedom.

7. *American Dreams* (1984) by James Benning

Once in a while, even avant-garde filmmakers find ways of making an obviously unusual approach accessible and interesting not only to those willing to try something new, but to a general audience. This is the accomplishment of James Benning's *American Dreams* and Su Friedrich's *Sink or Swim* (discussed next).

Benning grew up in Milwaukee in the 1940s–1960s (he was born in 1942) and, like many Milwaukee youths of his era, became a fan of Milwaukee Brave outfielder Hank Aaron, not simply because Aaron was a remarkable baseball player, but because he was one of the pioneers in breaking through baseball's color line. Benning's fascination with Aaron continued through Aaron's passing Babe Ruth's home run record, and in 1984 found an artistic outlet: in *American Dreams.* Benning presents his extensive collection of Hank Aaron memorabilia—baseball cards, pictures of Aaron on other products—one item at a time, front and back, one after another, for fifty-six minutes. The memorabilia are presented chronologically and thus track Aaron's career from his rookie year through his record-setting 715th home run; indeed each year of the Aaron story is introduced by a number—Aaron's home run total at the end of that year.

A careful review of Hank Aaron memorabilia would not maintain the attention of anyone but a baseball fanatic, but *American Dreams* provides three other sources of information that not only energize the experience of the film, but transform it into a provocative time capsule of the generation that came of age in the mid-1960s. As the Aaron memorabilia are presented, we also read a handwritten text that rolls across the lower portion of the screen from right to left. This text is a diary of a man's travels around the Midwest and Northeast, including stops at a massage parlor in New York City and at rallies by presidential candidates: first Richard Nixon and then George Wallace. At the beginning, this diary seems to be Benning's (the handwriting *is*), but as the man begins to talk seriously about assassinating one of the candidates, we assume he's not Benning. Few viewers in the current generation will know that the diary was written by Arthur Bremer—like Benning a Milwaukee native—who shot George Wallace in Laurel, Maryland, in 1972.

The viewer's attempt to keep up with the Aaron memorabilia *and* to read the rolling text causes the film to be unusually interactive: no sooner do we focus on the Aaron material than the rolling text draws the eye (as Hollis Frampton, one of Benning's film mentors, said, "Once we can read, and a word is put before us, we cannot not read it"[13]) and no sooner do we focus on the text than a change in the memorabilia distracts us from the rolling text.

The soundtrack alternates between moments of silence and two other sources of information: brief excerpts from popular songs, one per year from 1954—Aaron's rookie year—until his retirement from baseball in 1976; and brief excerpts from media moments—political speeches, responses to reporters' questions, advertisements—again, one per year (each singer and song, and speaker is identified with a visual text). If the triad of obsessions that dominate the visuals—the Aaron memorabilia, Bremer's quest to kill a political figure, Benning's rigorous and relentless structure—provide the central threads of *American Dreams,* the songs and speakers on the soundtrack create a context for them, revealing a wide range of personal and cultural dreams and nightmares that characterize the era. Benning's choice and timing of auditory information provide a good many opportunities for noticing intersections between the various sources of information. *American Dreams* concludes with a moment of "visual silence," during which we listen first to the sound of a gunshot, then to the play-by-play coverage of Aaron's "shot" to left center field that accomplished *his* dream.

American Dreams is, at least on one level, about gender. Just as Benning's presentation of the Aaron memorabilia involves showing the front and back of each item, *American Dreams* explores both sides of the "American Dream": Aaron's passing Ruth's home run record is an American triumph over adversity; and yet, is Aaron's obsession with the number 715 all that different from Bremer's obsession with entering the history books? Both seem quintessentially male obsessions, as does Benning's commitment to structure (what P. Adams Sitney called "structural film" had, by the early 1980s, been critiqued as a male form of exerting power over experience).[14] Benning seems to recognize himself as somewhere in between Aaron and Bremer, caught, like most of us, between our excitement about what we can and do accomplish and our frustration with our failures and with the forces we believe are holding us back.[15]

American Dreams can instigate valuable discussion in a wide variety of academic contexts. It's a rare class that won't find Benning's combination of a variety of strands of popular culture and an unusual, thoroughly rigorous, but engaging structure interesting and provocative. In a world that sometimes seems awash in sports events and the resulting media coverage, *American Dreams* offers the opportunity for an unusually deep discussion of the complex relationship of athletics and society.

8. *Sink or Swim* (1992) by Su Friedrich

Like *American Dreams,* Su Friedrich's *Sink or Swim* is thoroughly accessible to most filmgoers, and in particular to college students, despite its unconventional form; and like the Benning film, has already taught a lesson about the narrow range of pleasure ministered to by the commercial cinema even before a discussion of the film begins. Like *Zorns Lemma, Sink or Swim* is arranged alphabetically, but in reverse order: the film is divided into twenty-six sections, each of which is preceded by a one word title— "Zygote," "*Y* Chromosome," "*X* Chromosome," "*Witness*," "*Virgin*" . . . . Following each title, we hear a story about a young girl growing up, and especially about her relationship with her father. At first, the girl lives in what seems to be Edenic security, but when her father leaves the family, the girl must come to terms with her new life, including her mother's misery and her father's subsequent marriage.

As we hear the young girl's story, we are presented with a wide variety of visual imagery, including home movies of Friedrich's parents during the early years of their relationship; her parents' home movies of her and her sister; documentary imagery taken by Friedrich of various trips, her mother working as a secretary, swimming in Lake Michigan, and bits of television shows recorded informally from a TV screen. While the intersections between imagery and sound in *American Dreams* are intermittent rewards for viewer attention, in *Sink or Swim* Friedrich has arranged image and sound so that there is a constant, multileveled interconnection between them; and exploring the particulars of this interconnection is one of the most rewarding dimensions of the film.

Divorce is so usual in contemporary America and propaganda for the nuclear family is so pervasive in American media that Friedrich's openness about the real experience of divorce is a revelation and a relief for many students. That her family's break-up is presented in a film of remarkable intricacy and coherence is Friedrich's way of demonstrating that, despite the trauma of her family experiences, and despite her difficulties in retaining some semblance of a relationship with her father, she was able to grow into a fruitful maturity and exorcise some of the pain of her childhood, using the artistic skills she was able to develop. *Sink or Swim* is a painful and beautiful film, in many ways closer to the experience of poetry than to the conventional movie experience. That Friedrich is a lesbian—and this is implicit in *Sink or Swim*—provides a further avenue for discussion.[16]

9. *Unsere Afrikareise ("Our African Journey")* (1967) by Peter Kubelka

One of the most remarkable short films (twelve minutes) in the history of cinema, Austrian Peter Kubelka's exposé of several Austrian couples on safari in Africa can provide a powerful experience and generate valuable discussion in a variety of academic contexts. *Unsere Afrikareise* provides a powerful polemic against colonialism within a cinematic structure so intricate and precise that the horrors of what is exposed by the film are made all the more memorable by the beauty of the work of film art that Kubelka crafted over a period of years.

Hired originally to document the safari in a conventional travel film, Kubelka joined the safari because he was interested in seeing something of Africa and could not afford to take such a trip on his own. During the weeks of the safari (the group traveled to Egypt, then up the Nile to Kenya, where they hunted a variety of big and small game), Kubelka shot eight hours of film and recorded hours of sound. On his return to Vienna he began to familiarize himself with both and to decide what sort of film he would make.

It was clear to Kubelka early on that he could not make the sort of congratulatory travel film the group expected; indeed, he was alienated from the group even before they arrived in Kenya and began to kill animals. In the end he decided on a tightly constructed montage of the safari that would derive its power from his unusual handling of image and sound.[17] Having studied the imagery and sound he had recorded with great precision, Kubelka decided to forgo anything like conventional synchronized image/sound. Instead, he decided on an editing strategy that would cause one visual image to collide with the next, very different image, *and* that would cause each image to collide with the particular sound one hears with it, *and* that would cause each sound to collide with the next sound. Each of these three levels of collision creates its own implications, and together they reveal Kubelka's complex understanding of the ways in which this safari was typical of the activities of rich societies in regard to economically disenfranchised societies. When African women carrying bundles on their heads walk through the frame and we hear a gunshot, we understand that no one is actually shooting at these women (the gunshot was recorded during a hunt), but we also understand that, metaphorically, the European exploitation of this culture's natural resources does endanger the indigenous population, and that the achievement of "status" that allows these Austrians to take this safari and that is confirmed by each new "trophy" they kill, is an enactment of a particular male way of being in the world that does endanger women.

Virtually every image/image, sound/image, sound/sound juxtaposition in *Unsere Afrikareise* repays careful analysis; and as a result, the film needs to be seen more than once, in the same way any complex poem or painting requires careful attention over a period of time. In the current moment, the safari's destruction of wildlife is probably a more obvious and powerful theme than either colonialism or gender. Regardless of which theme one is focusing on, however, it is clear that Kubelka means not simply to condemn one group of Austrians for their activities, but to ask us to consider how their activities are an emblem for ours: as we sit in a college movie theater watching this film, are we really *not* part of these patterns? After all, it is *our* African journey, at least in the movie theater, not just the Austrian hunters' and Kubelka's.

10. *Line Describing a Cone* (1973) by Anthony McCall

For most students coming of age and coming to cinema in the new millennium, the technology of film exhibition is a mystery: nearly all of the "films" they see are experienced on TV, either through broadcast or on a VHS, or in a commercial theater. As a result, avant-garde film can be important not only because it models a broader articulation of motion picture art than a student will otherwise experience, but because actually presenting these films, and especially presenting them well, can model a more serious investment in cinema, and a greater awareness of its apparatus, than most students are accustomed to. A particularly valuable film in terms of what it has to teach, both directly and indirectly, about film exhibition is Anthony McCall's *Line Describing a Cone.*

Line Describing a Cone was made for exhibition in a gallery space, not a conventional theater (though for polemical and practical reasons, I have sometimes presented it in the front of a classroom theater space), and in a *smoky* environment. When the film came out, cigarette smoking was ubiquitous enough that virtually any space was a smoky space, but in more recent years, I've usually borrowed or rented a smoke-making machine from a theater department or a theater supply store. And finally, the exhibition space for McCall's film must be pitch dark.

The experience of *Line Describing a Cone* begins when the lights are turned out and the 16mm projector—which is *within* the screening space in this instance, *not* in a projection booth—is turned on; and students mill around in the darkness, conscious only of the machine operating in their midst and of each other. Soon they notice that a single beam of light is visible, coming from the projector and making a dot on the opposite wall. During the half hour that follows, the dot becomes more and more a circle, and the beam of light more and more a cone. And as this light sculpture takes shape in the smoky room, students tend to become more involved with the light, looking at it from various angles (I usually lead the way in this, if students are shy), interrupting the light, crawling under the cone (which seems to become increasingly material), and, when I've supplied incense sticks, making smoky interventions in the swirling shape of the developing cone. In most cases, students begin to cluster together at the end of the cone most distant from the projector, creating a human "circle" from within which to admire the increasingly striking shape of the cone. Indeed, the care necessary to move around in the darkened room involves students in a more fully participatory, more thoughtful, more audience-aware film experience than most of them have ever had.

Once the circle/cone is complete, and the lights come on, students are usually excited to talk about the experience of the film—noting, for instance, how dense and engaging this half-hour experience has been. Once one asks why McCall might have made such a film, and in what ways the experience of *Line Describing a Cone* critiques conventional cinema and media in general, discussion quickly reveals the implicit politics of the film.[18] Here the means of production are not hidden from the audience, but are, literally, in their hands; and instead of sitting in rows (hoping to have no particular interaction with other audience members) and seeing/hearing a film that requires virtually no activity/input from them, *Line Describing a Cone* invites the audience not only to be part of the production of the film, but to become both its directors and main characters. McCall's minimal film (it was produced for around $100) models participatory democracy and exposes undemocratic aspects of the conventional film experience.

Line Describing a Cone is an excellent film early in the semester, not only because its use of the most fundamental aspects of film exhibition—a projector with a film moving through it, the projector beam in a dark space—draws attention to basics, but because it is one of those experiences that tends to create a bond between students and between students and teacher. Further, since the experience of interacting with the film evokes childhood (and sometimes our early trips to movie theaters when we'd just as soon turn around in our seats and look at the audience or at the projection booth, or even crawl under the seats), *Line Describing a Cone* can serve as a metaphor for entering any new academic investigation. There is even a spiritual dimension to the experience, encoded in the evolving beauty of the cone, in our fascination with light, and even in the gentle interaction between viewers—or really *participants*—that develops in the darkness.

This discussion of some of the avant-garde films that have been most useful in my teaching only begins to suggest the value of this film history for academics. Indeed, I have found few kinds of research as satisfying as my ongoing exploration of developments in this field, not simply because of the pedagogical value of the films themselves, which I hope I have given some inkling of, but also because using *these* films provides direct support for alternatives to commercial media. It is one thing to rail against the various absurdities and excesses of mass-market film and television, a world that sometimes seems to grow more inhumane and intransigent with each new generation of critique by the academy. It is another to use those resources we *do* have—to use, support, and maintain progressive, challenging *alternatives*.

Roughly speaking, 16mm prints of avant-garde films rent for about $2 per minute: that is, a fifteen-minute film will rent for about $30, a ninety-minute film, for around $180. As expensive as these rates may seem, rental monies do more than provide one-time access to 16mm prints. Renting films from Canyon Cinema, the Film-makers' Cooperative, the Museum of Modern Art's Circulating Film Program, and other, smaller distributors of avant-garde film keeps these shoestring operations in business, allowing them to maintain the quality of their prints and our access to them. Without these institutions, any practical access to the full history of alternative cinema seems sure to disappear.

Academics can also support the field by inviting accomplished filmmakers to campus. Of course, the visiting filmmaker needs to be paid a reasonable fee (I try to pay any filmmaker with a substantial body of work an honorarium of $1,000), and there are transportation and housing costs as well. But in my experience, money to host filmmakers can virtually always be found somewhere within the academic system. Often, this involves making connections across disciplines and accessing extracurricular campus organizations. The result is both the expansion of our students' sense of what film-making is and can be, *and* a practical contribution to the filmmakers' economic independence, without which they cannot continue to make films.[19]

As with any new undertaking, using avant-garde films in the college classroom requires some extra work at the start, to create the necessary rental budget and to access an adequate screening space, as well as a period of adjustment in learning to work with students on these films. But in my experience few investments of time and energy have paid off pedagogically the way this one has, year after year, and in course after course.

FILM AVAILABILITY

In the United States there are three major distribution organizations for avant-garde film. Each is financially precarious and under-funded: as a result, some patience may be needed in dealing with the often harried staff. Further, since even some of the finest films exist in only a few prints, sometimes in a single print, a considerable lead time is necessary to be sure films will be available exactly when they're needed. The three distributors are:

Canyon Cinema (CC)
2325 Third Street, Suite 338
San Francisco, CA 94107
415-626-2255
films@canyoncinema.com
www.canyoncinema.com

Film-makers' Cooperative (FMC)
175 Lexington Avenue
New York, NY 10016
212-889-3820
film6000@aol.com
www.film-makerscoop.com

Museum of Modern Art Circulating Film Department (MoMA)
11 West 53rd Street
New York, NY 10019
212-708-9530

Each distributor provides an extensive catalogue with information about the films and with conditions for rental and distribution.

In Canada

Canadian Filmmakers Distribution Centre (CFDC)
Suite 220, 37 Hanna Ave.
Toronto, Ontario M6K 1W8
416-588-0725
cfmdc@cfmdc.org
www.cfmdc.org

Films Discussed and American Distributors

The Act of Seeing with One's Own Eyes: CC, CFMDC, MoMA
American Dreams: CC, CFMDC
Barn Rushes: CC, FMC
Un Chien Andalou ("An Andalusian Dog"): MoMA
Eaux D'Artifice: CC
Fireworks: CC
Fog Line: CC, FMC

Landscape (for Manon): CC

Line Describing a Cone: CC, FMC

Meshes of the Afternoon: MoMA

Riddles of the Sphinx: MoMA

Serene Velocity: CC, FMC, MoMA

Sink or Swim: CC, CFMDC, FMC, Women Make Movies (462 Broadway, Suite 500E, New York, NY 10013; 212-925-0606; info@wmm.com)

Snow: CC

Soft Rain: FMC

Take Off: CC, CFMDC

Unsere Afrikareise ("Our African Journey"): CC, FMC, MoMA

Window Water Baby Moving: CC, CFMDC, MoMA

Zorns Lemma: FMC, MoMA

NOTES

1. Actually, the complex history of "avant-garde" or "experimental" film has produced a considerable set of names, each of which defines one or another particular dimension of, or one or another attitude toward, the field. These include "poetic film," "film as art," "underground film," "film as a subversive art," " New American Cinema," "underground film," "expanded cinema," "abstract film," "the other cinema," "counter-cinema," "alternative cinema," "materialist film," "direct theory," "critical cinema," and a good many others. There is no point in reviewing the long and contentious history of naming what, for convenience, I will call avant-garde and experimental film, but it should be noted that the fact of so much terminology suggests both the size and diversity of the field.

2. Especially in the 1960s and early 1970s when most 16mm movie projectors had the built-in option of "sound speed" or "silent speed," many filmmakers preferred the slower, 18 frames per second rate, which creates a slight, nearly subliminal flicker. The hypnotic flicker of 18 frames per second is one of the important visual rhythms of *Barn Rushes*. Unfortunately, few contemporary film projectors provide the option of 18 frames per second. Often, college audio-visual specialists will know about the sound/silent speed distinction, and some will know how particular projectors can be adapted for the slower speed. The popular line of Eiki projectors up through the RM-1 model, for example, allowed for a change of belts to accommodate both sound and silent speeds.

3. Brakhage is widely recognized as the dean of avant-garde filmmakers, and his output is legendary. His more than two hundred films reveal a film artist fascinated with the potential of the movie camera to retrain perception. Among the best known of Brakhage's films are *Window Water Baby Moving* (1959), discussed later; *Mothlight* (1963), made by gluing moth wings, blades of grass, and tiny flowers onto a strip of celluloid and printing the result; and *Scenes from Under Childhood* (4 parts, 1967–70), which chronicles the perceptual acculturation of Brakhage's children. In 2003, the Criterion Collection presented a collection of his films on DVD, making Brakhage's work more accessible to general viewers.

4. My research has resulted in the Critical Cinema series of books, published by University of California Press (see the bibliography), each of which provides in-depth interviews with accomplished avant-garde filmmakers, along with introductions to their work and information about where to find it. This ongoing series means to provide teachers with a substantial resource for engaging the wide world of independent cinema.

5. Marx's book *The Machine in the Garden* (London: Oxford UP, 1964) explores the arrival of the locomotive (and the industrial revolution) in "edenic" America during the eighteenth and nineteenth centuries.

6. For discussions of "luminism" and "tonalism," see John Wilmerding, ed., *American Light: The Luminist Movement* (Washington: National Gallery of Art, 1980); and Wanda M. Corn, *The Color of Mood: American Tonalism 1880–1910* (San Francisco: M. H. DeYoung Memorial Museum and California Palace of the Legion of Honor, 1972).

7. See Gottheim's comments about *Fog Line* in Scott MacDonald, *A Critical Cinema* (Berkeley: U of California P, 1988): 82–85.

8. Brakhage, in the opening of "Metaphors on Vision," originally published in *Film Culture* 30 (fall 1963); and excerpted in P. Adams Sitney, ed., *The Avant-Garde Film: A Reader of Theory and Criticism* (New York: NYU Press, 1978), 120–28.

9. Several texts from *Zorns Lemma* and relevant to it are available in Scott MacDonald, ed., *Screen Writings: Scripts and Texts by Independent Filmmakers* (Berkeley: U of California P, 1993), 49–69. Frampton discusses the film in MacDonald, *Critical Cinema,* 48–60.

10. "Visual Pleasure and Narrative Cinema" is widely anthologized, including in Mulvey's own *Visual and Other Pleasures* (Bloomington: Indiana UP, 1989): 14–26.

11. Nelson discusses *Take Off* in Scott MacDonald, *A Critical Cinema 3* (Berkeley: U of California P, 1998), 190–93.

12. The most extensive discussion of particular avant-garde psychodramas and the forms of cinema that developed out of the psychodrama is P. Adams Sitney's *Visionary Film* (New York: Oxford UP, 1974; rev. ed., 1979).

13. Frampton, in MacDonald, *Critical Cinema,* 49.

14. Sitney defined "structural film" in his *Visionary Film,* 407–35.

15. Benning discusses *American Dreams* in Scott MacDonald, *A Critical Cinema 2* (Berkeley: U of California P, 1992), 241–45.

16. The text of *Sink or Swim* is available in MacDonald, *Screen Writings,* 241–58. Friedrich discusses the film in MacDonald, *Critical Cinema 2,* 308–18.

17. Kubelka discusses his working method in "The Theory of Metrical Film," in Sitney, *Avant-Garde Film,* 139–59.

18. See McCall, "Two Statements," in Sitney, *Avant-Garde Film,* 250–54; and McCall's discussion of the film in *Critical Cinema 2,* 157–65.

19. For more information on hosting filmmakers, see my "Visiting Filmmakers: Why Bother?" in *Journal of Film and Video* 46.4 (winter 1995): 3–12.

BIBLIOGRAPHY

(Included are books, periodicals, and catalogues that provide general introductions to avant-garde film history.)

American Federation of Arts. *A History of American Avant-Garde Cinema.* New York: American Federation of Arts, 1976. A catalogue for a touring show.

Canyon Cinema Film/Video Catalogue 2000. San Francisco: Canyon Cinema, 2000.

Curtis, David. *Experimental Cinema.* New York: Delta, 1971.

Film Culture, 1955 to the Present. Anthology Film Archives, 32 Second Ave., New York, NY 10003.

Film-makers' Cooperative Catalogue #7. New York: New American Cinema Group, 1989.

Fischer, Lucy. *Shot/Countershot: Film Tradition and Women's Cinema.* Princeton: Princeton UP, 1989.

Horak, Jan-Christopher. *Lovers of Cinema: The First American Film Avant-Garde, 1919–1945.* Madison: U of Wisconsin P, 1995.

LeGrice, Malcolm. *Abstract Film and Beyond.* Cambridge: MIT Press, 1977.

MacDonald, Scott. *A Critical Cinema.* Berkeley: U of California P, 1988.

———. *A Critical Cinema 2.* Berkeley: U of California P, 1992.

———. *A Critical Cinema 3.* Berkeley: U of California P, 1998.

———. *The Garden in the Machine: A Field Guide to Films about Place.* Berkeley: U of California P, 2001.

Millennium Film Journal, 1977 to the present. Millennium Film Workshop, 66 East 4th St., New York, NY 10003.

Museum of Modern Art, *Circulating Film Library Catalogue.* New York: Museum of Modern Art, 1984. Supplement, 1990.

Peterson, James. *Dreams of Chaos, Visions of Order: Understanding the American Avant-Garde Film.* Detroit: Wayne State UP, 1994.

Rosenbaum, Jonathan. *Film: The Front Line/1983.* Denver: Arden Press, 1983.

Sitney, P. Adams. *Visionary Film.* New York: Oxford UP, 1974; rev. ed., 1978.

———, ed. *The Avant-Garde Film: A Reader of Theory and Criticism.* New York: NYU Press, 1978.

Vogel, Amos. *Film As a Subversive Art.* New York: Random House, 1974.

Wees, William C. *Light Moving in Time: Studies in the Visual Aesthetics of Avant-Garde Film.* Berkeley: U of California P, 1992.

Youngblood, Gene. *Expanded Cinema.* New York: Dutton, 1970.

BIBLIOGRAPHY

Allen, Robert C., ed. *Channels of Discourse, Reassembled: Television and Contemporary Criticism.* 2nd ed. Chapel Hill: U of North Carolina P, 1992.

Alvarado, Manuel, and Oliver Boyd-Barrett, eds. *Media Education: An Introduction.* London: British Film Institute, 1992.

Aronowitz, Stanley. "Working Class Identity and Celluloid Fantasies in the Electronic Age." *Popular Culture: Schooling and Everyday Life.* Ed. Henry A. Giroux and Roger I. Simon. New York: Bergin and Garvey, 1989. 197–217.

Barthes, Roland. *Image, Music, Text.* Ed. S. Heath. New York: Hill and Wang, 1977.

———. *Mythologies.* London: Jonathan Cape, 1972.

Bazalgette, Cary, Evelyne Bevort, and Josiane Savino, eds. *New Directions: Media Education Worldwide.* London: British Film Institute, 1992.

Belsey, Catherine. *Critical Practice.* London: Methuen, 1980.

Belton, John, ed. *Movies and Mass Culture.* New Brunswick, NJ: Rutgers UP, 1996.

Benjamin, Walter. "The Work of Art in the Age of Mechanical Reproduction." *Illuminations.* Ed. Hannah Arendt. Trans. Harry Zohn. New York: Schocken, 1969. 217–51.

Bhabha, Homi K. "The Other Question: The Stereotype and Colonial Discourse." *Screen* 24.3 (1983): 18–36.

Bordwell, David, and Kristine Thompson. *Film Art: An Introduction.* 6th ed. New York: McGraw Hill, 2000.

Braden, Su. "Using Video for Research and Representation: Basic Human Needs and Critical Pedagogy." *Journal of Educational Media* 24.2 (July 1999): 117–30.

Bryson, Norman, Michael Ann Holly, and Keith Moxey, eds. *Visual Culture: Images and Interpretations.* Hanover, NH: Wesleyan UP, 1994.

Carey, James W. *Communication As Culture: Essays on Media and Society.* New York: Routledge, 1992.

Cartmell, Deborah, I. Q. Hunter, Heidi Kaye, and Imelda Whelehan, eds. *Classics in Film and Fiction.* Sterling, VA: Pluto Press, 2000.

Cartmell, Deborah, and Imelda Whelehan, eds. *Adaptation: From Text to Screen, Screen to Text.* New York: Routledge, 1999.

Chow, Rey. "A Phantom Discipline." *PMLA* 116.5 (October 2001): 1386–95.

Corrigan, Timothy, ed. *Film and Literature: An Introduction and a Reader.* Upper Saddle River, NJ: Prentice Hall, 1999.

Dalton, Mary M. *The Hollywood Curriculum: Teachers and Teaching in the Movies.* New York: Peter Lang, 1999.

De Lauretis, Teresa. *Alice Doesn't: Feminism, Semiotics, Cinema.* Bloomington: Indiana UP, 1984.

Evans, Jessica, and Stuart Hall, eds. *Visual Culture: The Reader.* London: Sage, 1999.

Fiske, John. *Introduction to Communication Studies.* London: Methuen, 1982.

———. *Media Matters: Race and Gender in US Politics.* Minneapolis: U of Minnesota P, 1996.

———. *Understanding Popular Culture.* Boston: Unwin Hyman, 1989.

Foucault, Michel. "Of Other Spaces." *Diacritics* 16.1 (spring 1986): 22–27.

Freire, Paulo. *Pedagogy of the Oppressed.* Trans. Myra Bergman Ramos. New York: Herder and Herder, 1970.

Friedberg, Anne. "The End of Cinema: Multimedia and Technological Change." *Reinventing Film Studies.* Ed. Christine Gledhill and Linda Williams. London: Arnold, 2000. 438–52.

———. *Window Shopping: Cinema and the Postmodern.* Berkeley: U of California P, 1993.

Galin, Jeffrey R., Joan Latchaw, Gail E. Hawisher, and Cynthia L. Selfe, eds. *The Dialogic Classroom: Teachers Integrating Computer Technology, Pedagogy, and Research.* Urbana: National Council of Teachers of English, 1998.

Giddings, Robert, Keith Selby, and Chris Wensley, eds. *Screening the Novel: The Theory and Practice of Literary Dramatization.* Basingstoke: Macmillan, 1990.

Giroux, Henry A. "Resisting Difference: Cultural Studies and the Discourse of Critical Pedagogy." *Cultural Studies.* Ed. Lawrence Grossberg, Cary Nelson, and Paula A. Treichler. New York: Routledge, 1992. 199–212.

Giroux, Henry A., and Robert I. Simon. "Popular Culture As Pedagogy of Pleasure and Meaning." *Popular Culture: Schooling and Everyday Life.* Ed. Henry A. Giroux and Robert I. Simon. New York: Bergin and Garvey, 1989. 1–29.

Gledhill, Christine, and Linda Williams, eds. *Reinventing Film Studies.* London: Arnold, 2000.

Grossberg, Lawrence, Cary Nelson, and Paula A. Treichler, eds. *Cultural Studies.* New York: Routledge, 1992.

Gurevitch, Michael, Tony Bennett, James Curran, and Janet Woollacott, eds. *Culture, Society, and the Media.* New York: Methuen, 1982.

Hall, Stuart, ed. *Representation: Cultural Representations and Signifying Practices.* London: Sage, 1997.

Hammer, Rhonda, and Douglas Kellner. "Multimedia Pedagogy for the New Millennium." *Journal of Adolescent and Adult Literacy* 42.7 (April 1999): 522–27.

Harraway, Donna. "The Persistence of Vision." *Simians, Cyborgs, and Women: The Reinvention of Nature.* New York: Routledge, 1991. 188–96.

Hebdige, Dick. *Subculture: The Meaning of Style.* London: Methuen, 1979.

Hill, John, and Pamela Church Gibson, eds. *The Oxford Guide to Film Studies.* Oxford: Oxford UP, 1998.

Hollows, Joanne, and Mark Jancovich, eds. *Approaches to Popular Film.* Manchester: Manchester UP, 1995.

hooks, bell. *Yearning: Race, Gender, and Cultural Politics.* Boston: South End Press, 1990.

Humm, Maggie. *Feminism and Film.* Bloomington: Indiana UP, 1997.

Jenks, Chris, ed. *Visual Culture*. New York: Routledge, 1995.

Katz, John Stuart. *Perspectives on the Study of Film*. Boston: Little, Brown, 1971.

Kellner, Douglas. *Media Culture: Cultural Studies, Identity, and Politics between the Modern and the Postmodern*. London: Routledge, 1994.

———. "Multiple Literacies and Critical Pedagogy in a Multicultural Society." *Educational Theory* 48.1 (winter 1998): 103–23.

Kolker, Robert. *Film, Form, and Culture*. Boston: McGraw Hill, 1999.

Lusted, David. *The Media Studies Book: A Guide for Teachers*. New York: Routledge, 1991.

Lyotard, Jean-Francois. *The Postmodern Condition: A Report on Knowledge*. Trans. Geoff Bennington and Brian Massumi. Minneapolis: U of Minnesota P, 1984.

Maynard, Richard A. *The Celluloid Curriculum: How to Use Movies in the Classroom*. New York: Hayden, 1971.

Metz, Christian. *Film Language: A Semiotics of the Cinema*. Trans. Michael Taylor. New York: Oxford UP, 1991.

———. *The Imaginary Signifier: Psychoanalysis and the Cinema*. Trans. Celia Britton et al. Bloomington: Indiana UP, 1982.

McFarlane, Brian. *Novel to Film: An Introduction to the Theory of Adaptation*. Oxford: Clarendon, 1996.

Mirzoeff, Nicholas, ed. *The Visual Culture Reader*. New York: Routledge, 1998.

Mulvey, Laura. *Visual and Other Pleasures*. Bloomington: Indiana UP, 1989.

Naremore, James. *Film Adaptation*. New Brunswick, NJ: Rutgers UP, 2000.

Nichols, Bill. *Ideology and the Image*. Bloomington: Indiana UP, 1981.

Ross, Andrew. *No Respect: Intellectuals and Popular Culture*. London: Routledge, 1989.

Ryan, Michael, and Douglas Kellner. *Camera Politica: The Politics and Ideology of Contemporary Hollywood Film*. Bloomington: Indiana UP, 1988.

Scannell, Paddy, Philip Schlesinger, and Colin Sparks, eds. *Culture and Power: A Media, Culture and Society Reader*. London: Sage, 1992.

Silverman, Kaja. *The Acoustic Mirror: The Female Voice in Psychoanalysis and Cinema*. Bloomington: Indiana UP, 1988.

———. *The Subject of Semiotics*. New York: Oxford UP, 1983.

Tinkcom, Matthew, and Amy Villarejo, eds. *Keyframes: Popular Film and Cultural Studies*. New York: Routledge, 2000.

Watson, Robert. *Film and Television in Education: An Aesthetic Approach to the Moving Image*. New York: Falmer Press, 1990.

Willeman, Paul. *Looks and Frictions: Essays on Cultural Studies and Film Theory*. Bloomington: Indiana UP, 1994.

Williams, Raymond. *Culture and Society*. London: Chatto and Windus, 1958.

———. *Television: Technology and Cultural Form*. Middletown, CT: Wesleyan UP, 1992.

CONTRIBUTORS

MARIA K. BACHMAN is an Assistant Professor of English at Coastal Carolina University. She is co-editor of *Reality's Dark Light: The Sensational Wilkie Collins* (University of Tennessee Press, 2003), and *Wilkie Collins's Blind Love* (Broadview Press, 2003), and has published articles on Samuel Richardson, Charles Dickens, Benjamin Disraeli, and Wilkie Collins.

ELYSE BLANKLEY is a Professor of English and Women's Studies at California State University, Long Beach, and has published essays on fin-de-siècle/modernist literature and contemporary American fiction and poetry. Her current project is a book-length study of the novels of E. M. Forster and their film adaptations.

CARMEN L. CHÁVEZ is a Visiting Professor and Director of the Lower-Division Language Program at Florida Atlantic University in Boca Raton. In addition to her research in Peninsular theater, literature, and film studies, she works in the areas of gender, cultural studies, and instructional technologies. Her book *Acts of Trauma in Six Plays by Antonio Buero Vallejo* presents a trajectory of Vallejo's body of work, bringing to light Spain's contribution to the performance arts written under Franco's regime. She is currently editing two projects: one is an anthology of Spanish short narrative and the second deals with the use of Hispanic film in the classroom.

THOMAS C. CROCHUNIS is an independent scholar whose work focuses on drama, theatre, and performance in Britain in the late eighteenth and early nineteenth centuries but also addresses theoretical issues in cultural performance, historiography, and media studies. He is co-editor of the *British Women Playwrights around 1800* Web project. He works as a research and evaluation specialist at the LAB at Brown University.

GERALD DUCHOVNAY is the founding and general editor of *Post Script: Essays in Film and the Humanities,* an international film journal, and the author of *Humphrey Bogart: A Bio-Bibliography* (Greenwood, 1999). A Professor of English and head of the Department of Literature and Languages at Texas A&M University–Commerce, he has published articles and reviews on film, Restoration and eighteenth-century British literature, twentieth-century American literature, and interviews with filmmakers. The recipient of a Dana Foundation Fellowship at Carnegie Mellon University, NEH summer fellowships at Johns Hopkins University and the University of North Carolina, and a Modern Media Institute Fellowship (Florida), he has also served as the coordinator for the Governor's Screenwriting competitions for the Motion Picture and Television Bureau of Florida's Department of Commerce and Disney/MGM Studios.

KAMILLA ELLIOTT is Assistant Professor of English at the University of California, Berkeley. She specializes in the interdisciplinary study of literature and film/television. She is the author of *Rethinking the Novel/Film Debate* (Cambridge University Press, 2003).

DALE JACOBS specializes in composition and rhetoric with interests in composition pedagogies, literacy, visual rhetorics, emotion studies, Sophistic rhetoric, and social justice. He is the editor of *The Myles Horton Reader* (University of Tennessee Press, 2003) and co-editor, with Laura Micciche, of *A Way to Move: Rhetorics of Emotion in Composition Studies* (Boyton/Cook, 2003). His articles have appeared in journals such as the *Journal of the Assembly of Expanded Perspectives on Learning, Composition Studies, National Writing Project Quarterly, North Carolina English Teacher,* and *The Writing Lab Newsletter*; he also served as guest editor for a special issue of *North Carolina English Teacher* on Assessing Assessment. In addition, he is the author of a book of poetry entitled *Beneath the Horse's Eye* and is the editor of *Ice: New Writing on Hockey.*

SCOTT MACDONALD is author of *The Garden in the Machine: A Field Guide to Independent Films about Place* (University of California Press, 2001) and *Avant-Garde Film/Motion Studies* (Cambridge University Press, 1993), and editor of *Cinema 16: Documents Toward a History of the Film Society* (Temple University Press, 2002). He is currently preparing volume 4 of *A Critical Cinema,* his series of interviews with independent filmmakers, published by University of California Press. He teaches at Bard College.

KECIA MCBRIDE is an Assistant Professor of English at Ball State University in Muncie, Indiana, where she researches and teaches cinema studies and American fiction after 1860. Her most recent publications include a study of early-twentieth-century folk plays and a materialist reevaluation of Ann Petry's novel *The Street.* Currently, she is working on a book-length manuscript examining the intersections of cinema and modernist American women writers.

ADRIENNE MCCORMICK is an Assistant Professor of English and director of the Women's Studies program at the State University of New York at Fredonia. She teaches in the areas of multi-ethnic American literature, women's studies, and film. Her publications include articles on the poetry of Marilyn Chin, Cathy Song, and David Mura, and she is currently working on two book manuscripts on contemporary multi-ethnic American poets and poetry anthologies.

WALTER METZ is an assistant professor in the Department of Media and Theatre Arts at Montana State University–Bozeman, where he teaches the history, theory, and criticism of film, theatre, and television. His previous publications focus on intertextual approaches to film adaptation, genre, and authorship, for such journals as *The Journal of Contemporary Thought, Film Quarterly, The Journal of Film and Video, Film Criticism,* and *Literature/Film Quarterly.* He is currently writing a textbook on film and theatre for Prentice Hall (forthcoming, 2004), entitled *Dramatic Intertexts: Encountering Theatre via Mass Media.*

JAMES W. MILES is a media designer and educator currently affiliated with the Virginia B. Ball Center for Creative Inquiry at Ball State University. His professional and pedagogical experiences with photography, graphic design, digital imaging, and writing inform his interest in media convergence and interaction.

BARBRA MORRIS is on the faculty of the University of Michigan's Residential College and English Department. She is co-editor of *The Encyclopedia of English Studies and Language Arts* and author of numerous articles about both television content analysis and focus group research.

DIANE NEGRA is Lecturer in Film and Television at the University of East Anglia, United Kingdom. She is the author of *Off-White Hollywood: American Culture and Ethnic Female Stardom* (Routledge, 2001), co-editor of *A Feminist Reader in Early Cinema* (Duke, 2002), and editor of *The Irish in Us: Irishness, Performativity, and Popular Culture* (Duke, forthcoming).

RAI PETERSON is an Associate Professor of English and the Director of Undergraduate Programs at Ball State University, where she has taught composition on television (among other things) for nine years. She is the founder of Poetry Goes to School, a poetry in the schools project that trains and places poetry reading and writing coaches in elementary and secondary classrooms throughout East Central Indiana. In addition to publishing poems in several small press magazines, she is the author of *The Writing Teacher's Companion* and *Real World Research: Sources and Strategies for Composition,* both at Houghton-Mifflin. She is also the founder of WebHead, a faculty web design seminar.

STEPHANIE LEWIS THOMPSON is a Visiting Professor in English at Peace College in Raleigh, North Carolina. She is the author of *Influencing America's Tastes: Realism in the Works of Wharton, Cather, and Hurst* (University Press of Florida, 2002).

JOONNA SMITHERMAN TRAPP is an Assistant Professor of English teaching in the interdisciplinary writing and rhetoric program at Northwestern College. Her most recent publication in film studies is an extended scholarly review of Derek Jarman's *Edward II,* which appeared in *Scope.*

STEPHANIE TRIPP is a Ph.D. candidate in English at the University of Florida. She has taught numerous literature, media, and composition courses in the University of Florida's Networked Writing Environment and is currently teaching at Rhodes College. Her dissertation project, directed by Gregory L. Ulmer, explores Jacques Derrida's work on hauntology as a basis for researching and writing in the age of electronic post-literacy.

BAN WANG is Associate Professor in Asian Studies and Comparative Literature at Rutgers University. Author of *The Sublime Figure of History: Aesthetics and Politics in Twentieth-Century China* (Stanford University Press, 1997) and *Narrative Perspective and Irony in Chinese and American Fiction* (Edwin Mellen, 2002), he has published numerous articles in scholarly journals and anthologies. He is also co-translator of the Chinese edition of the German critic Walter Benjamin's *Illuminations* (with Xudong Zhang). Recently he was a research fellow with the National Endowment for the Humanities and with the Center for Critical Analysis of Contemporary Culture at Rutgers.

JOHN ZUERN is an assistant professor in the Department of English at the University of Hawai'i at Manoa, where he teaches in the areas of literary theory and digital media. His research examines the intersection of philosophical traditions, particularly phenomenology and hermeneutics, and developing critical approaches to hypertext writing and other forms of computer-based literary production. He has published in *Computers and Composition, Literary and Linguistic Computing,* and *TEXT Technology.*

INDEX